CASS SERIES: STUDIES IN INTELLIGENCE
(Series Editors: Christopher Andrew and Michael I. Handel;
Wesley K. Wark and Richard J. Aldrich)
ISSN 1368-9916

# The Clandestine Cold War in Asia, 1945–65

Institute of Asia-Pacific Studies
in association with

Based on the Conference 'The Clandestine Cold War in Asia, 1945–65'
held at the University of Nottingham and in London 14–15 June 1999

# THE CLANDESTINE COLD WAR IN ASIA, 1945–65

## Western Intelligence, Propaganda and Special Operations

*Editors*

Richard J. Aldrich

Gary D. Rawnsley

Ming-Yeh T. Rawnsley

FRANK CASS

LONDON · NEW YORK

*First published 2000 in Great Britain by*
**FRANK CASS PUBLISHERS**
Reprinted 2004 by Frank Cass
2 Park Square
Milton Park
Abingdon
Oxon
OX14 4RN

Transferred to Digital Printing 2004

*Frank Cass is an imprint of the Taylor & Francis Group*

British Library Cataloguing in Publication Data

The clandestine cold war in Asia, 1945–65 : Western
intelligence, propaganda, security and special operations.
– (Studies in intelligence)
1. Cold War 2. Secret service 3. Asia – History – 1945–
4. Asia – Foreign relations
I. Aldrich, Richard J. II. Rawnsley, Gary D. III. Rawnsley,
Ming-Yeh
950.4'2

ISBN 0 7146 5045 5 (cloth)
ISBN 0 7146 8096 6 (paper)
ISSN 1368-9916

Library of Congress Cataloging-in-Publication Data

A catalog record for this book is available
from the Library of Congress

This group of studies first appeared in a Special Issue on 'The Clandestine Cold War in Asia,
1945–65' of *Intelligence and National Security* 14/4 (Winter 1999) published by
Frank Cass (ISSN 0268-4527).

Printed in Great Britain by
TJI Digital, Padstow, Cornwall

# Contents

## PART III: THE MALAYAN EMERGENCY

# Illustrations

# Foreword

During the war I served in the Special Operations Executive or 'SOE'. After a spell in the Baker Street headquarters building I worked to develop Operation *Massingham* with the French. Finally, between 1943 and 1945, I found myself in Admiral Lord Louis Mountbatten's South East Asia Command as Deputy Director of an organisation called Force 136, the Far Eastern manifestation of SOE. This organisation undertook some remarkable clandestine work in areas such as Burma and Malaya, organising resistance and gathering intelligence behind enemy lines. At the end of war, the Director of Force 136, Colin Mackenzie, returned home quickly to report on events to the new Foreign Secretary, Ernest Bevin.

There was much to report on. Across Asia the Second World War had left a trail of destruction and turbulence in its wake. Herein lay the seeds of many post-war conflicts, indeed in Vietnam the fighting that would stretch on through three decades had already begun. I remained in South East Asia long enough to preside over the liquidation of Force 136. However, such was the pace of developing conflicts in South East Asia that some SOE officers stayed on to assist Mountbatten with his difficult post-war tasks in parts of Asia where the early Cold War was already beginning.

During the last half century much has been written about the clandestine war against Japan. Now, with the welcome declassification of new documents, the story of the early clandestine Cold War in Asia can begin to be told. The Institute of Asia-Pacific Studies at the University of Nottingham has taken a lead in exploring these new materials. The fruits of that initiative are contained in this volume. It was to Nottingham that I returned following the war and when the University received its charter in 1948, I was invited to serve on the University Council and later as Pro-Chancellor. During my long and happy years of association I have watched the University develop strong links with many countries in Asia and acquire deep research expertise in the study of the region. It therefore gives me great pleasure to wish the Institute of Asia-Pacific Studies every success with its future programmes.

BRIGADIER SIR JOHN ANSTEY
*Southwell, Nottinghamshire*
*March 2000*

# Acknowledgements

Many people have assisted with this preliminary investigation into the clandestine aspects of the early Cold War in Asia. This began with a conference in the early summer of 1999 organised by the Institute of Asia-Pacific Studies at the University of Nottingham. The Institute provided an excellent framework for that event and many people from far and wide were generous with their time and effort in making it a success. Catherine Baxter, Ian Brown, Susie Carruthers, Eva-Lotta Hedman, Ralph Smith and Anthony Stockwell were very encouraging and supportive. Anthony Short was particularly helpful and served as a model chairman and adviser. The Department of History at the School of Oriental and African Studies, University of London, kindly offered to join us as partners for the conference, providing an invaluable London base for the second day of the proceedings and helping us to interact with practitioners. The presence of individuals with personal experiences and their willingness to share their thoughts generously made this a memorable occasion for us all.

Transcripts of documents from the Public Record Office and the India Office Library and Record appear by permission of Her Majesty's Stationery Office. The permissions of the Trustees of the Liddell Hart Centre for Military Archives and the Broadlands Archives at the Hartley Library, University of Southampton are also gratefully acknowledged.

# Abbreviations

| | |
|---|---|
| A-2 | US Air Force Intelligence |
| AFO | Anti-Fascist Organisations [Burmese] |
| AFP | Armed Forces of the Philippines |
| AFHQ | Allied Forces Headquarters |
| AFPFL | Anti-Fascist People's Freedom League [Burmese] |
| AFSA | Armed Forces Security Agency [American] |
| AFSS | Air Force Security Service [American] |
| ARVN | Army of the Republic of Vietnam [South Vietnamese] |
| ASA | Army Security Agency [American] |
| ASAPAC | Army Security Agency, Pacific [American] |
| ATIS | Allied Translation and Interrogation Service |
| BBC | British Broadcasting Corporation |
| BDCC/ME | British Defence Coordinating Committee, Middle East |
| BDCC/FE | British Defence Coordinating Committee, Far East |
| BIA | Burma Independence Army [Burmese] |
| BMH | British Military Hospital |
| BNA | Burmese National Army [Burmese] |
| BRIAM | British Advisory Mission (to Vietnam) |
| C | Chief of the British Secret Intelligence Service (MI6) |
| CAO | Civil Affairs Office (Filipino) |
| CAS (B) | Civil Affairs Staff (Burma) |
| CCE | Chief Controller Europe, SIS [British] |
| CCME | Chief Controller Mediterranean, SIS [British] |
| CEA | Controller Eastern Area, SIS [British] |
| CEP | Captured Enemy Personnel |
| CFE | Controller Far East, SIS [British] |
| CIA | Central Intelligence Agency [American] |
| CIC | Counter Intelligence Corps [American] |
| CID | Criminal Investigation Department, Malaya |
| CIG | Central Intelligence Group [American] |
| C-in-C | Commander-in-Chief |
| CINFE | Commander in Chief Far East [American] |
| CME | Controller Middle East, SIS [British] |

| | |
|---|---|
| CNA | Controller Northern Area, SIS [British] |
| CRPO | Combined Research and Planning Organisation, SIS |
| Comint | Communications intelligence |
| COS | Chiefs of Staff [British] |
| CW | Controller Western Area, SIS [British] |
| CX | Prefix for a report originating with SIS |
| DF | Direction Finding |
| DI | Directorate of Intelligence, CIA [American] |
| DMI | Director of Military Intelligence [British] |
| DOI | Director of Intelligence, Malaya |
| DPs | Directors of Production, SIS [British] |
| DRS | Document Research Section [American] |
| EDCOR | Economic Development Corps [Filipino] |
| EUSAK | Eighth US Army Korea [American] |
| FBI | Federal Bureau of Investigation [American] |
| FEAF | Far Eastern Air Forces [American] |
| FEC | Far Eastern Command [American] |
| FEC | Far Eastern Controller, SIS [British] |
| FECOM | Far Eastern Command [American] |
| FCO | Foreign and Commonwealth Office |
| FOIA | Freedom of Information Act |
| Force 136 | SOE in the Far East [British] |
| FPDP | Five Powers Defence Pact |
| FRU/FEC | Field Research Unit, Far East Command [CIA] |
| FRUS | *Foreign Relations of the United States* |
| G-2 | Military Intelligence [American] |
| GCHQ | Government Communications Headquarters [British] |
| GVN | Government of Vietnam |
| HFDF | High Frequency Direction Finding |
| HID | Higher Intelligence Department [S. Korean] |
| Humint | Human Intelligence |
| INSCOM | Intelligence and Security Command [American] |
| ISLD | SIS in the wartime Middle East and Far East [British] |
| JCS | Joint Chiefs of Staff [American] |
| JIC | Joint Intelligence Committee |
| JIC/FE | Joint Intelligence Committee, Far East [British] |
| JIC/ME | Joint Intelligence Committee, Middle East [British] |
| JSIC | Joint Special Intelligence Committee FECOM |
| JSOB | Joint Special Operations Branch [American] |
| JSM | Joint Services Mission, Washington [British] |
| JUSMAG | Joint US Military Advisory Group [American] |
| KLO | Korean Labor Organisation |

| | |
|---|---|
| KLO | Korean Liaison Organization [American] |
| KMAG | Korean Military Advisory Group |
| KMT | Kuomintang, Chinese nationalist party |
| KRB | Korean Research Bureau |
| MACL | MacArthur Memorial Library, Norfolk, Virginia |
| MCA | Malayan Chinese Association |
| MCP | Malayan Communist Party |
| MEC | Middle Eastern Controller, SIS [British] |
| MI5 | Security Service [British] |
| MI6 | Secret Intelligence Service (SIS) [British] |
| MLO | Military Liaison Officer, Malaya |
| MNLA | Malayan National Liberation Army |
| MPAJA | Malayan People's Anti-Japanese Army |
| MSS | Malayan Security Service |
| MTUC | Malayan Trade Union Congress |
| NKAF | North Korean Air Force |
| NKPA | North Korean People's Army |
| NSA | National Security Agency [American] |
| NSC | National Security Council [American] |
| NSG | Naval Security Group [American] |
| ONI | Office of Naval Intelligence [American] |
| OPC | Office of Policy Coordination [American] |
| OPDC | Overseas Policy and Defence Committee [British] |
| OSI | Office of Special Operations of the CIA |
| OSS | Office of Strategic Services [American] |
| OTP | One time pad cipher system |
| P Section | SIS Production Section |
| PKI | Indonesian Communist Party |
| POMEF | Political Adviser to Middle East Forces |
| PRC | People's Republic of China |
| PRO | Public Record Office, Kew Gardens, Surrey |
| RKG | Royal Khmer Government [Cambodian] |
| R1-8 | SIS Requirements Directorate Sections |
| ROC | Republic of China (Taiwan) |
| ROK | Republic of Korea |
| ROKA | Republic of Korea Army |
| RSM | Radio Squadron Mobile |
| SACSEA | Supreme Allied Commander South East Asia |
| SAS | Special Air Service [British] |
| SB | Special Branch |
| SCAP | Supreme Commander Allied Powers [MacArthur] |
| SD | State Department |

| | |
|---|---|
| SEAC | South East Asia Command |
| SEATO | South East Asia Treaty Organisation |
| SEP | Surrendered Enemy Personnel |
| SIDASP | Service of Documentation and Social and Political Action (Laos) |
| SIFE | Security Intelligence Far East (MI5/SIS V) [British] |
| Sigint | Signals intelligence |
| SIME | Security Intelligence Middle East (MI5/SIS V) [British] |
| SIS | Secret Intelligence Service (MI6) [British] |
| SIS | Special Intelligence Section [American] |
| SKLP | South Korean Labor Party |
| SOE | Special Operations Executive [British] |
| SSO | Special Security Office, FECOM |
| SSU | Strategic Services Unit [post-war OSS] |
| SWPA | South West Pacific Area |
| UMNO-MCA | United Malays National Organisation-Malayan Chinese Association |
| USAFIK | US Army Forces in Korea |
| USCIB | US Communications Intelligence Board |
| USIS | US Information Service |
| USNA | National Archives, Washington DC |
| WO | War Office [British] |
| W/T | Wireless Telegraphy |
| Y | Wireless interception, usually of a low-level variety |

# Introduction:
# The Clandestine Cold War in Asia, 1945–65

## RICHARD J. ALDRICH, GARY D. RAWNSLEY
## and MING-YEH T. RAWNSLEY

Asia represented the 'hottest' theatre in a global Cold War that lasted for half a century. Across this vast region there were usually several undeclared wars and numerous civil wars in progress, all with their clandestine elements. Among the five occasions when the US National Security Council seriously considered the use of nuclear weapons in this period, four of these instances were triggered by events in Asia.[1] The volatility of this conflict owed something to its additional complexities, for intertwining with obvious Cold War frictions were the pressures of nationalism and anti-colonialism, the politics of neutralism and non-alignment, together with the deep tensions of Sino-Soviet rivalry.

The Cold War in Asia was undoubtedly 'hotter' than its European counterpart, but it can also be distinguished in other ways. Our current knowledge about the European Cold War is more complete. The collapse of authoritarian regimes in East Germany and the Soviet Union, with the consequent opening of archives, has not been replicated everywhere in Asia and this has implications for what we know now. Although there have been substantial releases of new documentation from Beijing and from other Asian centres, the scope and scale of these releases has been more constrained. This is particularly true of the clandestine aspects of the Cold War. In Germany, individuals may consult their own former Stasi files, while in Russia, former KGB officers publish their memoirs with impunity. Remarkably, the former head of Soviet signals intelligence has recently offered detailed commentary on the role of his service and its achievements during the Cold War. By contrast our knowledge of the role and place of Communist Chinese and other Asian Communist secret services in the Cold War remains in its infancy.[2]

William Colby, Director of the CIA during the 1970s and a veteran of the clandestine Cold War in Asia, observed in his memoirs that: 'The great challenges to secret intelligence gathering were ... in Berlin, Vienna and Hong Kong.' Again the contrast between Europe and Asia is instructive. In Europe, we have witnessed the appearance of studies such as *Battleground Berlin*, in which senior CIA and KGB officers have come together to write a collaborative history of their mutually antithetical activities in that city, employing not only memory and interview, but reams of American and Russian declassified documents. We are unlikely to see the appearance of a similar volume dealing with Hong Kong or any other Asian city.

Equally, the history of the U-2 aerial reconnaissance programme over the Soviet Union, including the shoot-down of the Gary Powers aircraft in 1960, is now familiar to many. Yet the sight of photographs of the wreckage of four U-2 aircraft downed by the Chinese and eventually laid out in a neat row in a public park in Beijing in 1966 rarely fails to evoke surprise.[3] In short, the diet of material for the Cold War in Asia has been comparatively thin and many of its clandestine aspects are likely to remain poorly understood for some time to come.[4]

Notwithstanding the persistent problems relating to information in Asia, the moment for the reconsideration of some of these areas seems fortuitous. 'Glasnost' is increasingly a global phenomenon, triggering accelerated programmes of document release in Europe, the United States and Asia. Within this broader process of global declassification we might consider the decision of the authorities in United States to process rapidly documentation that were more than 25 years old, and even to move the declassification of some types of material out of the hands of the agencies that generated the documents. The latter was surely a landmark decision. Equally we might consider the sudden appearance of hitherto elusive Communist figures, such as Chin Peng, leader of the Malayan Communist Party, and their generous collaboration with scholars.[5]

These accelerated 'releases' have offered a fleeting opportunity to researchers and historians. The possibility of consulting intelligence materials, and other types of sensitive records, that are less than 50 years old has allowed a greater combination of archival work and interview work. Some of the documentation in areas such as intelligence, propaganda and special operations is often particularly arcane and therefore commentary and explanation by participants can be of special value. Sometimes the declassification of documents has prompted security-minded witnesses to speak on subjects which they would otherwise have been reluctant to address. Sadly, these witnesses will not be with us forever. The essays that constitute this volume represent a limited attempt to seize this opportunity. They arise from a conference organised to review work arising out of recent documentary releases on Asia and which was deliberately designed to draw together academics and former practitioners in fruitful discussion.

A prominent theme in this volume is that of intelligence. It is clear that Western intelligence services in Asia certainly shared a common state of dilapidation during the early Cold War. Damaged by the pressures of demobilisation, disrupted by decolonisation and further buffeted by summary ejection from one of its principal established areas of activity – mainland China – it was in a poor state by 1949. This was further exacerbated by the low status of Asian intelligence targets generally. Both London and Washington were primarily focused on Moscow and rated the likelihood of a Soviet incursion into Asia to be very low. Europe and the Middle East were considered to be the 'flashpoints' in the late 1940s.

Even the limited intelligence apparatus that was available in Asia showed a marked reluctance to examine Asian targets and the resources available were often focused on the Soviets in Asia. The examples are legion. At the end of the war, British signals intercept staff at Hong Kong found themselves shifting over to collecting Soviet traffic. When George Blake was sent to Seoul to open the first SIS station in Korea, he was told that his priority was to gather material on Soviet Asia, rather than China or North Korea, and his American opposite numbers were similarly Soviet-focused. Accordingly, both the Malayan Emergency in 1948 and the Korean War in 1950 took policy-makers by surprise.[6]

The rush to improve intelligence in Asia after 1950 did not produce immediate results and the construction of agent networks in particular is a matter for those with patient disposition. Human intelligence operations, whether launched into China, Soviet Asia or North Korea were especially dangerous. Local populations were sufficiently terrified to denounce any suspicious persons entering their area, even they happened to be from that particular locality, and the result in Korea and mainland China was a suicidal rate of failure. Poor survival rates were themselves a contributory factor and gradually prompted the authorities to surrender only indifferent human material for agent training. One officer engaged in running air-dropped agent penetrations of North Korea recalled the moment when he began his work. One morning the 'fifteen specially selected Koreans' he had been promised arrived at his facility for training. He could scarcely believe his eyes. Pathetic and malnourished, they were mostly shy rustic youths in their teens, some as young as 15. A week was enough for them to master the use of basic firearms, but they 'had only the haziest idea of the parachute drill'. Accompanying his 'agents' as far as their dropping zones over North Korea, this officer was overcome with a sense of black depression:

Never before had I taken unprepared men into battle and now I was about to do something far worse. I was sending untrained men into the most frightening and lonely of battles ... the cold night air rushed in through the open jump door. The tense queue of men waited to jump. Red light, green light, and the first man stumbled out into the night, then the next, then the next. The fourth hesitated and was pushed by those behind, and so the procession of fear went on until the fuselage was empty but for myself.[7]

Agent operations launched from Japan and Taiwan were equally unsuccessful. Eventually, in the early 1960s the head of the CIA station in Taipei, Ray Cline, pressed for the re-deployment of U-2 aircraft, which had ceased their increasingly hazardous flight over the Soviet Union, to Taiwan. His argument was that the rate of human agent attrition required a radical change in tactics. American U-2 pilots had already over-flown the Chinese coast from Japan during the Taiwan Straits Crisis of 1958, but now the CIA helped to launch a U-2 programme run by the ROC Air Force with pilots from Taiwan. The result was a comprehensive picture of Chinese missile development.

At the same time signals interception capability was continually expanded. Yet these new sources were not immune to countermeasures. Much Chinese communications traffic still went by landline and could not be intercepted, while the U-2s launched from Taiwan were becoming vulnerable by the mid-1960s. Satellites were the way ahead and in 1964 it was satellite photography that allowed the prediction of the first Chinese nuclear test.[8]

As with the Soviet Union, Western intelligence co-operation in Asia was encouraged by the nature of Communist China as a hard target. The close nature of Western co-operation in intelligence collection is often attributed to familiar patterns of co-operation established during World War II and indeed, in some cases, World War I. The legacy of close wartime personal associations – for example British and American intelligence officers working shoulder to shoulder in Eisenhower's SHAEF Command – was clearly important. But in Asia World War II, with its strongly imperial complexion, had left a legacy of tensions as well as friendships for many secret services and propaganda agencies employed by the British, Americans, French and Dutch.[9] Cold War pressures, particularly after 1949 helped to overcome these problems. The key factor driving co-operation was the extreme difficulty of collecting any intelligence from inside areas such as Soviet Asia, Communist China and North Korea where agents enjoyed a short life. In these conditions of famine, any allied contribution to the overall picture was considered valuable.

Although co-operation in the area of collection and sharing of raw data was considerable, the more complex area of intelligence analysis and interpretation was marked by distrust. While great volumes of agent reports, decrypts and finished analyses were exchanged, nevertheless the whole process of interpretation was characterised by justified suspicions that intelligence might be used to manipulate policy. Attempts to produce agreed 'Allied' reports often failed or resulted in compromise papers. These suspicions were exacerbated by deep disagreements over policy towards mainland China. On the one hand Washington suspected Britain and its Commonwealth allies as purveyors of material that would always suggest that Beijing's mentality was relatively defensive, while on the other hand Taiwan's secret services were anxious to impart a view of Beijing as extremely aggressive.

In Washington suspicions were heightened by clear examples of efforts to 'plant' material on the CIA by Taipei. One experienced CIA officer, who had served in many Asian locations, recalls how a Chinese agent recruited in Vietnam, with a supposed network of sub-agents working in southern China, eventually proved to be a officer in the Taiwanese intelligence service who was merely feeding him material that emanated from Taipei.[10] Within the vast United States national intelligence system there were also divisions and rivalries. National Intelligence Estimates were often ignored by policy-makers in favour of their own departmental studies that imbued the outlook of that particular section of the administration.[11]

Despite these uncertainties, intelligence in Asia was no less critical than it had been during World War II. Limited, but large-scale, military conflicts such as Korea, and later Vietnam, re-introduced many operational issues confronted during 1937–45. These ranged from the role of theatre commanders to the urgent demands for real-time intelligence on the battlefield.

As Matthew Aid makes clear in his extraordinary exposition on American human and signals intelligence and Korea, the extent to which the lessons of the previous conflict would, or would not, be successfully applied was crucially determined at the theatre level. Calamitous failures in the area of signals intelligence during the Korean War were central to Truman's decision to create the National Security Agency in 1952.

In a different context, Philip Davies explores the parallel complexities involved in the relationship between centre and region for the British SIS. Again, the problems of centre and region had impressed themselves between 1941 and 1945, but still remained live issues a decade later.[12]

What was the broader significance of the strategic intelligence effort in Asia? For the United States, faced with a continual state of war, near war, or proxy war, with mainland China until 1972, the premium was always upon military intelligence against the background of conflicts which often seemed to threaten to develop into a wider Asian war. For her allies, these conflicts provided both opportunities and dangers.

As Gary Rawnsley and Johannes R. Lombardo demonstrate, areas around the perimeter of China, especially Taiwan and Hong Kong, served as crucially important watchtowers looking into Communist China. The value of these centres was enhanced for the United States by the lack of even an American embassy in Beijing.

For the smaller powers, British, South Korean and also Taiwan's contributions to the Western 'pool' of intelligence in Asia were thereby enhanced and helped to offset the imbalance of these alliance relationships. Notwithstanding this, there are indications that 'minor' intelligence powers did not always receive their full credit. As Matthew Aid underlines, the linguistic contribution of signals intelligence personnel drawn from Japan, South Korea and from Taiwan, was critical to some of the achievements later in the Korean War and this debt remains largely unacknowledged.

In the areas of propaganda and special operations, the clandestine Cold War in Asia exhibited a distinctly local appearance. Whether we choose to focus on the bizarre sight of Chinese shelling each other with leaflets in the offshore islands crises of 1954 and 1958, or of Britons fighting on both sides of a conflict between Karen tribesmen and the central Burmese government, the Cold War in the Asian theatre seemed confined to the region in reach and intensity, and often had a uniquely local texture.

Yet beneath this facade lay a complexity of wider interests and involvement; the battle may have been regional, but the undercurrents of the war were no doubt global. These ostensibly local conflicts were quickly subsumed into the wider Cold War collision between East and West, between free-market liberal democracy and Communism. By accenting such divisions, it became much easier to package complex local political contests in readily digestible terms, and thus helped justify extensive involvement by non-regional actors. Indeed countries such as South Korea and Taiwan undoubtedly felt more secure, and indeed at liberty to engage in a degree of Cold War fighting, because of their place within a global pattern of alliance.

As in Europe, the Asian Cold War was characterised by the application of three opaque functional strategies – intelligence, propaganda, and special operations – that paralleled the transparency of diplomatic and conventional military activities. These three functional themes are complementary rather than separate, and form a symbiotic relationship. Chapters by Rawnsley and Lombardo as well as all the essays on the Malayan Emergency in this volume underline that intelligence is essential for effective propaganda. We learn from the contributions on Malaya by Kumar Ramakrishna and Karl Hack that publicity can often work with 'special operations' to generate a degree of popular support they might otherwise lack.

By 1960 propaganda, special operations and intelligence were moving out of the shadows and onto a centre stage, beginning to occupy the prominent place that they would assume during the Confrontation with Indonesia and the American phase of the war in Vietnam. As Michael McClintock has noted: 'This hidden dimension became the chosen instrument for permanent military action below the threshold of full-scale war or open intervention – another kind of war, that was waged continuously behind the false peace of the post-WWII era.'[13]

One of the most sustained areas of linkage between the essays in this volume is their concern with British and American interventions in the region. This suggests the deep post-colonial involvement of the Western powers in the area, and also their shared anxiety to prevent the spread of Communism through the region. Thus colonial problems quickly assumed a Cold War character, and the British and Americans decided to solve the problems they faced by employing a generic Cold War approach. For both Britain and the United States, propaganda and special operations seemed to offer answers to awkward power problems in the Third World. For the British these instruments were often employed in the context of military weakness and awkward imperial retreats, achieving by means of the 'hidden hand' what could not be achieved by the fancy footwork of informal imperialism, negotiated concession and the endless search for that elusive person, the 'moderate nationalist'. While for the United States they helped to address the equally awkward problem of the muscle-bound superpower confronted with a range of elusive problems in the Third World that an ever larger nuclear arsenal could not address.

Special operations are not always what they appear to be. This is strikingly apparent from the chapters by Mona Bitar and Lotta Hedman. Bitar's research on the CIA's operations during what she terms the Year of Coups in Cambodia and South Vietnam is a telling illustration of the problems of secret service activity amid troublesome allies. Prince Norodom Sihanouk has long-maintained that CIA planned to unseat him, in the same manner that the CIA and SIS had tried to apply pressure to Sukarno and other non-aligned leaders during the 1950s.[14]

In fact the reality was quite the reverse. CIA station chiefs in Saigon and Bangkok were doing everything in their power to restrain both Thailand and Vietnam in their own local animosities with Cambodia, a legacy of older regional rivalries that stretched back over centuries. These ancestral battles over control of the Annamite chain were, for the participants in mainland South East Asia, more important than the global Cold War struggle.

Despite Sihanouk's protestations of CIA activity against him, it was instead his opponent, Ngo Dinh Diem who fell in a coup that enjoyed at least CIA approval in 1963. The coup in South Vietnam resolved little and in March 1964, Robert McNamara told President Lyndon Johnson that since Diem's murder a year earlier, the situation had 'unquestionably been growing worse'.[15] While Viet Cong control and influence held steady, and was even increasing in some parts of South Vietnam, the new regime found its grip on the situation slackening. Casualties from among the ranks of the South Vietnamese Army (ARVN) steadily mounted, while attacks against American personnel, still acting ostensibly in an 'advisory' capacity, were likewise rising. The stage was set for the unplanned escalation of American commitment to Vietnam.

In his address to the nation in August 1964, Johnson drew parallels between Vietnam and the Cold War crises of Greece, Turkey, Berlin, Cuba and Lebanon. The Cold War historian Martin Walker has suggested that this revealed 'how thoroughly the US was misreading the political dynamics in South East Asia'.[16] Clearly this is a serious indictment either of the way America's intelligence community misunderstood Vietnam, failed (perhaps deliberately) to pass on its intelligence to key policy-makers, or the way the White House and Pentagon decided to ignore intelligence because its conclusions and recommendations contradicted American policy.

Eva-Lotta Hedman's discussion of one of the most famous American Cold War warriors, Major General Edward G. Lansdale is an instructive insight into the place of myth in the Cold War. It also highlights an important theme that runs throughout this volume, that so-called clandestine activities were often surprisingly high-profile, whether they were guerrilla raids against China, trumpeted in the Free China Press, or Lansdale's search for starring roles in both the Philippines and Vietnam. Hedman focuses on Lansdale's relationship with Ramon Magasaysay, 'a rising star in Philippine politics and a protégé of US advisers'.[17] In his 1972 memoirs, Lansdale provided a clear enunciation of his mission:

> My orders were plain. The United States government wanted me to give all help feasible to the Philippine government in stopping the attempt by the Communist-led Huks to overthrow that government by force. My help was to consist mainly of advice where needed and desired. It was up to me to figure out how best to do this.[18]

Hedman shuns a pedestrian narrative approach to Lansdale's activities in the Philippines, and focuses instead on how he has become part of the mythology of the clandestine Cold War. Lansdale was one of President Kennedy's principal advisers, a charismatic figure that lived up to the President's romantic vision of a prominent counter-insurgent and psychological warrior. Although disliked by many in the administration – he had his critics in the Defence and State Departments and while Vice-President Johnson was certainly not a fan – most of his eccentric and individualistic methods survived. They offer striking parallels with the 1980s when Ronald Reagan promised in his election campaign to unleash the CIA and went on to revive an American penchant for glamorous unconventional warfare.

The Philippines model of counter-insurgency left an indelible mark on American approaches to dealing with Asian communists, especially in Vietnam, which illuminated the contrasting British and American approaches. Lansdale's more devolved methods were criticised by British commentators on counter-insurgency, such as Sir Robert Thompson. Thompson had directed counter-insurgency operations in Malaya, and later headed the British Advisory Mission in Vietnam. Lansdale rejected the Malayan model, recalled in this volume by Karl Hack and by the valuable personal reminiscences of Brian Stewart, insisting that it was too colonial and more concerned with establishing order than defending democracy.

In doing so Lansdale was unconsciously echoing the familiar critique of other American practitioners who had developed close relationships with Asian proteges, for example Commander Milton 'Mary' Miles of Navy Group China and his partner Tai Li, who both loathed the mentality of the 'old China hand'.[19] The differences were not ones of approach but of context, since British-managed counter-insurgencies were always able to hold out the attraction of eventual strife-free road to independence, in contrast to the option of struggle. The United States often found herself offering security support in more problematic post-colonial context in which no such assurances were possible.

The Thompson Mission or British Advisory Mission (BRIAM) was described rather mundanely by one Foreign Office brief as a 'small group of civilian officers with Malayan experience' whose duties were to 'advise on administrative and police matters'.[20] The diplomatic aspects of BRIAM are now fairly well-established by scholars, but equally, significant sections of the records of this organisation remain closed to public inspection. This is hardly surprising given that BRIAM was required to have relations with the internal security organisation run by Diem's singularly unpleasant brother Nhu, at whose hands many political opponents of the regime met their end.[21]

BRIAM's failure to dissuade the authorities in South Vietnam from indulging in large-scale a programme of political liquidation is almost certainly one of the subjects still shielded from public inspection. Indeed, as Tony Shaw has pointed out in the context of Korea, propaganda organisations, such as Britain's Information Research Department, often found themselves dealing with the controversial aftermath of domestic security activity in Asia.[22]

The British intelligence community in Malaya certainly adopted a distinctly colonial approach to the insurgency. Yet as Brian Stewart underlines part of its responsibility was to bring the colonial government in Kuala Lumpur closer to the Chinese people and it was remarkably successful in that. In presenting the more human face of colonial government, the British were able to pacify the Chinese Communists and sow the seeds of disunity that would lead to their eventual collapse in 1958. As well as bringing out the more avuncular style of much British security activity in the colonies, we are also reminded of the holistic nature of this approach. Although Chinese Affairs in Malaya was especially concerned with intelligence, all aspects of the British administration were, to some extent, part of the intelligence machine, moreover, intelligence was especially important in informing propaganda. Information bred success and success, once well publicised, bred information.

The Chinese were likewise a central concern for the American intelligence community. The contributions to this volume by Lombardo and Rawnsley reveal, for the first time, the full extent of American-supported operations in Hong Kong and Taiwan directed towards the mainland of China. The Americans, still reeling from their 'loss' of China in 1949 were determined, once the Korean War broke out, to prevent Beijing from making further inroads into the region. While the CIA launched extensive secret operations in Taiwan in 1951, the vast American consulate in Hong Kong – the largest 'consulate' in the world – was a major conduit for intelligence about the mainland. Much to the consternation of the British authorities there who thought American activities were far too provocative, operatives were busy funding the Kuomintang and other anti-Communist organisations.

Many of their operations – intelligence gathering, propaganda and guerrilla raids against the Fukien coast of China – were launched from Taiwan's offshore islands, Kinmen and Matsu. It came as little surprise then, to America's intelligence community that in 1954 and 1958, the Communists should take offence at these 'provocative' actions, and respond by shelling the islands. Yet while the KMT under Generalissimo Chiang Kai-shek remained adamant that the mainland could be liberated by his forces with US assistance, the Americans were less convinced; intelligence reports suggested that sufficient resistance to the Communists had not developed, and that American opinion would not support a war for the islands.

Besides, the shelling of the islands were designed more to test the US commitment to Taiwan and as a protest against American involvement in the Middle East, than an attempt to expand Chinese influence across the Taiwan Strait. Taiwan's propaganda machinery published accounts of its special operations against the mainland, though Rawnsley suggests this was designed more to service Taiwan's diplomatic manoeuvres in the United States than intimidate the Communist authorities in Beijing.

Propaganda, more than intelligence, was central to the final destruction of the Malayan Communist Party (MCP), considered in detail here by Ramakrishna. While the government was enjoying far more military successes against the MCP by 1954, one can only acquire a full understanding of the surrender of the remaining hardcore terrorists in 1958 that brought the Emergency in Malaya to an end by examining the government's policy on surrendered enemy personnel or 'SEPs' between 1949 and 1958, which Sir Robert Thompson noted was the 'main base' of psychological warfare.[23] The surrender policy was part of a wider propaganda and psychological warfare offensive that combined traditional counterinsurgency tactics with a sophisticated amnesty programme that was liberal, credible and honourable in its treatment of the MCP. 'The whole idea', writes Ramakrishna, was to address the terrorists in 'a most palatable language'.

By contrast Hack takes a different approach and argues that we will fully understand the defeat of the MCP in Malaya only when we focus less on hearts and minds, and appreciate the role of population control, spearheaded by Lt-General Sir Harold Briggs, Sir Gerald Templer's predecessor as Director of Operations. Both propaganda and intelligence, he argues, should be viewed as 'important, but subordinate' ingredients of an approach that emphasised population control. While Hack concurs with Ramakrishna that policy towards the insurgents became more tolerant and 'palatable', he seeks to emphasise that political concessions were an important and effective part of the counter-insurgency as early as 1951. Hack argues that the turning point in the Emergency was not as late as 1958, but perhaps as early as 1951, gaining further momentum when Templer was appointed both High Commissioner and Director of Operations. In this way, the intelligence, propaganda, and counter-insurgency were not only combined with political approaches to the problems in Malaya, thus providing the essential consistency between means and ends, but it also meant that operations were centralised.

Both studies contribute to a fuller understanding of British activities in Malaya that contributed to the end of the emergency. They not only suggest different ways of interpreting a growing body of complex evidence, they also confirm that this area is likely to remain the subject of lively scholarly debate for a long time to come. Few would dissent form the view that the inability to identify a unicausal explanation for the defeat of the MCP lends support to the idea that, on the ground, is not only difficult, but also unwise, to completely separate intelligence, propaganda and special operations. The problem is combining them in a sophisticated system that provides for an accelerating cycle of victory, the key to success in counter-insurgency operations.

American scholars have observed that propaganda operations in Vietnam often lacked such sophistication. Propaganda there failed to understand and adapt to the local society, the cornerstone of victory in Malaya, and was inefficient in organising indigenous propaganda machinery that would guarantee that such problems would not arise.[24] Consider, for example, the level of expertise within the remnants of the Chinese Affairs Department within the British Colonial Office that contributed towards the propaganda victory over the Malayan Communist movement. The differences between the two conflicts are striking:

> In war, especially civil war, conventional propaganda and psychological warfare are only effective when victories are won on the field and morale-building political and economic reforms achieved behind the lines: There is no US government agency truly qualified and staffed to conduct psychological operations in a war the size of Vietnam. ... Propaganda cannot make bad policy palatable.[25]

Taken together, the contributions by Rawnsley, Bitar and Ramakrishna suggest that effective and credible propaganda is dependent on reliable intelligence, which in turn requires competent interpretation. The information gathered by intelligence activities may be accurate, but if its interpretation is wrong, misguided, or simply ignored all together, then the impact of propaganda strategies, special operations and relevant policies will be minimised.

Second, we begin to understand the importance of identifying resources and motivations. The reasons why particular powers became involved in regional conflicts are untangled by all of the essays in this volume. This then provides a more comprehensive insight into the relationships between policy and intelligence. Only when intelligence gathering and interpretations of the collected information are adequate will government machineries be able to detect the true motivations that lay behind some of the more puzzling episodes in Cold War history. This enables policy-makers to design satisfactory responses.

The issue of interests is at the core of David Easter's chapter on British policy towards Indonesian rebel movements during the 'Confrontation'. Unable to engage in overt military activities against Indonesia, the British favoured providing covert assistance to rebel groups that would carry out subversive operations against Indonesia. The few individuals involved in discussions arrived at a consensus that while such activity would not overthrow the Indonesian government, they would 'intensify existing political and economic strains within the country'. Thus Easter documents evidence that suggests Indonesians were trained by the British in various aspects of subversion, including weapons handling, psychological warfare and incitement.

This contribution reminds us that while Cold War historians are familiar with many of the high points of Cold War special operations, the coups and attempted coups, many instances of the clandestine application pressure short of overthrow remain unexamined, even unidentified.

All the analyses in this volume underline the problems of control in the area of clandestine activity. This final theme resonates particularly with Richard Aldrich's discussion of a renegade operation by SOE elements in Burma. In 1948 and 1949 ex-SOE operatives trained and armed Karen guerrilla units to fight the Burmese government, while a British Military Mission supported the government forces. Once MI5 had probed the affair, foreknowledge of the planned coup itself became an embarrassment and a problem. At various points London clearly considered switching sides and backing the SOE renegades if the fortunes of the central government seemed to be moving towards a terminal decline.

This privateer SOE operation in Burma has striking parallels with British operations in the Yemen in the 1960s, and even some operations in Africa in the 1990s.[26] However, privateer operations remain yet another aspects of Cold War history that is relatively neglected. In that respect this volume represents the opening words of new chapters of Cold War history. Much of this remains either unexplored or else still hidden from us.

## NOTES

1. These were Korea, Dien Bien Phu, and twice during the Taiwan Straits crises.
2. David Kahn, 'Soviet Comint in the Cold war', *Cryptologia* 22/1 (1998) pp.1–34; David Childs and Richard Popperwell, *The Stasi: East Germany's Secret Police* (London: Macmillan 1996).
3. William Colby, *Honorable Men* (London: Hutchinson 1978) p.103, see also Richard E. Johnson, interview transcript, 30 Jan. 1991, Foreign Affairs Oral History Program, 7. D.E. Murphy, S.A. Kondrashev, and G. Bailey, *Battleground Berlin: CIA vs KGB in the Cold War* (New Haven, CT: Yale UP 1997). One of these photographs from Beijing is reproduced in B.R. Rich and L. Janos, *Skunk Works* (Boston: Little Brown 1994).
4. The exception of course is Vietnam and Laos (but not Cambodia) on which much has been written. See for example, Timothy N. Castle, *At War in the Shadow of Vietnam: U.S. Military Aid to the Royal Lao Government, 1955-1975* (Ithaca, NY: Cornell UP 1993); Sedgwick Tourison, *Secret Army Secret War* (Annapolis, MD: Naval Inst. Press 1995); Roger Warner, *Backfire: The CIA's Secret War in Laos and Its Link to the War in Vietnam* (NY: Simon & Schuster 1995).
5. Anna Nelson, 'Opening the Door to Intelligence History: The Example of the Kennedy Assassination Records Review Board', paper to the 5th Annual Meeting of the International Intelligence History Study Group, Akademie für Politische Bildung, Tutzing, 20 June 1999.
6. George Blake, *No Other Choice* (London: Cape 1990) pp.120–4.
7. Ellery Anderson, *Banner Over Pusan* (London: Evans 1960) pp.34–5, 90–2, 160, 176–7, 199–201. Aspects of Anderson's account are challenged by Evanhoe, *Dark Moon: Eighth Army Special Operations in the Korean War* (Annapolis, MD: Naval Inst. Press 1995) pp.103–34.

8.  Ray Cline, *Chiang Ching-kuo Remembered* (Washington DC: US Global Strategy Council 1989) pp.83–92. See also Gregory W. Pedlow and Donald E. Welzenbach, *The CIA and the U-2 Program, 1954–1974* (Washington DC: CIA 1998) pp.211–33.
9.  Richard J. Aldrich, *Intelligence and the War Against Japan: Britain, America and the Politics of Secret Service* (Cambridge: CUP 2000) pp.201–46.
10. Ralph McGehee, *Deadly Deceits: My 25 Years in the CIA* (NY: Sheridan Square 1983) pp.50–1. See also Peer de Silva, *Sub Rosa: The CIA and the Use of Intelligence* (NY: Times Books 1978).
11. Patrick Mescall, 'The Triumph of Parochialism and Bureaucracy: Robert S. McNamara and the Birth of the Defence Intelligence Agency', in Rhodri Jeffreys-Jones and Andrew Lownie (eds.) *North American Spies: New Revisionist Essays* (Edinburgh UP 1991).
12. Christopher Andrew, *For the President's Eyes Only: Secret Intelligence and the American Presidency from Washington to Bush* (London: HarperCollins 1995) pp.196–7.
13. Michael McClintock, *Instruments of Statecraft: U.S. Guerrilla Warfare, Counter-Insurgency, Counter-Terrorism, 1940–1990* (NY: Pantheon 1992) p.xv.
14. On the American aspects see A.R. Kahin and G. Kahin, *Subversion as Foreign Policy: The Secret Eisenhower and Dulles Debacle in Indonesia* (London: I.B. Tauris 1995). On the British aspects see Matthew Jones, '"Maximum Disavowable Aid": Britain, the United States and the Indonesian Rebellion, 1957-8', *English Historical Review* 114/459 (1999) pp.1182–216. American encouragement of the clandestine war in Tibet looks more and more like an effort to push India away from non-alignment than against China, see S. Mahmud Ali, *Cold War in the High Himalayas* (London: Curzon 1999).
15. Michael R. Beschloss, *Kennedy v. Khrushchev: The Crisis Years, 1960–1963* (London: Faber 1991) p.693.
16. Martin Walker, *The Cold War* (London: Fourth Estate 1993) p.196.
17. McClintock (note 13) p.106.
18. Edward Lansdale, *In the Midst of Wars: An American's Missions to Southeast Asia* (NY: Harper & Row 1972) p.2. The author inevitably paints a somewhat quixotic portrait of himself, fuelled no doubt by the lavish praise heaped upon him by President Kennedy.
19. See McClintock (note 13) p.270; Yu Maochun, *OSS in China: Prelude to the Cold War in Asia* (New Haven, CT: Yale UP 1997) pp.88–9.
20. FO Brief for Lord Privy Seal's visit to Australia, 24 Jan. 1962, PRO, FO371/166726/DV1015/2/G.
21. Anthony Short, *The Origins of the Vietnam War* (London: Longmans 1994) p.00.
22. Ian Beckett, 'Robert Thompson and the British Advisory Mission to South Vietnam' *Small Wars and Insurgencies* 8/3 (Winter 1997) pp.41–63; Tony Shaw, 'The Information Research Department and the Korean War', *Journal of Contemporary History* 34/2 (1999) pp.263–81.
23. Robert Thompson, *Defeating Communist Insurgency: Experiences from Malaya and Vietnam* (London: Chatto & Windus 1966) p.90.
24. S.C. Sarkesian, *Unconventional Conflict in a New Era: Lessons from Malaya and Vietnam* (Westport, CT; Greenwood Press 1993).
25. Thomas Sorenson, *The Word War: The Story of American Propaganda* (NY: Harper & Row 1968) pp.291–2.
26. We are indebted to conference participants for drawing our attention to some of these parallels.

# PART I

# CHINA AND THE CHINESE PERIMETER

# 2

# US Humint and Comint in the Korean War: From the Approach of War to the Chinese Intervention

## MATTHEW M. AID

In May 1945, four months before the end of World War II, William F. Friedman, the 'father of American cryptology', wrote a Top Secret memorandum which stated, in part, 'Events in the past few years have also demonstrated that war in the future, if it comes, will come with devastating suddenness – unless the signal intelligence service is sufficiently competent to give adequate warning of impending disaster, for only by signal intelligence conducted in peacetime will we be in a position to know of the secret thoughts, actions, and machinations of a predatory and ruthless enemy.'[1] However, Friedman's prescient admonition was ignored or obscured by partisan internecine fighting within the US intelligence community following the end of World War II. Five years later, on 25 June 1950, the United States paid the consequences in a then obscure country in the Far East called South Korea.

American historians, perhaps correctly, have argued that the North Korean invasion of South Korea on 25 June 1950 ranks along with the Japanese surprise attack on Pearl Harbor in December 1941 as one of the worst American intelligence disasters in the twentieth century.

On the surface, the similarities between Pearl Harbor and Korea are striking. The North Koreans struck across the 38th Parallel on a Sunday morning; US foreign policy-makers in Washington were admittedly caught entirely by surprise by the attack; and there was a significant amount of intelligence data which should have indicated to American intelligence analysts that war in Korea was imminent. Yet somehow, this information was misinterpreted or never made its way to the people who needed it the most.

An examination of recently declassified documents shows that a myriad of factors contributed to the Korean intelligence disaster. The most important factor was the decrepit state of the American intelligence community in the Far East at the time of the North Korean invasion; as well as inexcusably poor intelligence collection, processing, analysis and reporting practices and procedures, both in the Far East and in Washington DC.

The commander of American forces in the Far East, General of the Army Douglas A. MacArthur, and his intelligence chief, Major General Charles A. Willoughby, have born the brunt of criticism in the past for America's failure to anticipate the North Korean attack. An examination of recently declassified documents suggests that Generals MacArthur and Willoughby indeed bear much of the onus for the Korean intelligence disaster. However, these documents also implicate other military and civilian intelligence officials within the Department of Defense, the Department of State, and the Central Intelligence Agency in the Korean fiasco. In particular the role of communications intelligence or 'Comint' forms a crucial, but as yet, poorly understood dimension of this subject.

## A DISASTER WAITING TO HAPPEN

The American intelligence situation in the Far East in June 1950 can only be characterized as a state of all-pervasive chaos. Five American military and civilian intelligence agencies, as well as a host of smaller intelligence collection units, were active in the Far East. Each of these various agencies operated independently of one another with little cooperation or coordination of effort, and the relationship among these units could hardly be described as harmonious. At the top of the intelligence 'food chain' in the Far East was General Douglas MacArthur, whose Far East Command (FECOM) headquarters in Tokyo was responsibile for monitoring military and political developments throughout the Far East.

MacArthur's intelligence chief was 58-year-old Major General Charles Andre Willoughby. General Willoughby is one of the most colorful and controversial officers in the history of American intelligence. Tall and stoutly built, former colleagues described him as the epitomy of the cold and haughty Prussian staff officer, who spoke with a heavy German accent despite the fact that he had left Germany 40 years before the beginning of the Korean War. One former member of Willoughby's staff in Tokyo described him as 'our Junker general', others in Tokyo referred to Willoughby as 'Sir Charles' or 'The Count' because of his studied regal comportment. Moody and prone to bouts of rage, Willoughby was feared and loathed by many who worked directly for him, as well as by many officers on General MacArthur's staff. Willoughby also inspired considerable loyalty from many who knew him. There is no doubt that Willoughby possessed considerable intellect. He spoke several foreign languages fluently, including German, Spanish and French, wrote books and monographs on military history, and was an accomplished actor.

Willoughby's professed right-wing political leanings were as controversial then as now. While stationed in the Philippines before World War II, Willoughby's circle of friends included Spaniards who were active supporters of the Spanish dictator, Generalissimo Francisco Franco, including individuals who were later accused of collaborating with the Japanese during the war. Willoughby made no secret of his admiration for Franco, whom he claimed to have met in Spanish Morocco in 1923, as well as the Portuguese dictator, Antonio Salazar. MacArthur on occasion affectionately referred to Willoughby as 'my little fascist'. Loyal to MacArthur to the point of sycophancy, one of MacArthur's senior staff officers at the time described Willoughby as '... the ideal man to be MacArthur's G-2. He knew exactly what MacArthur wanted to hear, and he told him exactly that, and no more.' The writer John Gunter later wrote that 'MacArthur is the only man in the world about whose opinion he cares anything.'[2]

General Willoughby commanded not one, but two separate and distinct intelligence staffs, both located in the Dai-Ichi Building in downtown Tokyo: the Far East Command (FECOM) G-2 staff, which focused on military intelligence matters in the Far East, and the Supreme Commander Allied Powers (SCAP) G-2 staff, which performed civil intelligence gathering and counterintelligence functions exclusively in occupied Japan. The vast majority of both G-2 staffs were composed of US Army personnel, despite the fact that they were supposed to be 'joint commands' composed of personnel from all branches of the US Armed Forces.

Like the rest of the American intelligence community, General Willoughby's intelligence organization had been decimated by the postwar defense budget cuts and demobilization of the American armed forces. Between December 1945 and June 1950, General Willoughby's SCAP and FECOM G-2 staffs in Tokyo had been reduced from 3,872 to 898 military and civilian personnel, and at the time of the North Korean invasion, Willoughby was in the process of further cutting the size of his G-2 staff.[3]

The relationship between Willoughby's two intelligence staffs was anything but harmonious. In the five years following the end of World War II, Willoughby had lavished most of his attention on the SCAP civil intelligence organization at the expense of the FECOM military intelligence staff, largely because of General MacArthur's postwar emphasis on the civil administration and restructuring of Japan.[4]

As a result, a disproportionately large percentage of General Willoughby's staff in Tokyo was devoted to civil intelligence and counterintelligence collection in Japan. Of the 864 personnel assigned to the

FECOM/SCAP G-2 offices in June 1950, fully 60 per cent were engaged in non-foreign intelligence related activities, such as monitoring Japanese ultra-conservative and Communist political activities, mail and newspaper censorship, operating the Japanese police, fire, coast guard and prisons, monitoring the Japanese press and public opinion, liaising with foreign embassies in Tokyo and the Japanese government, as well as maintaining a large historical office which was engaged in writing a multi-volume history of General MacArthur's military campaigns in the Southwest Pacific during World War II.

In addition, General Willoughby's SCAP G-2 staff controlled over 1,300 US Army Counter Intelligence Corps (CIC) and linguist personnel stationed throughout Japan, almost all of whom were engaged in peacetime counter-intelligence activities.[5]

FECOM G-2's highest priority was the monitoring of Soviet military activities in the Far East. FECOM's primary source of information about Russian military activities came from the interrogation of almost 1.5 million Japanese prisoners of war who had returned from captivity in the Soviet Union or Soviet-controlled areas in the Far East between the end of the Second World War and June 1950. Between December 1946 and June 1948, the FECOM Central Interrogation Center in Tokyo had screened almost 625,000 Japanese repatriates, briefly interrogated 57,000 former Japanese POWs at their port of entry, and more extensively interrogated 9,000 former POWs in Tokyo who possessed 'significant intelligence information about the Soviet Union'. Linguistic shortages, however, prevented all but the most important of the these interrogations from being reported in anything more than a cursory fashion.[6]

All Humint collection operations in the Far East were controlled by a secretive FECOM intelligence organization based in Tokyo called the Joint Special Operations Branch (JSOB), which was responsible for the planning, coordination and conduct of all espionage and counter-espionage activities in the Far East, including those of the US Army, Navy and Air Force, as well as the CIA's clandestine intelligence gathering unit in Japan, the Field Research Unit, Far East Command (FRU/FEC). JSOB's targets were focused narrowly upon the Soviet Union and typically included targets such as Soviet military and transportation activity along the Trans-Siberian railway, Soviet air activity in the region, Soviet naval activity in the Maritime Province, and fortifications along the Amur River.[7]

The US Far East Air Forces (FEAF) had only a small intelligence staff working out of the Meiji Building in downtown Tokyo. FEAF's intelligence staff and supporting units worked closely with its Army counterparts at FECOM G-2, but maintained considerable autonomy from Willoughby's staff, particularly in the field of aerial reconnaissance. Like its Army and

Navy counterparts in the Far East, FEAF's primary intelligence target prior to June 1950 was Soviet military capabilities in the Far East, particularly military, naval and industrial activities in Siberia.[8]

Prior to early 1949, most of FEAF's intelligence data on Soviet military activities came from FECOM G-2, particularly from the interrogation of returning Japanese POWs by FECOM's Allied Translator and Interrogation Service (ATIS). Air Force intelligence analysts, however, were unhappy about the quantity and quality of the information being received from ATIS about Soviet air force operations and dispositions. As a result, in May 1949, FEAF formed its own 12-man interrogation unit, separate and distinct from ATIS.[9]

FEAF also operated its own Humint collection program, which competed directly with comparable programs being undertaken by FECOM G-2 and the CIA. This program was directly managed by the 115-man FEAF Office of Special Investigations (OSI), which in addition to performing day-to-day counterintelligence functions throughout the Far East, also collected 'positive intelligence' (Humint) through overt and covert means. In particular, the FEAF OSI District Offices at Kimpo Airfield in South Korea (District No.8) and at Clark Air Force Base in the Philippines (District No.2) were tasked with collecting Humint after the Air Attaché offices in both countries were closed in November 1949.[10] FEAF aerial reconnaissance programs watched the waters contiguous to Japan.[11] US Navy intelligence capabilities in the Far East were practically non-existent at the time of the North Korean invasion.[12]

The Central Intelligence Agency (CIA) was supposed to have had an almost complete monopoly in the conduct of foreign clandestine intelligence collection in the Far East and elsewhere. The military, however, which had a longstanding vested interest in Humint collection, partly by virtue of its former control over the remnants of OSS as the Strategic Services Unit or SSU, insisted on its prerogative to operate its own clandestine intelligence collection resources to support military intelligence requirements. The CIA reluctantly accepted the military's contention that overseas military commanders had the inherent right 'to engage in such operations for protecting the safety of their commands', but fought tooth and nail to contain the military's ambitions in this field of endeavor. At the time of the North Korean invasion in June 1950, the relationship between the CIA and military in the clandestine intelligence field in the Far East was still unresolved, and military intelligence officials had become increasingly concerned about the poor quality of the intelligence product they were receiving from the CIA.[13]

General MacArthur's relationship with the CIA prior to the North Korean invasion can only be described as acrimonious and strained, a situation which had long prevailed. During World War II, MacArthur and his intelligence chief, Willoughby, had gone to considerable lengths to keep the CIA's predecessor organization, the Office of Strategic Services (OSS), out of their theater of operations in the Southwest Pacific, going so far as to arrest and deport OSS operatives found operating in the Southwest Pacific theater of operations.[14]

In the years immediately following World War II, MacArthur and Willoughby continued to deny the CIA substantive access to facilities in Japan as well as access to FECOM-generated intelligence data. In December 1946, the Central Intelligence Group (CIG), forerunner of the CIA, established a liaison office with MacArthur's headquarters in Tokyo under the command of a seconded Regular Army officer, Lt Colonel Robert J. Delaney.[15]

At the time of the North Korean invasion, most of the CIA's limited resources in the Far East were focused on mainland China, which had completely fallen to Mao Tse-tung's Chinese Communist forces by November 1949. During World War II, the OSS had conducted large-scale covert intelligence collection and paramilitary activities in mainland China, largely because MacArthur's authority did not extend to the Chinese theater of operations, which was commanded successively by Generals Joseph Stilwell and Al Wedemeyer.

Following VJ-Day, the OSS, then its successors, SSU, CIG and CIA, continued to operate in mainland China, despite interference from US military commanders and intelligence officials in the region. In the fall of 1946, General MacArthur and commander of the US Seventh Fleet in the Pacific, Vice Admiral Charles M. Cooke Jr, had unsuccessfully tried to seize control of these intelligence collection operations in China, but had been rebuffed by the then Director of the CIA, General Hoyt Vandenberg. The CIA's intelligence collection unit in China, which used the covername External Survey Detachment No.44 (ESD 44), had a large station at Shanghai, which continued to operate until the city fell to the communists in late 1949.[16]

With the fall of Shanghai and Chiang Kai-shek's withdrawal to Taiwan in November 1949, the CIA was finally allowed into Japan, albeit on a very limited basis. The first CIA unit to arrive in Japan from China was the Field Research Unit, Far East Command (FRU/FEC), which was the covername for the CIA's covert intelligence collection unit, the Office of Special Operations (OSO). Using a core of old China hands who had formerly worked for the OSO's External Survey Detachment in China, FRU/FEC established itself within the crowded confines of the US Navy base at Yokosuka, Japan, from where it ran agent operations throughout the Far East, albeit closely controlled by General Willoughby's staff.[17]

In January 1950, the Joint Chiefs of Staff (JCS) told MacArthur that they had authorized the CIA to 'provide liaison to your command in order that CIA plans for special operations may be coordinated to meet your operational requirements'. The JCS went on to say, however, that 'This liaison will be effected *only if you have such requirement and express desire to have it affected.*'[18] Not suprisingly, MacArthur was less than thrilled to have the CIA given entrée to his fiefdom. The Far East C-in-C liked the situation just the way it was and wanted to ensure that the CIA understood who was the boss in this part of the world.[19]

The next CIA unit to arrive in Japan was a small detachment from the Office of Policy Coordination (OPC), a covert operations organization which had only been created in the fall of 1948.[20] A small six-man OPC liaison staff called the FECOM G-2 Document Research Section (DRS), headed by George E. Aurell, arrived in Japan in May 1950.[21]

Here cooperation between Willoughby's FECOM G-2 staff and the CIA ended. Severe restrictions were imposed by Willoughby on CIA activities in Japan. FRU/FEC operations in the Far East were required to be 'coordinated' through General Willoughby's staff in Tokyo, and all CIA operatives entering the Far East had to obtain prior approval from FECOM/SCAP headquarters. Liaison between Willoughby's staff and George Aurell's DRS office 'barely existed'. For example, Aurell and his staff were only given limited access to FECOM-generated intelligence data and had virtually no involvement in FECOM's covert intelligence activities in northeast Asia.[22]

US Army intelligence officials, not surprisingly, evaluated the CIA's intelligence collection capabilities in the Far East prior to the North Korean invasion as being 'at a noticeable low level of accomplishment'.[23] At the time of the North Korean invasion, the CIA had few sources of its own in the Far East, being largely dependant on the Chinese Nationalist intelligence services for information, and was in the process of trying to build its own network of agents in the region when the North Koreans struck. Without its own sources of information, the CIA found itself largely dependent on handouts from its military colleagues in the Far East, plus whatever else they were able to obtain through liaison with local friendly intelligence services, which were rewritten and sent to Washington as CIA-generated intelligence product.[24]

There was a fifth intelligence source in the Far East – one which has not hitherto been subjected to sustained analysis – communications intelligence or 'Comint'. Extensive documentation obtained under the Freedom of Information Act has confirmed that at the time of the North Korean invasion, the US Comint infrastructure in the Far East was in a state of flux and disarray – a situation which had existed since the end of World War II.

FIGURE 1

HQ US Army Security Agency, Far East, Tokyo, Japan.

In the five years that followed, the American Comint infrastructure in the Far East had been allowed to dwindle to a shadow of its former self, in large part because of postwar fiscal austerity measures imposed on the US intelligence community as a whole. As of June 1950, the Comint collection and processing resources of the combined American and allied forces in the Far East were described in a Joint Chiefs of Staff document as 'far short of requirements' for peacetime Comint collection requirements, and that the available resources were incapable of handling the vastly greater requirements of wartime.[25]

The Army Security Agency (ASA) had the largest presence in the Far East of the three service cryptologic agencies, but was still feeling the disruptive effects of the 1949 reorganization of the American Comint community, which had resulted in ASA losing its best personnel and equipment to the newly created Armed Forces Security Agency (AFSA) and US Air Force Security Service (USAFSS), reducing ASA to a 'residual Army cryptologic agency searching for a new role'.[26]

All ASA units in the Far East were under the direct operational control of a regional command staff called Army Security Agency, Pacific (ASAPAC), whose headquarters was located within the confines of the Tokyo First Arsenal, an 18-acre former Imperial Japanese Army ordnance facility seven miles northwest of downtown Tokyo (see Figure 1).[27] With only 47 officers, 3 warrant officers and 192 enlisted men assigned, the ASAPAC headquarters staff was small but self-contained.[28] The commanding officer of ASAPAC at the time of the North Korean invasion was Lt Colonel Morton A. Rubin, an experienced and well-respected Comint officer who had commanded ASAPAC since May 1949.[29] There were four ASA listening posts in the Far East, three of which were situated in Japan and one in the Philippines.[30]

All ASA Comint collection and processing functions in the Far East were managed by the ASAPAC Operations Branch at the Tokyo Arsenal, headed by Major Clayton C. Swears, who would later in the early 1960s command the first ASA Comint troops in South Vietnam.[31] The ASAPAC Operations Branch supervised the day-to-day operations of all ASA Comint collection units in the Far East, providing detailed intercept tasking to all ASAPAC listening posts based upon instructions received from Armed Forces Security Agency (AFSA) headquarters in Washington DC. All intercepts from ASAPAC's Far East listening posts were teletyped directly to ASAPAC headquarters in Tokyo, where they were routed to the Operations Branch's processing center.

ASAPAC's traffic analysts extracted any immediately apparent information contained in the intercepts, such as the identities of the transmitters and the recipients based on frequency and call sign usage, direction finding plots, and other data contained in the intercepts. Next, the cryptanalysts attacked those intercepts that had been encoded using IBM tabulating machines, which had arrived in Tokyo in August 1949. Following analysis, the ASAPAC Operations Branch transmitted finished intelligence reports based on the intercepts to authorized Comint consumers in the Far East and the US. Apparently, the cryptanalytical capability at ASAPAC was small, necessitating that all but the most simple of enciphered intercepts be forwarded directly to ASA headquarters in Washington DC. for processing.

In addition, the ASAPAC Operations Branch coordinated Army Comint activities with those being conducted in the Far East by the US Navy and Air Force; and served as the point of contact for Comint consumer agencies in Washington DC as well as FECOM G-2 staff in Tokyo.[32]

The US Navy and Air Force, which had fewer resources than the Army, retained small Comint presences in the Far East, but these two services were barely capable of carrying out their peacetime mission of monitoring Soviet military activities, much less developments elsewhere in the Far East. For example, the US Air Force Security Service found itself in an abysmal state of preparedness. A declassified USAFSS report characterized the Command's capabilities at the outbreak of the Korean War as 'pitifully small and concentrated in the wrong places'.[33] USAFSS had only one Comint collection unit in the Far East, the 1st Radio Squadron Mobile (RSM), based at Johnson Air Base outside Tokyo.[34]

The Naval Security Group's (NSG) resources in the Far East were equally slim, consisting of a Comint intercept site at the Yokosuka naval base near Tokyo, and a small HFDF site at Tengan on the island of Okinawa. At the time of the North Korean invasion, the commander of NAVCOMMUNIT 35 was Commander Daniel W. 'Pop' Heagy, a 51-year old former enlisted man who had spent most of his Navy career as a pharmacist but who had commanded the Navy Comint intercept unit at Chungking, China during World War II. Afterwards, Heagy worked as a staff officer at CSA in Washington before returning to the Far East to take up command of NAVCOMMUNIT 35 in February 1949.[35]

It is important to emphasise that the few American Comint intercept facilities that were available in the Far East during summer 1950 were targeted almost exclusively against Soviet military radio circuits. The ASAPAC listening posts in Japan were busily engaged in intercepting Russian military, air, civil, and commercial radio traffic, as well as some developmental intercept coverage of Chinese military communications.

ASAPAC solved some low-level Soviet military cipher systems in 1949, but most of the intelligence data being churned out by ASAPAC and the other two Service Cryptologic Agencies in the Far East came from traffic analysis of Soviet military and civil radio traffic.

The Air Force's 1st RSM at Johnson Air Base outside Tokyo was dedicating almost all of its intercept resources against Soviet air and air defense forces, while the Naval Security Group's Naval Communications Unit No.35 at Yokosuka focused its resources on the surface and air activities of the Soviet Far East Fleet and Soviet shipping in the Pacific, which was the only threat to US Navy units operating off the North Korean coastline, and to a much lesser degree on the activities of the Chinese fleet. On the whole, American codebreaking efforts in the Far East against Soviet military cryptographic systems were deemed to be entirely unsuccessful by intelligence analysts in Tokyo who saw the resulting Comint product.[36]

All of the service Comint units in the Far East were suffering from serious personnel shortages at the time of the North Korean invasion. At the intercept sites, almost all units reported critical shortages of experienced supervisors, intelligence analysts, linguists, and radio intercept personnel.

With the exception of a sprinkling of junior operations officers and career NCOs, the quality of the military personnel assigned to the Far East listening posts was generally poor. With the notable exception of the Navy, most of the officers assigned to the listening posts in the Far East had little or no prior Comint experience. Morale, in general, among the career Comint officers and NCOs was low, caused in part by mediocre leadership, long duty hours due to personnel shortages, poor advancement possibilities in the Comint career field, and the general tedium that came with peacetime intelligence gathering operations.

Disciplinary problems abounded amongst the young enlisted conscripts who made up the majority of the Comint collection force, marked by alcoholism and rampant venereal disease. Turnover within the Comint units in the Far East was heavy, but not enough skilled replacements were arriving in the Far East to replace the personnel leaving the theater. Reenlistment rates among skilled enlisted Comint technicians were low.[37]

Moreover, Comint collection in the Far East was handled in a lackadaisical manner. The American Comint intercept sites in Japan only operated five and one-half days a week, eight hours a day, and participation in exercises and mobility deployments had virtually ceased because of severe personnel shortages in the Far East. Fiscal constraints had also created chronic shortages of equipment as well as the spare parts. Trained repair and maintenance personnel were also in short supply to keep the aging equipment up and running.[38]

It is important to note that neither the theater commander, General MacArthur, nor his FECOM G-2 staff had any authority or control over what ASAPAC and the other service Comint collection units in the Far East collected. Rather, operational control over the day-to-day operations of the American military Comint intercept sites in the Far East was exercised directly by the headquarters of the three service cryptologic agencies in the United States, and to a lesser degree by the Armed Forces Security Agency in Washington DC.[39] Not suprisingly, Generals MacArthur and Willoughby were extremely unhappy with this arrangement, and complained loudly and repeatedly to the Chief of ASAPAC, Lt Colonel Morton A. Rubin, about the situation.

The tension between FECOM and ASAPAC produced unfortunate situations. In July 1949, ASAPAC requested additional space at the First Tokyo Arsenal for its expanding Comint operations from Headquarters, FECOM. When staff officers at FECOM headquarters, who were not cleared for access to Comint, demanded detailed justification for the expansion, ASAPAC refused to provide data concerning the unit's mission because of classification concerns, prompting complaints to General MacArthur himself about ASAPAC's lack of cooperation. In the resulting storm, FECOM's Military Intelligence Service Division attempted to take control of ASAPAC, and was only thwarted when cooler heads prevailed.[40]

Despite the inherent tension, there was a 'working relationship' between MacArthur's FECOM intelligence staff and ASAPAC. In November 1949, ASAPAC assigned a permanent liaison officer to the FECOM G-2's Order of Battle Section.[41] The NSG intercept units in Japan and on Okinawa forwarded their intercepts to their command headquarters in Washington DC, while the USAFSS 1st RSM sent its intercepts not only to USAFSS headquarters in San Antonio, Texas, but also to the Comint liaison officer with the Far East Air Force (FEAF). All three of the service cryptologic agencies sent copies of their intercepts to AFSA in Washington DC.[42]

Access to Comint by FECOM intelligence analysts was a major problem. The stringent and all-pervasive secrecy surrounding Comint in the postwar years almost certainly impeded the effective analysis and timely reporting of what little Comint that was available in Tokyo prior to the North Korean invasion. The number of individuals on MacArthur's staff cleared for access to Comint appears to have been deliberately kept to a bare minimum. Besides the C-in-C, the only senior FECOM staff officers with regular access to Comint included his chief of staff, Lieutenant General Edward M. Almond and the deputy chief of staff, Major General Doyle O. Hickey; and the FECOM chief of intelligence, Willoughby. Even within the FECOM G-2 staff, access to Comint was strictly kept to a few senior staff officers, including Colonel Louis J. Fortier, Chief of the Theater Intelligence Division; and Lt Colonel Phillip B. Davidson, head of the Plans and Estimates Branch of the FECOM G-2 Theater Intelligence Division.[43]

Few intelligence officers in Tokyo appear to have been cleared for access to Comint, and many of those who were cleared did not know how to use it.[44] Only three intelligence officers assigned to the Plans and

Estimates Branch of the FECOM G-2 Theater Intelligence Division were cleared for access to Comint. These three officers, known as the Joint Special Intelligence Committee (JSIC), were assigned to the Order of Battle Section of the Plans and Estimates Branch, suggesting that the majority of the Comint forwarded by ASAPAC to the intelligence analysts at FECOM G-2 pertained to Soviet military order of battle data. JSIC's title suggests that the three man unit also functioned as FECOM's own Watch Committee, monitoring Comint reporting of Soviet military activities for signs of impending hostilities.[45]

Access to Comint within FECOM was strictly controlled by the GHQ FECOM Special Security Office (SSO), headed by Major O. L. Gentry. The SSO operated out of Room 703, a guarded windowless office on the seventh floor of the Dai-Ichi Building, which it shared with the Plans and Estimates Branch of FECOM G-2's Theater Intelligence Division. Under the operational control of the Order of Battle Section of the Plans and Estimates Branch, the FECOM SSO was the primary conduit for ground and air order of battle information as well as diplomatic Comint received from the Department of the Army's G-2 staff in Washington DC, which flowed into Room 703 over special encrypted teletype machines reserved exclusively for the SSO's use.[46]

Bureaucratic bottlenecks existed which prevented the free flow of Comint to those few individuals who were cleared for access to Comint. According to a recently declassified document, Willoughby had ordered that no Comint material be 'physically disseminated [by the theater SSOs] without his personal approval'. This meant that staff officers and intelligence analysts cleared for access to Comint had to physically go to the appropriate SSO's office and read the material there. Unless authorized by Willoughby, these individuals could not take a copy of the documents back to their offices, even if they were authorized to store Comint material. This system also meant that Comint cleared personnel had to visit the SSO's office every day, otherwise the value of the Comint would be lost because of the time-urgent nature of the material.[47]

INTELLIGENCE COLLECTION IN KOREA

North Korea was deemed to be an intelligence target of mere secondary, if not tertiary, importance in the Far East by the FECOM intelligence staff. All American combat troops had withdrawn from South Korea by 1 July 1949, and South Korea had been effectively placed outside the American defense perimeter by President Truman and Secretary of State Dean Acheson in January 1950.

As a result, far less emphasis was placed on intelligence collection regarding North Korea than on the Soviet Union and the People's Republic of China (PRC). Virtually everyone at FECOM headquarters in Tokyo, from MacArthur down to the lowest intelligence staff officer, later disclaimed any formal responsibility for monitoring events in Korea. A former senior FECOM intelligence officer recently stated that FECOM '... kept half an eye on Korea and collected intelligence on and in Korea as a distinctly secondary effort'.[48] Another former FECOM intelligence officer concurred, arguing that FECOM G-2 'felt no responsibility for Korea [because] it was outside our role of interest'.[49] In May 1951 after his relief from command, General MacArthur told a joint committee of the US Senate that he had no responsibility for Korea, and as such, had paid little attention to events there. Specifically, MacArthur stated: 'I had no jurisdiction whatsoever over Korea. I had nothing whatsoever to do with the policies, the administration, or the command responsibilities in Korea until after the war broke out.' When asked who had overall responsibility for monitoring North Korea, MacArthur replied: 'I fancy that it was the South Korean Government.'[50]

However, available evidence suggests that the MacArthur apologists and the former intelligence officers in Tokyo 'doth protest too much'. On 28 April 1950 a US Army Special Regulation, D/A SR 380-305-5, *Military Security, Army Intelligence Instructions* set out detailed intelligence collection responsibilities and stated 'The Commander in Chief, Far East, is responsible primarily in Japan, the Japanese Mandated Islands, and all other areas of the Far East Command except the Philippine Islands; and secondarily in all areas of strategic interest to his command, **including specifically Korea and the Philippine Islands'**.[51] Further, each issue of the FECOM *Daily Intelligence Summary* contained a detailed summary of all intelligence information concerning Korea, equal to the coverage being received by the Soviet Union and the PRC, suggesting that someone was closely watching events on the Korean peninsula, despite the explicit statements to the contrary by MacArthur and members of his staff.

The deliberately misleading statements that FECOM was not interested in or responsible for intelligence collection about events in North Korea is revealed when one looks at the myriad of FECOM Humint operations taking place in Korea prior to the North Korean invasion. Then as now, collecting hard intelligence about what was going on in North Korea was an extremely difficult proposition. Like the Soviet Union, Eastern Europe, and the Peoples Republic of China, North Korea was truly a 'denied area'. North Korea was, and still remains, a police state. The North Koreans controlled an extremely large and efficient counterintelligence service that made the running of clandestine intelligence gathering operations extremely difficult. Travellers to North Korea were few and far between, and there were very few defectors from that country. All-in-all, it was an extremely difficult environment in which to collect intelligence.[52]

The difficulty of gathering intelligence in North Korea did not keep the US from trying. From the fall of 1945 up until the withdrawal of American forces from South Korea in June 1949, the intelligence staff of US Army Forces in Korea (USAFIK) operated a small network of Korean agents in North Korea. The US Army had built up this network of agents in North Korea immediately after the surrender of Japan and the occupation of Korea in 1945. Agents were also infiltrated in North Korea for specific missions, such as the May 1947 infiltration of two agents across the 38th Parallel to collect intelligence on Soviet uranium mining operations at Chongjin and Nanam. However, after the withdrawal of American forces from Korea in July 1949, this network atrophied and was allowed to wither and die.[53]

Following the withdrawal of US forces from South Korea in summer 1949, responsibility for monitoring military and political events in North Korea fell to the intelligence services of the Republic of South Korea (ROK). A multitude of different South Korean military and civilian intelligence organizations were involved in intelligence collection in North Korea prior to the North Korean invasion. The ROK Army G-2, the ROK Navy Office of Naval Intelligence (ONI), the ROK Army Counter-Intelligence Corps, and the South Korean foreign intelligence organization, the Higher Intelligence Department (HID), were all operating agents in North Korea with varying degrees of success.[54]

Some ROK civilian intelligence agencies were also active in the field of intelligence collection in North Korea. The South Korean National Police, which was subordinate to the Ministry of the Interior, interrogated North Korean refugees and defectors who managed to escape from North Korea across the 38th Parallel. In August 1948, the South Koreans organized a civilian intelligence collection organization called the Korean Research Bureau (KRB), whose organizational structure and mission were largely copied from the US Army's Counter-Intelligence Corps (CIC). Between August 1948 and 1949, the KRB slipped agents into North Korea and conducted a variety of sabotage missions across the 38th Parallel.[55]

Accordingly, disparate South Korean guerrilla units and intelligence operatives were actively crossing the border on sabotage and intelligence collection missions from 1948 onwards. Beginning in early 1949, ROK intelligence agencies began infiltrating agents into North Korea equipped with old Japanese radios, but these agents were quickly discovered and executed by the North Korean security forces.[56] In January 1949, a 14-man South Korean team was captured by the North Koreans attempting to infiltrate across the 38th Parallel to sabotage military targets in the border town of Haeju.[57]

In May 1949, a South Korean guerrilla company crossed the 38th Parallel and attacked the North Korean town of T'aet'an, 10 kilometers inside North Korea.

In June 1949, two companies of South Korean guerrillas belonging to the Ho-rim ('Forest Tiger') Unit attacked across the 38th Parallel near the North Korean town of Inje. Within a week, North Korean security forces destroyed the Ho-rim Unit, killing more than 100 of the South Korean guerrillas and capturing 40.

In August 1949, North Korean put four captured South Korean intelligence operatives on trial in Pyong'yang. The four men had been captured attempting to infiltrate Pyong'yang in July 1949 after executing a successful sabotage mission in the North Korean capital the month before.[58]

In the year before the North Korean invasion, the ROK intelligence agencies were able to build up a comprehensive and detailed picture of North Korean military organization and capabilities. Reams of intelligence data made its way to Seoul from ROK agents and guerrilla teams operating in North Korea.

However, the vast majority of ROK intelligence data about the North Korean military came from North Korean People's Army (NKPA) troops captured during clashes along the 38th Parallel, an occasional defector, and from the interrogation of hundreds of refugees who crossed into South Korea from the North. Much of the information obtained from the NKPA prisoners captured along the 38th Parallel was the result of confessions obtained through torture. Secondary sources included analysis of captured enemy uniforms, insignias, personal identification cards and captured North Korean military documents.[59]

However, given the distinct emphasis on domestic political intelligence collection by all of the South Korean intelligence gathering organs, American intelligence analysts in Tokyo and Washington placed little credence in what KMAG and the American military attachés in Seoul were passing on. One former senior American military intelligence officer in Tokyo characterized the South Korean intelligence effort as 'puerile, tainted by internal politics, and thus, distrusted'.[60] Another intelligence officer who served on General Willoughby's staff in Tokyo agreed, stating that 'We didn't trust the ROKs at all.'[61] The official US Army historian of the Korean War concluded that American intelligence analysts and foreign policy-makers believed that President Syngman Rhee was prone to 'cry wolf,' hence much of the intelligence information received from Seoul was discounted as 'tainted'.[62]

The US ran its own limited and parallel network of Humint collection operations in Korea. Following the withdrawal of the US Army Forces in Korea (USAFIK) from South Korea in the summer of 1949, the newly created Korean Military Advisory Group (KMAG) assumed the responsibility of running the sole 'overt' intelligence collection agency in Korea in conjunction with the staff of the American Embassy in Seoul.

Although the G-2 Section of KMAG was not formally assigned an intelligence collection and reporting mission until December 1949, from the moment of KMAG's formation in June 1949 the organization's G-2 Section began forwarding to Tokyo and Washington intelligence information received from ROK Army sources. After December 1949, KMAG's intelligence responsibilities grew, and the organization was required to submit daily and weekly intelligence summaries and estimates.

KMAG itself did not run its own intelligence collection network, but rather depended almost entirely on South Korean military intelligence for virtually all of its intelligence data on North Korea. The KMAG G-2 officer was responsible for forwarding intelligence information provided to him by South Korean military intelligence to Tokyo. Yet as time went by, KMAG became increasingly responsible for preparing intelligence reports and estimates based on the information that it received from the South Koreans, copies of which were routinely forwarded to MacArthur's headquarters in Tokyo.

Finally, KMAG assumed the responsibility of acting as liaison for various American military and civilian covert agencies operating in Korea, principally FECOM and the CIA, and acted as cover for these organizations's activities in Korea on occasion. KMAG's intelligence staff of only four officers and two enlisted men, as such, was laughably undermanned and poorly equipped to perform all these critical functions.[63]

Assisting KMAG in providing intelligence coverage of Korea were the military attachés at the American Embassy in Seoul. However, recently declassified documents reveal that the service attaché offices in Seoul had been reduced to virtually nothing since the summer of 1949. The Air Attaché Office in South Korea had been completely eliminated, and the Army and Navy military attaché offices in Seoul had been reduced to but one officer apiece by June 1950, largely because Defense Department officials in Washington believed that the KMAG G-2 office could adequately replace the attaché's normal function of reporting intelligence information received from the South Korean Defense Ministry.[64] In the weeks before the North Korean invasion, some of the best and most experienced military attachés in Seoul were transfered to other posts.

In June 1949, General Willoughby secretly activated a small Humint collection and reporting unit in Seoul called the Korean Liaison Office (KLO) under the command of Major Lawrence J. Abbott. KLO was a small organization, consisting of only two officers, one warrant officer, and two enlisted clerks. KLO was tasked with infiltrating agents into North Korea in conjunction with South Korean military intelligence. According to one Army historical document, 'General Willoughby considered it essential to maintain this group in Korea even though FEC territorial boundries did not include the Korean peninsula'.

Most of KLO's initial stable of agents consisted of Koreans who had previously been on the USAFIK G-2 payroll before its departure in July 1949. According to Willoughby, when North Korea invaded, KLO had 16 operatives reporting from North Korea, whereas the CIA had but four agents operating north of the 38th Parallel.[65]

KLO's primary target was North Korean military activities, with lesser importance being placed on political and economic activity. KLO agents were infiltrated into several NKPA combat units and staff headquarters, as well as into the North Korean government and industry.

According to one source, one of KLO's most important agents was a 'Colonel Kim', who was the chief of staff of a regiment of the NKPA 105th Tank Division outside the North Korean capital of Pyong'yang. Colonel Kim's product was assigned the codename 'Bluebird', although the colonel was commonly referred to as 'Mr Y' within KLO. Colonel Kim's controller was a South Korean national named Kim Syu, who was Colonel Kim's nephew. Colonel Kim passed his information to KLO using carrier pigeons, who flew from Pyong'yang to a pigeon roost on a farm in the western part of North Korea, then were replaced by another pigeon who would fly to a farm house run by Kim Syu on the southern side of the 38th Parallel.

KLO also obtained intelligence information from more mundane sources, such as North Korean farmers, who would tie their reports to tree limbs and float the materials downriver to South Korea, as well as North Korean fishermen, who put their materials inside dead fish, or would sail over to South Korea to pass on their reports.[66]

KLO was a prolific provider of intelligence. Between 1 June 1949 and 25 June 1950, KLO filed a total of 1,195 reports, 417 of which were submitted in the six months immediately preceding the North Korean invasion.[67] According to Willoughby, these reports covered all aspects of the North Korean military, including preparations for the invasion of the South, the formation of new combat units, military movements, military training and preparedness, the development of the North Korean Air Force, as well as Soviet and Chinese military assistance to the North Korean People's Army.[68]

Despite the numerous intelligence reports generated by the unit, most sources agree that KLO was narrow in its focus and could not provide strategic intelligence or warning. KLO was most successful in reporting on military activities in the southern part of North Korea, but was unable to get its agents into the northern portion of North Korea where the vast majority of North Korean military forces were garrisoned and where most heavy industry was situated. According to one KLO report, '... our secret agents, both Army and KLO were not able to make deep penetrations and some of these men, who were sent into the northeastern corner of [North] Korea, adjacent to the Russian border, have disappeared'.[69]

Furthermore, the quality of the KLO sources and the information that they provided left much to be desired. A survey of 59 KLO intelligence reports submitted between January and June 1950 shows that only 13 of the reports came from sources deemed to be 'fairly reliable'. The remainder came from sources whose reliability could not be determined by KLO.[70] In part, this was because KLO officers 'held serious doubts' about the competence, motivation, and loyalty of their agents, many of whom were suspected of being double agents who were really working for the North Korean intelligence services. The fact that KLO's network of agents in North Korea disappeared without trace after 25 June suggests that most, if not all, of its agents were in fact working for or under the control of the North Koreans.[71]

For various reasons, the KLO Humint reports were given short shrift by intelligence analysts in Washington DC and Tokyo. The head of the KLO reported to Willoughby in 1951 that 'It appears that the KLO reports forwarded to Department of the Army were *not* considered to be of sufficient value to merit a thorough study of the material submitted.'[72]

MacArthur's biographer, D. Clayton James, attributes the lack of attention to KLO's reports as being due to (1) MacArthur and Willoughby's 'arrogant and irascible' attitude towards CIA and State Department intelligence collection efforts in the Far East; (2) Korea was not within GHQ FECOM's purview (KMAG was responsible for all intelligence reporting from Korea), therefore some analysts in Washington viewed the KLO as 'a brazen, extralegal creation'; and (3) KLO's previous warnings of an impending attack had consistently been discounted by Willoughby.[73]

Operating in direct competition with KLO was a small Air Force Humint collection operation being run by the FEAF Office of Special Investigations (OSI). District Eight of FEAF OSI, commanded by Chief Warrant Officer Donald Nichols, operated a three-man Humint collection unit from Kimpo Airfield just outside Seoul. CWO Nichols had been stationed in Korea since 1946, and commanded a unit comprised largely of Korean operatives. The OSI detachment focused its attention on the North Korean Air Force, but also produced intelligence on a multitude of other matters, placing it in direct competition with KLO's Humint collection efforts.

Unlike KLO and other intelligence agencies operating in Korea, which largely depended on the ROK Army for their raw data, the OSI detachment derived most of its intelligence information from the South Korean National

Police and the South Korean Coast Guard, which routinely interrogated refugees, repatriates, military deserters, defectors and other individuals who had fled from North Korea across the Han River by boat to South Korea. Nichols' detachment also sent a few agents into North Korea who had been recruited from the Democratic Young Men's Association in South Korea. Nichols also made covert overflights of North Korea in in unarmed South Korean L-4 and L-5 utility aircraft to photograph the North Korean military airfields at Haeju, Pyonggang, Pyong'yang, and Mirim-Ni. Nichols' unit also infiltrated the South Korean Labor Party (SKLP), with the OSI agents providing high level intelligence information concerning the SKLP's espionage operations in South Korea.[74]

In May 1950, FEAF OSI District No.8 lost its best intelligence personnel to normal personnel rotation. However, these personnel were not replaced, which had a severe impact on the unit's ability to collect and process the flow of incoming intelligence data from the ROK National Police.[75] Like the intelligence reports generated by the KLO, virtually all of the OSI Humint reports were given low evaluations for source and information reliability.[76]

Predictaby, a CIA Humint collection operation also ran parallel to this multitude of small-scale, uncoordinated, and rather threadbare, intelligence operations in Korea. Willoughby and other former army intelligence officials have suggested that the CIA was barely active in Korea prior to the North Korean invasion. Recently information suggests the contrary. According to retired US Army General John K. Singlaub, formerly the chief of the CIA station in Mukden, China, between 1946 and 1948 the CIA base at Antung, China had dispatched 'dozens' of Korean agents recruited in Manchuria across the Yalu River to collect intelligence in what was then Russian-occupied North Korea. The agents were instructed to infiltrate the North Korean military and civil government, and report their intelligence take through 'dead letter' drops in Manchuria. In an emergency, provisions were made to exfiltrate the agents across the 38th Parallel into American occupied South Korea. Opposition by MacArthur and Willoughby to a CIA presence in South Korea forced Agency operatives to establish safe houses covertly in Seoul without informing FECOM G-2.[77]

In late 1946, an old OSO China hand named Carleton Swift Jr established what would soon become the first CIA station in Seoul. Swift was later joined by James Kellis, a Greek-American who had considerable special operations experience with the OSS in China during World War II. Their first success in Korea came in February 1947, when a Russian sergeant crossed the 38th Parallel and defected to US forces in South Korea. After a series of careful briefings by Swift and Kellis, the sergeant was sent back to North Korea on several occasions, where he proved to be a most resourceful spy. Over the next ten months, the Russian sergeant conducted eight highly successful intelligence-gathering missions in North Korea, in the process producing the majority of the US intelligence community's information regarding the organization and capabilities of Soviet forces north of the 38th Parallel that year.[78]

Shortly after the withdrawal of the last American troops from South Korea in June 1949, the CIA's FRU/FEC formally opened a small station in Seoul. The CIA used Korea as a base from which to mount operations against Communist China. The chief of the CIA's Seoul station was now reportedly Kellis.[79] Following the departure of Russian forces from North Korea in December 1948, the CIA mounted a few covert intelligence collection missions across the 38th Parallel against the North Korean military and government, as well as used North Korea as a springboard to mount limited penetrations of Manchuria and the Soviet Union. However, former CIA officers admit that the CIA produced little useable intelligence from North Korea prior to June 1950.[80]

The preceding discussion makes clear that the Humint collection effort in Korea in June 1950 was far from perfect. Clearly there was no shortage of Humint collection resources in Korea. The problem was that they were highly fragmented, under-resourced, nor was there any coordination of effort among the various American and South Korean Humint units operating against North Korea. Two weeks before the North Korean invasion, the commander of FECOM's clandestine intelligence collection unit, JSOB, Colonel Charles C. Blakeney, was sent to Korea to assess ongoing intelligence operations in Korea.

Blakeney found that the activities of the American and South Korean military and civilian intelligence agencies in Korea 'were inadequately coordinated for obtaining maximum results'. Blakeney also determined that 'the South Koreans were not only failing to furnish much information of value about the Far Eastern situation but also demonstrating a decided lack of cooperation in helping the JSOB-sponsored and other American agents to get through the lines upon their return from intelligence trips to the north'.[81]

Other factors hindered the American and South Korean Humint effort in North Korea. The evacuation by the North Korean Army of all civilians from the area near the 38th Parallel in February 1950 made it virtually impossible for American and South Korean intelligence agencies to infiltrate agents into North Korea, leading to a dramatic reduction in the amount of intelligence information about North Korean military preparations north of the border in the months just before the invasion.[82]

Most Humint reports generated by KLO and OSI District No.8 were given the lowest possible reliability evaluation (F-6) since much of the information contained in these reports could not be verified by other intelligence gathering means. Further, there were often significant delays in getting these Humint reports from the field to the intelligence analysts in Tokyo and Washington DC, which only served to render these reports practically useless.[83] With virtually no agent sources in place in North Korea, American Humint units in South Korea were forced to rely upon 'dribbles of second and third hand information from low-level defectors, refugees, and the few Western diplomats stationed in Pyongyang'. As a result, the US intelligence community was operating virtually blind as to North Korean military capabilities and intentions prior to the invasion.[84]

Comint was equally ineffective in monitoring the North Korean military buildup before to the war. This is unsurprising since the US Comint presence in South Korea dwindled from small in 1945 to non-existent by 1950. When General Courtney H. Hodges' US XXIV Corps occupied the southern portion of Korea at the end of World War II, a small ASA Comint collection unit, 1st Operating Platoon of 126th Signal Service Company, was deployed to Korea from Japan on 20 December 1945 to provide Comint support to US forces in Korea. This small unit, which consisted of no more than 20 men by the spring of 1947, operated from a dilapidated former Japanese radio station eight miles from downtown Seoul. On 26 April 1947, 1st Operating Platoon, 126th Signal Service Company was replaced by the 111th Signal Service Company, which remained in South Korea until July 1948, when it was withdrawn to Okinawa. During its stay in South Korea, 111th established a semi-fixed listening post five miles east of Seoul, from which it monitored the communications traffic of the Soviet 25th Army stationed across the 38th Parallel in North Korea.

The withdrawal of 111th Signal Service Company from Korea coincided with the final stages of the Soviet withdrawal from North Korea. Following the withdrawal of 111th Signal Service Company, from July 1948 until the Korean War, there were no ASA personnel stationed in South Korea, and American Comint coverage of North Korean military and diplomatic radio traffic quickly dissipated to virtually nil.[85]

More broadly, across the Far East, the Comint collection emphasis on the Soviet Union left virtually no American radio intercept assets available for other targets, such as North Korea. Recently declassified documents reveal that: 'Prior to the [North Korean] attack there was virtually no COMINT concerning North Korea; what little North Korea radio traffic was intercepted was not being analyzed.'[86] The former commander of ASAPAC recalled that his organization received no instructions from either AFSA or ASA headquarters tasking him with the collection of North Korean radio traffic prior to the NKPA invasion.[87] Dr Louis Tordella, the former Deputy Director of NSA, stated that as of June 1950 North Korea was not targeted for Comint collection because of 'administrative confusion and inadequate resources' within the American Comint community, a situation not unlike that which existed prior to the Pearl Harbor attack.[88]

Although radio intercepts of North Korean communications were practically non-existent, ASAPAC was engaged in a 'special project' which generated some limited intelligence coverage of North Korea. Prior to the withdrawal of US forces from Korea in July 1949, FECOM Civil Censorship units in Japan forwarded to ASAPAC microfilmed copies of cable traffic or mail originating from Communist countries in the Far East, including North Korea. The FECOM Civil Censorship Detachment operated four cable and mail intercept sites in Japan at Tokyo, Osaka, Fukuoka and Sapporo, and one intercept site in Seoul, South Korea, which examined all mail, telegrams and cables, and telephone calls originating from or destined for Communist countries.

Following the withdrawal of American forces from South Korea in 1949, the project was briefly halted but started shortly thereafter, apparently with the tacit approval and cooperation of South Korean military intelligence. The last batch of intercepted cable and mail traffic was received from Seoul on 16 June 1950, nine days before the war began. One must believe, however, that the intelligence information came from these telegraph and mail intercepts was unlikely to offer attack warning.[89]

The South Korean military intelligence services had minimal Comint collection capabilities. The South Korean Army Signal Corps conducted a small-scale Comint collection and processing operation on behalf of ROKA G-2 with limited American assistance. In August 1949, a small South Korean Army Comint intercept and direction finding station was established outside Seoul, which monitored NKPA communications across the 38th Parallel. It is unlikely, however, that this unit was able to accomplish much given the poor equipment and lack of cryptologic training of its personnel. Details concerning the Comint activities of the ROK Air Force and Navy are unknown, but presumably each service had its own small Comint collection and processing unit which was also trying to monitor North Korean military activities.[90]

In retrospect, one cannot fault the American military Comint collection units in the Far East for failing to adequately cover North Korea since they had no control over the assignment of collection priorities, which dictated which targets were to be intercepted. The responsibility for the selection of Comint targets and the setting of collection priorities was the responsibility of the US Communications Intelligence Board (USCIB) in Washington DC, whose recommendations largely determined how AFSA's mission managers tasked out intercept assignments to the service-run listening posts around the world.

In the months prior to hostilities, the USCIB demanded increased Comint coverage of Soviet military activities, particularly the Soviet threat to Western Europe, and paid scant attention to the rest of the world. The *USCIB Monthly Intelligence Requirements* lists for the seven month period prior to 25 June 1950 mentioned Korea only once out of 124 specific intercept priority items; and in terms of ranking, Korea was last in frequency of mention among the areas of the world. As one official report later concluded: 'Since the intelligence agencies themselves failed to communicate to AFSA the extent of their growing interest in the Korean problem, it is small wonder that AFSA was so poorly prepared to handle Korean traffic when the invasion occurred on June 25, 1950.'[91]

This is not to suggest that intelligence analysts in Washington or Tokyo were not concerned by developments in Korea. A declassified 1952 study showed that prior to the North Korean invasion, intelligence consumer agencies in Washington DC were calling for greater intelligence coverage of North Korea, but somehow these requests were lost in the intelligence bureaucracy and were never translated into actual Comint coverage of North Korea.

The entity within the American intelligence community responsible for warning intelligence consumers of an impending attack was called the Watch Committee, which was responsible for collating all available intelligence information and warning US policy makers and military commanders about the threat of impending hostilities using all available intelligence data, including Comint. Remarkably, on 12 June 1950, two weeks before war, the CIA chairman of the Watch Committee had designated Korea as the fifth most likely area of conflict in the immediate future (the 'hit list' in order of ranking was as follows: Indochina, Berlin and West Germany, Iran, Yugoslavia, South Korea, the Philippines and Japan). But this had no effect on intelligence collection priorities.[92]

Even if greater Comint collection resources had been available in the Far East, and if a portion had been devoted to North Korea, it is still unlikely that Comint would have picked up any indications of North Korea's intentions to invade given the North Korean government and military's penchant for transmitting virtually all sensitive information, including sensitive diplomatic messages, by telegraph, landline telephone circuits or by couriers, which of course American Comint units in Japan and elsewhere could not intercept.

This practice was in keeping with Soviet communications security doctrine, which strongly discouraged the use of radio during peacetime because of 'its inherent security weakness'. When radio was used, the North Koreans closely followed Russian communications security procedures, including enciphering virtually all communications traffic, changing daily all operating frequencies and call-signs, dispersing or disguising all signal centers and equipment, and emphasizing strict communications security discipline. The NKPA also aped their Russian mentors by using specially trained units of the North Korean Ministry of the Interior to perform signal security and radio monitoring of all internal military communications.[93]

As at Pearl Harbor, the enemy forces preserved an effective radio silence. As a result was that none of the three service cryptologic agencies operating in the Far East provided, or could have provided, any warning prior to the invasion.[94]

### THE CRUCIBLE: JUNE–NOVEMBER 1950

The invasion had a devastating impact on American Humint efforts in Korea. The two principal American Humint organizations in South Korea, KLO and FEAF OSI District 8, had to hastily flee Seoul for the relative security of the port city of Pusan, and in the process, lost touch with their agents in North Korea. When attempts were made to reestablish contact with these agents, American intelligence officers discovered that shortly after the invasion began North Korean security forces had quickly rolled up virtually all American and South Korean Humint networks in North Korea. KLO and OSI's agents in North Korea disappeared without a trace and were never heard from again. All other existing FECOM and CIA intelligence nets in South Korea, including a hastily organized 'stay behind' network, were also quickly rolled up by the North Koreans as their forces advanced southwards.[95]

Attempts to reestablish a Humint capability in Korea during the early days of the war bordered on the humorous. On 9 July 1950, FECOM started an intelligence school in South Korea to train a new generation of Korean agents who were destined to be infiltrated behind enemy lines by air, land or sea. The Americans selected a small but dedicated group of Korean volunteers to undertake the arduous and sometimes dangerous agent training program. As the North Koreans continued their advance, the intelligence school was forced to retreat southwards, constantly interrupting the training program. Due to a shortage of parachutes in Korea, the Korean agents were forced to leap off the back of speeding jeeps in order to simulate parachute landings.

By late July, the Korean agents had completed a minimal number of night parachute jumps as well as rudimentary schooling in intelligence collection and radio transmission techniques. Throughout that summer the Korean agents were dropped behind enemy lines at night, sometimes using the personal aircraft of the commanding general of Eighth Army due to the shortage of available transport planes. On other occasions, Fifth Air Force liaison aircraft were used to drop agents behind enemy lines. For example, on 22 August 1950, the Fifth Air Force dropped a Korean agent behind enemy lines near Seoul without coordinating this mission with EUSAK.[96]

Not suprisingly, the loss rate for these Korean agents was horrendously high. According to one source, less than 50 per cent of the agents dropped behind North Korean lines ever managed to make their way back to American lines. The rest were either killed, captured or defected to the North Koreans, although there is no documentation to suggest what became of these agents. Those agents that did manage to return to American lines brought back information that was weeks old, often contradictory, and of little practical use to starved Army intelligence analysts in Korea.[97]

With no Humint capability to speak of, from the fall of Seoul to the NKPA to the beginning of the battle for the Pusan Perimeter in September 1950, most of Eighth Army's intelligence concerning NKPA troop movements came from interrogating refugees fleeing through the NKPA lines, and the few North Korean prisoners that fell into the hands of UN forces. Aerial reconnaissance was a vital source of information about NKPA activities, but much of the initial aerial reconnaissance was focused on supporting the intensive bombing of targets in North Korea rather than in support of ground forces in South Korea.

This placed considerable pressure on Comint to fill in the gaps left by the collapse of the military and CIA Humint networks. Once the news of invasion across the 38th Parallel was received in Tokyo, all US Comint intercept sites in the Far East were placed on a wartime footing, although ASAPAC and 1st Radio Squadron, Mobile were not placed on war alert status until 27 June. The delay in bringing American Comint units in the Far East to full alert status was due to the fact that it took almost two full days before FECOM determined that the NKPA incursion across the 38th Parallel was not a raid. By 30 June, all American listening posts in the Far East were operating 24 hours a day, seven days a week instead of the 5½-day work week which had been the norm prior to 25 June. All leaves were cancelled and those personnel scheduled for rotation back to the United States had their orders rescinded and were kept in the Far East indefinitely.[98]

The panic the ensued following the North Korean invasion is best demonstrated by the actions of the sole Air Force Comint unit in Japan, 1st Radio Squadron, Mobile. In the best tradition of the wild west, its commander, Major Lowell R. Jameson, placed his squadron on full-scale alert and ordered all of the squadron's vehicles placed in a circle around the base football field with their bumpers touching. The squadron's personnel were hastily armed with whatever weapons were available and placed inside the circle to await the impending assault. A former Air Force USAFSS intelligence officer recalled that 'It was a little bit like preparing for an attack by hostile indians.' Only when the threat of a North Korean parachute attack on the base subsided and a modicum of calm prevailed did normal operations resume, but not without some nervous laughter in many quarters.[99]

Interestingly, the US listening posts in the Far East were ordered to concentrate their Comint collection efforts not against North Korea, but rather against Soviet military radio traffic in the region to determine if the Russians intended to intervene in Korea, particularly after the first American troops were sent to South Korea. They found that the Russian forces in the Far East had been moved to a higher state of alert and that some 20,000 to 25,000 troops of the Russian 25th Army had been moved to the North Korean border, and Chinese Nationalist Comint detected the arrival at Mukden of a Soviet air division on 27 June, which had flown in from the Soviet Far East city of Chita. But at 0330 on 26 June, the Chinese Nationalists intercepted an urgent order from the Soviet Far East Fleet headquarters in Vladivostok for all Russian ships sailing from Dairen to return to port immediately, and American listening posts in the Far East found no further signs of any Soviet military preparations indicative of intent to intervene in Korea. Once the policy-makers and intelligence analysts were satisfied as to Russian intentions, Comint collection emphasis shifted to North Korean military activities, despite the fact that two weeks of precious Comint collection emphasis had been lost chasing the specter of Soviet intervention.[100]

The critical constraint upon the American Comint effort early on was the virtual absence of any Korean linguists with the service cryptologic agencies in the Far East. Few Americans could speak Korean, and the US armed services, failing to anticipate the need for such resources, had not initiated any training programs prior to the war.

According to one source, there were no more than 20 Korean linguists in the entire US Armed Forces in June 1950, and 14 of these were serving in the entire Far East Command, despite a standing requirement for 158 Korean linguists in the theater. Only seven spoke or understood the language well enough to be used in the field. General Willoughby's G-2 staff in Tokyo had only two Korean linguists on his staff, both civilians, who were assigned to FECOM's Allied Translator and Interpreter Section (ATIS). Following the invasion, both men, neither of whom were cleared for access to Special Intelligence, were press-ganged into Comint work at ASAPAC, then quietly transferred back to writing propaganda material once replacement personnel arrived from the United States.[101]

On 29 June CINCFE urgently requested that the Department of the Army send 30 Korean linguists immediately to Japan. Within a week, the Army managed to round up 17 Korean language officers from throughout the US and hastily put them on planes to Japan. By early August 1950, the Army had found 30 military Korean linguists and had managed to get 19 to

Japan. Upon arrival in Tokyo, intelligence officers at FECOM discovered that three of the 'linguists' could not speak or understand Korean other than a few words, which they had picked up by talking to Koreans that they had met. Faced by a pressing requirement for more Korean linguists than were available in the American military, CINCFE reluctantly asked that the Army 'requisition' 27 civilian Korean translators and send them to the Far East as quickly as possible.[102]

The absence of Korean linguists serving with the American cryptologic establishment in the Far East was only partially alleviated by the transfer from the US of whatever Comint-cleared Korean language personnel that were available. Within 36 hours of the North Korean invasion, the only Korean language officers in the entire US cryptologic community – Mr Norman Wild from AFSA and 2nd Lieutenant Richard S. Chun from ASA – were flown from the United States to ASAPAC in Tokyo to meet the urgent requirement in the Far Eastern theater for Korean linguists. Yet given the enormity of the problem at hand, it is clear that this was only a stopgap measure that fell painfully short of requirements.[103]

With virtually no qualified Korean linguists available at the start, both ASA and USAFSS turned to using Korean-speaking foreign nationals, principally Korean-speaking former Japanese intelligence officers, as well as religious missionaries who had served in Korea as a temporary measure until American servicemen could be trained to handle these duties. For example, shortly after the North Korean invasion, personnel of 1st RSM at Johnson AB approached FEAF and ATIS desperately seeking a 'clearable' individual to fill the unit's need for a Korean language officer. Neither FEAF nor ATIS were able to find such an individual, so 1st RSM was forced to privately recruit a missionary who spoke Korean, paying him what amounted to a princely sum at that time – $310 a month – which came out of USAFSS contingency funds.

Other intelligence organizations in Tokyo 'were continually approaching him [the linguist] with offers of more money'. Fortunately for 1st RSM, the missionary 'was more interested in congenial fellowship than money. This was the only thing which prevented our losing him at a most crucial time.'[104]

Desperate for information about North Korean Air Force activities, on 14 July, the intelligence staff of the Far East Air Force asked all three service cryptologic agencies operating in the Far East to provide any information concerning the location of NKAF air bases as well as the nature and extent of flight activities being conducted from these bases. This was fairly successful. Traffic analysis and high frequency direction finding of enemy ground-to-air radio traffic determined that the NKAF, which possessed 132 aircraft at the start of the war, was operating from three primary air bases, two of which were located near the North Korean capital of Pyong'yang and one at Yonpo on the east coast of North Korea south of the city of Hungnam. The NKAF also made use of the civil airfield at the port of Wonsan, and had deployed some fighter aircraft to forward dispersal airfields at Sinmak, Pyonggang, Kumchon and Kansong. Comint also confirmed that the NKAF was operating a few fighter aircraft from Kimpo airfield outside of Seoul, which the NKPA had captured early in the war.[105]

Remarkably, it would appear that General Willoughby, MacArthur's intelligence officer, issued orders that no American Comint collection units were to be sent to Korea, despite the urgent need for such critical intelligence information by General Walton Walker's Eighth US Army in Korea (EUSAK). Although Willoughby in his memoirs stated that FECOM provided Comint support to EUSAK, a recently declassified ASA document states clearly that

> Due to the lack of operational personnel, the complete lack of Korean translators, and the need to exploit every available intercept facility in Japan for support of General Headquarters, Far East Command, it was not possible to send any ASA personnel to Korea prior to September 1950.

The former commander of ASAPAC, Lt Colonel Morton A. Rubin, recalled that none of the ASAPAC Comint units in Japan at the time could be sent to Korea because they were operating in a fixed mode. US intelligence officers in Japan feared that any American Comint personnel or equipment deployed to Korea were likely to be captured by the advancing North Korean Army.[106]

In mid-July 1950, FECOM asked the Department of the Army and ASA to send a mobile tactical Comint collection unit to Korea from the United States since no comparable unit was available in the theater. Everyone in Washington knew that MacArthur was hoarding whatever Comint resources that were available in the Far East for his own use, and that any Comint resources for General Walker's use in Korea would have to come from the US. The only tactical Comint unit that ASA could find to send to Korea was 60th Signal Service Company, which was performing strategic Comint collection at Fort Lewis, Washington state on 25 June. The Army cabled MacArthur back in July telling him that it would take several months before the 60th could be made ready for deployment to Korea. The bitter bureaucratic wrangling between Tokyo and Washington coupled by the lack of preparedness within ASA for a wartime contingency was to cost the US dear in the months to come.[107]

The results were felt keenly on the ground in Korea. Denied access to Army and Air Force Comint from Japan, General Walker's Eighth Army was forced to rely solely on Comint supplied by a small South Korean unit known as ROK Intelligence Group 'M', which had been formed on 22 July from 'locally available resources'. It consisted of South Korean Army and Air Force intelligence personnel commanded by a handful of USAF Office of Special Investigations (OSI) personnel, who taught themselves the 'Comint trade' under fire. With little formal training and using a hodge-podge of 'scrounged' radio equipment, the ROK Comint Group proved itself in the months that followed to be highly adept at intercepting and processing North Korean Comint, generating vitally needed intelligence concerning enemy military capabilities and intentions during the intense fighting at the Pusan perimeter.[108]

Late in July, 1st RSM sent a small operational detachment known as 'Project Willy' to South Korea from Japan. 'Project Willy' consisted of TC-9 Comint intercept vans modified to hold four radio intercept positions, and few operations personnel under the command of Lieutenant Edward F. Murray. Upon arrival, the 'Project Willy' team ran headlong into the already established OSI Comint collection operation being conducted in Korea. Lt Murray, in the spirit of cooperation, 'made the 1st RSM equipment available' in return for access to the Comint data being produced by the OSI detachment. The OSI chose to accept the USAFSS equipment but did not make available to Murray or USAFSS any of the Comint data being produced, which was instead sent directly to MacArthur's FECOM headquarters in Tokyo. Accordingly, the USAFSS project '... faltered, primarily because the... officers on the scene (Army, Air Force, OSI, and South Korean) had organized their own [Comint] service and did not want to trade it for the "restrictive operation" proposed by the [Comint] professionals'. USAFSS made the understated observation that: 'This caused considerable friction and Lieutenant Murray withdrew back to Japan', leaving behind the USAFSS intercept equipment in the hands of the Eighth Army detachment.[109]

The ludicrous chain of events surrounding the travails of 'Project Willy', however, hide some very real accomplishments by Comint during the early stages. By August 1950, the NKPA communications system in South Korea had collapsed under the strain of the relentless attacks by USAF bombers. According to a declassified study of NKPA communications during the Korean War:

> The general and intrinsic shortage of signal equipment in the North Korean Army was greatly aggravated by initial supply deficiencies, notably in wireless equipment, as well as by combat losses. In particular, radio sets and spare parts for electronic equipment were not resupplied at any stage of the war, so that by the end of August [1950] an almost complete breakdown had occurred in radio communications. Coupled with the lack of technical training of signal

FIGURE 2
SIGNALS COLLECTION ON THE GROUND IN KOREA

replacement personnel, the rapid deterioration of wireless communications conditioned a pronounced loss in the combat efficiency of North Korean Army units. Most seriously affected were reconnaissance, tank and other elements who relied primarily on radio communications.[110]

As personnel and equipment losses mounted, NKPA radio discipline at the front fell into disarray. Recent memoirs by former NKPA officers confirm that the communications system, which was never very good to begin with, collapsed as the drive to the south continued. Communications and coordination among units was poor, and got progressively worse as losses mounted and supply lines grew longer and ever more strained. The few overworked radio operators who remained played into the hands of American cryptologists by becoming careless and making fundamental communications security errors. Perhaps as early as July 1950, Eighth Army's small ROK Comint detachment, with little or no help from the cryptologists in Japan, were able to solve the NKPA tactical cryptographic systems then in use in South Korea. A former US Army intelligence officer confirmed that South Korean military cryptologists were able to break the NKPA's tactical codes and ciphers, which were changed every week, within

24 hours of their issue, allowing General Walker's intelligence staff to read all North Korean communications traffic for the remainder of that week.[111]

It apears that the ability to read the NKPA tactical codes and ciphers gave Walker's G-2 section advance warning of impending attacks and provided crucial information concerning the movements and overall preparedness of the North Korean forces facing them. For example, Comint reportedly warned Eighth Army intelligence analysts several days in advance of an impending major NKPA offensive against the Pusan Perimeter scheduled to begin on 31 August 1950.

With Comint indicating that the primary NKPA thrust would come in the southwest corner of the Pusan Perimeter opposite the port of Masan, General Walker concentrated his entire strategic reserve, some eight American infantry regiments, opposite the threatened sector of the front, supported by tanks, artillery and strong air support. When the NKPA attack finally came, these forces were able to contain the North Korean attack, but only by the narrowest of margins. Without the warning from Comint, it is likely that the North Koreans would have punched through the American defenses in that sector of the Pusan perimeter.

Comint was also instrumental in pinpointing the location of an attack by the NKPA 15th Division near the villages of Kyongju and Yongchon on the northern side of the Pusan perimeter on 9 September. As a result of the warning provided by Comint, NKPA 15th Division was virtually destroyed by ROK forces in two days of heavy fighting. Comint and direction finding were also reportedly used to identify targets for air strikes during the furious fighting for the Pusan perimeter, with the principal targets being NKPA corps and divisional command posts and communications centers.[112]

Back in Tokyo, a small unit of General Willoughby's G-2 staff called the Special Intelligence Section (SIS) was formed to coordinate Comint research and reporting for FECOM. The SIS, which was subordinate to the FECOM G-2 Plans and Estimates Branch, had been formed in July 1950 from the already-existing Joint Special Intelligence Committee (JSIC) in the Plans and Estimates Branch. The head of SIS was Lt Colonel Phillip B. Davidson Jr, the former chief of the FECOM G-2 Plans and Estimates Branch. The SIS, which operated from a cramped suite of windowless offices on the fifth floor of the Dai-Ichi Building in downtown Tokyo, collated, analyzed and disseminated to authorized intelligence consumers all incoming Comint received from theater Comint collection agencies, as well as finished Comint reports received from AFSA in Washington DC over a special communications circuit operated by the FECOM SSO's office.[113]

Beginning on 18 August, the SIS began publishing for the first time since the end of World War II the *Special Intelligence Bulletin*, which contained an evaluated and interpreted digest of Comint material available to the section's analysts on a daily basis, strongly suggesting that one or more of the American cryptologic agencies operating in the Far East had scored some success *vis-à-vis* North Korean codes. In addition to the daily bulletin, the SIS also published a series of highly classified studies on the North Korean supply infrastructure and command installations, as well as numerous estimates focusing primarily on the NKPA order of battle and troop movements, all based on Comint.[114]

In September 1950, Lt Colonel Rubin, chief of ASAPAC, was transfered to SIS, where he became the head of the Operations Subsection of the SIS. With a staff consisting of only one Air Force and one Navy officer, Colonel Rubin's job was to read all incoming Comint reports received over the SSO communications links from Washington and collate this material with 'collateral intelligence' generated by Willoughby's G-2 staff and other intelligence sources. Rubin had no contact with ASAPAC, which forwarded its Comint take to FECOM via the ASAPAC liaison officer in FECOM G-2. Every evening Rubin personally briefed General MacArthur (and no one else) on all significant Comint forwarded to Tokyo from Washington.

Rubin's 'all-source' intelligence briefings for MacArthur, which were conducted orally at the Top Secret Codeword level, typically lasted no more than five to ten minutes. Rubin never indicated to MacArthur what the sources of individual intelligence items were, that is which came from Comint and which did not. Typically, General MacArthur listened to the briefing in silence, sometimes asking a few questions, then dismissed Rubin. How MacArthur used the intelligence is not known since nothing was committed to writing.[115]

Even at this stage, each of the three service cryptologic agencies generated their own intercept tasking without consultation with their sister services, often not knowing what they were doing. This resulted in the misuse of the precious few intercept resources available to AFSA in the Far East, including a great deal of duplication of effort.[116] This occurred because of split lines of command and authority amongst the service Comint units in the Far East. For example, while ASAPAC almost exclusively provided Comint to the FECOM G-2 staff in Tokyo, the Air Force Service Cryptologic Agency, USAFSS, serviced the Comint needs of the USAF theater command, the Far East Air Forces (FEAF). The only USAFSS Comint unit in the theater, 1st RSM, channelled all of its intercepts and Comint summaries to directly to FEAF through USAFSS headquarters in Texas. It was not until August that a USAFSS Liaison Officer, Major Robert S. Vandiver, was assigned to FEAF headquarters for the purpose of channelling Comint data directly to FEAF intelligence consumers.[117]

A certain degree of tacit cooperation among the three American military

Comint units in Japan did begin shortly after the war began. In July 1950, 1st RSM established direct teletype communication links with ASAPAC and with Navy Communications Unit 35 at Yokosuka, which were used to pass intercepted radio traffic back and forth among the units. Discussions were also initiated among the Army, Navy and Air Force Comint units in Japan about establishing a joint high frequency direction finding (HFDF) net. Resulting from these discussions, on 6 September, USAFSS placed in operation a HFDF network with only two stations (Johnson AB and Misawa) which served the HFDF needs of the ASA and NSG units in the Far East. In return, four enlisted USAFSS printer intercept operators were assigned to Navy Communication Unit 35 in order to be trained in the Russian printer intercept mission by Navy personnel. In 1952, more USAFSS personnel were sent to Yokosuka to be trained on the Navy printer intercept system.[118]

Shortly after hostilities, AFSA established a small regional headquarters, designated Armed Forces Security Agency Field Activity, Far East (FAFE), which the Naval Security Group agreed to host within the cramped confines of the Navy Communications Unit 35 facilities at Yokosuka, Japan. The establishment of AFSA Field Activity, Far East was due largely because senior AFSA officials in Washington had long argued that overseas Comint activities run by the military required coordination comparable to that provided by AFSA within the continental United States. The three military services, not surprisingly, opposed the establishment of regional AFSA headquarters because it was viewed as 'inconsistent with normal command relationships and with the responsibility of each Service to provide combat intelligence for its own operations'.[119]

Despite the objections of the three SCAs, AFSA Field Activity, Far East (FAFE) was activated in the fall of 1950 under the command of Captain Wesley A. 'Ham' Wright, a veteran Navy cryptologist and also commanding officer of the Navy communications station at Yokosuka. Wright held this position until August 1952, when he was replaced by his friend, Captain Thomas H. Dyer. Dyer served as chief of AFSA Field Activity, Far East (redesignated National Security Agency, Field Activity, Far East in October 1952) until December 1953.[120] The small staff of AFSA Field Activity Far, East, which was composed almost entirely of Navy personnel seconded from the Naval Security Group, was tasked with attempting to coordinate the activities of the three military Comint organizations in the Far East, serve as a medium for the transmission of Comint collection tasking for AFSA in Washington and the intelligence staff of FECOM in Tokyo, as well as provide 'technical support' for all military Comint activities in the Far East.[121]

Despite AFSA's attempt to instill some sense of order into the disparate Comint activities in the Far East, each of the three SCAs continue to maintain and expand their own Comint activities in the Far East, effectively ignoring the authority of AFSA. Only the Naval Security Group agreed to place its Comint intercept and processing unit at Yokosuka, Japan under the operational control of AFSA, but only insofar as it applied to the Comint processing activities being undertaken by the Navy's Advanced Exploitation Unit (AEU) at Yokosuka. Collection tasking continued to be derived from operational orders received from NSG headquarters in Washington DC.[122]

MacArthur and his intelligence chief, Willoughby, made no secret of the fact that they were extremely displeased with the quantity and quality of the Comint support that FECOM had been receiving. During the first six months, there were serious dissemination problems getting Comint from the SSO's office in Tokyo to key personnel on the FECOM staff. At the same time, General Walker and his commanders in Korea were also screaming about the lack of Comint support they were receiving from FECOM and ASA, which was largely the result of the rigid security barriers imposed on the dissemination of Comint to field commanders. Army regulations barred the release of Comint to field commanders below the Army level, and as such, Eighth Army corps and division commanders were receiving no Comint support throughout the critical first six months.[123]

In an internal memo dated 1 September 1950, General Willoughby expressed his feeling that the competitive and uncoordinated efforts being mounted by the three service cryptologic agencies in the Far East were making his staff's Comint tasking and analytical efforts 'extraordinarily complicated'. Acknowledging that the system was not working, Willoughby ordered the creation of a special unit within FECOM G-2 to coordinate Comint research, and demanded increased assistance and a temporary duty detail from Headquarters ASAPAC in order to fill this requirement (suggesting of course that he did not have the people on his own staff to do the job!). Finally, Willoughby ordered ASAPAC to deploy a field detachment to Korea in order to coordinate Comint matters in General Walker's Eighth Army headquarters at Taegu.[124]

Having ground to a halt in front of the combined US – South Korea defenses around the Pusan perimeter, the subsequent landing by General MacArthur's forces at Inch'on on 15 September 1950 caused the remaining NKPA forces to disintegrate and flee northwards. On 28 September, Seoul was recaptured by MacArthur's UN forces, and by the end of the month all of South Korea up to the old demarcation line at the 38th Parallel had been recaptured. Comint proved to be invaluable during the Inch'on landing and the subsequent recapture of Seoul. At 1330 on 13 September, two days before the scheduled landing at Inch'on, either an ASA listening post in Japan or the ROK Comint intercept unit in Korea intercepted and deciphered a NKPA message sent by the senior commander at Inch'on warning his troops that ten American warships were approaching Inch'on and that the offshore island of Wolmi-do was under intensive aerial bombardment. The message went on to state: 'There is every indication the enemy will perform a landing. All units under my command are directed to be ready for combat. All units will be stationed in their given positions so they may throw back enemy forces when they attempt their landing operation.' The message was hurriedly translated and forwarded to General Ned Almond, commander of the US landing force at 1730 the same day.[125]

Early the next morning, another message was intercepted by a listening post in Japan, this time the sender was the senior North Korean military commander in Seoul. The intercepted transmission stated

> According to an intercepted enemy [American] message, orders are now being transmitted for landing in the 196 (code, believed to be Inch'on) area. Enemy aircraft and 14 naval vessels bombarded the area today. Judging from enemy movements mentioned above, it is evident that the enemy is going to land in this area. It is directed that units at 230 (code unknown) complete preparations for the coming engagement so that we may succeed in repelling and eliminating the enemy in their attempt to land.

This intercept was also forwarded immediately to General Almond off Inch'on.[126]

Following the successful landing at Inch'on and the drive to recapture Seoul well underway, the JCS ordered FECOM to destroy all telegraph repeater stations throughout North Korea as a means of forcing the North Koreans to move their communications to the airwaves, where they could be intercepted and read. On 24 September, FECOM G-2 ordered the commander of FEAF to destroy eight telegraph repeater stations in North Korea, with particular emphasis placed on the destruction of the largest stations at Pyong'yang and Wonsan. The order added: 'It is requested that you advise G-2, GHQ, FEC of the plan of attack as far in advance as possible so that adequate preparations may be made to take advantage of the disruption of the enemy's communications.'[127]

Pressure had been building on the service cryptologic agencies since the war started to provide tactical commanders in Korea with more comprehensive Comint direct support. Walker's Eighth Army intelligence staff had been pressuring Willoughby for a mobile ASA tactical unit to provide his Army with critically needed Comint, as well as a permanent Special Security (SSO) representative so that he might receive high-level Comint being generated in Tokyo and Washington. Army regulations called for Eighth Army to have these units assigned to his staff for intelligence support, but Willoughby and senior ASA officials had steadfastly refused to give him what he asked for because of concern that they might be captured by the North Koreans. However, the landing at Inch'on changed everything, for suddenly the US and its allies were winning the war.

On 4 September, a small unit, ASAPAC Liaison Detachment (Provisional), consisting of three officers and five enlisted communications personnel, was activated in Tokyo for immediate deployment to Korea. The Liaison Detachment, commanded by Major Edward Dlusky, left Japan on 14 September by ship, landing at Pusan in Korea on the 18th. The Detachment was moved to Taegu, then transported by truck a few days later to the recently recaptured Seoul. On 28 September, ASAPAC Liaison Detachment, Provisional was redesignated Army Security Agency, Pacific, Advance (ASAPAC Advance) under the command of Major (later Lt. Col.) Jacob R. Degenhardt, former assistant operations officer at Headquarters, ASA at Arlington Hall Station, Virginia. Effective 1 October, ASAPAC (Advance) assumed control over all ASA units in Korea, which consisted only of the ASAPAC Liaison Detachment and a COMSEC detachment in Seoul. ASAPAC (Advance) also served as the conduit for Comint material destined for Walker's intelligence staff from ASAPAC in Tokyo, and was assigned the task of coordinating the crucial Comint support being provided Walker's G-2 staff by the South Korean Army Comint collection group.[128]

The importance of the contribution by the small ROK Army and Air Force Comint units during the fall of 1950 cannot be overemphasized. With no American Comint unit in Korea, Walker's Eighth Army was almost entirely dependant on the raw intercepts and decrypts supplied by the ROKs for the first six months. But despite the importance of the intelligence being produced by the ROKs, the US refused to expand the size and capabilities of the South Korean military Comint service. In early September, Eighth Army proposed the immediate formation of a South Korean Army radio intelligence company, modelled on ASA's signal service company. It would be composed entirely of South Korean personnel and would service the ROK Army only. All of the Comint collection equipment, however, would have to come from the US. The proposal was rejected out of hand by the Department of the Army in Washington because of equipment shortages and a reluctance to allow the South Koreans access to American Comint secrets.[129]

Only a few of the intercepts supplied by the ROK Comint units have been declassified. Two messages, both dated 9 October, contain information obtained from ROK Comint sources. The first message contained a verbatim copy of an intercept detailed the frantic NKPA preparations to defend the mouth of the Imjin River on the west coast of North Korea. The second message stated that 'A usually reliable source', which was a common phrase used to obliquely refer to Comint, identified the locations of the NKPA 17th and 24th Divisions and their subordinate units. A 22 November ROK intercept of a message from a senior North Korean official to the head of the NKPA Signal Department ordered each corps headquarter to produce 300 telegraphic cipher keys at local factories in their areas of operation, reflecting the desperation that the NKPA was experiencing trying to procure cipher materials.[130]

On 9 October, the first American Comint collection unit reached Korea. After three months of waiting, the 250-man 60th Signal Service Company and its radio intercept vans arrived at Pusan, having sailed all the way from Seattle, Washington state. The company was moved by truck to Seoul on 16 October, where a temporary listening post was set up in one of the few remaining concrete buildings still standing (albeit shell-pocked) in the South Korean capital, the former operations building of 111th Signal Service Company. The company's morse intercept operators were quickly divided into three shifts (known in Army parlance as 'tricks') of 21 operators apiece to man the unit's 20 morse intercept positions 24 hours a day, and morse intercept operations against North Korean military radio traffic began shortly after midnight on 17 October.[131]

The 60th began Comint collection just as units of Eighth Army were in the last phase of the drive to capture the capital of North Korea – Pyong'yang. On 17 October, units of the US 1st Cavalry Division had captured the villages of Sohung, Sariwon and Hwangju, the closest of which was just 10 miles south of Pyong'yang. Two days later, on 19 October, Pyong'yang fell and Kim Il-Sung's government fled to the industrial town of Kanggye in one of the remotest parts of North Korea.[132]

Like any green unit thrown directly into a wartime environment without any experience, the men of 60th Signal Service Company suffered through innumerable teething problems as the unit attempted to get its mission going. Results were slow in coming at first because of the inexperience of most of the company's personnel, as well as their unfamiliarity with the unit's new equipment and the vagaries of North Korean radio traffic. It took the unit more than a week before its intercept operators began to produce intelligence information, but the inexperience of the company's morse intercept operators severely hampered the unit's effectiveness. The lack of experienced morse intercept operators was partially rectified in late October when four senior operators familiar with North Korean radio traffic arrived from ASAPAC in Tokyo.[133]

Every other section of the 60th also experienced the same problems during their first month in Korea, in large part because of inexperience.

The company's Direction Finding Section spent weeks trying to establish a workable DF net after failing initially to properly locate their DF stations.

The Traffic Analysis Section was forced to hurriedly compile from scratch data on North Korean military call signs and frequency usage without the benefit of the knowledge in the hands of their counterparts in Tokyo.

No one in the company's small four-man Cryptanalysis Section had any previous experience with 'live' traffic and had been only partially trained in North Korean and Chinese ciphers prior to their deployment to Korea.

The Translation Section's ability to do its job was severely hampered by the fact that it did not have any Korean linguists, but instead had four enlisted Russian linguists fresh out of language school. Shortly after the unit's arrival in Korea, three Korean language officers from ASAPAC were assigned to the 60th, giving the unit a translation capability.[134]

In subsequent weeks, the 60th began producing North Korean Comint in quantity, helped in large part by the poor COMSEC procedures employed by the NKPA radio operators. The company's intercept operators quickly discovered that North Korean military communications were 'at a low ebb', due to the fact that the NKPA had largely disintegrated after the landing at Inch'on. On 20 October, Willoughby, no doubt referring to Comint obtained from 60th Signal Service Company, stated in the FECOM Daily Intelligence Summary that 'Communications with, and consequent control of, the enemy's field units have dissipated to a point of ineffectiveness.'[135]

CONCLUSIONS

The problems that beset American intelligence in Korea prior to November 1950 were complex. However, some key factors can be identified that were endemic to the entire US intelligence community at the time. First, there were the systemic problems caused by chronic under-resourcing resulting from the postwar retrenchment and fiscal austerity. Second, many of the problems stemmed from the lack of a strong controlling or centralizing organization in Washington DC. Third, bureaucratic problems that resulted from what might be broadly termed the vexed politics of regional commands.

From a regional perspective, American intelligence performed poorly during the early stages of the Korean War because of deficient leadership by the theater intelligence chief, General Willoughby. His intelligence organization, if it can be called such, was fragmented, uncoordinated, and its few resources misdirected. For example, too much of the theater's intelligence resources were focused on the Soviet Union, leaving little left for coverage of China and North Korea. The bitter petty bureaucratic infighting between Willoughby and the CIA only served to hamper the effectiveness of the US intelligence effort in the Far East.

Humint was never likely to deliver substantial dividends in an area characterized by highly-secure police states, and North Korea proved to be a particularly difficult target because of the paranoia of the Kim Il-sung regime. The American Humint collection program in the Far East and in North Korea itself was severely fragmented and poorly coordinated due to the infighting between Willoughby's FECOM G-2 staff and the CIA. There was little cooperation between the American and South Korean Humint organizations. They found themselves competing against one another for intelligence about the North. Most of the Humint being generated was given short shrift by intelligence analysts because of low reliability evaluations, and took weeks or even months to get from the field to intelligence analysts in Tokyo or Washington. This led to dependence on information from low-level defectors and refugees, whose reliability was given little credence because of the inherent racial bias of many of the American intelligence officials using the material.

Comint certainly helped the UN forces in engagements such as the Pusan perimeter and In'chon, but never came close to living up to its potential. In June 1950, the American Comint effort in the Far East was in flux because of the recent creation of the AFSA and USAFSS, and was but a shadow of its former self. All American Comint units in the Far East were suffering from serious personnel and equipment shortages, with a veritable dearth of Korean linguists in the theater resulting in virtually no Comint coverage of North Korea prior to the war.

Therefore, it should come as no surprise that Comint provided no prior warning of impending hostilities. The Comint collection and processing efforts of the three American services in Asia were not integrated into the Far East Command's intelligence structure, and were not coordinated, resulting in massive duplication of effort. Moreover, the AFSA failed to impose any form of discipline on the disparate Comint collection efforts of the three services.

Finally, security restrictions on the dissemination and use of Comint severely impeded the effective utilization of this perishable resource throughout the early stages of the Korean War.[136]

### NOTES

1. *Army Security Agency (ASA) Summary Annual Report: FY 1946*, Tab 5, p.2, INSCOM FOIA.
2. US Army Biography, Major General Charles Andre Willoughby, OCMH; Frank Kluckhohn, 'Heidelberg to Madrid – The Story of General Willoughby', *The Reporter*, 19 Aug. 1952, p.26; Roger A. Beaumont, 'The Flawed Soothsayer – Willoughby: General MacArthur's G-2', *Espionage* 1/4 (1985) pp.20–37; Clay Blair, *The Forgotten War: America in Korea, 1950–1953* (NY: Times Books 1987) p.1026; Joseph C. Goulden,

*Korea: The Untold Story of the War* (NY: McGraw-Hill 1982) pp.39–40; William Manchester, *American Caesar: Douglas MacArthur, 1880–1964* (NY: Laurel Books 1978) p.202; Bruce Cumings, *The Origins of the Korean War: The Roaring of the Cataract, 1947–1950* (Princeton UP 1990) p.104.

3. *SWPA/SCAP/FEC Intelligence History*, Vol.III, Part 2, Insert 31, Incls. 1 and 2 MacArthur Memorial Library (hereafter 'MACL'), Norfolk, Virginia.

4. MS, Bruce W. Bidwell, Col., USA (Ret.), *History of the Military Intelligence Division, Department of the Army General Staff* (hereafter 'Bidwell') 1962, Part 7, pp.II-18–II-19, X-6, Army FOIA.

5. *SWPA/SCAP/FEC Intelligence History*, Vol.III, Part 2 ff.

6. Ibid. Vol.V, Part 1, pp.72–4.

7. Ibid., Vol.III, Part 2, p.128, MACL; GHQ, FEC, Operations Instruction No.6, 1 April 1950, Annex No.6, pp.2–3, 6, MACL; Rad, C 54603, CINCFE TOKYO JAPAN to DA WASH DC, 26 Jan. 1950, RG-9, Box 152, Blue Binder Series P&O, MACL; Bidwell (note 4) p.II-20.

8. *History of FEAF, January 1, 1950 – June 30, 1950*, p.71, Roll A7244, Air Force Historical Research Agency (AFHRA), Maxwell AFB, AL.

9. *History of FEAF, July 1, 1949 – December 31, 1949*, pp.63–4, Roll A7244.

10. Ibid. pp.61–2, 137–8.

11. *History of FEAF, January 1, 1950 – June 30, 1950*, p.84, Roll A7244.

12. CINCPACFLT, *Interim Evaluation Report No.1, June 25, 1950 – November 15, 1950*, Vol.VIII, pp.1477–84, Vol.XII, p.A-27, Operational Archives, Naval Historical Center, Washington DC.

13. Bidwell (note 4) p.11–19.

14. R. Harris Smith, *OSS: The Secret History of America's First Central Intelligence Agency* (Berkeley, CA: U. of California Press 1972) pp. 250–1; Kluckhohn (note 2) p.29.

15. Delaney retired from the Army in 1970 with the rank of Colonel. Rad, C 54603, CINCFE TOKYO JAPAN to DA WASH DC, 26 Jan. 1950, P.O. 318, RG-9, Box 152, Blue Binder Series P&O, MACL; Letter, Vandenberg to Willoughby, 27 Nov. 1946, RG-263, Entry 36, HRP 89-2/00443, Box 13, File: 804A-804VV, NA, CP; Association of Graduates, USMA, *1976 Register of Graduates of the U.S. Military Academy*, p.440.

16. Letter, Vandenberg to Willoughby, 27 Nov. 1946, RG-263, Entry 36, HRP 89-2/00443, Box 13, NA, CP; Memo of Conversation, *CIG Activities in China*, 18 April 1947; Memorandum, Howe to Butterworth, 22 June 1949; and Memo, Howe to Merchant and Freeman, *ESD*, 14 Sept. 1949; and Memo, Howe to Freeman, 22 Sept. 1949, all in RG-59, Entry 1561, Lot 58D776, Box 7, NA, CP; Maochun Yu, *OSS in China* (New Haven, CT: Yale UP 1996) pp.251–62; A.B. Darling, *The Central Intelligence Agency: An Instrument of Government to 1950* (Pennsylvania State UP 1990) pp.119–20, 151; J.K. Singlaub, *Hazardous Duty: An American Soldier in the Twentieth Century* (NY: Summit Books 1991) pp.121, 135–6.

17. *North Korean Pre-Invasion Buildup*, Incl. 4, RG-23, Box 14, MACL; Jim G. Lucas, 'Intelligence Slur Called a Slap at MacArthur', *San Francisco News*, 15 Dec. 1950, p.1; SC-M-32, *CIA Staff Conference Minutes*, 10 Dec. 1951, RG-263, Entry 36, HRP 89-2/00443, Box 8, File: 725 DCI Staff Meetings, NA, CP; 25 April 1991 letter from Gen. James H. Polk.

18. Author's emphasis, Rad, WX 98293, JCS WASH DC to CINCFE TOKYO JAPAN, 10 Jan. 1950, PO 316, RG-9, Box 152, Blue Binder Series P&O, MACL.

19. Rad, C 54603, CINCFE TOKYO JAPAN to DA WASH DC, 26 Jan. 1950, RG-9, Box 152, Blue Binder Series P&O, MACL.

20. Cumings (note 2) p.128.

21. In 1952, George Aurell was named the head of the CIA's Far Eastern Division, and went on to become the Chief of Station in Bangkok, Thailand in the late 1960s. Joseph B. Smith, *Portrait of a Cold Warrior* (NY: Putnam's Sons 1976) pp.93, 245–6; Dept. of State, *The Biographic Register* (Washington DC: GPO 1956) p.41.

22. Cumings (note 2) p.127; Goulden (note 2) p.467.

23. Bidwell (note 4) p.X-6.

24. Ibid. p. II-19; 25 April 1991 letter to author from Gen. James H. Polk.

25. JCS 86211, DEPTAR (JCS) WASH DC to CINCFE TOKYO JAPAN, 10 March 1951, RG-9, Box 43, Radiograms, JCS, 30 June 1950 – 5 April 1951, MACL; ASA, *History of the Army Security Agency and Subordinate Units: FY 1951*, Vol.II, p.2, INSCOM FOIA.

26. John Patrick Finnegan, *Military Intelligence: An Overview, 1885–1987* (Arlington, VA: INSCOM History Office 1987) p.124, INSCOM FOIA.

27. Army Security Agency, Pacific, *Summary Annual Report, FY 1950*, p.60; Army Security Agency, Pacific, *Summary Annual Report, FY 1951*, pp.1, 25, all INSCOM FOIA.

28. Memo for Commander-in-Chief, General Headquarters, Far East Command from Headquarters, Army Security Agency, Pacific, *Proposed Expansion Plans, ASA Units and Installations*, 9 Nov. 1950, Inclosure 1, RG-6, Box 1, MACL.

29. 30 March 1992 and 5 May 1992 letters to author from Col. Morton A. Rubin; Army Security Agency Pacific, *Summary Annual Report, FY 1950*, p.1, INSCOM FOIA.

30. An intercept position, also known as a 'rack' within the SIGINT community, is essentially a seat next to an equipment console filled with radio receivers, transcription equipment (usually a typewriter) and other electronic equipment necessary for one intercept operator to perform his or her duties. Typically, an ASA signal service company operating in a 'fixed site' mode consisted of 27 intercept positions in June 1950. *History, Army Security Agency and Subordinate Units, Fiscal Year 1951*, Vol.II, p.4, INSCOM FOIA.

31. On 21 Dec. 1950, Swears was replaced as head of the Operations Branch by Lt. Col. Charles H. Hiser, the former Deputy Chief, Army Security Agency. Major Swears was named his deputy, ASAPAC, *Summary Annual Report, FY 1951*, p.31, *ASA Review*, May–June 1950, p.39. Hiser was perhaps the Army's premier cryptologist, having served most of his military career in signals intelligence, see *NSAN*, Aug. 1957, p.6; *NSAN*, Nov. 1988, p.15 (obit.). Fifteen years later, Col. Clayton Swears commanded 3rd Radio Research Unit (redesignated 509th Radio Research Group in June 1966), the Army Security Agency's primary COMINT collection unit in South Vietnam, Maj. Gen. Joseph A. McChristian, *The Role of Military Intelligence, 1965–1967* (Washington DC: OCMH 1974), App.D.

32. The IBM machinery sent to Tokyo in 1949 were 1 collator, 1 interpreter, 3 key punches, 2 printers, 2 reproducers, and 2 sorters. These machines were manned by 1 officer and 11 enlisted men (8 tabulating machine operators and 3 key punch operators). Army Security Agency, Pacific, *ASAPAC Summary Annual Report, FY 1950*, pp.36–8, 45, INSCOM FOIA; Army Security Agency, Pacific, *ASAPAC Summary Annual Report, FY 1951*, pp.31–2, INSCOM FOIA; *History of the Army Security Agency and Subordinate Units, FY 1951*, Vol.II, p.2, INSCOM FOIA; *AHR, ASA Plans and Operations Section, FY 1949*, Tab 10, INSCOM FOIA; JCS 2010/24, Memo by the Chief of Staff, USAF for the Joint Chiefs of Staff, *Division of Responsibility Between the Armed Forces Security Agency and the US Air Force*, Enclosure 'B', p.162, RG-218, CCS 334 (NSA), Section 4, NA, CP; 30 March 1992 and 5 May 1992 letters to author from Col. Morton A. Rubin.

33. At the time of the North Korean invasion, USAFSS had 1,832 personnel in the Continental United States (CONUS) and only 1,020 officers and enlisted men stationed overseas in Germany, Japan and Alaska (Alaska was until recently considered an overseas tour of duty). Headquarters USAFSS, *A Special Study: Securing Air Force Communications, 1948–1958*, Vol.I, dated 1 April 1966, p.37, partially declassified and on file at the National Security Archives, Washington DC. See also Headquarters US Air Force, *United States Air Force Statistical Digest, Fiscal Year 1951*, pp.426, 429, K134.11-6, USAFHRC, Maxwell AFB, AL.

34. HQ, USAFSS, *Historical Data, Headquarters, USAFSS, 1 January 1950 – 30 June 1950*, p.37, AIA FOIA; *Historical Data Report, 1st Radio Squadron Mobile, 1 May 1950 – 30 June 1950*, pp.1, 7, AIA FOIA; Robert F. Futrell, 'A Case Study: USAF Intelligence in the Korean War', in Lt. Col. Walter T. Hitchcock, USAF (ed.), *The Intelligence Revolution: A Historical Perspective* (Washington DC: Office of Air Force History 1991) pp.279–80.

35. Office of the Chief of Naval Operations, ibid., *Fiscal Year 1950*, 7 Nov. 1949, Annex A, p.28; and *Basic Naval Establishment Plan, Fiscal Year 1951*, 4 Jan. 1951, Annex A, p.15, both in Operational Archives, Naval Historical Center, Washington DC; Jay R. Browne,

*Kamiseya: Camelot of the Orient, A History* (1995) pp.1–3, Operational Archives, Naval Historical Center, Washington DC. See also *NCVA Cryptolog* 12/4 (1991) p.4; Austin Rutledge, 'COMM UNIT #35', *NCVA Cryptolog* (Spring 1995) p.5; Biographical Data Sheet, Capt. Daniel Webster Heagy USN (Ret.) Naval Historical Center, Washington DC.

36. *History, Army Security Agency and Subordinate Units, FY 1950*, p.28, INSCOM FOIA; ibid., Vol.II, p.3, INSCOM FOIA; US Naval Security Group, *US Navy Communication Supplementary Activities in the Korean Conflict, June 1950 – August 1953* (undated) pp.53, 56, COMNAVSECGRU FOIA; 25 April 1991 letter to author from Gen. James H. Polk.

37. Army Security Agency, Pacific, *Summary Annual Report, Fiscal Year 1950*, pp.14, 31–4, 35–6, Tab 82, INSCOM FOIA.

38. Army Security Agency, *Summary Annual Report, Army Security Agency and Subordinate Units, Fiscal Year 1949*, pp.47–8, INSCOM FOIA; *AHR, ASA Plans and Operations Section (AS-23), FY 1949*, p.56, INSCOM FOIA; Army Security Agency, Pacific, *Summary Annual Report, FY 1950*, pp.39–40, INSCOM FOIA.

39. SRH-123, *The Brownell Committee Report*, pp.59–60, RG-457, NA, CP; *History of the Army Security Agency and Subordinate Units, FY 1951*, Vol.II, p.2, INSCOM FOIA; 25 April 1991 letter to author from Gen. James H. Polk.

40. *History* (note 36) p.7; 30 March 1992 letter to author from Col. Morton A. Rubin.

41. SRH-123, *Brownell Committee Report*, p.60, RG-457, NA, CP; *SWPA/FEC/SCAP Intelligence History*, Vol.III, Part 3, Insert 32, Incl. 2, Plate 2, a copy of which is in the OCMH Library in Washington DC; Army Security Agency, Pacific, *Summary Annual Report, FY 1950*, pp.36–7 and Tab 83, INSCOM FOIA.

42. SRH-123, *The Brownell Committee Report*, p.60, RG-457, NA, CP.

43. Army Security Agency, Pacific, *Summary Annual Report, FY 1950*, p.23, INSCOM FOIA.

44. For one glaring example of the lack of knowledge about COMINT by one senior intelligence officer in the Far East, see *1st Radio Squadron, Mobile Historical Report, October 1, 1950 – December 31, 1950*, pp.7–9, AIA FOIA.

45. GHQ, Far East Command, Office of the Assistant Chief of Staff, G-2, *Historical Report, January 1, 1950 – October 31, 1950*, p.19, RG-407, Entry 429, Box 349, NA, CP.

46. Ibid., Plate 5; *SWPA/FEC/SCAP Intelligence History*, Vol.III, Part 3, Insert 32, Incl. 2, Plate 2; *SCAP/FEC Tokyo Telephone Directory*, 1 Oct. 1948 with 1949 supplement, p.2, RG-5, Box 121, MACL; SRH-032, *Reports By US Army ULTRA Representatives With Field Commands*, p.1, RG-457, NA, CP.

47. *1st Radio Squadron* (note 44) p.10, AIA FOIA.

48. Lt Gen. Phillip B. Davidson, USA (Ret.), *Secrets of the Vietnam War* (Novato, CA: Presidio Press 1990) p.94.

49. 25 April 1991 letter to author from Gen. James H. Polk.

50. *Military Situation in the Far East*, Hearings Before the Committee on Armed Services and the Committee on Foreign Relations, US Senate, 82nd Congress, First Session, p.37.

51. Author's emphasis, Bidwell (note 4) p.11–16;

52. Ralph E. Weber (ed.), *Spymasters* (Wilmington, DE: Scholarly Resources 1999) p.115.

53. Cumings, p.151 (note 2); S.L.A. Marshall, *The River and the Gauntlet* (Nashville, TN: The Battery Press 1986) p.2.

54. US Military Advisory Group to the Republic of Korea, *KMAG Command and Unit Historical Reports for 1949*, 20 Feb. 1950, Tab 10, p. 3, RG-407, Box 863, NA, CP; Ed Evanhoe, *Dark Moon: Eighth Army Special Operations in the Korean War* (Annapolis, MD: Naval Institute Press 1995) p.11.

55. Cumings (note 2) p.389; OH, Donald Nichols, 1989.

56. Draft manuscript of book by Norman E. Jones, p.522, RG-15, Box 29, MACL.

57. John R. Merrill, *Korea: The Peninsular Origins of the War* (Wilmington: Delaware UP 1989) p.210n.

58. Ibid., pp.138–41, 212n.

59. US Military Advisory Group to the Republic of Korea, *North Korean Armed Forces Order of Battle*, 26 May 1950, RG-338, Box 461, File North Korea 0100 Order of Battle, NA CP; Draft manuscript of book by Norman E. Jones, pp. 523–4, RG-15, Box 29, MACL.

60. Davidson (note 48) p.94.

61. 25 April 1991 letter to author from Gen. James H. Polk.
62. James F. Schnabel, *Policy and Direction: The First Year* (Washington DC: US Army Office of the Chief of Military History 1972) p.64.
63. Robert K. Sawyer, *Military Advisors in Korea: KMAG in Peace and War* (Washington DC: OCMH 1962) pp.50–1; *The North Korean Invasion of South Korea*, p.5, Geog. V Korea 370.3 Invasion, OCMH.
64. Bidwell (note 4) pp.II-17, X-6.
65. Ibid., pp.II-20–II-21; *The North Korean Invasion of South Korea*, Geog. V Korea 370.3 Invasion, OCMH; D. Clayton James, *The Years of MacArthur: Volume III: Triumph and Disaster, 1945 – 1964* (Boston, MA: Houghton Mifflin 1985) p.416; Jim G. Lucas, 'Intelligence Slur Called a Slap at MacArthur', *San Francisco News*, 15 Dec. 1950, p.1.
66. Memo for Gen. Willoughby from Lt Col. Leonard J. Abbott, *Korea Liaison Office Report* (hereafter Abbott Memo), 15 May 1951, RG-23, Box 1, MACL; Draft manuscript of unpublished book by Norman E. Jones, pp.517–19, 522, RG-15, Box 29, MACL.
67. Abbott Memo.
68. Charles A. Willoughby and John Chamberlain, *MacArthur, 1941–1951* (NY: McGraw-Hill 1954) p.351; *SWPA/SCAP/FEC Intelligence History*, Vol.3, Part 3, Insert 41: *Pre-Invasion Buildup of North Korean Forces*, pp.2–9.
69. KLO #518, dated 25 May 1950, in Abbott Memo (note 66).
70. The following is a breakdown of the source and information evaluations in the 59 KLO reports: C-2: 1; C-3: 11; C-6: 4; F-2: 2; F-3: 27; F-5: 1; F-6: 13, Abbott Memo (note 66).
71. William B. Breuer, *Shadow Warriors: The Covert War in Korea* (NY: Wiley 1996) p.21.
72. Abbott Memo (note 66).
73. James (note 65) p.416.
74. CINCFE TOKYO JAPAN TO DA WASH DC (for Irwin from Willoughby), 29 June 1950, in *North Korean Pre-Invasion Buildup*, RG-23, Box 14, Series 2, MACL; Bidwell (note 4), p.III-22; OH, Maj. Donald Nichols, 1989; Donald Nichols, *How Many Times Can I Die* (Brooksville, FL: Vanity Press 1981), pp. 116-124; Robert F. Futrell, 'A Case Study: USAF Intelligence in the Korean War', in Lt Col. Walter T. Hitchcok, (ed.), *The Intelligence Revolution: A Historical Perspective* (Washington DC: OAFH 1991) p.280.
75. *History of FEAF, January 1, 1950 – June 30, 1950*, p.85, Roll A7244, USAFHRC, Maxwell AFB, AL.
76. Bidwell (note 4) pp.III-12–III-20.
77. Singlaub (note 16) pp.143–4, 164.
78. Harry Rositzke, *The CIA's Secret Operations* (Boulder, CO: Westview Press 1988) p.52.
79. Singlaub (note 16) p.164; Smith (note 14) p.282; *The North Korean Invasion of South Korea*, Geog. V Korea 370.3 Invasion, OCMH.
80. Ralph E. Weber (ed.), *Spymasters* (Wilmington, DE: Scholarly Resources 1999) p.115; Cumings (note 2) p.129.
81. Bidwell (note 4) p.II-21.
82. Ibid. p.III-30.
83. Draft MS, *On the 20th Anniversary of the Korean War: An Informal Memoire by the ORE Korean Desk Officer, Circa 1948-1950*, undated, p.11, RG-263, HRP 89-2/01034, Entry 17, Box 4, NA, CP; Bidwell (note 4) p III-22.
84. W.R. Corson, *The Armies of Ignorance: The Rise of the American Intelligence Empire* (NY: Dial Press 1977) p.318; Goulden (note 2) p.40.
85. *Summary Annual Report, Army Security Agency and Subordinate Units, Fiscal Year 1949*, p.32, INSCOM FOIA; *History of ASA in Korea*, undated, p.1. The author is grateful to Joseph Bermudez for providing him with a copy of this document. See also 'Korea Sounds a GI Note', *ASA Review*, May–June 1947, p.18.
86. *History, Army Security Agency and Subordinate Units, Fiscal Year 1951*, Vol. II, p. 2, INSCOM FOIA; MS, *On the 20th Anniversary of the Korean War* (note 83) undated, p.22, RG-263, Entry 17, HRP 89-2/01034, Box 4, File: CIA Reporting on ChiComs in Korean War, NA, CP.
87. 5 May 1992 letter to author from Col. Morton A. Rubin.
88. Christopher Andrew, *For The President's Eyes Only: Secret Intelligence and the American*

*Presidency from Reagan to Bush* (NY: HarperCollins 1995) p.187.

89. Army Security Agency, Pacific, *Summary Annual Report, FY 1950*, pp.41–2, INSCOM FOIA; *SWPA/SCAP/FEC Intelligence Histories*, Vol.III, Part 2, pp.131–7; *Reports of General MacArthur* (Washington DC: GPO 1966) Vol.I Supplement, p.238.

90. US Military Advisory Group to the Republic of Korea, *KMAG Command and Unit Historical Reports for 1949*, 20 Feb. 1950, Tab 10, p. 3, RG-407, Box 863, NA, CP.

91. SRH-123, *The Brownell Committee Report*, p.70, RG-457, NA, CP; *History of the Army Security Agency and Subordinate Units, FY 1951*, Vol.II, p.2, INSCOM FOIA; US Naval Security Group, *US Naval Communication Supplementary Activities in the Korean Conflict, June 1950 – August 1953*, undated, pp.14–15, COMNAVSECGRU FOIA.

92. SRH-123, *The Brownell Committee Report*, p.67, RG-457, NA, CP.

93. ATIS *Research Supplement/Interrogation Reports – Enemy Forces #4*, pp.3–5, MACL; Department of the Army Pamphlet No.30-2, *The Soviet Army*, July 1949, pp.40–1, RG-6, Box 107, MACL; KLO #450-B, 18 April 1950, summarized in DIS #2812, 22 May 1950, p.2, and DIS #2815, 25 May 1950, p.2, both RG-6, MACL.

94. James E. Pierson, *USAFSS Response to World Crises, 1949-1969* (San Antonio, TX: USAFSS Historical Office, 22 April 1970) p.1, AIA FOIA; SRH-123, *The Brownell Committee Report*, p.29, RG-457, NA, CP.

95. Bidwell (note 2) p.V-4; *Officer Personnel to ADCOM*, 3 July 1950, RG-6, Box 4, Correspondence Korean War Misc., Folder #1, MACL; *History of the Inspector General Division, FEAF: June 26, 1950 – October 15, 1950*, p.2, K-720.294, USAFHRA, Maxwell AFB, AL; Hitchcock (note 34) p.280; Marshall (note 53) p.2.

96. Rad, G 21823 KGI, CG ARMY EIGHTH to CINCFE (G-2), 6 Sept. 1950, RG-9, Box 35, Army 8-IN, 1-15, Sept. 1950, MACL; Marshall (note 53) p.3.

97. Marshall (note 53) p.3.

98. Army Security Agency, Pacific, *Summary Annual Report, FY 1950*, p.48, INSCOM FOIA; ibid., *FY 1951*, p.5, INSCOM FOIA; *USAFSS Response to World Crises*, p.1, AIA FOIA; *Historical Data Report, 1st Radio Squadron, Mobile, 1 May 1950 – 30 June 1950*, 23 July 1950, pp.4, 6, AIA FOIA.

99. MSgt Bob Blackstone, 'Major Recalls USAFSS Career', *The Spokesman*, Oct. 1972, p.12.

100. *USAFSS Response to World Crises*, p.1, AIA FOIA; Department of Defense, *Soviet Military Power* (Washington DC: GPO, April 1984), p.10; Msg, G-2, Chinese Nationalist Ministry of National Defense (via Chinese Mission, Tokyo) to FECOM G-2 Foreign Liaison Branch, 3 July 1950, RG-6, Box 14, MACL.

101. *History, Army Security Agency and Subordinate Units, FY 1951*, Vol.II, p.3, INSCOM FOIA; Marc B. Powe and Edward E. Wilson, *The Evolution of American Military Intelligence* (Ft Huachuca, AZ: US Army Intelligence Center and School 1973) p.92; MS, *Intelligence and Counterintelligence Problems During the Korean Conflict*, Feb. 1955, p.26, OCMH, Washington DC; *SWPA/FEC/SCAP G-2 History*, Vol.III, Part 3, p.157.

102. Msg CX 56903, CINCFE to DA WASH DC, 29 June 1950, RG-9, Radiograms, WAR CX DA, June–Nov. 1950, Box 40, MACL; Msg W 84957, DA (CSGID) to CINCFE, 5 July 1950; Msg W 84958, DA (TAG) to CINCFE, 5 July 1950; Msg W 84959, DA (TAG) to CINCFE, 5 July 1950; Msg W 84938, DA (TAG) to CG USARPAC, 5 July 1950, all in RG-9, Radiograms, WAR WX, June–11 July 1950, Box 105, MACL; Msg C-59215, CINCFE TOKYO JAPAN to DA WASH DC, 2 Aug. 1950, RG-9, Radiograms, WAR CX DA, June–Nov. 1950, MACL.

103. At the time of the Korean War in 1950, Wild was probably the premier oriental languages specialist at AFSA. Wild remained at NSA until his retirement in 1980, specializing in several European and Asian languages, esp. Chinese. National Cryptologic School, *On Watch* (Ft Meade, MD: NSA/CSS 1986) p.24, NSA FOIA; Army Security Agency, Pacific, *ASAPAC Summary Annual Report, FY 1951*, p.63, INSCOM FOIA. Wild biography in *NSAN*, July 1970, p.10; *Washington Post*, 16 Oct. 1996, p.D6.

104. *SWPA/FEC/SCAP G-2 History*, Vol.III, Part 3, p.157; 1st Radio Squadron, Mobile, *Historical Report: 1 October 1950 – 31 December 1950*, pp.17–18, AIA FOIA.

105. *USAFSS Response to World Crises*, p. 1, AIA FOIA; Robert F. Futrell, *The US Air Force*

*in Korea, 1950-1953* (Washington DC: Office of Air Force History 1983) pp.19–99.

106.  Maj. Gen. Charles A. Willoughby, *MacArthur, 1941–1951* (NY: McGraw-Hill 1954) p.372; Army Security Agency, Pacific, *Summary Annual Report, FY 1951*, p.10, INSCOM FOIA; 1st Radio Squadron, Mobile, *Historical Report, October 1, 1950 – December 31, 1950*, p.24, AIA FOIA; 30 March 1992 letter to author from Col. Morton A. Rubin.

107.  Headquarters, 60th Signal Service Company, *Annual Report, 60th Signal Service Company for Fiscal Year 1950*, 25 Aug. 1950, pp.8–9, INSCOM FOIA; Msg W 90533, DA (CSGPO) to CINCFE, 3 Sept. 1950, RG-9, Box 105, Radiograms WAR WX, 1–10 Sept. 1950, MACL; Msg CX 62069, CINCFE TOKYO JAPAN to DA WASH DC, 4 Sept. 1950, RG-9, Box 40, Radiograms WAR WX, June–Nov. 1950, MACL; 'Two ASA Recon Companies Receive Meritorious Unit Commendation', *ASA Review*, Aug. 1952, p.2.

108.  *History, Army Security Agency and Subordinate Units, FY 1951*, Vol.II, p.3, INSCOM FOIA; Finnegan, *Military Intelligence: An Overview*, p.121, INSCOM FOIA; *History of ASA in Korea*, p.1; *USAFSS Response to World Crises*, p.2, AIA FOIA; USAF MS, Diane Putney, *Origins of USAF HUMINT in Korea*, undated, p.3.

109.  *USAFSS Response to World Crises*, p.2, AIA FOIA; *Historical Data Report, 1st Radio Squadron, Mobile, 1 July 1950 – 30 September 1950*, 21 Oct. 1950, pp.2–3, AIA FOIA; ibid., *1 October 1950 – 31 December 1950*, pp.40–41, AIA FOIA.

110.  ATIS, *Research Supplement/Interrogation Reports: Enemy Forces #4*, p.3, MACL.

111.  Sergei N. Goncharov, John W. Lewis and Xue Litai, *Uncertain Partners: Stalin, Mao and the Korean War* (Stanford UP 1993) p.155; Blair (note 2) p.171; 25 April 1991 letter to author from Gen. James H. Polk.

112.  Blair (note 2) p.240; DIS #2924, 11 Sept. 1950, pp.1-f–1-g, RG-6, MACL; Roy E. Appleman, *South to the Naktong, North to the Yalu* (Washington DC: Center for Military History 1986) pp.408–10; David Kahn, *Kahn on Codes: Secrets of the New Cryptology* (NY: MacMillan 1983) p.45; private information.

113.  GHQ, Far East Command, *Historical Report, Office of the Assistance Chief of Staff, G-2, Far East Command: 1 January – 31 October 1950*, Part I, p.19, Plate 6, RG-407, Entry 429, Box 349, NA, CP; 30 March 1992 and 5 May 1992 letters to author from Col. Morton A. Rubin.

114.  GHQ, Far East Command, *Historical Report, Office of the Assistance Chief of Staff, G-2, Far East Command: 1 January – 31 October 1950*, Part I, p.19, RG-407, Entry 429, Box 349, NA, CP.

115.  The Navy officer assigned to Col. Rubin's office was probably Lt. W.G. Hurley. The USAF officer was Maj. Robert S. Vandiver. 30 March 1992, 5 May 1992 and 1 June 1992 letters to author from Col. Morton A. Rubin.

116.  SRH-123, *The Brownell Committee Report*, pp.62, 78, RG-457, NA, CP.

117.  Maj. Vandiver worked out of a small office (Room SB14) in the sub-basement of FEAF headquarters. *History of USAFSS, January 1, 1953 – June 30, 1953*, pp.331–2. The author is grateful to Joseph Bermudez for making a copy of this document available.

118.  *Historical Data Report, 1st Radio Squadron, Mobile, 1 July 1950 – 30 September 1950*, 21 Oct. 1950, pp.6–8, AIA FOIA; *Historical Report for the 15th RSM: 1 January 1952 – 31 March 1952*, p.19, AIA FOIA.

119.  SRH-123, *The Brownell Committee Report*, p.79, RG-457, NA, CP.

120.  Biographical data sheets for Capt. Wesley A. Wright, dated 13 Au. 1957, and Capt. Thomas H. Dyer, dated 31 Jan. 1955.

121.  SRH-123, *The Brownell Committee Report*, pp.80–1, RG-457, NA, CP.

122.  Ibid. p.77n, RG-457, NA, CP.

123.  *Annual Report of the G-3 ASA: FY 1951*, pp.28, 75, INSCOM FOIA.

124.  *SWPA/FEC/SCAP G-2 History*, Vol.III, Part 3, Insert 32, Incl. 2, p.3.

125.  CX 63003, CINCFE TOKYO JAPAN to CG X CORPS, 14 Sept. 1950, RG-9, Box 51, Outgoing-Misc. (XTS), June–Oct. 1950, MACL.

126.  CX 63091, CINCFE TOKYO JAPAN to CG X CORPS, 14 Sept. 1950, RG-9, Box 51, Outgoing-Misc. (XTS), June–Oct. 1950, MACL.

127.  CX 64305, CINCFE TOKYO JAPAN to CG FEAF, 24 Sept.1950, RG-9, Box 51, Outgoing-Misc. (XTS), June–Oct. 1950, MACL.

128. *History of the Army Security Agency and Subordinate Units: FY 1951*, Vol.I, p.15, INSCOM FOIA; Army Security Agency, Pacific, *Summary Annual Report, FY 1951*, pp.3, 11–12, INSCOM FOIA; *Annual Report, 60th Signal Service Company for Fiscal Year 1951*, 15 Aug. 1951, p. 1, INSCOM FOIA; *History of ASA in Korea*, p.1; 'ASA Personnel Established in Korea', *ASA Review*, Nov.–Dec.1950, pp.2, 6.

129. Msg C 64796, CINCFE TOKYO JAPAN to DA WASH DC, 28 Sept. 1950, RG-9, Box 40, Radiograms, WAR CX DA, June–Nov. 1950, MACL; Msg W 95621, DEPTAR (g-3) to CINCFE TOKYO JAPAN, 3 Nov. 1950, RG-9, Box 106, Radiograms, WAR WX, 1–15 Nov. 1950, MACL.

130. Rad G-25659 KGI, CG ARMY EIGHTH (JOS/DICKEY) to CINCFE TOKYO JAPAN, 9 Oct. 1950; Rad G 25673 KGI, CG ARMY EIGHTH to CINCFE TOKYO JAPAN, 9 Oct. 1950, both in RG-9, Box 35, Army 8-IN, 1–15 Oct 50, MACL; Rad 221405 I, HQ ARMY EIGHTH (TACTICAL) to CINCFE (G-2), 22 Nov. 1950, RG-9, Box 36, ARMY 8-IN, 16-24 Nov 1950, MACL.

131. The SIGAD of 60th Signal Service Company was USM-35. Headquarters, 60th Signal Service Company, *Annual Report, 60th Signal Service Company for Fiscal Year 1951*, 15 Aug. 1951, pp.16, 22, 31, INSCOM FOIA; 'ASA Personnel Established in Korea', *ASA Review*, Nov.–Dec. 1950, p.6.

132. Appleman (note 112) pp.643–51.

133. 60th Signal Service Company, *FY 1951 Annual Report*, p.16, INSCOM FOIA; Army Security Agency, Pacific, *Summary Annual Report, FY 1951*, p.12, INSCOM FOIA.

134. Former 60th Signal Service Company Korean linguists included Capt. Youn P. Kim and an enlisted man. As of 30 June 1951, the Korean and Chinese linguists comprising the Translation Section were Capt. Samuel K.S. Hong, 1st Lt. Richard S. Chun, and 2nd Lt. Robert S.H. Lee. They were later joined by Capt. Robert A. Kobzina. *60th Signal Service Company, AHR FY 1951*, pp.18–19, 22, 25–6, INSCOM FOIA.

135. Ibid. p.17; *History, Army Security Agency and Subordinate Units, FY 1951*, Vol.II, p.7, INSCOM FOIA; DIS, FEC, 20 Oct. 1950, MACL.

136. The sequel to this article, dealing with the period from the Chinese Intervention to the Armistice, will appear in *Intelligence and National Security* 15/1 (Spring 2000).

# 3

# A Mission of Espionage, Intelligence and Psychological Operations: The American Consulate in Hong Kong, 1949–64

## JOHANNES R. LOMBARDO

After the Communist victory in China in late 1949, the Cold War manifested in Asia as a reoccurring confrontation between the United States and the People's Republic of China (PRC). This confrontational tendency was evident during the Korean War (1950–53) and the two Off-shore Island Crises (1954–55 and 1958). For the British colony of Hong Kong, its location on the southern coast, its relative degree of openness and the intensity of the Cold War in Asia, turned the colony into a miniature battleground of ideological conflict. The relative degree of openness facilitated the operations of foreign agents in Hong Kong, particularly agents run by Nationalist Chinese, the United States and Communist Chinese. Although the British government possessed a more accommodating policy towards Beijing, and authorities in Hong Kong were often at odds with American activities there, nevertheless the British discreetly facilitated and cooperated with American intelligence gathering operations.

Following the loss of all US diplomatic posts in mainland China in 1949, the American Consulate General in Hong Kong became the most important location for gathering human intelligence (Humint) on the activities of the Chinese Communists. This owed much to the vast efflux of refugees from the mainland, a phenomena that was similar to the outflow of Eastern Bloc refugees into Austria. As in Austria, elaborate arrangements were made to 'wring out' these refugees for their intelligence value. Moreover, Hong Kong also became crucial to US psychological operations that targeted the 'captive' population on the mainland. This study will examine these activities of the American Consulate in Hong Kong – the largest consulate anywhere in the world – during the 1950s and early 1960s. It will consider how its diverse activities factored into the divergent policies of the US, UK and also to some degree, Taiwan, towards Communist China.

## ANGLO-AMERICAN TENSIONS

From the outset, the emergence of a Communist China in 1949 placed significant strain on the traditional 'special relationship' between the United States and Britain. In the United States, the 'loss of China' was considered a great failure for the Free World. A common view in Washington was that Communism was a monolithic movement and Mao Zedong's China would be a satellite of the Soviet Union. At the time, the Truman administration had resisted propping up the Nationalists or investing in a recovery of the Chinese mainland because there was little confidence in Chiang Kai-shek's corrupt and unpopular regime. However, fervent criticism from the Republican opposition, the growing strength of McCarthyism in American domestic politics, and the perceived hostility of the Chinese Communist regime encouraged the US government to aid Taipei and adopt an adversarial policy towards the PRC.[1]

The British, on the other hand, believed that the Communist regime in Beijing would maintain control of the mainland for the long term. Economic and territorial interests in Asia, including Hong Kong, encouraged Whitehall to adopt a conciliatory policy towards the new regime. London also wished to take into account the views of Commonwealth states, including India, which were more sympathetic to Beijing. Even though the Americans had clearly opposed such a recognition of the PRC, the Labour government of Clement Attlee offered recognition to the People's Republic in early 1950.[2]

Nevertheless, the British attempted throughout the 1950s to consolidate the Anglo-American relationship with concessions on its China policy and general foreign policy in Asia. The British supported the US reaction to the invasion of South Korea and supplied combat units to United Nations actions against the North Koreans and the Chinese. However, regardless of their political orientation, London was anxious to present a more accommodating image to the new regime in Beijing.[3]

The Cold War and the divergent nature of British and American attitudes towards the PRC had a destabilizing affect on Hong Kong. Hong Kong's proximity to China and the British *laissez-faire* attitude of governing meant the American Consulate General in Hong Kong became a key post for collecting intelligence on the Communist regime in Beijing. Moreover, it is important to note that the British facilitated the collection of intelligence in Hong Kong by US officials and the use of the territory as a base for propaganda dissemination. However, some of the American anti-Communist operations in Hong Kong were considered by Hong Kong authorities as too provocative and detrimental to the colony's existence. In response, the British sought to limit US activities that might provoke the Communist regime.

British assistance to American intelligence gathering in Hong Kong came in two forms: human intelligence (Humint) and communications or signals intelligence (Sigint). Regarding human intelligence, the British frequently allowed US officials to interview refugees fleeing China. British officials also provided information collected by their own intelligence, military and paramilitary services operating in Hong Kong. In addition to Humint, British and American officials also cooperated in the gathering of Sigint in Hong Kong. In 1948, the UKUSA agreement linked the Sigint agencies of the United States, United Kingdom, Australia, New Zealand and Canada. In 1949, a joint British-Australian listening post was established a Little Sai Wan in Hong Kong with the primary purpose of monitoring Chinese Communist communications. The US intelligence community had open access to the intelligence gathered at this facility. The listening post in Hong Kong served as a complement to intelligence gathered from human sources.[4]

Hong Kong permitted the US authorities to use the American Consulate as a processing plant for human intelligence received from the British or collected independently. American officials, including the Consulate's political and economic sections, its military liaison officers and local CIA operatives, collected intelligence by cultivating sources in the Crown Colony and examining Chinese language newspapers. Human sources included British military officials, Hong Kong government officials, Kuomintang (KMT) representatives and agents, local and foreign businessmen, and refugees coming across the border from China. American officials used these sources primarily to acquire information regarding political, social, economic and military developments on the Chinese mainland, and secondarily, to gain information regarding Chinese Communist underground activities in Hong Kong.

American officials considered their intelligence gathering activities were necessary to counter the operations of Communist agents in Hong Kong and frequently reported that Beijing was trying to influence internal developments there. These activities encouraging 'Communist underground' movement in Hong Kong by instigating labour unrest and exerting influence over schools, businesses, social groups and the media.[5]

British officials did not seem to be tough enough on this sort of activity. One American Consul General of the early 1950s, Karl Lott Rankin, suggested that the British were partially to blame for the strengthening pro-Communist movement in Hong Kong. Rankin believed that, to the Hong Kong people, the British recognition of the People's Republic in February 1950 had 'given a measure of legality' to the 'new homeland regime'.[6]

Furthermore, there is evidence to suggest that American officials in Hong Kong were funding KMT and other anti-Communist organizations that were engaged in sabotage and guerrilla campaigns against both the Communist mainland in China and pro-Communist elements in Hong Kong. The American Consulate in Hong Kong was thus not only using some KMT agents but were also encouraging more violent activities. In many cases, such American backed operations contravened British law in Hong Kong. After recognizing the People's Republic in early 1950, the British had outlawed flagrant anti-Beijing activities. In January 1951, for example, the Hong Kong police arrested a KMT agent whom the Consul General considered 'one of the more respected contacts of the Consulate's Political Section'.[7] To officials in the US State Department, the incident presented 'an example of the sensitiveness with which the British viewed various American 'activities in Hong Kong'. It was also seen as evidence of British suspicions of American intentions in Hong Kong.[8]

Nevertheless, the Americans continued to encourage and take advantage of anti-Communist activities of the KMT and other groups in Hong Kong. For example, in February 1951, Consul General Walter McConaughy described how the Consulate and US military attachés were cultivating sources among other anti-Communist organizations in Hong Kong, including the so-called 'Third Force' group.[9] During the 1950s, the Third Force group was created by the CIA as anti-Communist movement of Chinese, that would also be a possible alternative to the KMT.[10] McConaughy also described how the Consulate was receiving intelligence from 'Nationalist agents' regarding 'Soviet Intelligence Activities' in Shanghai.[11] Moreover, the American chargé d'affaires in Taiwan explained to Assistant Secretary of State Dean Rusk in some detail about how the CIA was financing active anti-Communist groups in Hong Kong while the British were cracking down on them by arresting their leaders.[12]

In March 1952, the mounting confrontation between pro-Communist and anti-Communist elements in Hong Kong contributed to an outbreak of civil unrest. The ensuing riot evidently occurred after a Communist Chinese 'comfort mission' was refused entry into Hong Kong when trying to deliver aid to the victims of a village fire. American officials from the Consulate reported to Washington that the riot was 'planned' by the 'Chinese Communist authorities', and that Westerners were the targets of violence, with two American officials from the Consulate injured.[13]

PSYCHOLOGICAL WARFARE

The United States expanded its psychological operations capabilities in Hong Kong through the American Consulate. The US Information Service in Hong Kong (USIS-Hong Kong) became the key operating unit for the dissemination of anti-Communist and pro-democratic propaganda in Asia.[14]

The main function of the USIS-Hong Kong was to direct its anti-Communist message at the population in China, but it also had the secondary targets of the overseas Chinese operation in Asia, any areas thought to be under threat by Communists and the local population of Hong Kong. Although the British colony was convenient for American propaganda operations against the Chinese Communists, the British were often displeased with the overt way the Americans carried out such activities.

In the early 1950s, the USIS used various media such as pamphlets, bulletins, periodicals, radio broadcasts, films and a library set up in Hong Kong that was full of anti-Communist and 'American material'. While USIS engaged in mainland with pamphleteering and radio broadcasting, the population of Hong Kong, including the growing number of refugees and the expatriates, were targeted with all forms of propaganda media.[15] Within Hong Kong, USIS focused most of its efforts on the local population, categorized into 'target groups': businessmen, merchants and shopkeepers; students and teachers; and labour in public utilities and important industries.

Specifically, USIS issued grants from the American government and private institutions, such as the Ford Foundation, to support the work of local scholars and educators. They used audio-visual programmes in primary and secondary schools, and published general and specific magazines and newspapers that were intended to reach the target groups. These publications include general Chinese language magazines, like *American Today* and *America Today Pictorial*, and more specific papers that appealed to workers, students and businessmen. Additionally, other propaganda tools included 'the American Library', which stocked American literature and showed American movies, and the international radio station, the Voice of America (VOA), which broadcast to the mainland.[16]

In some instances, USIS was conducting operations to counter specific activities on Hong Kong that were sponsored by the Chinese Communists. During the 1950 Hong Kong Tramway Strike, USIS distributed 'movies and literature' to tramway union representatives at the same time that 'communist agitators' were influencing the union. USIS-Hong Kong believed its efforts contributed to ending the strike.[17] Nonetheless, the British found that the Americans' overt anti-Communist propaganda activities in Hong Kong put them in a difficult position with Beijing. Therefore, in 1951 the British told the Americans that 'no official agency or group or organization' was to 'use the colony as an anti-Communist base'.[18]

Anglo-American differences over Hong Kong were not as detrimental or important to the 'special relationship' as the fundamental differences in their foreign policy in Asia. This was evident in Anglo-American approaches towards the end of the war in Korea. In November 1952, General Dwight D. Eisenhower won the US presidential elections because of his popularity with the American people as a successful wartime general, his promise to end the Korean War, and his political embrace with McCarthyite Republicans, signified by his frequent references to a strategy of liberation.[19] Although there is archival evidence that indicates that Eisenhower later considered relaxing tensions between the US and China, his administration went further than his predecessor in antagonizing Mao's regime to gain a strategic edge. To bring the Chinese to the bargaining table on the Korean hostilities, Eisenhower released restraints on KMT activities against the mainland and menaced the Communist Chinese with the prospect of a total embargo. Eisenhower threatened to use atomic weapons against targets in mainland China if hostilities resumed,[20] a strategy that alarmed the British.[21]

## THE EISENHOWER YEARS

The intelligence role of the American Consulate in Hong Kong during the Eisenhower administration (1953–60) continued in the direction it had followed under Truman, but on an expanded scale. The Consulate remained primarily a nexus for the collection of information on political, military, social and economic developments on the mainland. Furthermore, as in the past, the Consulate gathered intelligence on Communist elements within the colony. The Consulate grew as intelligence, propaganda, consular and trade operations expanded there. According to Sir Alexander Grantham, Governor of Hong Kong from 1947 to 1957, the American Consulate grew significantly during his tenure. Evidently, it became the largest consulate in the world, much to Beijing's displeasure.[22]

The CIA station had likewise increased in size and significance. Its production of intelligence rivalled that of the 600-man CIA station in Taiwan.[23] However, it apparently went beyond gathering intelligence. Later, in a 1968 radio interview, Grantham described how he had taken 'a poor view' of the size and the purpose of the Consulate at the time which, he said, was 'at enmity with the lawful government of China'. Grantham explained how the CIA had been 'extremely ham handed' in Hong Kong during his tenure as governor and that he had 'to take very strong line to stop them being so stupid'.[24]

Despite nascent problems and budget difficulties, the Americans began to formulate a more articulate set of objectives and methodology for propaganda activities. The purpose and method of US propaganda policy was set down in an annual country plan or prospectus authored by USIS officials in Hong Kong and approved by the parent agency in Washington.

The June 1953 USIS 'Country Plan' reveals that the objectives of USIS-Hong Kong were 'unusual' when compared to other USIS offices because they focused on a common language, Chinese, rather than a geographical location. The intended audience of USIS-Hong Kong included the people on the Chinese mainland, overseas Chinese populations and Hong Kong itself.

The Country Plan identified three primary psychological objectives: undermine 'Chinese Communist sources of power and support on mainland China' and give 'hope and encouragement to anti-Communist elements'; induce 'Chinese in Southeast Asia to support US and Free World policies and actions, and to produce among them anti-Communist sentiment and action'; and to obtain 'in Hong Kong increased understanding and support of US and Free World policies and actions, and increased anti-Communist sentiment and action'.[25] To achieve these objectives in Hong Kong, the Country Plan listed nine tasks:

1. Increasing the output of pro-'Free World' and anti-Communist publications and motion pictures.
2. Reducing the circulation of Communist publications and motion pictures.
3. Fostering the understanding and cooperation of British officials, businessmen and Armed Forces.
4. Engendering anti-Communist and pro-'Free World' attitudes among Chinese intellectuals.
5. Fostering anti-Communist policies among businessmen and wider acceptance and understanding among them of economic measures taken against Communist China.
6. Increasing pro-'Free World' influences in schools.
7. Strengthening anti-Communist influence in labour unions.
8. Furthering anti-Communist and pro-'Free World' sentiments among refugees from Mainland China.
9. Countering and refuting anti-US propaganda by Communists among all segments of the population.[26]

It is apparent from these objectives that the views of Hong Kong's population continued to be of interest to the United States. The Americans were particularly interested in countering the influence that Beijing had amassed in Hong Kong's schools, labour unions and the media. Another part of the US psychological operations policy that targeted the population of Hong Kong was the educational exchange programme. The exchange programme offered selected Chinese scholars from Hong Kong, whether legal residents or refugees, the opportunity to study or temporarily work in the United States. In turn, the programme would export American scholars to Hong Kong to conduct research or to lecture at Hong Kong universities. The programme was established through US Public Law 535 which stated that its goal was 'to provide assistance to Chinese of academic standing who wished to avoid returning to China at this time and making their skills available to the Communist regime'. However, the programme often failed to meet this goal because it only provided a one year grant to individual Chinese scholars, thus forcing their return after that year was complete.[27]

USIS-Hong Kong faced major obstacles in these objectives. In 1953, American officials lamented 'the increasingly uncooperative attitude' of the British towards the information programmes of the USIS. In the first half of 1953, the Hong Kong authorities apparently protested to the American Consulate about USIS activities. The director of USIS responded these protests were unjustified since these activities had been continuing 'for some time with British knowledge'. The British position was that they were contrary to the agency's 'agreed function' in Hong Kong which was to 'explain, by overt, means, American policies and American life'. The Hong Kong authorities wanted USIS to cease publishing anti-Communist material as it did not 'come under the scope of the Agreement'. Although they did not press the matter with the British, USIS officials in Hong Kong told Washington that they knew of no such agreement. As a result, some publications were terminated, some books were removed from the American Library, and pamphleteering was curtailed.[28]

Anglo-American disagreements over propaganda policy in Hong Kong were minor compared to the high level divergence over security policy in Asia. In 1954, following the end of the Korean War, French difficulties in Indochina drew world attention. Although the Eisenhower administration wanted to avoid sending troops to Southeast Asia as it might result in another Korea, continued Vietminh victories against French forces put pressure on Eisenhower to intervene. The US government called for a united Allied effort to prevent French Indochina from falling to the Communist insurgents.[29]

However, the British rejected any Allied military involvement. The Conservative government of Winston Churchill believed that collective intervention on behalf of the French might provoke the PRC and ruin the Korean settlement in Geneva. British officials were also concerned that, if there was American intervention in Indochina, Eisenhower might go further than in Korea and use nuclear weapons. Without collective support, there was no Allied intervention in Indochina, and French forces suffered a decisive defeat in May 1954.[30]

THE OFFSHORE ISLANDS CRISES

With the expansion of Communism in Southeast Asia, American officials in Hong Kong became more concerned with what they saw as Communist infiltration of the British colony, particularly in businesses, trade unions, schools and the media.[31] Hong Kong's situation grew more awkward as the Communist–KMT conflict escalated in September 1954. The two sides exchanged artillery barrages over the Nationalist held islands of Kinmen (Quemoy) and Mazu (Matsu). The Eisenhower administration was drawn into the confrontation in support of the KMT. Eisenhower publicly hinted that nuclear strikes might be used to settle the conflict. Although the President attempted to gain British support by informally committing the US to the defence of Hong Kong in the event of significant conflict, the Churchill government contended that the islands were insignificant and were afraid that the US would use nuclear weapons if there was an escalation.[32] However, tensions were eased after Zhou Enlai, the Chinese premier, called for negotiations at the Bandung Conference in April 1955.[33]

For Hong Kong, the international situation affected its internal stability. The political struggle between Communist sponsored elements and KMT sponsored elements in Hong Kong intensified, culminating in terrorist campaigns and outbreaks of civil unrest. Before the first Offshore Islands Crisis ended in April 1955, the KMT bombed an Air India aircraft carrying Communist journalists from China to the Bandung Conference in Indonesia. The explosion occurred after it had refuelled in Hong Kong.[34] Eisenhower's National Security Council discussed the incident, while in Beijing, Mao Zedong accused the British government of being responsible as it had warned the British *chargé d'affaires* in Beijing 'prior to the departure of the Indian aircraft...that efforts would be made to sabotage the aircraft'.[35] Moreover, according to Governor Grantham, the aircraft was supposed to be carrying Zhou Enlai, but Zhou's travel plans to the conference had been rescheduled at the last minute.[36]

The alleged Nationalist saboteur had escaped from Hong Kong to Taiwan. In August 1955, investigations led the Hong Kong authorities to conclude that the aircraft did indeed explode due to a 'time bomb placed aboard' by 'a Chinese Nationalist' in Hong Kong. The British embassy in Washington informed the Eisenhower administration that the Hong Kong authorities had issued a warrant for the arrest of the saboteur.[37] The British were perturbed by the bombing and the possibility of the American involvement. Not only did Beijing and Indonesia accuse the CIA of having funded the saboteur, but they were also unhappy that the saboteur had escaped to Taiwan on a plane belonging to Civil Air Transport Incorporated (CAT), an airline that had very close links to the CIA.[38] In Washington,

British officials urged the US to put pressure on the 'Nationalists to return the saboteur' to Hong Kong. The American Consulate in Hong Kong recommended to Washington that the British should be 'politely advised to pursue their own remedies'. The Consulate indicated that such an answer 'would prevent lending "colour" to British charges which may or may not be true'.[39] In the end, the British were never able to secure the saboteur's extradition, because Her Majesty's Government did not recognize the Nationalist government in Taipei and therefore no extradition treaty existed between them.[40]

The 'Kowloon Riots' of October 1956 could also be attributed to Cold War tensions. They had 'started spontaneously among refugee elements', but civil unrest was intensified by conflict between anti-Communist groups and pro-Communist groups. In discussions between American officials and British officials in Hong Kong, Governor Grantham claimed that, although neither the Nationalists nor the Communists had 'instigated' the riots, pro-Nationalist labour elements had been responsible for some of the most significant outbreaks of violence.[41] After the meeting, Consul General Everett Drumright reported to Washington that he had done his 'best ... to exculpate the right-wing [or pro-Nationalist] unions for the riots'.[42] Yet regardless of events such as the Air India bombing and the Kowloon Riots, the British and the Americans maintained a cooperative relationship in Hong Kong with the British providing a great deal of intelligence for the Americans.

## PROPAGANDA AND PSYCHOLOGICAL WARFARE AFTER 1956

During the late 1950s, USIS-Hong Kong continued to disseminate anti-Communist messages to Chinese audiences in China and Southeast Asia, but described the impact of the related exchange programme as 'limited'. Its view agreed with the American Consulate that the programme seemed to be limited by factors including a shortage of worthwhile candidates, visa restrictions that disqualified many of the worthy candidates, lack of interest among some candidates, and the Hong Kong Governor's lack of 'receptivity' to the exchange programme. The Consulate emphasized that programme targeted at groups in Hong Kong were subordinate to the operations which were directed at the overseas Chinese and the mainland. Nevertheless, the Consulate requested that resources devoted to the educational exchange programme be increased in the 1956 and 1957 budgets.[43]

Moreover, USIS-Hong Kong 'reassessed the objectives and potentials' of the educational exchange programme and implemented policies that it deemed effective. First, USIS sought to use grants available through the programme to influence media which would reach Hong Kong and overseas Chinese. Second, the USIS post devoted more attention to strengthening the 'refugee colleges' in Hong Kong that were designed to accommodate refugees. Finally, the post sought to use the strengthened social programmes in Hong Kong, an area that could guarantee cooperation from governmental officials.[44] In other words, these efforts not only had the intended purpose of 'saving' individuals from Communism, but also to gain dividends in public relations.

During Eisenhower's second term, 1957–60, the Communist press in China and the pro-Communist press in Hong Kong were particularly vehement in their accusations that the American Consulate in Hong Kong was a base for administering espionage, sabotage and guerrilla war against the People's Republic. Moreover, the pro-Beijing press accused the British of colluding with such American operations. American officials at the Consulate and in Washington became concerned over the damage that the campaign was doing to American prestige among Hong Kong and overseas Chinese.

Some examples of such accusations are evident in articles published in various 'local [Hong Kong] Chinese-language Communist papers' during the period. On 4 and 6 December 1957, Hong Kong papers, *Ta Kung Pao* and *Wen Hui Pao* , alleged that the American Consulate in Hong Kong was involved in joint US-KMT 'terrorist activities in and based in Hong Kong'. The pro-Communist dailies accused the American Consulate of aiding the Chinese Nationalists in 'training agents and sending them to the mainland' to conduct espionage and sabotage. One of the papers claimed that 'the American aggressors' had converted 'their "listening post" into a base for assassinations, robbery, shipping arms, and training and despatching [*sic*] agents'.[45] In January 1958, *Ta Kung Pao* contained another scathing article that attacked the American consulate as 'a miniature Washington' and that it surpassed the size of any embassy including the one in Moscow. The article then accurately listed all of the offices and agencies that were based in the Consulate General.[46]

Anti-American attacks in Hong Kong's pro-Communist press had occurred previously and would continue until America's recognition of the Chinese government in 1972. Nonetheless, at the end of 1958, officials at the US Department of State were apprehensive about what they considered the 'unprecedented virulence' of the Hong Kong papers' defamation campaign against the Consulate. The State Department was particularly concerned that there might have been a 'loss of influence on [the] part of US Government agencies and private organizations sufficient [to] have [a] lasting effect [on] their future operations'.[47] This concern however, was insignificant to the re-emergence of hostilities over the Off-shore Islands in the summer of 1958.

## THE 1958 CRISIS

In 1958 Mao Zedong had responded to Chiang Kai-shek's massing of troops of Kinmen and Mazu, and to commando raids into the mainland, by shelling the offshore islands. Washington once again backed the KMT and ferried troops and supplies to the islands with the Seventh Fleet. For the second time, the US and the PRC had reached the brink, and once again, the Eisenhower administration made ominous threats.[48] During the crisis, the British government, under Harold Macmillan's leadership, continued to oppose an escalation of the conflict over the islands which his government regarded as insignificant. However, Macmillan gave Eisenhower moral support and did not advertise Allied differences over China policy. Fortunately, in October 1958, Beijing and Washington mutually withdrew from the brink and hostilities subsided.[49] Macmillan's policy was consistent with a re-strengthening of the 'special relationship' that had been initiated a year earlier during meetings with Eisenhower in Washington. The British and Americans had agreed to cooperate on issues that included nuclear weapons technology, policy towards the PRC, and defence arrangements for Hong Kong. On China, Macmillan had agreed not to press for the PRC's membership in the United Nations and not to overtly appear contradict US policy towards China.[50]

Nevertheless, Hong Kong continued to be exploited by the US intelligence gathering and propaganda apparatus into the 1960s. American agencies in Hong Kong carried on a primary mission of collecting, translating, analyzing and processing information on internal political and economic developments in the PRC. In a classified NSC policy paper implemented on 11 June 1960 the Eisenhower administration stated that the American Consulate in Hong Kong was 'the most important source of hard economic, political and military information on Communist China'.[51]

In addition to intelligence gathering, the US information programme was also deemed significant. Three NSC policy papers, dated 20 June 1957, 17 July 1957, and 11 June 1960, emphasized the importance of the propaganda programme's main objective in Hong Kong to 'alienate the Overseas Chinese from the Chinese Communists'.[52] An NSC policy paper of July 1957 described how the operation in Hong Kong continued to place 'a major emphasis on the production of news periodicals, books, movies, radio scripts, and other anti-Communist materials directed at the overseas Chinese'.[53] According to NSC 6007/1, the programme was a 'main source of materials' that were 'designed to counteract Chinese Communist propaganda by putting mainland developments in realistic perspective and making clear the heavy price that the Chinese people' had to pay for 'the material advances achieved by the Communists'.[54]

The importance of the US information programme in Hong Kong was also apparent from the size of its budget. From 1958 to 1961, the US government invested US$3.2 million in its Hong Kong operations.[55] Furthermore, by the 1960s, the programme also provoked less hostility from the British authorities who in many ways assisted such operations or supplemented them with their own public relations programme.[56]

However, the Anglo-American 'special relationship' was still being tested in other areas, particularly by developments in Southeast Asia. In the United States, John F. Kennedy had inherited the containment policy of the previous administrations. Partly as inheritance and partly in response to an openly hostile PRC, the Kennedy administration chose to continue the diplomatic and strategic containment of China, and to maintain American support for the KMT.[57] Moreover, Kennedy was, like his predecessor, under pressure to intervene against Communist insurgencies in both Laos and Vietnam. Once again, British and American policies diverged in Asia, and the Macmillan government attempted to prevail upon the Kennedy administration not to intervene in Southeast Asia with large scale military forces.[58]

When the situation in Laos grew worse, the British did reluctantly participate with the United States, Australia and New Zealand in sending a small number of troops to defend Thailand in the spring of 1962 in accordance to the SEATO treaty. However, the Laotian situation was temporarily neutralized. In Laos, the United States began to build up a vast CIA-sponsored Army while the British withdrew their forces from Thailand.[59] American attention now turned to Vietnam and Kennedy went against British recommendations. By 1963, Kennedy had escalated American involvement there by sending some 15,000 troops.[60] Despite disagreements over policies in Asia, Macmillan and Kennedy reaffirmed the special relationship.[61]

Nevertheless, American support for Chiang Kai-shek impacted upon Hong Kong when the colony was rocked by KMT terrorism. The surge of Nationalist sabotage in or through Hong Kong raised concern even in America as it began to threaten their objectives. Some believed that intelligence gathering and propaganda operations were jeopardized by a loss of American prestige, that was caused by knowledge of how the American Consulate and the CIA had operative and financial ties to the Nationalist Chinese organizations responsible for the sabotage and guerrilla warfare.[62] Nationalist attacks included the mailing of postal bombs into China, the bombing of Communist targets in Hong Kong, and commando raids into south China. The Hong Kong authorities did their best to apprehend Nationalist agents as when the Royal Navy arrested 11 Nationalist commandos in the waters around Hong Kong.[63]

Such incidents prompted discussions between Americans and British in January and February 1963. From the meetings, it was evident that the Hong Kong authorities wanted Washington to actively prevail upon the KMT to stop its campaign of violence.[64] At the same time, a British Labour opposition in the House of Commons called upon the Macmillan government to put pressure on the American government to make 'representations' to the KMT leadership. Labour also claimed that KMT 'banditry' in or near Hong Kong was carried out by 'agents armed and trained by the US'.[65] In response, the Hong Kong authorities were forced to adopt a policy that included prosecuting apprehended Nationalist saboteurs, and levying stringent prison sentences on those found guilty, instead of simply deporting them to Taiwan as in the past.

American officials in Washington and Hong Kong worried that the Hong Kong government's prosecution of Nationalists agents in Hong Kong would damage US prestige and operations. The American Consulate reported that the criminal prosecution of KMT operatives could 'stir things up' between the Communists and the Nationalists and lead to a loss of US 'intelligence dividends'.[66] Moreover, the Consulate believed that public disclosure of evidence from prosecutions could implicate the US government, while many of the explosives and weapons seized by Hong Kong authorities were of US origin.[67]

The Macmillan government made both informal and formal requests for American assistance in pressuring the Nationalist to cease their campaign of violence in Hong Kong.[68] British pressure and ceaseless Nationalist terrorism in Hong Kong forced the Kennedy administration to use the State Department and the American Consulate to 'approach' KMT elements in Taiwan and Hong Kong concerning the violence.[69] At the time, the Americans were also seeking British support after the *coup d'état* in Vietnam and the assassination of Kennedy. By 1964, the KMT's campaign of violence in Hong Kong or near Hong Kong subsided because of its ineffectiveness, the international condemnation it had provoked, and because of pressure from the United States.

CONCLUSION

The significance of American operations in Hong Kong throughout the 1950s and early 1960s was summarized best by Allen S. Whiting in 1965. Then in the State Department, Whiting wrote that the American Consulate General in Hong Kong was 'for all intents and purposes' the US 'Peking embassy'.[70] Historical evidence demonstrates that the British colony became a very important location for American intelligence operations and propaganda policy in Asia. It is also apparent that some of the American

Consulate's activities in Hong Kong at this time put a strain on the Anglo-American relationship. The most damaging American activities were those that encouraged Nationalist Chinese operations in Hong Kong. It is difficult to determine the extent to which American officials were involved, if at all, in the actual planning and execution of the KMT's campaigns of violence and sabotage in Hong Kong and China. However, it is clear that US agencies funded Nationalist and anti-Communist elements in Hong Kong and used them as sources of intelligence.

Moreover, Anglo-American differences over Hong Kong's usefulness can be attributable to their differences in their policies towards the Far East. Despite British irritation with some of the more aggressive American operations in Hong Kong, the 'special relationship' was maintained throughout the 1950s and early 1960s in the area of sharing Humint and Sigint gathered in the colony. The British also continued to allow the Americans to use Hong Kong as a base for massive anti-Communist propaganda operations. Although the American intelligence and propaganda operations in Hong Kong retained some size and importance right up to the British handover of Hong Kong in 1997, these operations were never again as virulently opposed to the Chinese Communist regime as during the era of Eisenhower and Kennedy.

### NOTES

1. Edwin Martin, *Divided Counsel: The Anglo-American Response to Communist Victory in China* (Lexington: UP of Kentucky 1986) pp.231–7; Robert Accinelli, *Crisis and Commitment: United States Policy towards Taiwan, 1950–1955* (Chapel Hill: UNC Press 1996) pp.3–17; James Tuck-Hong Tang, *Britain's Encounter with a Revolutionary China, 1949–54* (NY: St Martin's Press 1992) pp.5–5.
2. Peter Lowe, *Containing the Cold War in East Asia* (Manchester UP 1997) pp.99–112; Martin (note 1) pp.63–70; Tang (note 1) pp.53–5.
3. Qiang Zhai, *The Dragon, the Lion and the Eagle: Chinese/British/American Relations, 1949–1958* (Kent, OH: Kent State UP 1995) p.114.
4. Jeffrey T. Richelson and Desmond Ball, *The Ties that Bind: Intelligence Cooperation between the UKUSA Countries* (London: Unwin Hyman 1990) pp.40, 142–3, 190–1. For more on the Sigint facility in Hong Kong, see: Desmond Ball, 'Over and Out: Signals Intelligence (SIGINT) in Hong Kong', *Intelligence and National Security* 11/3 (July 1996).
5. Karl Rankin, Hong Kong, to Department of State, #166, 28 Feb. 1950, Subject: Political Report for Jan. 1950, 746G.00/2-2850, Record Group (RG) 59, US National Archives (USNA).
6. Karl Rankin, Hong Kong, to Dept. of State, #228, 16 March 1950, Subject: Political Report for Feb. 1950, 746G.00/3-1650, RG 59, USNA.
7. Walter McConaughy, Hong Kong, to Dept. of State, #113, 15 Feb. 1951, Subject: Arrest of Chinese Contact of Consulate General by Hong Kong Police, 746G.00/2-1551, RG 59, USNA.
8. Mr Strong to Mr Clubb, Office Memo, Dept. of State, #113, 15 Feb. 1951, FW 746.00/3-151, RG 59, USNA.
9. Walter McConaughy, Hong Kong, to Secretary of State, #2291, 16 Feb. 1951, 746G.00/2-1551, RG 59, USNA.

10. Richard J. Aldrich, 'The Value of Residual Empire: Anglo-American Intelligence Co-operation in Asia after 1945', in idem and Michael F. Hopkins (eds.) *Intelligence, Defence and Diplomacy: British Policy in the Post-War World* (London/Portland, OR: Frank Cass 1994) p.234.

11. Walter McConaughy, Hong Kong, to Dept. of State, #1139, 21 Feb. 1951, Subject: Political and Military Intelligence Concerning Communists, 746G.001/2-2151. RG 59, USNA.

12. The Chargé in the Republic of China (Karl Rankin), Taipei, to the Asst. Sec. of State for Far Eastern Affairs (Dean Rusk), 13 Aug. 1951, *Foreign Relations of the United States (FRUS)* 1951, Vol.VII, pp.1778–85. British had, at the time, arrested eight Nationalist leaders.

13. Walter McConaughy, Hong Kong, to the Secretary of State, 15 Feb. 1952, 746G.00(W)/2-1552, RG 59, USNA.; idem to Dept. of State, 10 March 1952, 746G.00/3-1052, RG 59, USNA.

14. The United States Information Service (USIS) is the overseas service of the United States Information Agency (USIA), essentially the public relations organization for US foreign policy aims.

15. James R. Wilkinson, Hong Kong, to Dept. of State, #617, 3 Nov. 1950, Subject: Semi-annual USIS Evaluation Report for the period ending 31 May 1950, 511.46G/11-350, Record Group (RG) 59, USNA.

16. Walter McConaughy, Hong Kong, to Dept. of State, #337, 27 Aug. 1951, Subject: USIE Semi-annual Evaluation Report for the period ending May 1951, 511.46G/8-2751, RG 59, USNA.

17. Wilkinson to Dept. of State, 3 Nov. 1950.

18. McConaughy to Dept. of State, 27 Aug. 1951.

19. Stephen E. Ambrose, *Eisenhower: Soldier and President* (NY: Simon & Schuster, 1990), pp.269, 281–2.

20. Ibid. p.325; Qiang (note 3) p.123; Edward C. Keefer, 'President Dwight D. Eisenhower and the End of the Korean War', *Diplomatic History* 1/3 (Summer 1986) p.281.

21. Callum MacDonald, *Britain and the Korean War* (Oxford: Blackwell 1990) pp.82–5; Kevin Ruane, 'Containing America: Aspects of British Foreign Policy and the Cold War in South-East Asia, 1951–54', *Diplomacy & Statecraft* 7/1 (March 1996) pp.160–2.

22. Alexander Grantham, *Via Ports: From Hong Kong to Hong Kong* (Hong Kong UP 1966) pp.169–70.

23. Aldrich (note 10) p.233; Joseph. B. Smith, *Portrait of a Cold Warrior* (NY: Scribner's 1976) pp.147–8.

24. Frank Welsh, *A History of Hong Kong* (London: HarperCollins 1993) p.446.

25. Julian F. Harrington to Dept. of State, Hong Kong, 9 June 1953, #2526, Subject: Draft Country Plan for USIS Hong Kong, 511.46G/6-953, RG59, USNA.

26. Ibid.

27. USIS Hong Kong to USIA Washington, USIS Semi-annual Evaluation Report, #1, 19 Aug. 1953, 511.46G/8-1953, RG 59, USNA.

28. Ibid.

29. George C. Herring, *America's Longest War: the United States and Vietnam, 1950–75*, 2nd ed. (NY: Knopf 1986) pp.28–30; Lloyd C. Gardner, *Approaching Vietnam: from World War II through Dienbienphu* (NY: Norton 1988) p.202.

30. Ruane, 'Containing America (note 21) p.142; Herring, pp.34–5; Gardner (note 29) p.203.

31. Office Memo, A. Guy Hope to Mr. McConaughy, CA, 15 Jan. 1953, Subject: Chinese Communist Activities in Hong Kong, 746G.001/12-1552, RG 59, USNA; American Consulate General, Hong Kong, to Dept. of State, 8 April 1953, #1989, Subject: Information on Chinese Communist Insurance Companies, 746G.001/4-853, RG 59, USNA; Julian F. Harrington, Hong Kong, to Dept. of State, 4 May 1954, #2009, Subject: May Observances in Hong Kong, 746G.00 MAY DAY/5-454, RG 59, USNA; Everett F. Drumright, Hong Kong, to Dept. of State, 3 Jan. 1955, #1030, 746G.001/1-355, RG 59, USNA.

32. Michael Dockrill, 'Britain and the Chinese Off-Shore Islands, 1954-55', in idem and John W. Young (eds.) *British Foreign Policy 1945–56* (Basingstoke: Macmillan 1989) pp.180–9. For Eisenhower's comments on Hong Kong's security, see the letter: Eisenhower to Churchill, 18 Feb. 1955 in Peter G. Boyle (ed.) *The Churchill-Eisenhower Correspondence, 1953–55* (Chapel Hill: UNC Press 1990).

33. For more on the first Offshore Islands Crisis, see: Gordon Chang, 'To the Nuclear Brink: Eisenhower, Dulles and the Quemoy-Matsu Crisis', *International Security* 12/4 (Spring 1988) pp.86–98; H.W. Brands Jr, 'Testing Massive Retaliation: Credibility and Crisis Management in the Taiwan Strait', ibid. 12/4 (Spring 1988) pp.124–5.

34. Daily Intelligence Abstracts No.348, 14 April 1955, File Folder: OCB 350.05 [Intelligence Abstracts] (File #2) (3), Box 111, OCB Central Files, NSC Staff Papers, Dwight D. Eisenhower Library; Daily Intelligence Abstracts No. 447, 2 Sept. 1955, File Folder: OCB 350.05 [Intelligence Abstracts] (File #2) (7), Box 111, OCB Central Files, NSC Staff Papers, Dwight D. Eisenhower Library.

35. Daily Intelligence Abstracts No. 348.

36. Grantham (note 22), p. 180. See also Nancy Bernkopf Tucker, *Taiwan, Hong Kong and the United States, 1945–1992: Uncertain Friendships* (NY: Twayne 1994) p.206.

37. Daily Intelligence Abstracts No. 447; Grantham (note 22) p.180.

38. Grantham (note 22) p.180; Tucker (note 36) p.206; For evidence of CAT Inc.'s ties to the CIA, see William M. Leary Jr, 'Aircraft and Anti-Communists: CAT in Action, 1949–52', *China Quarterly*, Oct./Dec. 52 (1972) pp.654–69.

39. Daily Intelligence Abstracts No.447.

40. Grantham (note 22) p.181.

41. Everett F. Drumright, Hong Kong, to Dept. of State, 1 Nov. 1956, #364, Subject: Conversation with Governor of Hong Kong, 746G.00/11-156, RG 59, USNA.

42. Everett F. Drumright, Hong Kong, to Dept. of State, 8 Nov. 1956, #384, Subject: Discussion with Hong Kong Government Political Adviser, 746G.00/11-856, RG 59, USNA

43. Maurice S. Rice, Consul in Charge, Hong Kong, to Dept. of State, #2904, 16 June 1955, Subject: Educational Exchange: FY 1956 Prospectus, 511.46G3/6-1655, RG 59, USNA.

44. Everett F. Drumright, Hong Kong, to Dept. of State, '424, 13 Sept. 1955, Subject: Semi-annual Report on Educational Exchange Program, 511.46G3/9-1355, RG 59, USNA.

45. Everett F. Drumright, Hong Kong, to Dept. of State, 10 Dec. 1957, #456, Subject: Hong Kong Communist Press attack on 'US-Chiang' Activities Here, 746G.001/12-1057, RG 59, USNA.

46. Everett F. Drumright, Hong Kong, to Dept. of State, 12 Jan. 1958, #572, Subject: Hong Kong Communist Press Attack on the American Consulate General, 746G.001/1-2258, RG 59, USNA.

47. Christian Herter, Secretary of State, to the American Consulate General, Hong Kong, 12 Dec. 1958, 746G.001/12-958, RG 59, USNA.

48. Qiang (note 3) pp.178–89; Tucker (note 36) pp.42–3.

49. Qiang (note 3) p.54.

50. Alistair Horne, *Macmillan: 1957–1986, Volume II of the Official Biography* (London: Macmillan 1989) p.56.

51. NSC 6007/1, 'US Policy on Hong Kong', National Security Council, 11 June 1960, NSC 6007/1-Hong Kong Folder, Box 28, Policy Paper Subseries, NSC Series, Office of the Special Assistant for National Security Affairs Records, White House Office, Dwight D. Eisenhower Library.

52. Quote from #206, NSC 5720, Status United States Programs for National Security as of 20 June 1957, *Foreign Relations of the United States, 1955–57*, Vol.IX, p.610. See also NSC 5717, 'US Policy on Hong Kong', National Security Council, 17 July 1957, USNA; NSC 6007/1, 11 June 1960 and 10 Nov. 1960.

53. NSC 5717.

54. NSC 6007/1.

55. Ibid.

56. NSC 5717; NSC 6117/1. See also Johannes R. Lombardo, United States' Foreign Policy Towards the British Crown Colony of Hong Kong during the Early Cold War Period, 1945–1964, PhD thesis, Aug. 1997, U. of Hong Kong, pp.73–7, 160–3.

57. James Fetzer, 'Clinging to Containment: China Policy', in Thomas G. Paterson (ed.) *Kennedy's Quest for Victory: American Foreign Policy, 1961–1963* (NY: OUP 1989) pp.178–79.

58. Richard Lamb, *The Macmillan Years 1957–1963: The Emerging Truth* (London: John Murray 1995) p.396.

59. Ibid. pp.392–3.
60. Horne (note 50) p.418.
61. Lamb (note 58) p.303; Horne (note 50) pp.288–92, 438–9, 525–6.
62. Harold W. Jacobson, Hong Kong, to Det. of State, 19 Dec. 1961, #556, Subject: Pro-Nationalists in Hong Kong Discuss Hong Kong Political Events, 746G.00/12-1961, USNA.
63. Dept. of State to the American Consulate Hong Kong, 1 Nov. 1962, #CA-4762, 746G.00/11-162, RG 59, USNA; Lynn H. Olsen, Hong Kong, to Dept. of State, 29 Nov. 1962, #A-563, Subject: Hong Kong/Macau Weeka No. 48, 746G.00(W)/11.7962. Regarding the British arrest of the Nationalist commandos, the Hong Kong government 'received a note of thanks' from the Beijing government for its action. Marshall Green, Hong Kong, to Sec. of State, 5 Feb. 1963, #1309, POL 24 HK, USNA.
64. Marshall Green, Hong Kong, to Dept. of State, 23 Jan. 1963, #a-723, Subject: Hong Kong Chief of Staff's Commentaries on (1) Future of Hong Kong; (2) Chinat Raids on the Mainland; (3) May 1963 Border Crossing Incident, 746G.00/1-2363, USNA; Green to Sec. State, 5 Feb. 1963.
65. American Embassy, London, to Sec. of State, 15 Feb. 1963, #3180, POL 24 HK, USNA; Alfred Harding, London, to Dept. of State, 2 March 1963, #A-1194, Subject: Parliamentary Question on KMT Activities in Hong Kong and US Involvement, POL 24 HK XR POL 24 US, USNA.
66. Marshall Green, Hong Kong, to Sec. of State, 15 Feb. 1963, #1389, POL 24 HK XR DEF 6-7 CHINAT, USNA; idem to idem, 15 Feb. 1963, #1380, POL 24 HK XR DEF 6-7 CHINAT, USNA.
67. Marshall Green, Hong Kong, to Sec. of State, 13 June 1963, #2145, POL 24 HK, USNA.
68. American Embassy, London, to Sec. of State, 15 Feb. 1963, #3181, POL 24 HK, USNA; Ambassador Bruce, London, to Sec. of State, 7 May 1963, #4410, POL 24 HK, USNA; Marshall Green, Hong Kong, to Sec. of State, 10 May 1963, #1891, POL 24 HK XR DEF 6-5 CHINAT, USNA; idem to idem, 24 May 1963, #2003, DEF 6-5 CHINAT XR POL 23 HK, USNA; American Embassy, London, to the Sec. of State, 25 May 1963, #4760, DEF 6-5 CHINAT POL 24 HK, USNA.
69. Lynn H. Olsen, Hong Kong, to Dept. of State, 11 Oct. 1963, #a-294, POL 1 HK XR POL 7 INDIA, USNA; Dean Rusk, Sec. of State, to American Consulate Hong Kong, 29 Nov. 1963, #520, POL 24 HK, USNA. Marshall Green, who had just been appointed the Asst. Sec. of State for Far Eastern Affairs, had recommended that the approach be made and drafted the telegram of instruction to Hong Kong.
70. Allen S. Whiting to William P. Bundy, Dept. of State, 29 July 1965, Subject: The Hong Kong Consulate General and China Analysis, Box 13, James C. Thomson Papers, John F. Kennedy Library.

# 4

# Taiwan's Propaganda Cold War: The Offshore Islands Crises of 1954 and 1958

### GARY D. RAWNSLEY

In 1952, an American journalist stationed in Taiwan, H. Maclear Bate, wrote, 'if any Government ever lacked an adequate propaganda organisation, it is Chiang Kai-shek's. ... a clever propagandist he said, would find an inexhaustible fund of material in Formosa [Taiwan] which could be capitalized', and he concluded by observing how 'Never has so little been done with so much.'[1]

In many respects, Bate was correct. For much of the early Cold War, Taiwan's propaganda lacked sparkle and originality; it did not respond to vacillations in the international environment; and while it depended far too heavily on the United States for *material* support, failed to heed their advice when offered. The Republic of China (ROC) on Taiwan even declined to explore sufficiently the opportunities presented by covert propaganda; few of its activities were hidden from view, and its international media even publicized the activities of Taiwan's guerrilla units on the mainland. Remarkably, while most governments sought to hide their special operations, Taiwan was anxious to tell the world. Clearly, the government of the ROC imagined that the security of the operations themselves was less important than the propaganda about them which, as most propagandists will agree, was a reckless assumption.

Taiwan possessed three characteristics that should have given its propaganda a distinctive edge. First, American support cannot be neglected. After the outbreak of the Korean War in 1950, the Truman administration finally (though reluctantly) acquiesced to demands that Chiang's regime be considered a vital strategic ally in the war against Asian Communism. Dean Rusk talked of the need to roll-back Communist authority on the mainland, 'to get China unhooked from Russia'.[2] Taiwan thus became the destination of American manpower, aid and intelligence expertise.

Second, we must be mindful of Taiwan's geographic location. Situated just 100 miles from the mainland of China (a distance that also separates Cuba from the United States), Taiwan was in a favourable position to project itself as 'Free China'. Thus the proximity of the two Chinas narrowed significantly the distance that propaganda had to travel, whether by balloon, loudspeaker, radio, or word-of-mouth. It also allowed the authorities and CIA agents in Taiwan to gather detailed intelligence on unfolding events in the mainland, and incorporate into its propaganda the many Communist blunders and U-turns it discovered there. The disastrous famine after the Great Leap Forward, and the turmoil of the Cultural Revolution, were welcome propaganda fodder.

Third, propaganda towards the mainland was structured *by* Chinese *for* Chinese, lending it a plausible and authentic texture. However, the meaning of Chinese, and the use of Chinese symbolism, heritage, and value-systems, would remain a point of contention between the propagandists and their American advisers. This also meant that American advice about how to structure propaganda was overlooked.

The nature of this propaganda turned on the ROC's projection of itself as the legitimate government of China, and thus depicted the 'illegal' seizure of power by Communist rebels. The Kuomintang (KMT) had galvanized its power on Taiwan through its pursuit of political tutelage, a strong state to protect the island from the Communist menace, and the eventual recovery of the mainland on its own terms. 'We are going back to the mainland', the *Free China Weekly* vowed repeatedly throughout the 1950s and 1960s.[3]

However, the political realities of martial law, the suppression of the Taiwanese identity, and a one-party state sat in obvious discomfort alongside the propaganda image of 'Free China'. Until 1986, when the ROC launched itself upon the road of political transformation, the government experienced crippling public relations difficulties: How could 'Free China', even in the Cold War, be so authoritarian?

Upon the advice of their friends in the United States, the KMT devoted considerable time and energy to convincing its international audience that it alone was the true heir of Sun Yat-sen and therefore of the Chinese Revolution: 'To win [the overseas Chinese] over to Chinese culture was, it was hoped, to win them over to Taiwan, for it was the boast of the Nationalists that they, rather than the Marxist iconoclasts of the Chinese mainland, were the orthodox guardians of the Chinese cultural tradition.'[4] Thus the KMT government was conscious of the need for a concerted effort to appear less militaristic. In 1958, the American Department of State advised the ROC to concentrate on promoting itself as the 'custodian of Chinese culture, virtues and education':[5]

> Its seems to us [US government] that there is a great and assured
> future for the [ROC] if it makes clear to the world that the bases for
> [ROC] counterattack against the mainland are ... in the minds and
> souls of 600 million Chinese people on the mainland who hope and
> pray for delivery from their present bondage. They derive hope and
> are sustained during these dark days by the very existence of the free
> Chinese Government and the preservation by that government of the
> culture and tradition of the Chinese people. The [ROC] helps to keep
> alive the flame of freedom within the world's largest nation.[6]

However not everybody within the US government agreed that this strategy
was appropriate. For example George Allen, once Director of the United
States Information Agency, 'did not think there was much pay dirt in
making Taiwan the custodian of traditional Chinese culture. To obtain the
regard of the Far East, Taiwan must picture itself, not as the guardian of the
past, but as the dynamic leader of the future. ...'[7]

Given Taiwan's extraordinary progress towards a prosperous future,
presenting the contradiction between capitalist Taiwan and Communist
China was certainly a sensible strategy. But the timing was not right. Taiwan
was only just beginning to lay the foundations of the economic miracle that
would materialize in the 1970s, and the Cold War environment persuaded
the government to adopt a more militant style of propaganda.

Hence, Taiwan opted to package its propaganda in the familiar rhetoric
of the period, that which propagandists themselves knew would be most
appealing to both domestic and overseas audiences. Taiwan's projection of
the People's Republic of China (PRC) was decidedly negative, evoking
images and stereotypes designed to convince audiences that China was an
evil enemy deserving to be challenged. The Asian People's Anti-
Communist League's Printing of *A Decade of Chinese Communist Tyranny*
in 1960, begins by comparing 'the Communist controlled area' with a zoo,
'with people there being placed under ruthless exploitation by the aggressor
and traitor alike'. It describes the 'gangsters' (a familiar term used in
reference to the Chinese Communists, suggesting the illegality of their
power and the brutality of their methods) as 'inhuman and devoid of all
moral scruples' – all of this in the first two paragraphs of a closely-typed
book of 483 pages![8]

Cold War propaganda encouraged the use of such stereotypes and the
substitution of names which reinforce the stereotype – 'reds' instead of
Communists, for example. The 1957–58 edition of the *China Yearbook* even
went so far as to refer to the Communists as 'the sons of Satan'.[9] Such
religious imagery was prominent in selling Chiang Kai-shek and his wife,
Madam Chiang to American audiences who delighted in these Chinese

Christians: 'Churches in every township in America offered ready-made and inexpensive vehicles for the dissemination of news concerning the leading Christian family in China. ... [A] victory for Communists in China meant a triumph for the anti-Christ in Asia'.

Whenever Congress was scheduled to debate further aid measures for China, stories that centred on the Chiangs' 'rich spiritual life' appeared in the vocal pro-Taiwan press.[10] It was an image readily accepted by the Western powers, especially the United States. The satanic evil that challenged God-fearing Christians throughout the 'free world' was brought home by the apparent Communist aggression first in Korea and Vietnam, and then against the offshore islands of Mazu (Matsu) and Kinmen (Quemoy).

## THE OFFSHORE ISLANDS CRISES

US policy towards China vacillated after the Communist victory in 1949, and the Truman administration was reluctant to offer the ROC any appreciable support. In January 1950, Secretary of State Dean Acheson announced that the US would not provide the KMT government with military aid or advice, despite warnings that Taiwan could be expected to soon fall to the Communists. Such fears seemed justified when Communist forces attacked and occupied the island of Hainan in May 1950. Acheson told Ernest Bevin, the British Foreign Secretary, that Chiang's regime was 'washed up', and promised that the US 'henceforth will pursue a more realistic policy respecting China'.[11]

In describing these deliberations, Warren I. Cohen has written that such sentiments expressed the widespread view that the US should administer the last rites to Chiang's regime: 'On the 2 [1949], when the China Aid Act expired, the United States would cease wasting its resources. Kuomintang China was dead', while it was only a matter of time before Taiwan fell to the Communists.[12] In January 1950, President Truman formally announced this 'hands-off' policy:

> The United States has no predatory designs on Formosa [Taiwan] or on any other Chinese territory. The United States has no desire to obtain special rights or privileges, or to establish military bases on Formosa at this time. Nor does it have any intention of utilizing its armed forces to interfere in the present situation. The United States will not pursue a course which will lead to involvement in the civil conflict in China ... Similarly the United States will not provide military aid or advice to Chinese forces on Formosa ... [13]

Dean Acheson gave this approach his full support: 'We are not going to get involved militarily in any way on the island of Formosa. So far as I know, no responsible person in the Government, no military man, has ever believed that we should involve forces in the island.'[14] The Chinese Nationalists felt they had been well and truly betrayed by the United States.

However, such American diffidence quickly evaporated with the outbreak of war in Korea. As Chinese forces crossed the Yalu river, the Western powers seized the opportunity to reappraise and then demonstrate their commitment to Taiwan: the US sent the Seventh Fleet to neutralize the Taiwan Strait. Washington's actions now aimed at preventing Mao from attacking Taiwan, and preventing Chiang Kai-shek from launching a premature invasion of the mainland. In President Truman's words the policy was designed to prevent the enlargement of 'the area of conflict'.[15]

This was a dramatic reversal of policy within the space of a mere five months. The Korean War served to propel Taiwan to the forefront of America's Cold War strategy. As a vital component in the global containment of Communism, the island became the CIA's main operational base in Asia, eventually boasting 600 CIA staff, and enjoyed copious amounts of military and economic aid from the US.[16] American policy considered Taiwan 'an important anchor in the defensive chain from the Aleutians to Australia', and an 'unsinkable aircraft carrier ... ideally located for offensive or defensive purposes'.[17]

Most worrying for the Defense Department was that the PRC viewed Taiwan in the same way; the loss of Taiwan to the Communists would be a blow to US military strategy in the Asia-Pacific region. Besides, America remained the subject of virulent Chinese propaganda activity throughout the world. Most worrying was the rapid increase in radio broadcasts to Latin America, with Spanish ranking only below English as the most dominant foreign language in China's transmissions. Targeting the opinion leaders of Latin America, this Communist propaganda was considered a direct threat to American interests in its own backyard.

In their own propaganda, however, Americans had little to gain from suggesting how helping Taiwan would serve only American interests. Rather, they couched justification in familiar Cold War language – the clash of ideologies (good versus evil), containment, and the possibility of liberation from within followed by the eradication of Communism. All these themes had structured America's Cold War in Europe and were now transferred lock, stock and barrel to Asia:

> Communism runs counter to Chinese culture. The two can never exist together. The Maoist seizure of the mainland is only temporary. A genuine revolution among the Chinese people on the mainland is now in the making. With the help of the free Chinese in Taiwan, they will

> wipe Communism from the face of China. China, then, will again regain her rightful position and contribute to the peace of the world.[18]

Such propaganda could be rooted in reality when the Communists began shelling the offshore islands of Kinmen and Matsu in 1954. As Frank Welsh has written so eloquently: 'Taiwan, and the offshore islands ... became in American mythology beleaguered outposts of democratic decency in a wicked, Communist-dominated East.'[19]

Still, any hopes that President Eisenhower, hero of World War II and the champion of liberation, would be less reticent than Truman, soon dissolved. He rebuked his military advisers who assumed that the US would rush to the defence of Taiwan in the event of a military invasion of these islands. Eisenhower was unsure whether Kinmen and Matsu were within America's defence perimeter, and if it was, were the waters that surrounded the island too shallow for a show of naval force? In fact, Matsu and Kinmen were so geographically close to the mainland that many in the administration could see no problem with letting them go to Beijing.

However, Eisenhower decided to sign a Mutual Defence Treaty with the ROC after the Chinese gave jail sentences for espionage to 13 American airmen, shot down in the Korean War.[20] This was a direct contravention of the Korean War armistice, and Eisenhower felt he had to do something to satisfy public opinion at home. Like other front-line Cold War states, for example East Germany, Taiwan thrived on an acceleration of tensions.

But tension subsided by April 1955 following a series of adroit diplomatic moves that have secured Eisenhower's place in Cold War history.[21] The Communists claimed they did not want to go to war with the United States and announced their willingness to negotiate, though their propaganda promised that they would continue to seek the 'liberation' of Taiwan by 'peaceful means'. Overcome by the spirit of Bandung and Geneva, representatives from the PRC and the United States met to defuse the crisis.

Representatives from the ROC were not invited to participate, a decision that only strengthened both American and Chinese propaganda: the US thought Taiwan an important but junior ally that serviced American interests; at the same time, Chinese impressions of Taiwan as nothing more dangerous than an American lackey were confirmed. Neither power thought Taiwan was important enough to be involved in such high-level diplomatic proceedings. Talks continued over the next three years, usually in Poland, but such diplomatic activity could not prevent military action indefinitely.

The crisis resumed in 1958 when Chinese Communist forces once again bombarded the islands of Kinmen and Matsu. Propaganda originating in Taiwan exaggerated the power of the latest attack: 'Over 300 Russian-make

shore guns ringing Kinmen started the most furious shelling in war history
...'[22] However, Joseph McCarthy had been discredited,[23] the Korean War had
ended in an inglorious stalemate, and the Red Scare of the early 1950s had
largely dissipated; the 1958 crisis could not recapture the mood that had
engulfed the US between 1950 and 1954 when two American nationals had
been killed on the first day of shelling. Instead, many began to advocate a
reversal of American policy towards Chiang Kai-shek. The *Wall Street
Journal* spoke for many when it said:

> It is one thing for this country to undertake the defense of Formosa
> itself, although the passing years are taking our Formosan policy also
> further from reality. But it is something else again to act as though the
> Nationalists are on their way back to China and that these islands are
> priceless pawns to be held at any cost, including a war.[24]

In other words, politics, war, the objectives of foreign policy, and the
perception of what constitutes the national interest, all impose their own
limitations on what propaganda can achieve. Even the vociferous China
lobby in the United States, the grassroots diplomacy of the ROC embassy,
the millions of dollars spent by the Soong dynasty on cultivating personal
relationships with influential Americans and their media, and (from 1956
until 1967) the CIA's covert involvement with the ostensibly private Asia
Foundation,[25] could not prevent a reversal in public attitudes when the
international climate changed.[26] At the time of the second Communist
shelling of Matsu and Kinmen, the State Department and many
Congressmen received daily telephone calls and letters from anxious
Americans worried by the prospect of being dragged into a nuclear war over
two small islands. Of the 626 letters received in the State Department in just
one week, 322 opposed the US becoming involved.[27]

Both public and political opinion in the United States were ambivalent
on important issues arising from the crisis. First, Americans did not want to
appear to support the ROC's explicit militarism. As Secretary of State, John
Foster Dulles noted: 'We are, in effect, demanding that the islands be a
privileged sanctuary from which the [Chinese Nationalists] can wage at
least political and subversive warfare against the [Communists] but against
which the [Communists] cannot retaliate.'[28] After all, the KMT continued to
use the offshore islands for gathering intelligence about the mainland,
launching guerrilla operations, harassing Chinese fishermen, and of course
propaganda.[29]

Second, the administration questioned the strategic importance of the
islands. Allen Dulles, the CIA's Director, described how the ROC had
'overplayed and overdramatized the situation for their own purposes. US
military observers saw no immediate threat of invasion'. In fact the US

Ambassador in the ROC, Everett F. Drumright, confided to the State Department on 7 August 1958, that the Communist activity could be considered a natural consequence of the ROC's guerrilla operations against the mainland. 'We can hardly expect Commies to remain wholly passive ...'

The US military conceded that Kinmen and Matsu were not worth the risk of even limited war, but declared that the symbolic significance of defending the islands far outweighed military factors. Others were more vociferous: at the height of the islands crisis the Commander of the US Taiwan Defence Command, Vice Admiral Roland Smoot, demanded that the PRC be told they risked getting into a 'shooting war' with the US within two weeks. 'This is our private fight: the US and Red China ... Talk first, yes – but talk fast and fierce and hold a gun right between their eyes.' Smoot even considered that the US should perhaps have been tougher with the ROC. Before signing off, he announced: 'I feel better.'[30]

However, Americans were uneasy with the prospect of being dragged into another war over the islands; and they were uncomfortable with Chiang Kai-shek's repeated intention to reconquer the mainland, as the following passage from a 1958 'Memorandum of a conversation' between officials from the ROC and the US clearly illustrates:

> President Chiang had been accustomed to saying every year that this year would be the year in which the [ROC] would go back to the mainland. These statements had been counter-productive as far as the public here [in the US] was concerned. [ROC] Ambassador Yeh said that these New Year messages of the Generalissimo had been quite an ordeal for him. He felt in the last two or three years they had been much better. While he was Foreign Minister he conscientiously avoided using the word 'reconquest' in connection with the [ROC]'s going back to the mainland. He stressed that the [ROC] can only go back to the mainland in response to the desires and wishes of the people.[31]

Hence much of the American support at this time was conditioned upon the ROC taming its aggression in favour of more political methods of engaging the mainland.[32] In fact the Americans tried to persuade Chiang Kai-shek to withdraw altogether from the disputed islands of Kinmen and Matsu. However, the State Department had to admit that the military repulsion of invasion in 1958, plus the support provided by the US 'provided a tremendous lift to the morale of the Free Chinese, making even more difficult any voluntary relinquishment ...'[33]

America need not have worried. The shelling of the offshore islands were designed to have more symbolic value than to push the US to the brink of war with China. In fact, Zhou Enlai had told the Soviet foreign minister,

Andrei Gromyko, that the Chinese did not intend to take either Taiwan or the islands by force. The purpose of the shelling was to send a clear signal of China's strength to Washington.[34] The shelling of the islands became central to the PRC's psychological warfare against Taiwan. It had little military value beyond reminding Taipei of Beijing's existence and commitment to 'liberate' Taiwan at an unspecified time in the future.

This was the view of the American Secretary of State, John Foster Dulles. Referring to Beijing's decision to shell Matsu and Kinmen only on odd-numbered days – a practice that continued until 1979 – Dulles told Selwyn Lloyd, the British Foreign Secretary, that it seems to confirm our analysis of the Chinese Communist attitude as being 'essentially political and propaganda rather than military'.[35]

Needless to say the ROC returned fire. Often the shells that originated on both sides would contain nothing more harmful than printed propaganda that 'explained' the Communist 'defeat', conveniently glossing over the diplomatic intricacies: ' ... the defenders [on Kinmen] held the Reds at bay. Their dream of invasion shattered, the Communists started a peace offensive. ... Having reached the end of their rope the Reds finally introduced the unique alternate day shelling pattern in October to cover their ignominious defeat.'[36] The ROC also continued to use loudspeakers to broadcast propaganda from the islands. Inevitably, Communist forces on the mainland reciprocated in kind.[37]

Such methods had been at the forefront of Taiwan's psychological warfare since the Korean War, and the offshore islands had provided the most appropriate location from which to launch it. *The China Handbook* for 1953–54 contends that many Communist soldiers surrendered after hearing the loudspeakers, 'which accounted for much of the completeness of the victory on our side'.[38] It also prompted the ROC to study seriously the potential of psychological warfare, including the possibility of using loudspeakers in aeroplanes that flew over the mainland. By 1958, psychological warfare was considered so important in Taiwan's pressure on the mainland that it was integrated into the policy-making process, achieving equivalent status with the more conventional forms of statecraft. The 1958–59 *Republic of China Yearbook* (as *The China Handbook* was now called) noted how the Ministry of National Defence had strengthened its psychological warfare capabilities during the offshore islands crisis: 'Each month aircraft flew deep into the mainland to drop leaflets, proclamations, charts, safe conduct passes and food. The air-droppings have borne fruit in influencing a fair number of mainlanders to flee from behind the Bamboo Curtain.'[39] We should not read too much into the impact of such propaganda. On 26 September 1958, Dulles told Selwyn Lloyd, that rumours' of leaflet raids were used as a cover for American reconnaissance flights over the mainland.[40]

Radio was also pressed into service on both sides of the Taiwan Strait. In August 1954, the PRC launched a series of programmes for audiences in the ROC 'to keep pace with the struggle for the liberation of Taiwan'. In late 1958, Communist transmissions from a station on the 'Fukien Front' included programmes for KMT 'personnel' on Kinmen. In fact, 21 per cent of all radio broadcasts from the PRC were designed for Taiwan in the island's main languages – Hakka, Amoy and, of course, Mandarin; a further 10 per cent broadcast in Mandarin and Amoy directly towards Kinmen.[41]

The KMT, however, had taken an early lead over its Communist rivals. Taipei's Voice of China was created in 1949, broadcasting in Mandarin, English, Japanese, Korean, Arabic, Russian and French via a 50kw transmitter. Yet the Chinese on the mainland were not forgotten, and on 17 July 1949, the Voice of Free China also broadcast to the PRC in Mandarin, and other dialects – Amoy, Chaochow, Hakka, Cantonese, Shanghainese – and English for four hours every evening. During the Korean War, the Voice of Free China engaged in what the deputy director of the CBS has admitted to as propaganda for 'psychological purposes'.[42] This can be detected in the titles of some of its programmes, for example 'The Free World', and ' Home Sweet Home ' (i.e. mainland China).

In an effort to make this propaganda more effective and efficient the Broadcasting Corporation of China, responsible for all of Taiwan's broadcasting activities, established the Mainland Chinese Service Department in May 1954. Until 1970, the total number of transmitters numbered 16 (five short-wave and 11 medium-wave) and included broadcasts to all parts of China in Mandarin 24 hours per day, even though both Taipei and Washington knew that radio sets were in short supply on the mainland.[43] It is not surprising that the station should claim that:

> Many of the mainland Chinese fighter pilots, People's Liberation Army personnel, musicians and anti-Communists who defected to Taiwan or other neighbouring countries in the 1960s noted that they regularly listened to the VOFC mainland Chinese service programmes, especially the 'Mailbag Time', though it was heavily jammed and could bring on big trouble such as being reformed through forced labour or even capital punishment for themselves and other family members.[44]

During the Cold War, defectors and refugees from behind the Iron Curtain in Europe said more or less the same thing when talking to representatives of Radio Free Europe, the Voice of America and the BBC. Often they said what their interviewers wanted to hear, and determining whether they fled in response to radio programming is difficult to verify.[45] Polling and surveys of listeners could not be performed to measure the size of audience in China.

However, informal conversations with foreign diplomats, travellers and refugees provided evidence of widespread listening.

These testimonies, together with letters that escaped the censor, suggested that radio did have a positive impact on the 'hearts and minds' of the Chinese. Radio Free China (RFC), however, was less popular than the Voice of America; only ten per cent of an elite group of defectors interviewed by the US Information Agency in 1958 said they listened to broadcasts from RFC.[46]

None mentioned the CIA-sponsored Radio Free Asia (RFA), broadcasting from Manila, though this is not surprising. Unlike its European counterparts, Radio Free Europe and Radio Liberty, RFA did not aim to undermine the existing Communist governments, but rather to shore-up the region's anti-Communist regimes. The CIA knew that China's masses had few opportunities to listen to overseas broadcasts due to the shortage of radio sets.[47]

AMERICAN PROPAGANDA SUPPORT

Unfortunately, we still know very little about just how much covert help the US gave the ROC at this time as part of its anti-Communist strategy in Asia. Nevertheless, a few pieces of the jigsaw indicate something of the overall picture. In 1951, CIA operatives started to 'stream' into Taiwan under the cover of Western Enterprises Inc. Robert Accinelli has discovered that there were more than 600 on Taiwan, training guerrillas, gathering intelligence and providing propaganda facilities. By 1953, the Americans recognised Taiwan to be 'an ideal base for a greatly intensified overt psychological warfare campaign directed to the China mainland'. In July, General Charles Cabell, Deputy Director of the CIA, assured a joint State-Department-JCS meeting that the offshore islands were proving useful to the CIA 'for infiltrating and exfiltrating intelligence agents'. He added that 'as long as we have responsibility for hit and run raids, we should point out that the islands are useful for that purpose'.[48]

The CIA had dispatched 'resistance teams' to China from Taiwan to contact dissidents and build a 'viable resistance to Mao Tse-tung's government'. Commando teams were responsible for attacking and destroying key installations on the Chinese mainland. However, American involvement in such operations dissipated by 1954; information about these activities leaked after two Americans were shot down in 1952 on a mission over the PRC. Thereafter, the Chinese Communists became proficient in crushing such subversive operations.[49]

American Special Forces training teams were present in Thailand, South Vietnam and Taiwan from 1956 onwards, though Chinese Nationalists had been visiting Fort Bragg in North Carolina on a regular basis since 1953. In 1957, the ROC was given American help and advice in setting up its own Special Forces centre at Lung Tan in Taiwan. Ray S. Cline, formerly the CIA station chief at Taipei and a long-standing advocate of the ROC, has been most open about the CIA's involvement, describing in his memoirs 'agent penetration' of the mainland, the training of U2 pilots to fly over China, the CIA's control of Air America, Civil Air Transport and Air Asia, and how the agency encouraged Chinese MIG pilots to defect to Taiwan.[50]

The American government did support a 'Third Force' alternative to the Communists and the KMT.[51] In fact, American support after China entered the Korean War was directed towards aiding guerrilla groups already working on the mainland, since most operated independently and without guidance or control from the KMT.[52] This allowed the American government to remain detached from 'Nationalist' China and avoid open confrontation with Beijing. It was imperative to avoid participation in any activities that might lend credibility to Communist accusations that the US was responsible for the ROC's attempts to subvert the Communist government of China.

Nevertheless, we now know that Washington limited its involvement to training and modernizing the ROC's defence forces, and never provided any reason to believe that it would assist in any offensive action against the mainland from Taiwan.[53] The United States worried that the already extensive CIA operations on the island only tied it closer to Taiwan and made American disengagement difficult.[54]

Such considerations did not extend to propaganda that was frequently used as a substitute for the kind of military activity the US had refused to endorse. During the Cold War the ROC's propaganda and psychological warfare activities, often directed by the CIA, assumed a character familiar to anyone acquainted with propaganda in Europe at this time. In fact Marchetti and Marks have suggested a sense of *deja vu* when, in 1967, the CIA Far East Division encouraged the launch from Taiwan of balloons loaded with propaganda leaflets, pamphlets and newspapers that would drift across the Strait to the mainland.[55] This has been described a 'knick-knack bombardment', with the balloons carrying 'pens, can openers, bright T-shirts, and other cheap items' which would 'pop and shower the mainland with the flotsam of capitalism'.[56]

The stated objective of this propaganda barrage was to take advantage of a perceived backlash against the Cultural Revolution and stir up 'domestic turmoil'. Chiang Kai-shek had already tried to take advantage of the failures of the Great Leap Forward in his psychological warfare programme intended for the PRC. By 'disseminating facts about Mao's failures', he hoped to 'dissolve Communist power'.[57] Such propaganda policies were activated even though in 1958 Secretary of State Dulles had already dismissed the promise that such propaganda and psychological warfare could easily deliver the liberation of captive people. Dulles believed that change in China (as in Eastern Europe), would be the result of forces within the country 'rather than stimulants without'.[58]

All along, the Americans were more appreciative of how propaganda and psychological warfare work than the ROC, and their own experiences, first in Eastern Europe and then in Cuba, meant that they were deeply sensitive to the limitations of propaganda. They knew not to expect too much from propaganda, and that both the medium and the message must be adapted to suit the audience. They understood, for example, the consequences of ignoring the characteristics of the Chinese audience, and how the indoctrination they were believed to receive every day could affect their receptivity to foreign propaganda. Rather than political diatribe, captive audiences responded more to music and entertainment.

Propaganda should also avoid making unrealistic promises. The Chinese would not be liberated from outside, and internal unrest was sporadic. Data suggesting high levels of dissatisfaction inside China – a favourite theme of Chiang Kai-shek – were incomplete, and were therefore unreliable. The Americans therefore advised the ROC's propagandists to avoid raising the expectations of the Chinese.[59]

Why the government of the ROC itself was not convinced of this strategy remains a mystery. We know that a Panel on Special Operations and Psychological Warfare, part of the US Department of Defense and led by America's leading expert on propaganda, Professor Wilbur Schramm, met with the ROC's psychological warfare experts in Taipei in 1957. Their deliberations suggest that the Americans had the opportunity to impart their skill in determining the type of propaganda, images and themes that would appeal to different audiences and in specific conditions.[60] However, this was not the kind of advice Chiang wanted to hear. He knew exactly what he wanted to achieve, American help in the liberation of the mainland, and he believed that he would succeed. His disposition – ambitious, obsessed with control, impulsive, stubborn and impatient – is legendary. His 'unbounded confidence in his political and military judgement, his faith in his infallibility, and his mystic sense of identity with the nation made him arrogant and unsusceptible to advice and argument'.[61]

Greater success lay in exploring the kind of black propaganda techniques that had been tried and failed in Eastern Europe. With the CIA's endorsement, the ROC resurrected them for use against China. Publications carried by balloons across the Taiwan Strait were designed to appear as near as possible to the few dissident publications already circulating through parts of China, and to add to the confusion, they used fictitious names of anti-revolutionary organisations as the source of the propaganda. Of course the US denied all knowledge of these operations, assigning all responsibility to Chiang Kai-shek, the CIA's 'willing and cooperative host for the operation'.[62] Refugees arriving from the PRC in Hong Kong carried the leaflets with them, thus providing for the agency apparent evidence of the success of its propaganda.[63]

Similarly the CIA was involved with organising the broadcast of disinformation and black propaganda to the PRC from Taiwan. It has been suggested, though no evidence is forthcoming, that during the 1958 Kinmen crisis, these stations broadcast to the PRC on a frequency that was a mere 1MHz away from domestic stations in the mainland, a propaganda technique known as 'cuddling' or 'snuggling'.[64] The true source of the transmissions was not revealed, and audiences had no way of knowing they were listening to black propaganda. The problem was that the CIA (which had an outpost on Kinmen[65]) used the Foreign Broadcast Information Service (FBIS)[66] to keep track of its own black propaganda stations, and to monitor genuine Chinese dissident stations, but kept FBIS completely in the dark about its own operations. In this way, China-watchers in the US were often misled by FBIS reports of transmissions from the black stations. There was no attempt to rectify the situation since American policy benefited from the publicity given to the broadcasts by sympathetic journalists and academics who treated the FBIS material as genuine.[67]

Other suggestions about how best to intensify America's covert involvement in Taiwan's propaganda activities were dismissed. The State Department advised the Psychological Strategy Board that any efforts to widen such operations to involve other Asian countries or the overseas Chinese in Asia risked jeopardising American political interests in the region. Few of Taiwan's neighbours supported the KMT and would not wish to be drawn into the 'China question'.[68] These deliberations and their outcome reveal that the Americans were mindful of how propaganda and related activities were subordinate to political and diplomatic objectives. Even covert operations were restricted by the need to maintain a visible and careful diplomatic position in the region. In turn, American objectives took priority over those of the ROC.

Chiang Kai-shek compensated for the lack of American support by strengthening the ROC's propaganda. Central to his strategy was the dissemination of the idea that he possessed a strong military force that was willing and capable of first defending Taiwan from the PRC, and second of striking against the Communist mainland. The estimates of the ROC's military capabilities were erroneous, but fulfilled a specific propaganda objective of building support for the ROC within the United States. Similar conclusions can be drawn about Chiang's over-optimistic expectation of the

number of men (one million) on the mainland 'waiting to spring to arms'
against the Communist regime.[69]

This spirit was fed by propaganda that highlighted the success of guerrilla
raids on the mainland. The Special Forces in question were known as the
Anti-Communist National Salvation Army – 'the commando and guerrilla
forces which have cast a pall of fear over the enslaved defenders of Red
China'.[70] Such units had been active since the Nationalists retreated to Taiwan
in 1949, but until 1962, their work had focused on gathering information and
planning the creation of underground organisations inside China. After 1962,
'the information is being used, and the plans are being carried out'.[71]

Actually, the Chinese were very successful during the early 1950s in
'nipping' such guerrilla operations 'in the bud',[72] which explains why the
Americans had withdrawn their support for such activity by 1954.[73] *The
China Handbook*, together with the *Free China Weekly*, were far from
reticent about such nominally secret operations:

> Free Chinese seaborne guerrillas, with the cooperation of amphibious
> raiding units, staged many raids against the important islands and
> ports along the coast of Chekiang, Fukien and Kwangtun. They served
> as the forerunner of the counteroffensive to be launched in the future.
> Because of the high morale of the guerrillas, every raid produced
> excellent results. Enemy casualties during 1952 were 110% more than
> in 1951; enemy prisoners of war, 108% more; and weapons captured,
> 210% more.[74]

This passage is followed in the book by three pages describing in graphic
detail the raids, their victories and the weapons that the guerrillas captured.
As part of their duties, the guerrillas were required to participate in
propaganda and psychological warfare that offered hope of liberation to the
'enslaved' Chinese people, that is to encourage optimism for *pien tien*, or a
change in the weather.

Such themes are important for propaganda that is directed at an enemy.
It builds a profile based on projected strength, determination, and inevitable
victory. However, the ROC made the mistake of using such imagery in its
diplomacy with the US, when in fact Washington's intelligence community
already knew that Chiang Kai-shek's optimism in unrest on the Chinese
mainland were exaggerated. Dissidence had increased, but no organised
resistance had been able to develop.[75] In September 1958, Free China's
Premier said that his government did not seek the overthrow of the
Communist government by force, but rather by 'internal revolts'. Hence the
importance of 'political' rather than military measures: 'In view of
continuous and expanded Red oppression, mainland people are dissatisfied
and want to know when they will be liberated ...'[76]

Chiang remained optimistic that China could be liberated during the Kennedy administration. The documentary record reveals that Chiang and his government continued to try and convince Washington that the mainland was ripe for liberation via covert and overt military operations, and that they deserved full American support.[77] It seemed inevitable that American enthusiasm for such activity, never all that great anyway, should hit an all time low after the failure of the 1961 Bay of Pigs invasion in Cuba.[78]

CONCLUSIONS

The undemanding imagery that was central to Taiwan's propaganda could be effortlessly transposed to the Cold War environment. However, the offshore islands crises of 1954 and 1958 suggest that the twists and turns of international politics were far more significant than such propaganda itself. Popular, if not political American support for Chiang Kai-shek and his regime on Taiwan solidified after the outbreak of war in Korea, which coincided with the zenith of anti-Communism in the country at large. In 1951, 60 per cent of surveyed Americans 'wanted the United States to give Chiang's forces all the help they needed to attack the mainland'.[79] Henry Luce's *Life* magazine in July 1950 referred to the ROC as 'an all-out ally',[80] while the *New York Times* described the government on Taiwan as

> more viable now than it was six months ago. Its spokesmen have stated recently that with even modest economic assistance from the outside world they can hope to hold the island almost indefinitely. ... Since this government is the largest, active, committed, military, anti-Communist force in east Asia, its capacity to resist is of the gravest concern to all of the still free world.[81]

But such comment had little influence on Truman's attitude towards the Nationalist regime on Taiwan. Privately, he is said to have despised Chiang Kai-shek and his family, allegedly describing them all as 'thieves'.[82] It took the Korean War to change *policy* rather than attitude: 'Only after the PRC's intervention in Korea and Peking's rejection of the UN cease-fire offers did the United States in effect become committed to preserving the *status quo* on Formosa, *more because it was at war with the People's Republic than out of pro-Nationalist sentiments*' (emphasis added).[83]

Similarly MacArthur sent a memorandum to the Joint Chiefs of Staff in June 1950 claiming that 'the domination of Formosa by an unfriendly power would be a disaster of utmost importance *to the US* ...' (emphasis added).[84] Hence the shelling of Kinmen and Matsu in 1954 coincided with the popular mood of anti-Communism. The imprisonment of US airmen on spying charges in direct contravention of the Korean War armistice, and the deaths of two Americans on the first day of shelling, sent shockwaves through Washington. Thus propaganda from and about the ROC found a willing audience, especially among the CIA and US military whose interests in Taiwan were clearly defined. The Eisenhower administration, unconvinced of the value of the offshore islands, nevertheless felt obliged to respond.

By 1958, political realities had overtaken hopes that China might be liberated from without. Even the renewal of Communist action against Matsu and Kinmen could not regenerate sufficient popular support for American intervention.

However, the ROC's propaganda did not respond to these changes. It was too caught up in the Cold War rhetoric that had structured propaganda since the KMT's retreat to Taiwan. They ignored American advice that the Chinese were unsympathetic to the kind of rhetoric that the ROC's propagandists were pumping out day after day. And this oversight is remarkable, since the ROC enjoyed a distinct advantage over its allies: Chinese should know how to structure propaganda for Chinese audiences. The ROC remained convinced that the liberation of China was not only possible, but also that it was the KMT's duty to achieve the liberation with US assistance. Hence most of the ROC's propaganda at this time was designed for American, rather than Chinese audiences.

The US realized that the liberation of China would not happen in the foreseeable future, and certainly not with American help. Liberation was only possible once the Chinese people 'stood up' against the Communist regime, and in the 1950s, Washington's intelligence community could detect no signs of organized resistance or unrest on the mainland of China that might offer the ROC hope. Propaganda that repeated the promise of liberation would not only antagonize Beijing, but risked also creating false expectations among the Chinese people.

Moreover, the habitual projection in propaganda of 'Free China' as a militaristic regime determined to foment trouble in the Taiwan Strait only made potential allies less sympathetic to the ROC's cause. For a political system in a such a delicate diplomatic position as the ROC, there must have been easier and more profitable ways to win friends and influence people.

NOTES

1. H. Maclear Bate, *Report From Formosa* (London: Eyre & Spottiswoode 1952) p.151.
2. Quoted in Robert Accinelli, *Crisis and Commitment: United States Policy Towards Taiwan, 1950-1955* (Chapel Hill: UNC Press 1996) p.65.
3. See e.g., *Free China Weekly* (FCW), 3 Jan. 1965.
4. Lynn Pan, *Sons of the Yellow Emperor: The Story of the Overseas Chinese* (London: Mandarin 1991) p.222.
5. 'Talking paper prepared by Secretary of State Dulles, 21 October 1958', *Foreign Relations*

*of the United States* (FRUS), 1958-1960, XIX, China (Washington DC: Dept. of State 1996) pp.413–17.

6. Sec. of State Dulles, 'Memorandum of Conversation', 22 Oct. 1958, ibid. p.425.

7. Ibid.

8. Asian People's Anti-Communist League, *A Decade of Chinese Communist Tyranny* (Taipei 1960).

9. *China Yearbook, 1957–1958* (Taipei: GIO 1958) p.i.

10. George H. Kerr, *Formosa Betrayed* (London: Eyre & Spottiswoode 1966) pp.400–1, 414.

11. 'Memorandum of Acheson-Bevin conversation', 4 April 1949, FRUS, 1949, VII, pp.1138–41. Quoted by Warren I. Cohen, 'Acheson, His Advisers, and China, 1949-1950', in Dorothy Borg and Waldo Heinrichs (eds) *Uncertain Years: Chinese-American Relations, 1947–1950* (NY: Columbia UP 1980) pp.23–-4.

12. Borg and Heinrichs (note 11) p.28.

13. Quoted in Kerr (note 10) pp.386–7.

14. Quoted in Gerald H. Corr, *The Chinese Red Army* (London: Purnell 1974) p.72.

15. Harry S. Truman, *Memoirs: Years of Trial and Hope* Vol.2 (Garden City, NY: Doubleday 1956) p.334. See also Steve Tsang, 'Chiang Kai-shek and the Kuomintang's Policy to Reconquer the Chinese Mainland, 1949–1958', in idem, *In the Shadow of China: Political Developments in Taiwan Since 1949* (London: Hurst 1993) pp.48–72. The Korean War interfered with Mao's plans for the invasion of Taiwan. Apparently he ordered several army units to the Taiwan Strait only 48 hours before North Korea invaded the South. See John Lewis Gaddis, *We Now Know: Rethinking the Cold War* (Oxford: OUP 1997) pp.70–5.

16. For details of US aid to the ROC during the Korean War see Hung-Mao Tien, *The Great Transition: Political and Social Change in the Republic of China* (Taipei: SMC 1989) p.230. Estimates of American military aid 1950–70 range from $2.5 billion to $3 billion. Allen S. Whiting, 'Morality, Taiwan and U.S. Policy', in Jerome Alan Cohen *et al.* (eds) *Taiwan and American Policy* (NY: Praeger 1971) p.86; A. Doak Barnett, *China and the Major Powers in East Asia* (Washington DC: Brookings 1977) p.244. It is thought that the ROC also received more than $1 billion in economic aid. Shirley W.Y. Kuo, *The Taiwan Economy in Transition* (Boulder, CO: Westview Press 1983) p.14. A discussion of the US-ROC relationship can be found in Accinelli (note 2), Nancy Bernkopf Tucker, *Taiwan, Hong Kong and the United States, 1945–1992: Uncertain Friendships* (NY: Twayne 1994), and A. James Gregor and Martin Hsia Chang, 'Taiwan: The "Wild Card" in US Defense Policy in the Far Pacific', in James C. Hsiung and Winberg Chai (eds) *Asia and US Foreign Policy* (NY: Praeger 1981). For details of CIA operations in/from Taiwan, see Victor Marchetti & John D. Marks, *The CIA and the Cult of Intelligence* (NY: Knopf 1974) esp. pp.302–3; Ray Cline, *Secrets, Spies and Scholars: Blueprint of the Essential CIA* (Washington DC: Acropolis Books 1976).

17. US Senate, Committee on Foreign Relations, *Report on Mutual Defence Treaty with the Republic of China*, 8 Feb. 1955, Senate, 84th Congress, 1st Session, Executive Report #2, US GPO, 1955, p.8; Dept. of Foreign Affairs and Trade, Canberra, *Current Notes on International Affairs*, 22/7 (1951) p.375.

18. *China Yearbook 1978* (Taipei: GIO 1978) p.33.

19. Frank Welsh, *A History of Hong Kong* (London: HarperCollins 1994) p.442.

20. Stephen E. Ambrose, *Eisenhower: Soldier and President* (NY: Simon & Schuster 1990) pp.374–5.

21. Ibid. pp.382, 385

22. See note 8, p.319.

23. Many of McCarthy's allegations, esp. against prominent Sinologists (Owen Lattimore being the prime target), were 'reinforced' by rumours, forged documents and 'intelligence' emanating from Taipei. See Robert P. Newman, 'Clandestine Chinese Nationalist Efforts to Punish their American Detractors', *Diplomatic History* 7/3 (1983) pp.205–22.

24. *Wall Street Journal*, 5 Sept. 1958.

25. See Marchetti and Marks (note 16) p.172.

26. See Conclusions.

27. Leonard A. Kusnitz, *Public Opinion and Foreign Policy: America's China Policy, 1949–1979* (Westport, CT: Greenwood 1984) p.79fn.

28. 'Memorandum by Secretary of State Dulles', 23 Aug. 1958, FRUS 1958–60, XIX, China, p.69; pp.40–2.
29. Accinelli (note 2) p.147.
30. Allen Dulles at 375th meeting of NSC, 7 Aug. 1958, FRUS 1958-60, XIX, China, pp.42–3. Telegram from Commander in Chief in Pacific (Admiral Harry Felt) to Joint Chiefs of Staff, 25 Aug. 1958, ibid. pp.79–80, 224–5.
31. Ibid. p.467.
32. See ibid. in *passim.*
33. See ibid. in *passim*, and Memo from Asst. Sec. of State for Far Eastern Affairs (Parsons) to Sec. of State Herter, 10 Aug. 1960, p.707.
34. Gaddis (note 15) pp.250–52.
35. 'Letter from Secretary of State Dulles to Foreign Secretary Lloyd', 24 Oct. 1958, FRUS 1958–60, XIX, China, p.451.
36. See note 8, p.319.
37. 'Dulles in conversation', 12 Sept. 1958, FRUS 1958-60, XIX, China, pp.168–71
38. *The China Handbook, 1953–4* (Taipei: GIO 1954) p.203.
39. *The China Yearbook, 1958–9* (Taipei: GIO 1959) p.182.
40. 'Memorandum by Secretary of State Dulles' (note 28) p.280.
41. USNA, RG 306, USIA Special Reports, 1953–1963, 4/87/30/4-5. S-49-59, '12 Years of Communist Broadcasting, 1948–1959'.
42. Daniel Dong Yu-ching, Deputy Director of the BCC's International Department, in correspondence, 20 October 1997. He kindly provided most of this information.
43. USNA, RG306, Program and Media Studies, 1956-62; PMS31: 'Listening to the VOA in Communist China', Sept. 1958.
44. See note 42.
45. See G.D Rawnsley, *Radio Diplomacy and Propaganda: The BBC and VOA in International Politics, 1956–64* (Basingstoke/NY: Macmillan/ St Martin's Press 1996) Ch.3.
46. See note 43.
47. Walter L. Hixson, *Parting the Curtain: Propaganda, Culture and Cold War, 1945–1960* (NY: St Martin's Press 1998) p.65.
48. USNA, State Department Lot Files, 64 D563 – Policy Planning Staff, Box 77, File SD-JCS Meetings, Meeting of 31 July 1953.
49. Ralph W. McGehee, *Deadly Deceits: My 25 Years in the CIA* (NY: Sheridan Sq. Publications 1983) p.25.
50. Michael McClintock, *Instruments of Statecraft* (NY: Pantheon 1992) p.45; Cline (note 16).
51. Accinelli (note 2) p.66. David Wise and Thomas B. Ross, *The Invisible Government* (London: Jonathan Cape 1965) p.109, claimed that 'at least in the past, the CIA trained, equipped and financed Chinese Nationalist commando raids on the mainland'.
52. Accinelli (note 2) pp.64–5. Advocates of a 'Third Force' sought an alternative government to both Communist and Nationalist. In 1958, e.g., US Sec. of Defense, Neil McElroy suggested to Eisenhower that Chiang be assassinated and replaced. See www.islandnet.com/ ~emerald/upc/readings/nuheuse.htm
53. Accinelli (note 2) p.257.
54. Marchetti and Marks (note 16) p.302.
55. As of Aug. 1956, around 280 million leaflets had been covertly dispatched by the CIA in approximately half a million balloons to Poland, Czechoslovakia and Hungary. See Cord Meyer, *Facing Reality* (NY: Harper & Row 1980) and Allan Michie, *Voices Through the Iron Curtain* (NYY: Dodd Mead 1963).
56. M.S. Dobbs-Higginson, *Asia-Pacific: Its Role in the New World Disorder* (London: Longman 1994) p.152.
57. Marchetti and Marks (note 16) pp.156–7. This required American support for a 'token military campaign', which Washington refused to give. Ray S. Cline, *Chiang Ching-kuo Remembered* (Washington DC: US Global Strategy Council 1989) pp.50–1.
58. 'Memorandum by Secretary of State Dulles' (note 28) p.69.
59. Dwight D. Eisenhower Library, Abilene, Kansas (DDEL), C.D. Jackson Records, Box 2, Submission on China 8/1/1954: VIII, Brainwashing, p.45.

60. DDEL. PMA Linebarger files, Box 22, China: Psychological Warfare, 30 Jan. 1957.
61. Tang Tsou, *America's Failure in China, 1941–1950* (U. of Chicago Press 1963) pp.122–3.
62. Marchetti and Marks (note 16) p.158.
63. Ibid.
64. Roy Godson, *Dirty Tricks or Trump Cards: US Covert Action and Counter Intelligence* (London: Brassey's 1995) p.152 reports that the Nazis 'snuggled' the Americans in World War II, while the Americans themselves 'snuggled' in Vietnam. On p.153 he also reveals that the ROC was involved with 'grey' broadcasts to China, but does not elaborate. I would like to thank Professor Donald Browne for his confirmation that Taiwan's military did indeed 'cuddle' Chinese broadcasts, probably from Matsu or Kinmen. In correspondence, 18 March 1998.
65. Cline (note 16) p.174.
66. The American equivalent of the BBC Monitoring Service at Caversham Park, Reading, UK, the FBIS is an open source of information on radio and TV broadcasts from around the world. It then sells this information to libraries, the press, the academic community and of course government. Further information can be found in Gary Rawnsley's chapter on 'The Importance of Monitored Broadcasts', in Jan Melissen (ed.), *Innovations in Diplomacy* (Basingstoke: Macmillan 1998).
67. Marchetti and Marks (note 16) pp.158–60.
68. USNA, SD Lot Files, Lot 55D 388, Bureau of Far Eastern Affairs 1953, Box 4, 'Nationalist Chinese'.
69. Kerr (note 10) pp.300, 382, 402–3.
70. The *Free China Review* (Taipei), Jan. 1965, p.11.
71. Ibid.
72. FRUS, 1958-60, XIX, China, pp.19–20.
73. Accinelli (note 2) p.138.
74. *The China Handbook 1953–4* (Taipei: GIO 1954) p.197.
75. FRUS, 1958-60, XIX, China, pp.7–-15. Communist rule remained firm and in control of the coercive powers in China.
76. Ibid. pp.23–7.
77. Ibid. *in passim.*
78. For example, see FRUS, 1961-1963, XXII, Northeast Asia, p.317, 387.
79. Rosemary Foot, *The Practice of Power: US Relations with China Since 1949* (Oxford: Clarendon 1995) p.88.
80. *Life*, 24 July 1950 p.26.
81. *New York Times* 23 April 1950.
82. See Merle Miller, *'Plain Speaking': An Oral Biography of Harry S. Truman* (NY: Putnam's 1974).
83. Edwin W. Martin, *Divided Counsel: The Anglo-American Response to Communist Victory in China* (Lexington: Kentucky UP 1986) p.236.
84. Quoted in ibid. pp.155–6.

# PART II

# SOUTHEAST ASIA

# 5

# The SIS Singapore Station and the Role of the Far East Controller: Secret Intelligence Structure and Process in Post-War Colonial Administration

## PHILIP H. J. DAVIES

### INTELLIGENCE AND INFRASTRUCTURE

For 20 years, between the end of World War II and Singaporean independence, the Singapore station of the British Secret Intelligence Service (SIS, aka MI6) served as that agency's main regional headquarters, and for much of that as what was termed its area 'controlling station'. In effect, this meant that command and control of the other stations in the region was routed to the station commander in Singapore, designated the Far East Controller (FEC), and only secondarily to the operational organisation at the main headquarters in London.

This management structure is of more than just historical interest, and the following discussion will examine the development, and eventual demise, of the postwar Far East Controller in terms of its implications for our understanding of the role of intelligence within the machinery of government in general and the role and status of the SIS in Britain's postwar colonial administrations in particular. The relationship between central, national intelligence services and the peripheral machineries of government in imperial administrations or occupation governments is a weakly developed area in the literature, and often a somewhat fraught matter in practice.[1]

In the case of Britain's postwar presence in the Far East, the key issue to be addressed is the fact that FEC in Singapore existed to serve two different masters. On the one hand, it was part of the SIS operational or 'Production' organisation, and as a result was part of the central intelligence machinery focused on the Joint Intelligence Committee and the direct tasking and dissemination mechanisms which linked SIS' London HQ to its main intelligence consumers in Whitehall and Downing Street. On the other hand, FEC was also answerable to the regional administration under the

Commissioner-General for Southeast Asia. In that capacity, FEC was a member of, was tasked by, and collected intelligence for the Joint Intelligence Committee, Far East (JIC/FE) *entirely apart from* the requirements issued from what recent government publications have termed the 'central intelligence machinery' in London.

The JIC/FE in turn generated all-source intelligence assessments for the British Defence Co-ordinating Committee, Far East (BDCC/FE), all of which came under the ultimate authority of the Commissioner-General for the United Kingdom in Southeast Asia.

FEC and the Singapore controlling station were not, it has to be noted, unique. The Singapore system was actually modelled on a similar, pre-existing arrangement in the Middle East which was itself a rather more direct carry-over from World War II than was the Singapore system. Here, the Middle East Controller (MEC) was set up to serve the Middle East JIC (JIC/ME), Defence Co-ordinating Committee (BDCC/ME) and the Commander in Chief, Middle East, originally in Cairo, but later in Ismailia in the Canal Zone, and after nationalisation of the Suez Canal in Episkopi, Cyprus.

In other words, the regional controlling station was a standard model for setting up remote headquarters linked to regional JICs, much as the creation of regional JICs was a standard model for dealing with regional the all-source intelligence assessment needs of British colonial and occupation administrations. It is precisely the governmental conditions or mechanisms that drove the development of such a standard model[2] which constitutes the central interest in the following discussion.

The central proposition advanced here is that an examination of FEC brings into stark relief a particular and crucial feature of the relationship between the SIS and the machinery of British government, both central and colonial. The feature is that the SIS is characterised by what American intelligence literature calls a 'pull' architecture. In other words, that the SIS is fundamentally a demand-driven organisation with its operational goals and priorities set, not by itself, but by its consumers in government. This 'pull' architecture results not merely from the existence of a series of formal arrangements by which consumers can articulate their intelligence needs to SIS, but because of a fundamental *decentralisation* of intelligence in the British state. To be sure, the operational work of covert collection may be centralised through agencies like the SIS or Government Communications Headquarters (GCHQ, Britain's signals intelligence agency), but intelligence *analysis* is dispersed throughout Britain's departments of state, as is the gathering of information from non-covert[3] sources.

As a result, the covert collection agencies exist primarily as a clandestine armature for overt government. Consequently, the internal structure and process of the SIS tends to reflect the interests, structure and process of wider government, and the evolution, and eventual dissolution, of FEC illustrates that dynamic particularly clearly. To fully appreciate the implications of a 'pull' architecture and its appearance within British governmental machinery, it is necessary to examine in some detail the literature and debates which surround the benefits and limitations of this approach to intelligence management.

*Intelligence Architectures 'Push' and 'Pull'*

The notions of push and pull intelligence architectures derive from a series of running debates about performance and structure within the US intelligence community since World War II.[4] Broadly, the distinction is between the production of intelligence on the basis of explicit demands laid down by consumers, in other words a *demand-driven* relationship or consumer-led 'pull' architecture, and alternatively one in which the producers set their own targets and provide consumers with what they think the consumers need, in other words it is a *supply-driven* 'push' architecture.

There are often strong sentiments expressed on either side of the two approaches, although within American literature there is a common tendency to advocate the former while decrying the existing American system as being the latter. Peter Scharfman, for example, has presented 'pull' architectures as being all but a panacaea for the intelligence community. He describes the 'push' architecture as being 'frustrating' for both producer and consumer, since the producer is forced to guess about the needs of the consumer, and the consumer is stuck with a product which they may, or may, not be need or want and have little ability to tailor the process to their needs.[5] What is needed, he argues, is a 'pull' architecture in which 'decisions about which information gets to the user, the level of detail, the format ... and above all else the timing will be made by the user rather than the producer'.[6] This 'pull' architecture is something he believes can be most effectively provided by electronic dissemination methods such as electronic mail, networked databases, on-line reports, real-time and non-real-time conferencing and so forth.

Even the CIA's Directorate of Intelligence (or DI, nominally responsible for all-source analysis on a national footing) has expressed a similar sentiment about the 'push' oriented nature of intelligence production in the American system. In a 1996 articulation of an agenda for reform, the DI admitted that 'a decade ago, the DI's communication with collectors was, on balance, constructive but passive – we took and evaluated whatever came along without pushing "consumer demand"'. That report subsequently promises that 'a decade from now, the DI, as a primary, all-source nexus in the [Intelligence Community], will actively drive collection – articulating requirements, assiduously identifying gaps, and rigorously evaluating raw reports – for all the intelligence disciplines'.[7]

By the same token, however, while the DI advocates a greater role for its own demand as consumer, the same document consistently casts the DI itself as a 'push' supplier of 'finished' (evaluated, collated, interpreted and analysed) intelligence to the various departments of the US government, albeit one guided by 'extensive insight into the concerns and objectives of our consumers'.[8]

The notion of the 'pull' architecture is not without its critics. Britain's Michael Herman, for example, has argued that where 'large-scale intelligence production is involved, the "push" factor has to be emphasised, together with seeking reactions rather than "pulls"'.[9] For the most part, intelligence consumers, he argues, do not always know clearly what they need to know, while on the other hand, they are often not in a position to really know what it is that intelligence is capable of providing – until the intelligence producers show them.[10] There is, perhaps, a certain irony that participants in a 'push'-oriented system should favour the notion of a 'pull' architecture while one from a 'pull' architecture expresses preference for the 'push'. The British system can be said to be 'pull' system because, within it, intelligence production is based around the national requirements formulating process centred on the Joint Intelligence Committee (JIC) in the Cabinet Office. According to the UK government's account of its own 'central intelligence machinery', the 'principal collection Agencies for secret intelligence', SIS and GCHQ, undertake their operations on the basis of national intelligence requirements issued by the JIC.

> The JIC agrees the broad intelligence requirements and tasking to be laid upon SIS and GCHQ. These are reviewed annually in a process managed by the Intelligence Co-ordinator. This combines a rigorous analysis of the need for secret intelligence with extensive consultation with customer Departments and consideration of the financial and other resources required. The resulting requirements are submitted to Ministers for approval.[11]

However, the implementation of a 'pull' architecture is achieved not by the latest information technology, but by the 'jointery' and collegiality which Herman describes as 'symptomatic' of the defence community's preference for 'jointery' and the British government's ethos of interdepartmentalism.[12] Moreover, both the SIS and GCHQ have historically maintained divisions in their organisation which act as liaison links with their consumers in order to receive detailed requirements on a continuous basis. In the case of the GCHQ, this has been in the form of Z Division, within the Directorate of Sigint Plans and Operations.[13] Within the SIS, that liaison arrangement was originally articulated after World War I in what the official history has termed the '1921 arrangement',[14] and which, during the Cold War, constituted the 'Requirements Directorate' (however, this will be discussed in greater detail below).

There is, however, a potential danger in trying to transpose the concepts of American 'intelligence theory' to the British case too directly. The danger is the fact that the British and the Americans tend to attach profoundly different meanings to the term 'intelligence'. The official US definition is remarkably broad, consisting of the 'product resulting from the collection, evaluation, analysis, integration and interpretation of all available information which concerns one or more aspects of foreign nations or of areas of operation which is immediately or potentially significant for planning'.[15]

While no comparably formal definition of intelligence appears in British literature, Herman traces the British notion back to a fifteenth century definition as 'knowledge as to events, communicated by or obtained from another',[16] although the British attitude has been captured most succinctly perhaps by Ken Robertson as 'the secret collection of someone else's secrets'.[17] A similar sentiment was expressed by a senior British official who once remarked 'intelligence is about secrets, not mysteries'.[18] While one might be concerned that such a fundamental difference in basic definitions might lead to a pervasive incommensurability of concepts, it does instead play directly into the analysis being developed herein. The conditions for a demand-driven system are embodied in the very narrowness of the British definition.

With its emphasis on intelligence as *finished* intelligence, the American approach arguably predisposes itself towards a highly centralised architecture, and one geared towards analytical producer 'push'. Indeed, Scharfman's advocacy of a 'pull' architecture is explicitly concerned with *analytical* production, and as noted above, the DI's desire for a 'pull' scheme reaches only as far its own ability to 'pull' in the raw information it wants in order to 'push' out the finished assessments which are its product. On the other hand, in the British system analysis is comprehensively *de*centralised.[19]

This decentralised quality of the intelligence process is expressed in Foreign Office terms by former Foreign and Commonwealth Office (FCO) official Reginald Hibbert. Discussing the British intelligence system and the role of the Foreign Office, Hibbert distinguishes between secret intelligence, and a spectrum of non-secret (but not necessarily overt) sources. Of the total information to the FCO, these comprise '50 per cent ... drawn from overt published sources ... privileged material which is not strictly speaking classified ... is some 10 to 20 per cent ... [and] material classifiable as confidential [which] is a product of normal diplomatic activity', leaving perhaps ten per cent being information from secret sources.[20] As a consequence, he argues:

> The Foreign Office is itself a huge assessment machine ... with its elaborate organisation of over 60 departments, some geographical in scope and some functional, it constitutes a capacious and versatile digestive system fed by the massive intake of information [composed of] the 50 per cent or so overt, the 10 per cent or so privileged, the 20 or 25 per cent confidential and the 10 per cent secret. It chews the cud of this material day by day, reacts to it as it becomes available, 'in real time' as the expression goes, and applies it in the decision-taking and policy-forming process which is the end product of the system.[21]

Much the same is true of other departments of state such as the Ministry of Defence, Department of Trade and Industry and HM Customs and Excise,[22] and to a more limited degree, the Home Office and its National Criminal Intelligence Service. And the same might also have been said of the colonial and regional administrations in places like pre-1947 India, the Middle East and the Far East prior to the withdrawal from Empire. As a consequence, the central role of consumer demand in the British system is not merely a veneer of formal procedure, as one might be inclined to suspect of the DI report's rationalisations and promises, but a fundamental structural relationship in the British system.

Thus even the 'central' collegiality of the JIC is a manifestation of decentralisation. SIS, GCHQ and MI5 were all relative latecomers to the JIC, composed originally (and still mainly) of overt departments of state pooling raw information and formulating agreed collective assessments on the basis of their particular departmental evaluations. In the British system, the producers of finished intelligence are also the consumers of finished intelligence. Herman has commented that this dual role 'may seem a Gilbertian comedy. A FCO official attends ... JIC meeting and plays his part ... then back in his office he changes his role and waits for the intelligence assessment to arrive as the "objective" input to his policy recommendations and decisions.'[23]

The process is not quite as absurd at it may appear at first sight because that final report will include input at least from the other overt departments of state involved in the assessment, as well as a potentially crucial ten per cent from the secret intelligence agencies. Herman concludes of the British system that 'pedantry would suggest that, unlike the US system, what they produce is not strictly "*intelligence* assessment" but "government assessment"'.[24]

What is crucial in this process is the fact that intelligence analysis, as well as collection from non-covert sources such as publications and diplomatic confidential contacts, is dispersed throughout Whitehall. Agencies like SIS, GCHQ and MI5 are ultimately relatively minor and highly specialised players.

In the last analysis, in the British system, the function of a secret service is, as Nicholas Elliott has put it, 'to find out by clandestine means what the overt organs of government cannot find out by overt means'.[25] The function of Britain's intelligence and security agencies is defined and circumscribed by lacunae in the information available from non-secret sources. It is this relationship which underlies the structure and process of those agencies, and is so acutely apparent in the development and role of the regional controlling stations serving postwar colonial administrations.

## ORIGINS OF THE REGIONAL CONTROLLING STATIONS

The antecedents of the SIS controlling stations in the Middle and Far East were the wartime Interservice Liaison Departments (ISLDs) in Cairo, Algiers and Delhi (later Kandy). The title 'ISLD' was simply a cover-name for the SIS headquarters based with the relevant theatre GHQ. As such, the three were designated ISLD/Cairo, ISLD/Algiers (although these two were later consolidated under ISLD/Cairo), and ISLD/FE and serviced Middle East Command, Allied Forces Headquarters (AFHQ), and Supreme Allied Commander Southeast Asia (SACSEA) respectively. The purpose of the theatre ISLDs was, in the first place, to collect secret intelligence as per the needs of the theatre GHQ and theatre JICs, although out of the constant wrangling between the diverse wartime secret services, they also eventually took on a central collation and dissemination role handling any secret intelligence generated by all of the operational agencies.[26]

In the case of ISLD/ME, SIS already had a small cluster of stations in the Middle East, prior to the Italian entry in the war (June 1940), at Athens, Jerusalem, Istanbul and Cairo.[27] However, with the outbreak of fighting in the Middle East there arose the need to co-ordinate SIS work under the regional GHQ, and so the SIS despatched what the official history refers circuitously to as 'senior men' to GHQ Middle East in Cairo,[28] led by Captain Cuthbert Bowlby RN.[29] Although it got off to a slow start, failing to achieve a great deal by the end of 1940[30] this began to pick up in 1941 and 1942 with ISLD setting up new stations in Tehran, Baghdad, Damascus and Beirut.[31]

Although ISLD's first point of contact was the GHQ Director of Military Intelligence (DMI (ME)), ISLD also maintained its own three-man Collation Section.[32] According to one officer interviewed, the ISLD collation group were supposed to deal with everything from military order of battle to political intelligence,[33] although Nigel Clive, an SIS clandestine operator in wartime Greece, was absolutely convinced that his lengthy political reports on the partisan groups were essentially ignored by a Cairo headquarters whose 'whole professional upbringing had schooled them to treat politics as an arcane art, best left to others'.[34]

The Algiers ISLD began with an SIS unit which was attached to Allied Forces HQ at Norfolk House, providing information to the Anglo-American Combined Intelligence Section during preparation for Operation 'Torch', the landings in North Africa.[35] After the 'Torch' landings the new regional SIS HQ under AFHQ in Algiers adopted the ISLD designation as well.[36] With the surrender of Axis forces in the Middle East and North Africa in May 1943, ISLD/Cairo took over control of ISLD/Algiers.[37]

ISLD became responsible for operations in Italy during the invasion and liberation of that country, setting up an ISLD office there concerned with infiltrating intelligence cells and W/T operators into Northern Italy.[38] However, although ISLD/Italy was operating in continental Europe, it experienced no day to day control from Broadway (the SIS London HQ), but instead come under the direct control of Advance AFHQ in Italy, and was answerable within the SIS chain of command to ISLD/Cairo.[39]

ISLD/FE took shape in the first instance from a review of intelligence organisation in the Far East by Commander in Chief Far East Air Marshal Sir Robert Brooke-Popham. At the outbreak of war, the SIS maintained only three stations in the Pacific: Singapore, Hong Kong and Shanghai. These stations were subject to the direct control of a very distant Broadway, and weakly at that, with little or no co-ordination between the three. Sir Stewart Menzies ('C'), aware of the limitations of his Far East organisation, had already dispatched an officer to conduct an internal review during (but not before) Brooke-Popham's January 1941 review. Brooke-Popham's investigation resulted in a scathing assessment wired back to the Chiefs of Staff on 6 January, which concluded:

> Recent visit to H.K. [Hong Kong] completes my view of intelligence in the Far East. Weakest link undoubtedly is SIS Organization. At present, little or no reliance is placed upon SIS information by any authorities here and little valuable information in fact appears to be obtained. I am satisfied that identity of principal officers at Shanghai, HK and Singapore is known to many. Their subordinates are in general local amateurs with no training in Intelligence duties nor adequate knowledge of military, naval, air or political affairs ... I am aware that representative is being sent out to investigate but consider that action is required at once. I recommend immediate appointment of head for SIS organization in Far East to supervise and coordinate work for existing three sections and with power to make changes in personnel without delay.[40]

Brooke-Popham and the SIS representative, businessman Geoffrey Denham, agreed that Denham should take on the role of regional head of the SIS Far East organisation, attached to the Far East Combined Bureau in Singapore. With the December 1941 Japanese offensive overrunning Hong Kong and Singapore in 70 days, SIS retreated to India where it was based in New Delhi, with a forward station in Calcutta.[41] It was at this point that SIS FE adopted the SIS Cairo designation ISLD.

ISLD/FE remained in Delhi until 1944 when, under a new head, it relocated to Kandy, Ceylon (Sri Lanka) where Mountbatten's South East Asia Command (SEAC, created in August 1943) had relocated along with Force 136 (SOE Far East) in early 1944.[42] Like ISLD/Cairo, ISLD/FE was answerable directly to the theatre GHQ, in this case SEAC, and received no operational direction from London.

From December 1943, the co-ordination of the various UK and allied 'clandestine services' came under the oversight of SEAC's P (Priorities) Division, which sought to co-ordinate not only SIS and the Special Operations Executive (SOE), but also the British agencies with the work of the American Office of Strategic Services (OSS). To process the raw intelligence gathered by ISLD cells behind enemy lines into source reports for SEAC, ISLD/FE maintained its own Collation Section, which was also empowered to collate and disseminate any and all raw intelligence generated by any of the clandestine services operating under SEAC's control.[43]

INTELLIGENCE AND POSTWAR REGIONAL ADMINISTRATION

With the end of World War II, the theatre GHQs were wound down, and civilian regional and colonial administrations re-installed. In the Middle East, the old cover name ISLD/Cairo was abandoned in favour of a new title, the Combined Research and Planning Organisation, Middle East (CRPO/ME) and ISLD/FE in Kandy was relocated to Singapore with the re-establishment of the British presence there, where it was referred to more directly as SIS/FE.[44] Within the SIS, CRPO/ME and SIS/FE acted as regional headquarters with direct control over the other stations in their areas. They were termed 'controlling stations' (colloquially sometimes 'longstop' stations), and each was headed by its own area controller, Middle East Controller (MEC) and Far East Controller (FEC) respectively.[45]

Even as a new field organisation was being planned and installed in Cairo, the Egyptians were demanding a revision of the 1936 Treaty with Britain. In 1946, British forces were withdrawn from Egypt to the Canal Zone, and in 1949, faced with riots and general hostility from the populace, the British completely abandoned Cairo and Alexandria and MEC was relocated to Ismailia.[46] Then, with the Egyptian seizure of the Canal Zone, MEC was relocated to Cyprus, from 1951 to 1955 in Nicosia, and then moving with the staff of the Political Adviser to Middle East Forces (POMEF) to the British Military Hospital (BMH) Compound at Episkopi.[47] A 1948 'Review of Intelligence Organisation in the Middle East' noted on the matter of 'Provision and Control of Certain Intelligence Sources' that 'The Heads of Combined Research and Planning Organisation Middle East (CRPO(ME)) and of Security Intelligence Middle East (SIME) are responsible to MI6 and the Security Service respectively, but may also be called upon by JIC(ME) to fulfil local intelligence requirements.'[48]

In Southeast Asia, the end of the war ushered in a reassertion of British civilian government over her former possessions in the region. A Governor-General for Southeast Asia (concerned primarily with the Federated and Unfederated Malay States, the Straits Colonies and British Borneo) as well as a Special Commissioner for the UK in Southeast Asia and a Governor of Singapore were installed. The governmental situation in Southeast Asia was somewhat vexed as the region included both British-governed colonial possessions (which fell within the remit of the Colonial Office) and an assortment of independent 'native states' such as Burma and Thailand (strictly the concern of the Foreign Office). As a result, the Special Commission potentially fell between two governmental and constitutional stools, and the resulting administrative arrangements had to reflect this dual nature.

The individual chosen as Special Commissioner was Lord Killearn from the Foreign Office, described by one historian as an 'old Imperialist' but also well familiar with regional and colonial intelligence administration problems from his wartime experience as British Minister in Cairo.[49] Killearn remained on as Special Commissioner until 1948. After his departure, in May of that year, the posts of Governor-General of Malaya and Special Commissioner were consolidated into a new Commissioner-General for the United Kingdom in Southeast Asia (Singapore retained its own Commissioner during the 1950s). The dual nature of the Commission became thus even more pronounced, and was reflected by the fact that the newly appointed Commissioner-General received two deputies, one each for his colonial and foreign affairs staff.[50]

Under the Commissioner-General, the Far East intelligence arrangements, which had been mainly carried over directly from World War II,[51] underwent a review in which they were consciously modelled on those in the Middle East. One significant difference was that where JIC/ME was responsible directly to the Commander in Chief Middle East, the JIC/FE came under the auspices of the British Defence Co-ordinating Committee (BDCC/FE) in the first instance, rather than the Far East C-in-C or

Commissioner-General.[52] A 1948 'Draft Charter for JIC(FE)', not only discussed the role of SIS and MI5 in the Far East, but also proposed upgrading their relationship with the JIC(FE) to one roughly comparable with SIS itself on the London JIC.

> As regards the composition of the Joint Intelligence Committee (Far East), the Head of SIFE, the Head of SIS(FE), and the [Joint Intelligence Bureau] Representative are shown only as observers on the instructions of the Defence Coordinating Committee ... on the grounds that they have not hitherto been signing members and that the last two have responsibility only for producing intelligence and not for appreciating it. The Joint Intelligence Committee (Far East) had proposed that they should all be full members (but not signing members)....[53]

As a result, the SIS and Security Service were to contribute to any 'government assessments' generated by the British colonial administrations. However, on the grounds that the two covert organisations were responsible only for the gathering of information, and not its assessment, they were not 'signing members', that is, they were not signatories to any joint assessments made by the JIC/FE. In this capacity, however, they were required to produce information to be contributed to the joint assessment process, and as a result, were tasked by the regional colonial administrations, and disseminated their product directly to consumers within those administrations. In order to do so, the SIS/FE headquarters in Singapore could issue JIC/FE requirements to the subordinate field stations under FEC's control in the region.

FEC AND THE PRODUCTION/REQUIREMENTS SYSTEM

There was, however, an additional level of complication in the process, and that is hinted at in passing by the JIC/ME review. As quoted above, the JIC/ME arrangements state that 'The Heads of Combined Research and Planning Organisation Middle East (CRPO(ME)) and of Security Intelligence Middle East (SIME) are responsible to MI6 and the Security Service respectively', as well as fulfilling 'local intelligence requirements', and in the case of the SIS, thereby hangs a tale of some convolution. The 'dual control' architecture that was developing over the regional controlling stations in the postwar years involved a peculiar degree of duplication and parallelism within the operational command and control hierarchy within SIS' London headquarters. To place this convolution in context it is necessary to examine the general structure and process of the SIS in London.

The SIS headquarters in London was centred around two main 'sides' to the organisation which, between 1946 and 1979,[54] constituted two separate directorates. These two aspects of the organisation were the Directorate of Production, which handled operations, and the Directorate of Requirements, which mediated the SIS relationship with its consumers in Whitehall and Downing Street. Requirements Directorate had, as noted above arisen out of what the official history of British intelligence calls the '1921 arrangement', in which the SIS' main consumers attached sections of their own staff to the SIS headquarters staff to present their home departments' requirements to the agency, while acting as a secure conduit for SIS product to be circulated back to those home departments (Figure 3).

FIGURE 3
SIS BOARD OF DIRECTORS CIRCA 1948

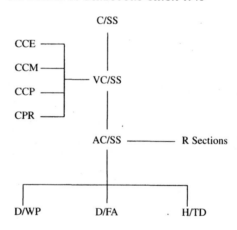

*Legend*:
AC/SS – Assistant Chief of Secret Service
CC – Chief Controller (CCE Europe; CCM Mediterranean; CCP Pacific)
CPR – Controller, Production Research
C/Ss – Chief of Secret Service
D/FA – Director, Finance and Administration
D/WP – Director, War Planning
H/TD – Head of Training and Development
R Sections – Requirements Sections
VC/SS – Vice-Chief of Secret Service

For most of the agency's history Requirements Directorate (and its evolutionary precursors the 'Circulating Sections') had been organised along functional lines, with one R Section representing each main customer. As a result, there were R1 representing the Foreign Office, R2 Air

Intelligence, R3 Naval Intelligence, R4 Military Intelligence and R5 was the counter-espionage section (of Philby notoriety). R6 handled industrial, financial and contraband intelligence on behalf of a brace of consumers that included the Board of Trade, Treasury, Bank of England and the newly-formed Joint Intelligence Bureau's Directorate of Economic Intelligence. R7 handled scientific and technical intelligence, initially on behalf of the Joint Scientific/Technical Intelligence Committee, later the JIB's Directorate of Scientific Intelligence, while R8 was the liaison with GCHQ.[55]

Many of these sections, in particular R1, R6 and R7 were also liable to participate in the assorted Joint Intelligence Staff subcommittees which collated specialist assessments for approval and circulating by the London JIC to its 'high-powered consumers' in the form of senior civil servants and ministers of state. The function of these sections was to receive detailed intelligence requirements from their customers, relay those requirements to the SIS' operational Production side, and then receive and interpret the resulting source reports from the Production side, and pass those results back to their customers attached to an indication of how reliable the information was likely to be.

On the other hand, the Production side of the agency was generally organised geographically around the location of the various field stations abroad.[56] Indeed, the fact that operational control was based on the locale of the station rather than the state being targeted reflects a fundamental principle in SIS operational organisation, that of the 'Third country rule'. According to the 'third country' rule, stations are supposed to target neighbouring states, rather than the host nation. As put by one former SIS officer interviewed in this research, 'in principle a station's first point of contact is the local security service'. Supposedly, the SIS station is there primarily by way of liaison with the local services to share information and co-ordinate action dealing with common concerns and targets.

To be sure, there was relatively little question of stations in the old Soviet Bloc engaging in liaison and co-operation with the various Communist secret police organisations. However, in nominally friendly countries the 'third country' rule remains an approximate norm and station cover constitutes little more than what the late John Bruce Lockhart, a former Deputy Chief of Service, has described as 'the fig leaf of convention'. By the same token, however, Lockhart argues that in hostile areas, that cover should be a 'suit of armour'.[57] As a consequence, the main purpose of SIS residencies in colonial (later Commonwealth) capitals was as staging points for operations against neighbouring states. Thus stations in Singapore, Kuala Lumpur and Hong Kong had as their targets countries like Thailand, Burma, Indonesia, Mainland China and so forth.[58]

As a result, Production Directorate grouped the various stations under Production Sections, and then generally one or more Production Sections, which provided mainly administrative support to the stations abroad, under an Area Controller, with two or more Area Controllers under a regional Chief Controller. Between the late 1940s and the late 1950s there were three Chief Controllers. Chief Controller Europe (CCE) oversaw three Controllers for the Western Area (CW: France, Italy and Iberia), Northern Area (CNA: Scandinavia and Denmark) and Eastern Area (CEA: Germany Switzerland, Austria).

However, things were more complex with the next two. Chief Controller Mediterranean (CCM) had under him both the Middle East Controller in the region, but also a London-based *Controller Middle East* or CME, who oversaw the relevant Middle East P Sections at Broadway.

Similarly, the Chief Controller Pacific (CCP) had under him both the Singapore Far East Controller *and* a Controller Far East in London performing the same task as CME under Chief Controller Mediterranean.[59]

There was also a fourth senior controller responsible for operations in North America and for operations mounted against 'denied areas' like the Soviet Union and Eastern Europe from within the UK, entitled Controller Production Research.[60] As a result, there was arguably a somewhat peculiar duplication between MEC and CME under CCM, and between FEC and CFE under CCP. However, in practice MEC and CME played distinct, even complementary roles under the overall authority of their Chief Controller as did FEC and CFE, but those distinct and complementary roles hinged on the basic 'pull' dynamic described above coupled to the geographical dispersal of governmental functions under the postwar colonial administrations (Figure 2).

The relationship between the Requirements and Productions sides, indeed the '1921 arrangement' itself, constitutes the original 'pull architecture' with which this discussion is concerned. Operations were mounted primarily in response to explicit enquiries which consumers issued to their liaison officers from the appropriate R sections. These would, for example, take the form of 'Standing Questionnaires' issued by Military Intelligence sub-sections to R4, occasionally supplemented by 'Special Questions' and 'Supplementary briefs'.[61] As recalled by one officer, this process ran roughly:

> ...if the War Office ... required to know whether a new type of Soviet tank shown off at the May Day Parade in Moscow was yet in service in Eastern Germany [*sic*], the officer in the Directorate of Military Intelligence ... responsible wrote a brief for R4 ... the Army officer attached to the SIS to make up the R4 section would then send out a request to the overseas station most likely to be able to provide the answer.[62]

FIGURE 4
PRODUCTION DIRECTORATE CIRCA 1948

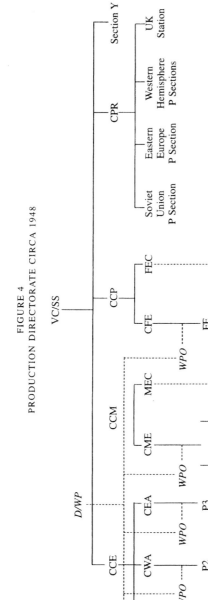

Legend:
CC – Chief Controller (CCE Europe; CCM Mediterranean; CCP Pacific)
CEA – Controller Eastern Area
CFE – Controller Far East
CME – Controller Middle East
CNA – Controller Northern Area
CWA – Controller Western Area
CPR – Controller, Production Research
D/WP – Director, War Planning
FEC – Far East Controller
JIC – Joint Intelligence Committee (ME Middle East; FE Far East)
MEC – Middle East Controller
P Section – Production Section
VC/SS – Vice Chief of Secret Service
WPO – War Planning Officer

One-time Iberian P Section officer Desmond Bristow has recounted the process from the Production side point of view, suggesting that the request to head of station would be routed via the relevant P section. The P officer would receive the result and pass the result to the relevant consumer where 'the report would then be digested by its recipients and returned to me marked with an A, B, C or D according to its importance, usually accompanied by a request for further information'. On top of the circulation of specific requests, Bristow recalls that 'every six months, I and my colleagues in [the Iberian P section] would evaluate each agent in collaboration with the recipient departments of his or her reports and the head of station supplying the reports'.[63]

This demand-driven process became considerably more sharply defined after the JIC moved to the Cabinet Office in 1957, and thereafter produced an annual National Intelligence Requirement Document with the authority of the Cabinet Office behind it. Under the JIC annual national intelligence requirements, there was a single set of general needs and priorities which, as recently described by the government, 'combines a rigorous analysis of the need for secret intelligence with extensive consultation with customer Departments and consideration of the financial and other resources required'.[64] For the SIS, their portion of the national requirements were (and are) formulated in a document called the 'SIS Red Book', circulated to stations abroad and in terms of which any operation must be justified (or can even be refused if the proposed operation does not address any of the Red Book requirements).[65]

There was, therefore, considerably more rhyme and reason to the arrangement than might appear at first glance. SIS/FE and SIS/ME both had to serve two masters, in the form of the regional JICs *and* the London tasking and dissemination mechanism that ran via Production Directorate through to Requirements Directorate, and thence to consumer departments and the London JIC. This is because there were *two different levels of intelligence needs to be served* (Figure 5). On the one hand, there were the regional intelligence needs of the Middle East and Far East British Defence Co-ordinating Committees, as well as the Commissioner-General, but on the other there were national intelligence requirements which lay outside the interests of the colonial administrative machinery but which could still be addressed through operations in the region.

This might easily be illustrated in the Far East situation by the need of the Commission for the UK in Southeast Asia to assess the intentions and capabilities of neighbouring states like Indonesia or China *vis-à-vis* British possessions in the Asia-Pacific region, and might task SIS/FE do provide secret intelligence in support of these needs. On the other hand, London might also wish to mount operations against Communist bloc nationals and

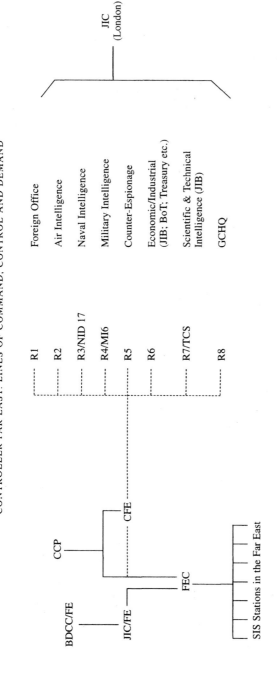

FIGURE 5
CONTROLLER FAR EAST: LINES OF COMMAND, CONTROL AND DEMAND

| | |
|---|---|
| R1 | Foreign Office |
| R2 | Air Intelligence |
| R3/NID 17 | Naval Intelligence |
| R4/MI6 | Military Intelligence |
| R5 | Counter-Espionage |
| R6 | Economic/Industrial (JIB; BoT; Treasury etc.) |
| R7/TCS | Scientific & Technical Intelligence (JIB) |
| R8 | GCHQ |

JIC (London)

BDCC/FE
CCP
CFE
JIC/FE
FEC

SIS Stations in the Far East

*Legend*:
BDCC/FE – British Defence Co-Ordinating Committee, Far East
CCP – Chief Controller, Pacific
GCHQ – Government Communications Headquarters
JIC – Joint Intelligence Committee
JIC/FE – Joint Intelligence Committee, Far East
TCS – Technical Coordinating Section

interests in the Asia-Pacific region in support of the more global concerns of the Cold War and emerging nuclear balance of terror.[66] The latter operations would lie outside the interests and needs of the JIC/FE, while the former would be of a purely 'local' interest and not required by the JIC or any of the Whitehall consumers back in the UK. To a very real degree, the Commission for Southeast Asia functioned like a separate public administration (as had the then defunct Indian Civil Service) from that in London, and one which also required secret intelligence to formulate its own 'government assessments'.

## THE DEMISE OF THE CONTROLLING STATIONS

During the late 1950s, Britain's progressive withdrawal from its interests east of Suez led in due course to a comprehensive re-organisation of the Production side of the SIS. As noted above, the somewhat intricate assortment of area 'controllerates' was a consequence of the distribution of global operations on the one hand, and of diverse governmental consumer needs on the other. The progressive scaling-down and eventual dissolution of the UK's colonial administrations coupled to the increased centralisation of consumer requirements negotiation and formulation in the Cabinet Office. Together, these constituted a fairly extensive series of changes to the wider machinery of the decentralised, all-source intelligence process Michael Herman has termed 'government assessment' and therefore the specific demand for secret intelligence in that process.

An extensive restructuring of the consumer-side of the equation would naturally imply a concomitant reformulation of the SIS' own infrastructure. Therefore, between 1958 and 1959, the hierarchy of Area Controllers and regional Chief Controllers was abandoned, Production Directorate was broken up into four separate directorates, and the subordinate Area Controllers abolished. Production sections answered directly to the four Directors of Production and their immediate Deputy Directors. The four-fold division of geographical interests, however, remained relatively unchanged. Under this reorganisation, CCE became DP1, CCM became DP2, CCP became DP3 and CPR became DP4.[67]

The reorganisation of Production in London also carried with it the discontinuation of the two Area Controllers abroad, MEC and FEC, and the direct subordination of the stations in the Middle and Far East to their respective DPs in London. However, the dynamics leading to this reform did not originate with the SIS itself, but with the reduced role and importance of Britain's colonial administrations in Cyprus and Singapore.

In Cyprus, MEC was part of the FO's Political Office to Middle East Forces (POMEF) in Episkopi. Between 1958 and 1960 negotiations were undertaken between the Middle East High Command and the government of Archbishop Makarios to secure Cypriot independence, the termination of British administration, and the confinement of British strategic interests to the British Sovereign Base Areas. The FO's Political Representative (and head of POMEF) on the High Command involved in these negotiations was former SIS Foreign Office Adviser Geoffrey McDermott who recounts the fate of MEC (not referred to as such) in his *The Eden Legacy*. Far from being abolished to increase direct control from London, MEC fell prey to what McDermott in retrospect views as 'a ridiculous bit of Whitehall warfare'. Cyprus elected to become a member of the British Commonwealth, and as a result it fell not within Foreign Office and SIS jurisdiction but instead under that of the Commonwealth Relations Office (CRO) and as a result, in 1958

> the MI6 man, who had provided much useful intelligence, was immediately removed because gentlemen of the Commonwealth do not spy on one another. According to CRO custom an MI5 man was substituted to work in liaison with the Cyprus government.[68]

The Middle East Controller was replaced with a Middle East Liaison Officer, who was to act simply as a conduit for intelligence of 'area interest' to British Middle East forces in Cyprus, and as one officer interviewed put it 'MEC became MELO'.[69] By 1959, the Chief Controllers in London had been abolished and replaced with Directors, and operational control of the Middle East and African Stations fell to DP2.

The Far East Controller in Singapore suffered much the same fate. By 1957, the assorted Malay states and British Borneo became fully independent as the Malaysian Federation while Singapore acquired effective self-rule by 1959. With their roles steadily dwindling, the post of Commissioner-General for the UK in Southeast Asia and the UK Commission for Singapore were amalgamated. For the most part, the British role, apart from defence and security arrangements, was chiefly concerned with mediating the transition to independence for Malaysia and, after an assortment of false starts and ethnic complications, Singapore.

Hence, the need for a relatively autonomous intelligence system was steadily dwindling while requirements were overall becoming increasingly centrally managed in the Cabinet Office. As a result, Controller Far East was phased out at around the same time as Controller Middle East, and operational control routed directly to DP3 at Broadway.[70] However, as one officer interviewed recalled, 'we still copied reports of "area interest" to Singapore',[71] where they were subsequently circulated to JIC/FE. Even that limited role essentially ceased with Singapore's abrupt 1965 declaration of independence.

As a result, the post-1965 role of the Singapore station became that of a staging point for operations against neighbouring states and, perhaps more crucially, against Soviet and Chinese personnel and interests in the region. There has been some suggestion that the Singapore office has, at times, had a larger role to play as a handler and collator of SIS product required for British participation in regional combined military arrangements like the Five Powers Defence Pact (FPDP),[72] but this sort of role is more reminiscent of the work of wartime Special Liaison Units holding and disseminating highly sensitive information than it is of the overarching regional role of the wartime ISLDs or postwar 'longstop' controlling stations.

CONCLUSION

It can be seen from the preceding, therefore, that the institutional mechanisms of a 'pull' intelligence architecture in the British state as having driven – or, perhaps more appropriately *drawn* – SIS' Far East organisation and its residency in Singapore through three distinct stages.

In the first stage, when secret intelligence in the Far East was of a relatively low priority (as compared with the mounting tensions with the Soviet Union on one hand and Fascism in Western Europe on the other), the SIS system in the region was allowed to languish, starved of funds and weakly overseen and managed, and almost entirely unaffected by the dynamics of the '1921 arrangement' in London.

The second stage came with World War II, and the appearance of highly autonomous theatre commands in the Middle East, North Africa and the Far East which created their own regional analogues to the '1921 arrangement' with their respective ISLD organisations. Under these conditions, the ISLDs were essentially servicing only their immediate theatre commands, and had only minimal dealings with SIS' London HQ. During this period, ISLD/FE was based in India, and later Ceylon.

The third stage in the development of SIS in the Far East rested upon the postwar British colonial administrations in the Middle and Far East. Under these conditions, SIS global operational organisation was headquartered in London, but subsidiary headquarters were set up to respond to regional intelligence requirements laid down by JIC/FE and JIC/ME, in turn serving the requirements of the Middle and Far East British Defence Co-ordinating Committees (BDCC/ME and BDCC/FE).

The common theme throughout this entire trajectory has been the essentially subservient role of the SIS. Its regional headquarters did not merely operate on behalf of wartime theatre commands and postwar colonial administration. They were set up in the first place on the basis of those needs, and their operations driven by the demands laid upon them by two distinct and separate sets of consumers, both in-theatre, and in London. The underlying relationship between SIS and its regional and central consumers has, since 1919 at least, been based on, and organisational infrastructure developed to implement, a consumer-led *pull architecture*. That 'pull' dynamic is nowhere more apparent than where SIS elements have been required to serve a plurality of consumers, as they were so required in the Middle East and Far East regional controlling stations. What MEC and FEC both embodied with such clarity was that, within the British system, secret intelligence agencies in general, and the SIS in particular, exist not as independent operational entities but ultimately a *covert armature of overt government*.

## NOTES

I would like to express my gratitude to Sheila Kerr at the University of Salford and Richard Aldrich at Nottingham for the opportunity to present this paper at the 1999 'Clandestine Cold War in the Asia-Pacific 1945–65' conference held at Nottingham's Institute of Asia-Pacific Studies on 14 June. Additional thanks also to the editors for advice and suggestions concerning the final version of this article.

1. It is a matter that has developed in several national contexts, see for example, Roger Faligot and Paul Krop, *La Piscine* (Oxford: Blackwell 1989) pp.85–6, or Matthew Aid's study in this volume.
2. It might also be argued that a similar set of conditions and mechanisms surrounded the very large (reportedly 100+ officers) SIS station at the Olympic Stadium in West Berlin and its relationship along with the Bonn Station to the JIC in Germany during the postwar occupation. However, such an analysis lies beyond the purview of the present discussion.
3. As will become apparent below, 'non-covert' is *not* the same thing as *overt*.
4. Possibly the earliest articulation of this principle appears in H.S. Rowen, *Reforming Intelligence: A Market Approach* (Washington DC: Consortium for the Study of Intelligence 1993). However, the notions of supply, demand and the relationship between producer and consumer is of a considerably older vintage and arises out of the notion of the 'intelligence cycle'; see, e.g., Walter Laqueur, *A World of Secrets* (NY: Basic 1995).
5. Sharfman, 'Intelligence Analysis in an Age of Electronic Dissemination', in David Charters, Stuart Farson and Glenn Hastedt, *Intelligence Analysis and Assessment* (London/Portland, OR: Frank Cass 1996) pp.202–3.
6. Ibid. p.203
7. CIA, *Analysis: Directorate of Intelligence in the 21st Century* (Washington DC: CIA 1996) p.1.
8. Ibid. p.10
9. Michael Herman, *Intelligence Power in Peace and War* (Cambridge: CUP 1996) p.295
10. Ibid. p.289
11. Cabinet Office, *Central Intelligence Machinery*, available on line at: http://www.cabinet-office.gov.uk/cabsec/1998/cim/cimrep2.htm#intel (16 June 1999). It is worth noting that the Cabinet Office views the tasking and dissemination process sufficiently important to warrant its own headlined link on the CIM homepage.
12. Herman (note 9) pp.262, 278.
13. James Bamford, *The Puzzle Palace: The American NSA and its Special Relationship with Britain's GCHQ* (London: Sidgwick 1983).
14. F.H. Hinsley *et al.*, *British Intelligence in the Second World War: Its Impact on Strategy and*

*Operations, Volume I* (London: HMSO 1979) pp.17–18.

15. *Dictionary of United States Military Terms for Joint Usage* (Washington DC: Depts of Army, Navy and Airforce 1979) p.2 cited in Jeffrey T. Richelson, *The US Intelligence Community* (NY: Ballinger 1989) p.1.
16. Herman (note 9) p.9.
17. K.G. Robertson 'Intelligence, Terrorism and Civil Liberties', in *Conflict Quarterly* 7/2 (Spring 1987) p.46.
18. Private information.
19. Philip H.J. Davies, 'Organisational Politics and the Development of Britain's Intelligence Producer/Consumer Interface', *Intelligence and National Security* 10/4 (Oct. 1995) pp.111–32.
20. Reginald Hibbert, 'Intelligence and Policy', *Intelligence and National Security* 5/1 (Jan. 1990) p.112.
21. Ibid. p.113.
22. All three of these, along with the FCO were, of course, players in the 1994 Matrix-Churchill fiasco, and one might be tempted to forward the tentative hypothesis that the very dispersal and relative isolation of four, or more, distinct intelligence assessment architectures may have contributed to the kind of crossing of lines which led to the arrest of SIS sources by Customs officials.
23. Herman (note 9) p.275.
24. Ibid., emphasis in the original. It would be tempting to suggest that what the DI produces in its all-source assessments is a would-be government assessment devoid of the credibility and 'buy in' which might otherwise result from interdepartmental consensus.
25. Nicholas Elliott, *With My Little Eye* (Wilton, UK: Michael Joseph 1993) p.22; Elliott also adds additional functions which include 'to support and strengthen friendly regimes and to weaken hostile ones; to assist friendly foreign services [and] act as an informal link between governments whose overt relationships are in a delicate state'. Or, as also put by one of Elliott's contemporaries, one time Deputy C John Bruce Lockhart: 'The essential skill of a secret service is to get things done secretly and deniably' in Lockhart, 'Intelligence: A British View'; in K.G. Robertson (ed.) *British and American Approaches to Intelligence* (London: Macmillan 1987) p.46.
26. At this point, by 'secret intelligence' I am referring primarily to human intelligence. The Middle East and Far East organisations for signals intelligence were a somewhat different, and often somewhat entangled, affair, in which the collation and dissemination arrangements were typified by the Special Communications Unit/Special Liaison Unit (SCU/SLU) system. This complexity was further contorted by the fact that the SCU/SLU system was actually controlled and operated by the SIS' Communications Section (Section VIII), although they served the Government Codes and Cipher School (GC&CS; predecessor to GCHQ). F.W. Winterbotham, *The Ultra Secret* (London/NY: Weidenfeld/Dell 1974) pp.41–2.
27. Interview with I-12.
28. Hinsley *et al.* (note 14) p.207.
29. Nigel West, *MI6: British Secret Intelligence Service Operations 1909–45* (London: Weidenfeld 1983) p.156; I-12 interview.
30. Hinsley *et al.* (note 14) p.207.
31. Interview with I-12.
32. Ibid.; unlike other stations abroad for which the local security service was the first point of contact, links with the Egyptian government and police lay with the Security Service representative in the theatre, the Cairo Defence Security Office (DSO), F.H. Hinsley and C.A.G. Simkins, *British Intelligence in The Second World War: Security and Counterintelligence*, Vol.IV (London: HMSO 1990) p.150.
33. Interview with I-12.
34. Nigel Clive, *A Greek Experience 1943–1948* (Wilton, UK: Michael Russell 1985) p.29. In a later meeting with Malcolm Woolcombe, head of Section I (R1), Clive learned that *none* of his political reports had been forwarded to London by ISLD Cairo (p.146). However, it should be noted that British policy concerned with Greece and the Balkans was essentially a matter for the Commander-in-Chief Middle East and his Foreign Office Political Adviser in

Cairo, so (without even invoking security compartmentalization), Section I did not really need to know.

35. Hinsley *et al.* (note 14) pp.13, 50.
36. Interview with I-12 suggested that SIS Algiers did not adopt the ISLD designation until after the Middle East and African forces combined, although SIS documents released with SOE papers concerning SIS at AFHQ Algiers in 1942 carry ISLD letterhead, HS 3/59 PRO.
37. Interview with I-12 identified the consolidation of ISLD Cairo and Algiers, but suggested the transfer of ISLD control to Algiers; however, an SOE organisation chart outlining Allied secret organisation work in Italy clearly placed ISLD Italy under the direct control of ISLD Cairo, not AFHQ. HS 3/170 PRO.
38. Organisation chart in HS 3/170 PRO; I-12 interview.
39. Interview with I-12, Organisation chart in HS 3/170 PRO.
40. Telegram from Commander in Chief Far East to Air Ministry of 6 Jan. 1941, CAB 81/900, PRO.
41. A potential source of complication was the fact that ISLD/FE was based in Delhi, but India and the Gulf States fell under the auspices of the Indian government. Although this had the potential for difficulties and conflicts within the defence and intelligence communities (see e.g. Patrick French, *Liberty or Death* (London: HarperCollins 1998) or Milan Hauner, *India in Axis Strategy* (Stuttgart: Klett-Cotta 1981)), it was entirely consistent with the SIS Third Country Doctrine discussed below.
42. Richard J. Aldrich, 'Britain's Secret Intelligence Service in Asia during the Second World War', *Modern Asian Studies* 32/1 (1998) pp.188, 192–3. Aldrich's piece is a comprehensive review of SIS development in the wartime Far East. Peter Elphick has also provided a general overview of the covert conflict in the Asia-Pacific region in his *Far Eastern File: The Intelligence War in the Far East 1930–1945* (London: Coronet 1997).
43. Memo from Capt. G.A. Garnons-Williams RN, Head of P Division to Director of Intelligence, Head of SOE in India, Advance HQ Force 136, ISLD and Chief of OSS of 2 Oct. 1944. HS 1/303 PRO.
44. For CRPO(ME), JIC (48) 60 'Review of Intelligence Organization in the Middle East' in L/WS/1/1051; for SIS(FE) WS/7065 'Appendix A: Draft Charter for JIC(FE)' of 7 Jan. 1948, L/WS/1/1050, both IOLR, the existence of both also first published by Richard J. Aldrich 'Secret Intelligence for a Post War World' in idem (ed.) *British Intelligence, Strategy and the Cold War* (London: Routlege 1992).
45. Interviews with I-10, I-15, I-17.
46. For the withdrawal of British forces from the 'Delta cities', to the Canal Zone, see Keith Kyle, *Suez* (London: Weidenfeld 1991) p.21; I-10 interview.
47. Interview with I-10; for documents concerning the re-designation of the British Middle East Officer (BMEO) to POMEF, see 'New Directive for POMEF to replace BMEO' Draft, V1052/48 of 20 Sept. 1955 FO 371/115478.
48. JIC (48) 60 'Review of Intelligence Organization in the Middle East' in L/WS/1/1051, IOLR.
49. For a detailed account of the development and complication surrounding the Special Commission and Commissioner-General for the UK in Southeast Asia, see Tilman Remme, *Britain and Regional Cooperation in South-East Asia, 1945–49* (London : Routledge 1995) esp. pp.116–19.
50. Ibid. p.117
51. Plus or minus the 1945-46 demise of Force 136, the SOE Far East presence, primarily absorbed into the SIS (although not completely, as demonstrated by Richard Aldrich in his 'Unquiet in Death: The postwar Survival of the Special Operations Executive 1945–1951' in Anthony Gorst *et al.* (ed.) *Contemporary British History 1931–1961: Policy and the Limits of Policy* (London: Pinter 1991) pp.193–210.
52. WS/7065 'Appendix A: Draft Charter for JIC(FE)' of 7 Jan. 1948, L/WS/1/1050, IOLR
53. Ibid.
54. Shortly after Sir Arthur Franks became CSS in 1979, Requirements and Production were consolidated into under a single combined Director of Production and Requirements, who also served as Deputy Chief of Service. The R Sections retained their own Deputy Director

of Requirements until after the end of the Cold War when the R Sections came under the authority of their relevant Area Controllers. The consolidated Directorate first appeared publicly in Duncan Campbell 'Friends and Others', *New Statesman and Society* 26 Nov. 1982, p.6; Interviews with I-20 and I-28.

55. For close detail of the emergence of this aspect of SIS organisation, see Davies, 'MI6's Requirements Directorate: Integrating Intelligence into the Machinery of Government', forthcoming in *Public Administration*.

56. In recent years, the SIS has set up several of Controllerates along functional lines, such as those for Counter-Proliferation and 'Global Issues' (e.g. the environment and transnational serious crime), even more recently consolidated into a single Controller Global and Functional. Mark Urban, *UK Eyes Alpha* (London: Faber 1996) pp.229, 237, 262; BBC, 'On Her Majesty's Secret Service', *Panorama*, 22 Nov. 1993. Interview 28.

57. Lockhart (note 25) p.44.

58. In fairness, the literature on the SIS is replete with examples of stations apparently violating the Third Country Rule, such as Moscow Station handling GRU agents like Oleg Penkovsky and Oleg Gordievsky (see e.g. Jerold Schechter and Peter Deriabin, *The Spy Who Saved the World* (NY: Scribner's 1992) or Oleg Gordievsky, *Next Stop Execution* (London: Macmillan 1995)) or Vienna Station's 1949 tunnelling operation against the Soviet telephone lines in that city (George Blake, *No Other Choice* (London: Jonathan Cape 1990) pp.5–16). However, it should be pointed out that both Penkovsky and Gordievsky were contacted and recruited *outside* the USSR, with Moscow Station handling only clandestine communications and escape routes, while the Vienna tunnel was targeted against the Soviet sector of occupied Austria. As a result, most apparent exceptions tend to appear out of unavoidable ambiguities which tend to emerge in what one former SIS officer (Interview 15) described with an almost sociological turn of phrase as 'doing spying'.

59. Anthony Cavendish, *Inside Intelligence* (London: Collins 1991) p.39; Interviews with I-10, I-15, I-17.

60. Blake (note 58) p.184; Tom Bower, *The Perfect English Spy*, p.159; Interviews with I-9, I-11, I-15.

61. Documents laying this process out in some detail have recently been published by Richard J. Aldrich in his *Espionage, Security and Intelligence in Britain 1945–1970* (Manchester UP 1998) pp.27–9, 63–4. It should be kept in mind that most R sections had something of a 'double identity' carrying one designation in the Requirements scheme at Broadway, and another in their home Department of State. Hence, R4 within MID was, after 1941, designated MI6; see 'Reorganisation of MO and MI' DMO&P 307 in WO 208/4696 PRO.

62. Cavendish (note 59) p.40.

63. Desmond Bristow, *A Game of Moles* (London: Bodley Head 1993) pp.175–6. The mechanics of the processes described by Cavendish and Bristow were also borne out in interviews with nine former SIS officers between 1993 and 1998 who answered questions on this particular matter.

64. As drawn from the most recent version of the Central Intelligence Machinery statement on the 'open government' webpage, downloadable HTML at http://www.cabinet-office.gov.uk/cabsec/1998/cim/cimrep2.htm#intel, 23 June 1999.

65. For discussion of the SIS Red Book, not to be confused with the weekly JIC all-source survey called the Red Book, see Anthony Verrier, *Through the Looking Glass: British Foreign Policy in an Age of Illusion* (London: Jonathan Cape 1983) p.4. Interviews with I-20 and I-28.

66. A classic example of this is provided in Donald McCormick's biography of Maurice Oldfield under the pen-name Richard Deacon. Therein he traces an operation to track down illegal shipments of wolfram, tungsten ore, a controlled strategic material under the 1948 COCOM regime (although McCormick attributes the operation in the first instance to a world-wide shortage of the metal). He traces how Oldfield tasked the Hong Kong station, among others, with locating foreign buyers and tracing their connections back to the crown territory. However, McCormick inaccurately describes Hong Kong has having been outside Oldfield's 'patch' at the time, evidently unaware that Oldfield was not merely a station commander but Far East Controller at the time. Donald McCormick, *'C': A Biography of Sir Maurice*

*Oldfield, Head of MI6* (London: Futura 1985) pp.90–1.

67. This development is traced fairly explicitly in Blake (note 58) pp.182–4. The remaining DPs are identified by West in parallel with the CC titles, Nigel West, *The Friends: Britain's Post-War Secret Intelligence Operations* (London: Weidenfeld 1988) pp.13–15, a scheme also cited by Richard Norton-Taylor in his *In Defence of the Realm?* (London: Civil Liberties Trust 1990) p.50, although this completely contradicts the organisation chart of area controllers which Norton-Taylor provides on p.62 of the same volume (derived from the Campbell chart referred to above). The DP designations were confirmed, approximately dated (to c. 1958/59) during interviews with: I-008; I-010; I-015; I-019; I-020 and I-028.

68. Geoffrey McDermott, *The Eden Legacy and the Decline of British Diplomacy* (London: Leslie Frewin 1969) p.175.

69. Interview with I-10.

70. Officers interviewed were vague about the exact date when FEC was abolished, but there was a general consensus that FEC and CFE both disappeared when, or by the time, the controllerates were replaced by the various directorates.

71. Interview with I-15.

72. Stephen Dorril, from press reports, in *Silent Conspiracy* (London: Mandarin 1994). Private information.

## APPENDIX: A NOTE ON SOURCES

The following discussion had been based on three main classes of resources: public archives, published firsthand accounts, and interviews with former intelligence officers. Due to the obvious difficulties of referring to persons who cannot be identified by name, the sociological (and, indeed, intelligence community) practice has been adopted of assigning informants serial numbers (e.g. I-12 interview, note 27), and referring to them on the basis of those numbers. Interview data in this discussion was drawn from a series of interviews with 20 former officers conducted between Aug. 1993 and Sept. 1997. During a recent stay in Singapore I have also been privileged to discuss intelligence matters with regional defence officials. Because these individuals, and in some cases UK officials giving briefings to UK academics, were at the time, or remain active in governmental capacities, such information in that case has been enshrouded in the hoary, and vague, old convention 'private information'.

# 6

# Legacies of Secret Service: Renegade SOE and the Karen Struggle in Burma, 1948–50

## RICHARD J. ALDRICH

### SOE LEGACIES ACROSS ASIA

In late 1947, Basil Liddell Hart, Britain's leading strategic thinker, was contacted by Air Chief Marshal Sir John Slessor, soon to become Chief of the Air Staff. Slessor consulted Liddell Hart on his blueprint for accelerating the Cold War against the Eastern Bloc through aggressive measures. He described this programme as the creation of a 'Fifth Column of Freedom', and spoke of the revival of the Special Operations Executive (SOE) and the Political Warfare Executive for this purpose. In early 1948 Basil Liddell Hart gave his encouragement for these schemes and seemed enthusiastic about the blueprint for a clandestine war against the Soviets.[1] But by the end of 1949 Liddell Hart had changed his mind and set himself firmly against the concept of resistance and insurgency by civil populations. What had triggered this strange reversal?

In a dozen different countries around the world, the legacy of long-term wartime resistance work was gradually becoming clear. During 1948 and 1949, in Malaya and Burma, the painful aftermath of guerrilla tactics employed against the Japanese became all too apparent for policy-makers in Whitehall. This could hardly have escaped Liddell Hart's attention. Wars of insurgency were easy for secret services to ignite, but now looked very difficult to extinguish. Clandestine struggle might help to evict an occupying enemy, but only at the risk of rendering the territory ungovernable.

Brigadier R. G. B. Prescott, who had served in the Mediterranean in 1944 and then in Asia in 1945 offered candid observations on the subject. Prescott was Deputy Head of Civil Affairs in Burma. In Europe, he explained, the worst of these problems of remnant resistance forces had to be solved by the returning governments of the country concerned. However, 'in Burma, if our clandestine organisations leave awkward legacies, *they leave them for ourselves*'. Civil Affairs was particularly anxious about plans to distribute 3,000 further weapons to Karens in the Delta region of Burma, which had always been 'a criminal area'. This, it argued would result in a wave of serious crime, the suppression of which 'will be in the nature of a minor military operation'.

Moreover, many of the Karen hill tribes had been massacred by the lowland Burmese in 1942 and, if armed, the temptation to 'pay off old scores' would be overwhelming. Arming guerrillas, he argued, would only result in them expecting large political favours from the postwar settlement. They were not, he argued like the Maquis – the mountain resistance in France – but were instead 'disgruntled elements who have backed the wrong horse, and who are endeavouring to cover their bets'. These were prescient observations.[2]

However, in 1945 the Civil Affairs officers and former colonial policemen who advanced such views against SOE's programme of arming guerrillas lost the argument. SOE offered the counter-argument that only by arming and training the guerrillas could these forces be kept under British control. SOE were persuasive and in the summer of 1945, London finally authorised as much assistance to the Malayan guerrilla forces as was necessary to achieve control. Similar decisions were taken in Burma. Building up continued, but SOE's central purpose was now retardation of these irregular forces which it barely controlled.[3]

Admiral Lord Mountbatten's own arguments for the arming of the guerrillas, which were more sophisticated and more persuasive than those of SOE had helped to win London over. As Supreme Allied Commander, South-East Asia, Mountbatten had freely conceded that the potential dangers of support included lending the guerrillas enhanced status, might translate into high political expectations after the surrender. Yet, he insisted that this could be countered by making Britain's constitutional plans clear at an early stage.[4] Meanwhile Mountbatten had spotted an invaluable publicity opportunity. Writing to the Colonial Secretary, Oliver Stanley, he explained:

> I very much hope that the War Cabinet will see their way to agreeing with my new proposals. The question of Resistance Movements within the British Empire is in a special category. Presumably we have not previously found Colonial Subjects rising to fight on our behalf when we were about to occupy their territory, and the fact that they are doing so today seems to me a wonderful opportunity for propaganda to the world in general, and to the Americans in particular, at a time when we are being accused of reconquering colonial peoples in order to re-subjugate them.

Mountbatten accepted that many of the guerrillas in Malaya and Burma were anti-British but, ever the optimist, he hoped that many of them could be won over by revised constitutions.[5] However by 1948, Mountbatten, aptly described by one historian as the 'imperial undertaker who never wore black', had left the Asian scene while some of the guerrillas once under his command were still fighting.[6]

In postwar Greece, Palestine, Indochina, Burma and Malaya, former SOE personnel sometimes found themselves pressed into service against groups which the Allies had previously armed and trained. In Indochina, the British and the French fought Viet Minh forces who were armed with tons of new British weapons dropped into Thailand in the last stages of the war, but never used because of the truncation of a conflict that many believed would continue until November 1946. Instead they had been quickly sold on by ubiquitous Chinese merchants.

Even though many of the weapons dropped into Thailand were later exported at a profit into neighbouring Burma and Indochina, enough weapons remained to cause trouble in Thailand. Postwar Thai politics were heavily militarised and the 'coup trap' culture that characterised Thailand was not unconnected to this. In 1947, as faction fighting became worse the British and the Americans were obliged to evacuate the democratic leader whom they had backed, separately but energetically, during the war – the Thai Regent, Luang Pridi or 'Ruth' – for fear that he would be assassinated by equally well-armed rival factions.[7]

On 9 November 1947 a military coup directed by Luang Phibul, the wartime pro-Japanese collaborator, displaced the moderate government and restored the Thai wartime leader to power. Ten days later the new regime moved against Pridi and the Free Thais, seizing Free Thai arms caches and increasing surveillance.[8] In London, Ernest Bevin, the Foreign Secretary, feared 'a long period of civil war'.[9] Former Office of Strategic Services (OSS) officers still in Bangkok were distressed and reported to William J. Donovan that their old wartime associates were now being purged with many thrown into jail on 'absurd charges'.[10] With Free Thai elements being rounded up, and in some cases executed, the issue for British and American officials was the discreet exfiltration of Pridi from Bangkok in order to save his life.[11]

Early on the morning of 19 November 1947, Pridi arrived at the house of the British Naval Attaché, Captain Dennis, 'disguised in naval uniform, wearing thick glasses and a new moustache and missing his upper dental plate'. Then, Dennis and his American colleague, Commander Gardes, used an American naval launch to rendezvous with a Shell tanker which took him to Malaya. In Dennis' house, Pridi discarded two or three machine-guns, several other weapons and two hand grenades. Britain's Ambassador Thompson did not like the 'dangerous melodrama' but felt that they had discharged their 'humanitarian obligation' to the wartime resistance leader.[12]

The authorities in Malaya over-reacted somewhat and were relieved when Pridi departed for China.[13]

However, the problem of the SOE legacy in Asia was more fundamental than simply arms and training. After all, vast quantities of weapons were, in any case, available in 1945 from the Japanese who surrendered their weapons more readily to Asiatics than to Europeans. Instead Liddell Hart complained that the whole strategy of resistance had an 'amoral effect on the younger generation as a whole'. It taught them to defy authority and to break the rules of civil morality in their fight against the occupying forces that remained long after they had gone.

Even the Soviets, with their draconian methods, were having trouble extinguishing the partisan culture in areas of the Ukraine and the former Baltic states and would fight a counter-insurgency war in those places until the early 1950s. This experience would be repeated during the Cold War, with the current situation in 'liberated' Afghanistan seemingly confirming the wisdom of these observations.[14]

SOE LEGACIES IN BURMA

SOE legacies in Burma were probably more important than in other countries of Asia and were certainly complex. Although the political issues confronting the Allied secret services and the indigenous resistance groups in Burma bore some similarities to those in Thailand and Malaya, the context was different. Burma was the sole area of concentrated fighting in mainland Asia, and this lent all decisions a more military texture. By late 1944 the morale of Japanese forces in Burma was low and, from March 1945, this collapsed quickly.[15]

The most controversial issue was, as elsewhere, the handling of resistance forces. From autumn 1944 the forces of the Burmese National Army (BNA) and other Anti-Fascist Organisations (AFO) deserted to the British in droves. British responses to these deserters varied markedly. SOE readily recruited them behind Japanese lines, while in liberated areas the officers of Civil Affairs Service (Burma) or CAS (B), supported by large Field Security contingents, sought their arrest as collaborators. Uneasy truces between officials of SOE and CAS (B) had be negotiated locally by senior army commanders.[16] In November 1944, Colin Mackenzie, Head of SOE in the Far East, had decided to go ahead with the arming of the BNA without consulting CAS (B), whom he knew would object strenuously. But controversy loomed for, as in Yugoslavia, Greece and Malaya, SOE was arming groups that were inimical to Britain's postwar policy.[17]

Colin Mackenzie had to work hard to counter these powerful arguments. He stressed expediency, pointing out that the AFO had rebelled against their

Japanese masters and sought contacts with the British of their own accord, thus 'it would be politically most unwise to refuse this offer of co-operation'. The Lowland Burmese in the BNA would arm themselves anyway with materials discarded by the retreating Japanese, but would bear a grudge, knowing that the British had already armed the hill tribes, thus 'sowing the seeds of post war communal grievance'. Moreover, alluding to the SOE experience in Greece, he warned of press revelations of 'the Drew Pearson type' about the reactionary British refusing to co-operate with these anti-fascist forces of the left.[18] In the event Mackenzie joined up with American OSS to persuade Mountbatten to continue arming all groups.[19]

However, their victory on the issue of arming *disaffected* pockets of guerrillas was now overshadowed by a much larger question, whether SOE should enter in a formal alliance with Aung San, the BNA leader. Both General Sir William Slim, commander of the advancing British-Indian 14th Army, and Mountbatten were favourably inclined.[20] Mountbatten stressed that he was starved of military resources and any help that would speed his drive south towards Rangoon was, as he told the British Chiefs of Staff during March, 'a welcome bonus'. They would be doing no more than the Allies had done for Italy in taking some Italian forces into Allied service. Most importantly, he insisted, when figures such as the resistance leader, Aung San, became national heroes as they 'are bound to become', they would have achieved this with the British, rather than against them.

Mountbatten's Public Relations Division now gave wide publicity to Aung San as an 'example of patriotic resistance within the British Empire'. Again, these decisions were informed by Mountbatten's keen desire to counter the American critique of the British Empire in Asia.[21]

SOE were acutely aware of the potential legacy of civil affairs problems in Burma. Yet they insisted that previous experience in Europe and the Mediterranean had shown that the key was 'a positive policy'. During April 1945 they argued that the problem in Burma fell naturally into two parts. First, in the staunchly anti-Japanese hill tribes areas, the Kachin and Karen would give little trouble. All that was required here was 'a clear promise from H.M.G. that their special status will be preserved and their undoubted and unwavering loyalty recognised'. This simple, but important, criteria, we should note, would remain tragically unfulfilled.

Second, in the lowland Burmese areas, the main group, Aung San's BNA, were increasingly anti-Japanese and had SOE liaison teams working with them, but control was clearly going to be difficult. Having been both communistic and pro-Japanese, they were mostly now very disaffected. Nevertheless, SOE insisted that control 'is possible', especially if their SOE liaison officers were gradually transferred into CAS (B), to ensure continuity.[22] As Mountbatten had rightly observed as early as February

1944, there were few indigenous groups in South East Asia who had not treated with the Japanese in some way.[23]

These arguments reverberated at the highest level. In the War Cabinet during May 1945, Anthony Eden, Foreign Secretary, warned of the difficulties that most SOE-backed groups eventually caused, adding: 'Surely we must not boost these people too so much. They will give us great trouble hereafter.' Churchill agreed. However, Mountbatten skilfully couched his appeal in military terms and achieved some leeway. The Chiefs of Staff consented to a purely military agreement in which Aung San's forces were to 'work their passage home', a phrase that appeared with increasing frequency in British policy in Asia. Yet London cautioned against any degree of encouragement 'beyond what is strictly necessary for operational reasons'. Mountbatten secured these permissions just in time, for the BNA were turning on the Japanese and he barely retained a semblance of control.[24]

Dissidents in SEAC had to be restrained, including Air Chief Marshal Sir Philip Joubert, Deputy Chief of Staff for Information and Civil Affairs, who wanted Aung San arrested and shot. Joubert had to be forbidden by Mountbatten from communicating with the Governor of Burma.[25] By June 1945, Mackenzie was reporting that the various AFO groups were much larger than they had suspected, and action against them would have been, in his opinion, almost impossible.[26]

However, although SOE won this argument, SOE's big successes in Burma lay elsewhere. During early 1945 SOE in Burma carried out its most spectacularly successful military operations of the war. Their main focus was a series of operations employing the fiercely loyal Burmese hill tribes codenamed 'Nation' and 'Character'. The guerrilla levies recruited from these minorities in the hills now scented victory and were hard to restrain as the Japanese attempted to flee southward down the river valleys towards the coast. Guerrilla intelligence also multiplied the effect of Allied air attacks. Japanese casualties in SOE's Operation 'Nation' were estimated at between 3,582 and 4,650, while Allied casualties were estimated at between 63 and 88.[27]

SOE's Operation 'Character', conducted in the Karen area, met with even greater success and consisted of three main groups under Lt-Colonel Cromarty Tulloch, Lt-Colonel Peacock and Major Turral. By 13 April 1945, Tulloch's Northern Group commanded a local force of 2,000 Karen guerrillas. As the Japanese 15th Division tried to move south through the Karen areas in a race with the British for the key town of Toungoo, it was repeatedly ambushed. Toungoo controlled the strategic road south to Rangoon.[28]

Extended fighting developed with a force of 50,000 Japanese troops which continued into July. Remarkably, on 21 July 1945, Lt-General Sir

Montagu Stopford, commander of the British-Indian 33rd Corps, conceded that SOE's Karen forces had inflicted more casualties in the last month than the regular army.[29]

## SOE RENEGADES IN POSTWAR BURMA

By 1948, elements armed and trained by SOE or OSS during the war were ranged in battle against British forces in several disparate parts of the world. Yet no predicament was more curious than that existing in Burma, where renegade Britons from SOE still fighting alongside the Karens found themselves on the opposite side to regular British forces during a post-independence civil war that flared during 1949 and 1950. The renegade Britons were led by one of SOE's most distinguished officers and they now fought to assist the Karen hill tribes against the central Rangoon government.

The Karens had worked loyally with SOE against Japan during World War II, and SOE now considered them to be betrayed by the independence settlement of 1948, which also took Burma out of the Commonwealth. The Karens were one of the few Asian peoples who had proved to be unflinchingly anti-Japanese from the outset of the war. They had also been responsible for a jewel in SOE military crown, Operation 'Character', which had stopped the Japanese 15th Division in its tracks, the most substantial military achievement of SOE's war in Asia, perhaps in any theatre of World War II.

From 1948 the Karen cause was supported by network of senior figures in London, including Winston Churchill, now in opposition; Sir Reginald Dorman-Smith, wartime Governor designate of Burma; and Major-General Sir Colin Gubbins, the wartime head of SOE. The scheme to revive SOE assistance was masterminded and funded in part by Frank Owen, who had run Mountbatten's SEAC Command newspaper during the war and who was now Editor of the *Daily Mail*, a leading Conservative newspaper. Some funds from the newspaper were diverted to the Karen cause, while a former SOE officer was sent out to Burma as a *Daily Mail* journalist.

This 'private' SOE unit was formed on an entirely independent basis some two years after SOE was disbanded. It was driven by anger on the part of senior SOE officers and others from Mountbatten's SEAC HQ who had worked with the Karens in Burma and who felt that the Karens had been promised a degree of autonomy, or at least a state of security after independence, in return for their military efforts against the Japanese.

During the postwar independence negotiations in London, British officials were anxious to hand power to a unified central government, which in effect meant the lowland Burmese. Meanwhile, Aung Sang's socialist credentials were welcomed by Clement Attlee's new Labour government.

As in India and many other newly independent states, few guarantees were offered to minorities or small semi-independent states, and the new Constitution offered little to the Karens. After independence, and despite Burma's decision not to join the Commonwealth, London authorised loans, arms and the dispatch of a British Services Mission to smooth the transition to independence and assist in the smooth running of more technical elements such as the Burmese Air Force.

In February 1948, as tensions increased between the Karens and the predominant lowland Burmese elements in Rangoon, the Karens sought assistance form their old allies in SOE. The key individual was an extraordinary SOE figure called Lt-Colonel Cromarty Tulloch who had led one of the three main groups during SOE's wartime Operation 'Character'. 'Pop' Tulloch was an colourful character and typical of the strange figures collected by SOE during the war. Standing only five feet tall he was over 50 years old when he joined SOE in Burma.

Tulloch was almost a caricature of a British Army officer complete with a waxed moustache and a monocle. He claimed a remarkable history. Beginning World War I as a pilot serving under the Canadian fighter ace Billy Bishop he then insisted he had left in 1916 in order to drive the first tank into battle on the Somme in 1916. In the 1920s he claimed to have carried out pioneer parachute work in the United States.[30] By the 1930s, so he said, he was serving as an agent for SIS, moving through Nazi Germany in the 1930s disguised as an Arab carpet-seller. His close friends came to regard him as a teller of tall but amusing tales, although the claim of SIS work before the war seems to have some substance.[31]

In 1948 he began to organise air drops of supplies to the Karen flown out from Thailand and India and promised renewed assistance with training. His main go-between was Alexander Campbell, another ex-SOE officer who had fought alongside the Karens and whom Frank Owen had posted to Rangoon as a journalist for the *Daily Mail*. Meanwhile a steady stream of reports of mysterious air drops and shadowy European figures training the Karens in the jungle alerted the Burmese authorities and alarmed British diplomats trying to stabilise British relations with the touchy post-independence regime.[32]

In August 1948, Frank Owen, who controlled the London end of the scheme, decided that he would try and bring the British government on board by suggesting that they support a Karen-led effort oust the central government in Rangoon. Owen contrived a meeting at the bar of the Carlton Hotel, with Esler Dening and the senior official superintending all of British policy throughout South-East Asia. Like a rabbit out of a hat, Owen then produced Lt Colonel Tulloch. Dening was not ready for this and later

complained that the meeting was more than he had been led to expect and
the whole thing was 'thrust upon me'. Tulloch set out his ideas vigorously,
explaining that the Burmese Minister of Defence, the only Karen in a senior
ministerial post in Rangoon, and elements of the Burmese Army, were in on
the scheme. He insisted that the current Rangoon government would soon
collapse 'and plans were complete for his people to take over'.

Dening was possessed of an orthodox mind and was inclined to view the
world from behind a collar stud. He was not accustomed to discussing plots
against a sovereign state over beer in a hotel bar. His first instincts were to
warn Tulloch off. He had heard reports of Tulloch before, he had already
taken the precaution of checking that Tulloch had no current SIS
connections, and so felt free to threaten that HMG would 'put an end to his
activities' and, Dening added, there would be 'unpleasant consequences for
him' if he continued, but far from being intimidated, Tulloch seemed to
enjoy the vigorous exchange.

But the next day, Dening has second thoughts. Mr Abrahams, the
Managing Director of the Burma Oil Company had rung up 'somewhat
mysteriously' to request a private meeting outside the Foreign Office to
discuss the matter. If 'matters had gone so far' what, Dening asked, should
British policy towards this nascent rebellion be? Should they warn the
Burmese Prime Minster, assist Tulloch, or just let matters take their course?
Dening counselled that:

> The main thing to be avoided is that H.M.G. should appear in any way
> to be giving their blessing ... One the other hand, if the move is
> inevitable, it is not impossible that advantage may derive from it,
> though for all we know it may be ill-conceived and unlikely to meet
> with success. Colonel Tulloch is of course convinced that the new
> Burma will come back into the Empire.

Sir Orme Sargent, the Permanent Under Secretary, caught the essence of
the dilemma. The problem was having unwelcome foreknowledge of a
coup. If they did not warn the Burmese Prime Minster, and then the coup
failed, the plotters would claim in their defence that they had been in contact
with London. But if they did warn Rangoon then it would cause a wave of
arrests and 'this might easily precipitate the *coup d'état*'. In either case they
worried that in the confusion the Burmese Communists might make gains.
After much agonising the Foreign Office decided to tell Rangoon in vague
terms, while hoping to make clear that London was not backing the
renegades.[33]

Either way the scheme seemed to be on as substantial scale. It became
clear that Tulloch's ambitions included using the issue of nationalisation to
recruit long-term British business support for his efforts to overthrow the

central government in Rangoon. In the short term the scheme seemed to be financed by the Karens' ring of London supporters and by smuggling out gemstones from the region which were used to purchase arms from Australian black market suppliers operating through Bangkok.[34] Dening had enjoyed almost daily contact with SOE during the war as Chief Political Adviser to Mountbatten. He was therefore well positioned to appreciate the possibilities. He observed that SOE officers, by 'the very nature of their task' were often wild men and 'a law unto themselves'.[35]

London now sought more information about Karen support on the ground. In Rangoon, the head of the British Services Mission to the Burmese government, Major-General Geoffrey Bourne, held discreet talks with General Smith Dun, Minster of Defence and the only Karen in the Cabinet. Smith Dun was clearly implicated and asserted that the Karens 'definitely intend to attempt a *coup d'état*' adding that they were 'well organised and very confident'.[36]

The Burma experts in the Foreign Office were now required to make some careful calculations. 'However much we may sympathise with the Karens and prefer them to the Burmese' they were convinced that the Karens were simply too fragmented to gain control of Burma. They therefore appeared the wrong horse to back. After lengthy calculations, The Foreign Office concluded in September 1948 that 'we shall have to try and stop all this Force 136 [SOE] plotting'. However, Foreign Office legal advisers rummaged in vain for legal power to restrain figures such as Tulloch once they were outside British territory. All they could suggest was to warn Tulloch's group that 'if they fall into Burmese hands, they can expect no protection whatever from H.M.G. from anything which the Burmese Government chooses to do to them'.[37] By mid-September the Foreign Office had received reports of aircraft landing at jungle airstrips in Karen areas carrying supplies from airfields at Bangkok and Calcutta and 'with the connivance of the authorities there'. Meanwhile British Military Intelligence had uncovered Tulloch's plans to move more ex-SOE people into Burma.[38]

Dening's policy was primarily one of expediency. He told the Americans that although he did not like Tulloch, and was instinctively opposed to such freebooters – 'any legal action possible would be taken against them' – nevertheless the main reason for British opposition was that London just did not believe they could win. Dening conceded that if the Karen, or a combination of hill tribes should win, London would reconsider its policy.

Broadly speaking Burma was in a terrible mess and London 'would welcome any GOB [Government of Burma] that would crush Communists'. Rapid restoration of order was especially important for the British, given that the disturbances were interfering with rice exports to Malaya, and the last thing they wished to do was reduce the rice ration in Malaya with the Communist-driven Emergency having broken out there only a few months before.[39]

In October 1948 there was a new turn of events. The Tulloch scheme was a classic *coup de main* operation, using covertly smuggled arms and training to overthrow a government. It came close to success, but as with so many operations of this type, it did not remain covert for long enough. The weak link was Tulloch's communications. In Rangoon, the Burmese Special Branch, only recently transferred to Burmese control, were closing in on Alex Campbell. Tulloch's group knew all international mail would be opened and read routinely by the authorities in Rangoon. Accordingly, Campbell sent his messages to Tulloch by safe hand using an airline steward as a courier, but the courier sold them out to the Burmese authorities for $500 and an all-expenses paid holiday.

At this time Tulloch was in Calcutta, arranging further arms supplies. Tulloch corresponded with Campbell regularly using a British Overseas Air Corporation (BOAC) steward named Rowland Symons as a courier. But the inquisitive airline steward steamed one of the letters open and, on realising its significance, sold it on to the Burmese ambassador in Karachi. He then continued to work for the Burmese under a covername handing over further material. Thereafter, Tulloch's plans began to unravel. The intercepted letter revealed two recent arms shipments from Brisbane, paid for by smuggled gemstones. It also named other British SOE officers working with Tulloch in Burma.

MI5 in London uncovered the Symons connection when he was interrogated by Special Branch at Southampton. Their suspicions had been triggered by the fact that he was carrying large quantities of currency. Symons, whom they characterised as weak, shifty and 'a thoroughly despicable character', explained that he had acted partly out of political motives. He was sympathetic to the current Labour government in Britain and to the Socialist government in Burma. By contrast, he considered that:

> British business interest, possibly even the Tory Party as a whole, have organised and financed the Karen revolt, using Tory ex-Force 136 [SOE] officers as their instruments of this policy, in order to prevent the Burma Government from carrying out their nationalisation scheme.

In the words of Sir Percy Sillitoe, the Head of MI5, it was clear that the work of Symons was the principal 'pillar' on which the Burmese government had built their case against the SOE renegades.[40]

Once the Burmese had Symons' information they closed in on Alex Campbell in Rangoon. The Special Branch discreetly searched his hotel room in his absence and found further incriminating materials. He was arrested and confronted the prospect of a long spell in a Rangoon jail. The Burmese press exploded with anger when the story broke. For the Foreign Office, who had been attempting to persuade Burma to join the Commonwealth, and more generally trying to portray Britain as a liberal power, willingly retreating from empire, this was a disaster.[41]

The Foreign Office now identified Tulloch's activities as a major problem for British policy. This triggered a concerted effort by MI5 against the London end of the conspiracy. MI5 investigated at some length the group that was supporting Tulloch, who called themselves 'The Friends of the Burma Hill People'. To their surprise they discovered that this included none other than Sir Colin Gubbins the wartime head of SOE. It included Sir Reginald Dorman-Smith, a former Cabinet minister and Governor of Burma until 1946. Other founder members included Colonel Bernard Fergusson, a wartime special forces officer, various generals from the Burma War of 1941–45 and some Conservative MPs. Churchill's sympathies for the Karens do not seem to have been identified by the authorities at this time. Nevertheless the sensitivity of probing a scheme run by these senior figures was obvious, and so the investigation was directed by Sir Percy Sillitoe, the Head of MI5, and supervised on a day-to day basis by Dick White, then a leading figure in MI5 and head of the prestigious B Division, the counter-espionage section.

Dick White was possessed of an acute mind and quickly identified the most dangerous aspects of the developing situation. While Tulloch's activities were limited to Burma and neighbouring countries, the British government could plausibly disown this activity as the work of irritating renegades and hope to maintain good relations with Rangoon. However, White pointed out that MI5's latest discoveries revealed new developments that jeopardised this. He warned the Foreign Office that two former British Army signals experts, who had served in Burma, had been recruited to reinstate SOE's radio links between London and the Karens in Burma.

The Karen cipher had recently been smuggled into Britain, inscribed on a small piece of silk and hidden in the barrel of a fountain pen. MI5 knew the Burmese government operated wireless interception units and they would soon identify this radio traffic. White warned that: 'The Burmese government are likely soon to become aware that wireless contact has been established between the Karens and persons in the UK.' He continued: 'Should they become aware of [this] they could not help concluding that the British Government were conniving with the secret supporters of the Karen party.' Yet MI5 wished to proceed carefully because of the level at which the whole scheme was being played out. Dorman-Smith, for example was 'undoubtedly fully aware' of the radio link.[42]

In December 1948, Dick White and the JIC chairman William Hayter met with Esler Dening to talk tactics. For them, one of the most surprising lessons of the whole Tulloch episode, was the inability of the British government to take legal action against a British citizen abroad engaged in launching a conspiracy based in a third country. Even the radio net appeared to be legal, although they decided that MI5 should try and close this down by trying to 'catch them out' on some technical infringement of Post Office regulations.[43] In the event this proved somewhat easier than expected as they were found to making illegal use of Army equipment. Meanwhile, MI5 were active following up the backgrounds of other SOE officers alleged to be assisting the Karens.[44]

The most obvious step was quickly taken. The Foreign Office turned on the proprietor of the *Daily Mail*, Lord Rothermere, and asked him to answer for the actions of his staff. Michael Geddes, the *Daily Mail*'s legal adviser freely admitted the newspaper's involvement, but insisted that Rothermere was personally ignorant of the proceedings. Geddes insisted that the key figures there were the Chief Editor, Frank Owen and the Foreign Editor, Ewan Butler. Inevitably perhaps their days at the *Daily Mail* were numbered. Already suspected of being too close to Rothermere's wife, the Karen episode resulted in Owen's departure. Rothermere had apparently returned from a trip abroad to discover the Karen flag was flying from the flagpole at the front of the *Daily Mail* building. Inside the building a Karen delegation had been installed in an unused office, which they were using as their London headquarters.[45] Butler and Owen were quickly fired.

By now the whole affair was talked about freely in some London circles and journalists enjoyed it immensely. Philip Jordan, Clement Attlee's Press Adviser, recounted to his friends how Owen and Butler, 'had engineered a revolt in Burma, about which Rothermere the proprietor of the paper, knew nothing'. The episode was greeted with excitement: 'End of the affair was to be Owen marching on Rangoon with the victorious Karen Army.' However, now the plot had been uncovered, the senior staff of the *Daily Mail* were lying low for a while. Once dismissed, Frank Owen 'went off to Africa' while Rothermere decided to keep a low profile and 'went to the South of France to recuperate'.[46]

### 'IF CIRCUMSTANCES REQUIRE'

There are clear indications that the policy of the Foreign Office towards Tulloch and his renegades was ambiguous. Although London remained committed to supporting the central government in Burma for the time being, politics in Burma were volatile and the central government was clearly unstable. There was the possibility that the central government in Rangoon, which was socialist, might contract a relationship with the Burmese Communists, equally it might simply collapse. London wished to constrain Tulloch but at the same time keep its options open. This was underlined by the relatively gentle manner in which London dealt with Tulloch, who was still based in India.

British security officials in India used their local contacts with the Commissioner of Police in Calcutta to put pressure on Tulloch. They decided to proceed with care for they perceived Tulloch as both a problem and a potential asset. London was now only tentatively committed to the Rangoon government, a commitment felt more strongly by ministers in Attlee's Labour government than by officials. On 22 September 1948 one such official explained the dilemma, adding that:

> If, however, the present Burmese Government came to an arrangement with the Communists, there might be advantage to us in a Karen rising and consequently ... it would be preferable from our point of view that they should keep their activities in suspense rather than that their whole organisation should be broken up.

The approach therefore was one of 'frightening Colonel Tulloch out of India' but at the same time to avoid his arrest by Indian security. This was 'because, if detained, he would not be available if circumstances require a change of policy on our part towards the Karen movement'.[47]

Accordingly, the Calcutta police set about 'frightening' Tulloch. They had searched his room at the Spence's Hotel to see 'whether or not he had any wireless equipment' and then laid on heavy and conspicuous surveillance. Later, in a private meeting with British officials Tulloch explained he was in India to meet with Vallabhai Patel, India's Deputy Prime Minster. However, now he was leaving for London because, he conceded, 'things were getting too hot for him'. Tulloch was an unhappy man and was 'disgusted' with his treatment at the hands of British officials who felt they had missed a great opportunity. In a meeting with the Chief Security Officer at the British High Commission he recounted an alleged earlier meeting with Ernest Bevin, the Foreign Secretary, in the Ritz Hotel in London to explain his plans before setting out. However, is had not gone well as Bevin did not like covert activities. He claimed that 'in spite of the young nit-wits in the Foreign Office and Bevin's ignorance about South East Asia, he could guarantee to stamp out Moscow's sphere of influence in South East Asia so long as he was provided with the best part of £1,000,000 sterling'. Although he was departing , he boasted that 'his removal from the scene would make little difference to "the organisation"'.

Tulloch's presence in Calcutta had worried the authorities in London on other counts. It was clear that he was supported in Calcutta by a group consisting both Britons and Indians. Already coping with the Indo-Pakistan hostilities in Kashmir, they feared that he might be trying to exploit equally explosive tensions between India and Burma. One foreign official noted:

> I am afraid we have not finished with Col.Tulloch and his friends, and will have our work cut out to stop their pro-Karen fanaticism from setting Burma aflame. I wonder what Tulloch wanted to see Patel about, and whether it was to offer Karen assistance to an Indian invasion?

The Commissioner of Police in Calcutta had been most co-operative with the staff of the British High Commission, but he had acted without instructions from the Government of India. Delhi's attitude to the Karens remained unknown.[48]

Tulloch's friends were true to their word and an uprising followed. On Christmas Eve 1948, 300 Karen were massacred at a church service at Palaw by Burmese Military Police. The long-awaited Karen rebellion launched itself in January 1949. Even in 1948 the British Service Mission could hardly hide its pro-Karen sympathies, speaking of the Karens' strong military tradition, their leaning towards British ideas, loyalty during the war and of 'the widespread massacres of Karens by Burmese'. They also emphasised in their reports to London that the Karen rebellion sought not only a separate state but also to 'prevent at all costs Burma having a Communist Government'. Meanwhile they regarded the Premier, Thakin Nu, as a crypto-communist, notwithstanding the fact that the Rangoon government was simultaneously battling two other insurgencies by small Communist groups. The Rangoon government was not unaware of these latent sympathies among the British Services Mission which was nevertheless there to support their armed forces.[49]

Notwithstanding this mutual antipathy, the British Services Mission dutifully assisted in the counter-insurgency campaign against the Karens in 1949. Technical support to the Burmese Air Force, which inflicted severe blows on the Karens, was potentially decisive in stemming the Karen tide.[50] Meanwhile, on the ground, the British Services Mission witnessed the collapse of the Burmese Army, many of whom were irregulars, in the face of the more disciplined Karen force stiffened by Gurkhas who had lent their services. One fleeing government soldier remarked: 'I've had no food for three days. These Karens are killing us, and calling us sons of dogs. Today is the last day I shall fight for my country, tomorrow I shall go back to my village.' By mid-February 1949, Burmese government control was reduced to the area around Rangoon only.[51]

The Burmese Air Force received considerable assistance from RAF personnel in the British Services Mission, but the Burmese Army were more wary, rightly detecting a pro-Karen attitude among the British Army officers there. In May 1949 an American diplomat asked the Head of the British Services Mission, Major-General Bertram Temple, if he thought the coming monsoons would impede the government troops more than the Karens. Temple replied unhesitatingly: 'I certainly hope so.'[52]

The Karen advance of 1949 drew more ex-British personnel to their cause. The Karens later claimed that 18 British officers and NCOs were helping to train their forces. This included the notorious gun-runner Captain David Vivian, jailed in July 1947 for smuggling Bren guns and associated with the assassination of the first Burmese Prime Minster Aung Sang. Vivian was liberated from Insein Central Gaol, close to Rangoon, then the world's second largest prison, by the advancing Karen. He had then fought alongside them for two years. In August 1950 he was caught in an ambush at Moulmein and killed alongside the military leader of the Karen movement, Saw Ba U Gyi.[53]

The Karen successes in mid-1949 prompted further agonising in London. Should they continue to back the Burmese government or should they switch to Tulloch and the Karens, neither option was overly attractive. London pursued a policy of wait and see but in the meantime opened discussion with the Americans about the best course if the central government in Burma became weaker. In September 1949 Dening travelled to Washington for discussion with an American team led by George McGhee of the State Department. McGhee emphasised that the United States was taking more interest in Burma now that 'the dark shadow of Communism was creeping over Asia'. Dening stressed that the only viable course for time being was to back the central government and remained dead set against dealing with the Karens who he felt 'constituted the number one problem in Burma'. However, they had to consider the possibility that the central government might disintegrate and that Burma may descend into 'anarchy'. In this case, Dening argued, intervention by India might not only be possible but desirable. Dening believed that India alone was capable of the sizeable task of restoring law and order across Burma.[54]

In the spring of 1950 the Rangoon government began to claw its way back, recovering the road and rail axis from Rangoon to Mandalay. Malcolm MacDonald, Britain's charismatic Commissioner-General in South East Asia visited and tried to ease Defence Minister Ne Win's 'almost pathological suspicions' of the British. But their day-long river excursion was marred by the mortal wounding of one of Ne Win's party by a Burmese Army officer carelessly unloading his pistol. The incident was thought symbolic of the need for professional training from the British Services

Mission, but this remained under a cloud.[55] Nevertheless by the end of 1950 the Rangoon government had stabilised the situation.

The full extent of Churchill's support for these schemes remains a mystery. 'The Karens,' Churchill wrote to one of his staff in May 1950, 'who were our faithful allies in the War and fought better than anyone else, in fact the only ones that fought at all, were oppressed by the new Burmese Government and rebelled. I want to know more about the Karens.' Certainly, he took every opportunity to attack Attlee's military and financial assistance to the Rangoon government in the House of Commons and was visited by MPs close to the Karen group in London. Yet his support melted away in November 1951 as he resumed office. The Karen governing body now wrote to Churchill, expressing their thanks for his efforts while in opposition, and asking that he now intervene on their behalf. The letter was forwarded to Churchill by Tulloch, who was then residing in London at the Special Forces Club. However, the Foreign Office pressed Churchill not to reply to the Karens.[56]

The Karen insurgency, launched in early 1949, was blunted rather than defeated. Instead it lasted in the 1990s and constitutes one of the longest civil wars of the twentieth century. SOE officers who have survived to watch the ebb and flow of this struggle remain unrepentant. Campbell recently recalled that during the war SOE officers were advised to tell Karen chiefs that if they would fight with the British against the Japanese, their autonomy would be guaranteed. However, the Karens had not demanded such assurances and instead had simply fought alongside the British unquestioningly and out of loyalty. Many in SOE regarded the Karens as their most distinguished allies and certainly Alex Campbell felt that the renegade Tulloch operation was simply a matter of SOE paying its dues.[57]

## ACKNOWLEDGEMENTS

I am grateful to numerous individuals and organisations for assistance in the preparations of this study. Most importantly I mention Paul Elston and Rebecca Lewis of BBC Timewatch with whom I worked on the documentary *Forgotten Allies* (1997), documenting the Karen struggle into the 1990s. Members of the Fifth Indian Division Association and former members of SOE have also kindly shared their memories with me. Materials from the Public Record Office, the India Office Library and Records and the Hartley Library, University of Southampton and the Liddell Hart Centre for Military Archives appear with the usual permissions. I should also like to thank all those responsible for the implementation of the Open Government Initiative.

## NOTES

1. Slessor to Liddell Hart, 6 Sept. 1947, 1/644, Liddell Hart Papers, Liddell Hart Centre for Military Archives; Liddell Hart to Slessor, 8 Jan. 1948, ibid; Slessor to Liddell Hart, 22 Jan. 1948, ibid. Liddell Hart's change of view was clear from *Defence of the West: Some Riddles of Peace and War* (London: Cassell 1950).

2. Brigadier Prescott, CAS (B), 'Assistance to ALF Burma by Pro-Allied Burmese Elements', 13 Feb. 1945, HS 1/13, PRO.
3. Charles Cruickshank, *SOE in the Far East* (Oxford: OUP 1983) pp.208–9.
4. Mountbatten to COS, 11 May 1945, WO 203/2967, PRO.
5. Mountbatten to Stanley, 11 May 1945, WO 172/1763, PRO, quoted in Cheah Boon Kheng, *Red Star Over Malaya* (U. of Singapore Press 1981) p.156.
6. David Canadine, *The Perils of the Past* (London: Viking 1992) p.67.
7. The political background to these events is explored in depth in Judith A. Stowe, *Siam Become Thailand: A Story of Intrigue* (London: Hurst 1991) and in Michael Fineman, *A Special Relationship: The United States and Military Government in Thailand, 1947–1958* (Hawaii: U. of Honolulu Press 19997).
8. Thompson to FO, 17 Nov. 1947, F15320/1565/40, FO 371/63911, PRO.
9. Bevin minute, n.d. [18 Nov. 1947?], F15182/1565/40, ibid.
10. Bird to Donovan, 20 Dec. 1947, File 680, Box 73A, Donovan Papers, US Military History Institute, Carlisle Barracks, Pennsylvania. Donovan was head of OSS 1941–45.
11. Thompson to FO, 23 April 1947, F508/1563/40, FO 371/63910, PRO.
12. Thompson to FO, 19 and 20 Nov. 1947, F15371 and F15387/1565/40, FO 371/63911, PRO.
13. Entry for 2 Jan. 1948, Killearn diary, St Antony's College Oxford.
14. Liddell Hart (note 1) pp.53–9.
15. HQ 'A Group' Force 136 to Kandy, 1 Sept. 1944, HS 1/10, PRO.
16. Cruickshank (note 3) pp.176–7.
17. Bickham Sweet-Escott, *Baker Street Irregular* (London: Methuen 1965) p.245.
18. Mackenzie memo, 'Political Factors Affecting Co-operation with Anti-Fascist Organisations in Burma', 31 Jan. 1945, HS 1/16, PRO.
19. Conversation with Mackenzie reported in Coughlin to Donovan, 21 Feb. 1945, File 20, Box 20, Entry 110, RG 226, USNA.
20. Cruickshank (note 3) p.178; Sweet-Escott (note 17) pp.244–6.
21. Mountbatten to COS, 27 March 1945, HS 1/16, PRO. See also Dorman-Smith to Mountbatten, 20 May 1945, ibid.
22. B/B210 to AD4, 'Draft Letter for SO', 18 April 1945, HS 1/13, PRO.
23. Mountbatten to Hone, 4 Feb. 1944, C123, Mountbatten Papers, Hartley Library, University of Southampton.
24. COS to Mountbatten, 22 May 1945, HS 1/16, PRO.
25. Cruickshank (note 2) pp.180–1.
26. Mackenzie to Mountbatten, 'AFO and "Provisional Government"', 5 June 1945, HS 1/16, PRO.
27. Mountbatten, *Report to the Combined Chiefs of Staff* (London: HMSO 1951) p.173; Cruickshank (note 2) pp.184–5.
28. Over 10,000 casualties, Cruickshank (note 2) pp.189–90.
29. Stopford to Browning, 21 July 1945, WO 203/4398, PRO; see also 'Note of Operation Character up to 25.4.45', WO 203/54, PRO.
30. Terence O'Brien, *The Moonlight War: The Story of Clandestine Operations in South East Asia, 1944–45* (London: Collins 1987) pp. 242–9.
31. Bowker to FO, 28 Feb. 1948, F4171/1087/97, FO 371/69509, PRO; Glass minute, 13 Oct. 1948, FO 643/119, PRO.
32. The earliest report was probably the warning by Thakin Nu of British 'intrigues' and airdrops of arms to the Karens, reported in *The Rangoon Daily Herald*, 19 Jan. 1947.
33. Dening and Sargent minutes, 18 Aug. 1948, F10053/1087/97, FO 371/69509, PRO.
34. Minute by Dening, 17 Sept. 1948, F13277/1087/G, FO 371/69510, PRO.
35. Dening to Bowker, 16 March 1948, F4171/1087/79, FO 371/69509, PRO.
36. Bowker to FO, 31 Aug. 1948, F12017/1087/79, FO 371/69509, PRO; Bourne minutes of meeting, 28 Aug. 1948, F12730/1087/79 ibid.
37. Murray minute, 16 Sept. 1948, and legal adviser minute, 17 Sept. 1948, F12457/1087/97, FO 371/69509, PRO.
38. Bowker to Grey, 15 Sept. 1948, F12802/1087/79, FO 371/69509, PRO.
39. London to Sec. of State, 8 Sept. 1948, 8450.00/9.848, RG 59, USNA.

40. MI5 to FO, 26 Oct. 1948, F16055/1087/79, FO 371/69512, PRO: Sillitoe, Director MI5 to Head of SIFE, 26 Oct. 1948, ibid.
41. Harrison minute of discussions with D.I.G. Special Branch, Burma Police, 21 Sept. 1948 and 'Copy of Police Search List', FO 643/119, PRO.
42. MI5 to FO, 10 Dec. 1948 enclosing 'The Friends of the Burma Hill People', F17365/1087/79, FO 371/69513, PRO.
43. Hayter (JIC) minute of mtg. with Dening and White, 4 Dec. 1948, F17365/1087/79, FO 371/69513, PRO.
44. MI5 to FO, 11 Nov. 1948, F16054/10871/79, FO 371/69512, PRO.
45. M. Smith, 'Why Briton Faced Briton in Burma', *Daily Telegraph*, 31 March 1997.
46. Entry for 30 Nov. 1948, John Bright-Holmes (ed.), *Like It Was: The Diaries of Malcolm Muggeridge* (London: Collins 1981).
47. Minute to Laithwaite, 22 Sept. 1948, L/P&S/12/1378, India Office Library and Records.
48. Addison to FO, 1 Oct. 1948, F14416/1087/79, FO 371/69511, PRO; Shattock to FO, 6 Oct. 1948, ibid; Murray (FO) minute, 16 Oct. 1948, ibid.
49. BSM (48) P/9 14 Sept. 1948, DEFE 7/863, PRO.
50. BSM (49) P/4 31 March 1949, DEFE 7/864, PRO.
51. BSM (49) P/11 30 June 1949, DEFE 7/865, PRO.
52. Huddle (Rangoon) to Sec. of State, 1 May 1949, 8450.00/5-149 JAD, RG 59, USNA. see also London to Sec. of State, 1 July 1949, 845C.002/7-149, ibid.
53. *Empire News*, 20 Aug. 1950.
54. Memo of a Conversation at the State Department, led by Esler Dening and George McGhee,14 Sept. 1949, 845C.00/9-1449, RG 59, USNA.
55. Bowker to Bevin, 4 May 1950, DEFE 7/364, PRO.
56. Saw Michael to Churchill, 1 July 1949, 2/82, Churchill Papers, Churchill College Cambridge; Churchill to Conservative Research Dept. 4 May 1950, 2/39, ibid.; 475 H.C. DEB. 5s, 9 May 1950, pp. 235-8; I Po Kee, Sec. Kawthoolei Governing Body to Churchill, 9 Nov. 1951, F1015/72, FO 371/921238, PRO; Wilford minute, 2 Jan. 1952, ibid.
57. BBC Timewatch, *Forgotten Allies* (1997).

# 7

# Bombs, Plots and Allies:
# Cambodia and the Western Powers, 1958–59

### MONA K. BITAR

In 1954 Cambodia achieved independence from France. From that point in time the leader of Cambodia, Prince Norodom Sihanouk, conducted a foreign policy of neutrality. He believed that this was the only policy option that would guarantee Cambodia's independence in the alarming atmosphere of an accelerating Cold War. Yet Sihanouk's concept of neutrality was not merely an extempore Cold War construct, but instead reflected a much deeper experience of Southeast Asian history. In the early 1950s, Sihanouk had defined Cambodian neutrality as a bulwark against the age-old hostility of his irridentist neighbours, Vietnam and Thailand. It is worthwhile stressing at the outset that tensions between the regional players in mainland Southeast Asia – Vietnam, Thailand, Laos and Cambodia – have a long historical tradition. Moreover, the clandestine aspects of these deeper struggles frequently cut across the requirements of anti-Communism, as identified by London and Washington.

During 1958 and 1959, Sihanouk began to practice his policy of neutrality in order to counter the threat which he perceived from his neighbours, Thailand and especially South Vietnam. During the early 1950s, relations between Cambodia and her neighbours had deteriorated badly, fuelled by the tensions that were engulfing the entire world with division of nations into a bipolar structure. Increased tension between Cambodia and her neighbours had a significant impact on relations with the West, in particular the United States. It is crucial at this point to understand that Sihanouk held the US and other Western allies accountable for actions undertaken by both Thailand and Vietnam. Consequently, the response of the Great Powers to Sihanouk's grievances against his neighbours was hinged to the development of Sihanouk's conduct of foreign policy, and the protection of Great Power interests in Cambodia.

It is this complex triangle which is analysed here. It is asserted that the relationship between Cambodia and the US was terminally linked to Cambodia's difficult relationships with her neighbours. A key question is why Sihanouk held the US, and more specifically the CIA, responsible for Vietnamese aggression. The response of the United States to these tensions and disputes between Cambodia and Vietnam are examined in detail here. Remarkably, this was the case of a small tail wagging a large dog. Free World interests in Cambodia were largely determined by the level of tension that existed between Cambodia and her neighbours, indeed they became hostage to Vietnamese policy towards Cambodia. The importance that these issues exerted upon all those involved in US policymaking has not hitherto been fully appreciated by other historians who have tended to see the conflicts of this region in an exclusively Cold War framework.

Of primary concern is the reaction of the Western Powers, especially the United States, to these regional tensions. It will be suggested that the response of the Western Powers was counter-productive and further damaged Western interests in Cambodia. This essay will consider in some detail the problems that Washington encountered in the formulation of policy towards neutral Cambodia in light of complex regional disputes. Of primary significance, is the division that existed amongst the different levels of the US policymaking machine. It will be argued that these divisions caused, in part, a deterioration of US-Cambodian relations. The inability of the American State Department to form a cohesive policy, due to the conflicting recommendations made by the various embassies, caused Sihanouk to be increasingly suspicious of US motives. Confusion and inconsistency was read by Sihanouk as indicative of something more sinister lurking beneath Washington's overt policy and frequent reassurances. This had deleterious effects on the interests of the US, because it ultimately led to the formal recognition of Communist China by Sihanouk.

However, it was not only the divisions within the US policymaking machine that contributed to this outcome. The tensions between the US and France also greatly contributed to the disadvantaged position that the West faced in 1959. Notwithstanding that fact that the focus of this essay is primarily upon Britain and the United States, the tangential insights into the role of France remain interesting. Indeed because of the limited scope and scale of this essay, a comprehensive discussion of the issues of the period is not possible, and so selected and illustrative examples of tensions between Cambodia, Thailand and Vietnam during 1958 and 1959 are employed here to develop the main contention.

## THE SOUTH VIETNAMESE BORDER INCURSION INTO CAMBODIA, JUNE 1958

In June 1958, Sihanouk was outraged by a South Vietnamese incursion into Cambodia that set up a border two kilometres inside Cambodian territory. It was reported by Cambodian intelligence services that Saigon troops had invaded the northeastern province of Stung Treng.[1] The Cambodians called on the United States to intervene and obtain the withdrawal of the South Vietnamese troops. Sihanouk, in a personal audience with the US Ambassador, Carl Strom, requested that the US use its influence to convince President Diem to withdraw his troops. However, Strom is reported to have told Sihanouk that 'the United States could not interfere in a dispute between neighbouring states, both friends of the United States'.[2]

It is clear that Strom was under direct instructions from the State Department not to commit his country in any involvement in territorial disputes between the two countries. This was deemed of such importance that instructions were sent personally by the Secretary of State, John Foster Dulles, who emphatically stated that the 'Department wishes avoid danger both governments lean too heavily on US to attempt to settle disputes rather than taking action directly with other government reduce tension'.[3] The obvious consequences that involvement in this dispute would have on the numerous disputes between Cambodia and her neighbours was a clear determining factor.

Unavoidably perhaps, the incursion into Cambodian territory by South Vietnam had important consequences for US policy towards Cambodia. Although Dulles was extremely circumspect about involving the United States in mediating between Cambodia and Vietnam, it became clear to all concerned that the increased tensions between Vietnam and Cambodia would jeopardise Cambodian neutrality, indeed, it was plausibly argued that such incidents would push Sihanouk into a closer alliance with the Communist bloc, and in particular with China. This prospect generated alarm among senior circles in Washington. A full decade after the 'loss' of China, this event continued to reverberate on Capitol Hill, and any further Communist success in extending influence over the states of Indochina would cause enormous embarrassment to the Eisenhower regime. Therefore, the State Department reluctantly concluded that it had to confront the wider issue of Cambodian/Vietnamese relations in order to safeguard its interests in Cambodia.

A significant obstacle faced by Washington in formulating any policy on how to resolve Cambodian-Vietnamese tensions was the serious division of opinion that existed between the American embassies in Phnom Penh and Saigon. This division in policy caused, in part, a deterioration in the US relationship with Cambodia, for which America had to pay heavily, and resulted in Cambodia formally recognising China. The lack of decisive action and support from Washington convinced Sihanouk that he would have to call on the support of China, one of Vietnam's traditional enemies, to counter the threat of Vietnamese incursions into Cambodian territory, and thus formal recognition, became considered essential by Cambodia.

The US embassy in Phnom Penh was aware of the serious implications that the South Vietnamese incursion would have on American interests in Cambodia. This period was deemed crucial, and the embassy warned that Cambodia had reached an important 'crossroad', insisting that its future policy would be determined by the reaction of the West to what Cambodia saw as a hostile invasion, and a total disregard to its territorial integrity. Ambassador Strom was sympathetic to Sihanouk's ambition to find a solution to his problems with Vietnam through the instrumentality of the Western Powers. Strom was in no doubt that Sihanouk would fulfil his threat to call for support from China if Washington failed to take action with its Vietnamese ally.

These fears were strongly put to the State Department; Strom argued that although Sihanouk did not really want to enlist the support of China 'he feels put upon and abandoned. He believes that Cambodia's Western friends have been indifferent in his times of trouble...'.[4] Typically the embassy staff in Phnom Penh had assessed the incursion against the bigger picture of historical tensions between Cambodia and Vietnam. Unlike many at the State Department, the embassy team had learnt from the experiences of 1956 and 1957, namely that Sihanouk's neutrality was created with the specific purpose of countering Vietnamese aggression, and those on the ground clearly understood that Sihanouk's greatest concern had always been his fear of his large and powerful neighbour and not the unlikely advance of international Communism.

Therefore, the US embassy, in Phnom Penh, acutely aware of the need to reassure Sihanouk that Vietnamese intentions were not hostile, nor condoned by Washington, advocated a settlement between Cambodia and Vietnam. Strom proposed positive action by the State Department to this end and advised that pressure had to be applied on Saigon to settle its differences with Cambodia. Seeking to counter State Department arguments, expressed by the Secretary of State himself, that the United States could not tell the South Vietnamese government what to do, he argued that:

> In absence firm action by US, GVN [the Government of Vietnam] has acted and, in effect, established policy for West *vis-à-vis* Cambodia which is exactly contrary to policy desired by all Western Powers

represented here. Even if negotiations can be rescheduled, they will not succeed unless Diem can be persuaded GVN's self-interest makes success desirable. I do not believe we have any choice but to present matter to Diem as vital to his own interest and to that of West and to insist on negotiations with Cambodia in good faith.[5]

Predictably, the US embassy in Saigon firmly rejected Strom's proposals. Like the Secretary of State and others in the State Department, Ambassador Elbridge Durbrow was not sympathetic to neutralism. He told the State Department that 'from here Cambodia does not appear to be at crossroads but rather somewhat past that point along road to left'.[6] Durbrow argued that Sihanouk was using the guise of neutrality to further his own interests against Vietnam, and so was hindering the Free World fight against Communism. He argued that the tensions between Cambodia and Vietnam were being spuriously exaggerated, and that any accommodation of Sihanouk's grievances would encourage him to play East against West to his advantage, and at the expense of the United States. Durbrow expressed these sentiments frankly:

> ... I have personal conviction that Sihanouk for whatever motives he may have has deliberately elected to exacerbate Cambodian-Vietnamese relations and that time has clearly come for us to call his bluff... If, as may be case, Sihanouk is drifting more and more towards Communist China any efforts to appease him will only encourage him in his game of playing both ends against the middle. On the other hand if we bring him up abruptly I think we have a good chance of making him face the situation with greater realism.[7]

Durbrow failed to understand that Sihanouk had instigated threats to ally more closely with China, as a direct measure against Vietnamese hostility. At this point Sihanouk's tendency to appeal for support from China rather than the US is captured well by Leifer, who argues that 'the one-sided approach was a consequence of the apparent one-sided threat'.[8] There is no doubt that this was indeed the crux of Sihanouk's foreign policy, but Sihanouk's recognition of China has to be assessed against wider regional developments. Neighbouring Laos, governed by Souvanna Phouma, had pursued a policy of neutrality since the Geneva Agreements of 1954, however, in 1958, Souvanna Phouma was removed from power. His fall had been instigated by the United States, who had cut all aid to Laos as a protest against the strong showing of the Communist Pathet Lao in the May elections.

The new right wing government was determined to establish military control on all provinces that had served as regroupment bases for the Pathet

Lao. The CIA had been active in Laos as early as 1956, when it assisted in rebuilding the Royal Lao government's intelligence agency, the Service of Documentation and Social and Political Action (SIDASP) against the Pathet Lao. By 1959 both the CIA and the American 7th Special Forces Group had a substantial presence in the country, developing one of the largest military assistance programmes in Asia. This firmly entrenched Laos into the Vietnam War.[9]

Not surprisingly this caused great anxiety to Sihanouk. Sihanouk's greatest fear was, with a right wing, US backed government in Laos, the factional conflict would spill over into Cambodian territory and Washington would instigate similar measures against Cambodia. Therefore, any threat of aid reduction was anathema to Sihanouk. The recognition of China served as a safeguard against such an outcome.[10] After the fall of Souvanna Phouma, Sihanouk expressed his deep concern at attempts to involve neutral states in the ideological war: 'The Great Powers which aspire to be masters of thought to the whole contemporary world should understand that it would be no use trying to change our policy and to delude themselves that they will have won a victory if they can drag our country into one camp or other.'[11]

While the US attempted to identify what the best approach to the tensions between Cambodia and South Vietnam were, Sihanouk began to publicly threaten closer relations with China. Further to these developments it had become clear that Sihanouk was convinced that the United States not only condoned Vietnamese aggression but was also placing obstacles in the way of negotiations with Vietnam. Strom emphatically warned the State Department that immediate measures would have to be taken with the Vietnamese government in order to ensure that Sihanouk did not lurch to the left in a fit of anger.

There is no indication that the State Department had condoned Vietnamese action, the more likely scenario was that it was baffled by these developments and the accusations levelled by Sihanouk, but its inaction had been considered highly suspicious by Sihanouk. The State Department was 'astounded that Sihanouk believed US would not want talks between himself and Diem; that the US had induced Diem create obstacles to talks and that we attempting bully him with threat of reducing aid'.

It is evident that the State Department was greatly frustrated by Sihanouk's continued attempts to link US policy with that of Vietnam. This frustration was expressed to the embassy in Phnom Penh: 'It difficult know how to remove "dichotomy" in US and Vietnam policy towards Cambodia. We cannot require Diem to do what we wish.'[12] This frustration was a classic problem in US-Cambodian relations. Sihanouk had always remained convinced that the governments of Thailand and South Vietnam were puppet states of America and would not therefore accept that it could not control their actions. On the other hand, Washington was experiencing great difficulty in ensuring Diem followed US policy inside Vietnam let alone in respect to other nations. American aid and military support to Vietnam had not delivered political control. Indeed President Diem was legendary within the Saigon diplomatic community as man with whom it was impossible to get a word in edgeways. Contrary to Sihanouk's opinion, Diem was certainly not a biddable creature of the United States.[13]

The problem of getting Diem to comply with US wishes was perhaps most apparent at the American embassy in Saigon. Most likely frustrated by his inability to tell Diem what to do, Durbrow reacted to the tensions between Cambodia and South Vietnam by placing the blame firmly on Sihanouk, and he urged that Sihanouk's 'remarks accusing us of sabotaging his meeting with Diem are insulting and call for a very sharp protest'.[14] The problems faced by Durbrow are linked to the problems he faced in dealing with Diem. It had become increasingly difficult for Durbrow to persuade Diem to change his reforms that had created the ill-fated 'agroville' programme which had relocated peasants in order that the army could protect them. This forced migration had greatly withered support for the Diem regime, and had created further difficulty in the fight against Communism.[15] Durbrow wanted the United States to take a firm hand with Sihanouk, partly to leverage more cooperation from Diem. Counseling against this, Strom purported that 'Cambodia had legitimate grievances against South Vietnam and clearly Diem did not want a settlement'.[16] Therefore, Strom insisted that if a firm hand should be taken it would have to be with the government of South Vietnam.

The continuing tension between Vietnam and Cambodia and Washington's inability to respond to this dispute in a clear and determined manner, created a dilemma for the State Department and cost a departure from the Cambodia policy held since 1954 which stated that it would not recognise divided countries, under its policy of strict neutrality. On 25 July 1958, in a public radio announcement Sihanouk formally recognised Communist China.[17] American fears had been realised, and to a great extent, policy in the following months was centred upon damage control resulting from the formal recognition of China. And Washington feared that this move would mark ever closer relations between Cambodia and China, which would have serious consequences as the US had begun to consider larger-scale armed intervention in Laos. However its efforts continued to be hampered by indecision and division among policymakers.

In discussions about the recognition of China, Sihanouk had explained to Ambassador Strom that the Cambodian departure from its policy on recognition of divided countries was a direct result of 'Vietnamese attitudes over the last two years'.[18] Strom expressed concern over this departure and dutifully explained Washington's line. He highlighted the danger of new colonialism represented by Soviet and Chinese expansionism, and stressed that tensions between Cambodia and Vietnam would have to be resolved.

Yet Sihanouk put his response very clearly explaining that Cambodia's chief concern was hostility from Vietnam, he told Strom: 'despite US view, no Cambodian would ever believe Chinese were more dangerous than Vietnamese'.[19] The recognition of Communist China by Cambodia ensured that an important lesson had been driven home for the United States. Its containment policy in Southeast Asia had not taken into account the local 'systems' which involved deeper, long-established rivalries and tensions. After the recognition of China, Washington had to reassess its policy towards Cambodia, finally taking into account these fundamental regional tensions. Thereafter, great efforts were made at various different levels within the American policymaking machine to take into account the recent developments, in formulating policy towards Cambodia.

In an urgent meeting called to examine Cambodian recognition of Communist China, Brigadier General Hartshorn, Chief of the Military Aid and Advisory Group (MAAG), Cambodia, stated that the C-in-C Pacific (CINCPAC) 'considered Cambodia as the hub of the wheel in Southeast Asia in view of its location south of Laos and on the flanks of Vietnam and Thailand'.[20] Captain B.A. Robbins, USN, Regional Director, Far East, OASD/ISA, confirmed that although the Joint Chiefs of Staff had made no formal statement, 'one of them had recently expressed informally a view identical with that of CINCPAC'.[21] Pressing the point more firmly, Ambassador Strom encouraged the State Department not to 'eliminate or reduce its military or economic aid to "punish" Cambodia' in view of its strategic importance.[22]

Threats of aid reduction greatly alarmed Sihanouk, because of the drastic effect they had in Laos. Furthermore, there was a determined effort to avoid a similar situation to that which had helped trigger the Suez Crisis in 1956. These concerns were the basis on which US policy was formed and in a summary, the Assistant Secretary for Far Eastern Affairs, W. Robertson, expressed the State Department's opinion: 'we are all agreed that we should not terminate our aid program as a result of the recognition action since that would mean abandoning Cambodia to the Communists'.[23] However, it was agreed to give the Cambodian government that the aid program would be re-examined in light of its future actions, General Hartshorn stressed the importance of this 'because of Cambodia's neighbours who are watching the US reaction to this development'.[24] The United States could not be seen to be soft on Sihanouk because it had to prove that it was a controlling force in Southeast Asia, especially as the situation in Laos began to escalate.

Sihanouk's decision to recognise China had exposed a lack of control and had resulted in American loss of face.

The US military had deep reservations about Sihanouk's conduct of neutrality. As far as the military was concerned, some action had to be taken to prevent a deterioration of the balance of power in Indochina. The Chairman of the Joint Chiefs of Staff (JCS), General Nathan Twining, advised that American interests in the area would be best served by remaining in a position to 'influence the forces upon which Prince Sihanouk must eventually depend to take action to prevent further Communist encroachments in Cambodia'.[25] Naturally, these were the armed forces, which were the only possible stabilizing force if Sihanouk's drift to the left continued. The US military was pursuing alternatives to Sihanouk, after all, by the end of the 1950s support of military dictatorships was regarded as a tried and tested formula. Therefore, Twining advised that 'the United States must seek further to improve US-Cambodian military relationships rather than risk the sudden loss of hard-earned gains by withdrawing from them'.[26]

Such a relationship was thought to counter Sihanouk's personal power in Cambodia, and was considered essential, should an opportunity to remove Sihanouk from power present itself. Chandler and Field have both argued that the United States actively sought alternatives to Sihanouk. While this had been considered, such measures had ultimately been rejected because of Sihanouk's powerful and popular status in Cambodia. It is important to remember that Sihanouk's monarchical status was inimitable, his popularity with the people almost insurmountable and consequently Washington did not envisage that attempts to replace him were likely to be successful.

The consequences of the formal recognition of China on Cambodian policy was carefully monitored, and awaited. The United States was particularly interested in the outcome of Sihanouk's visit to China following recognition, but lack of American diplomatic representation in China rendered this difficult to observe first hand. There was great concern lest Sihanouk accept Communist military aid which would seriously threaten Western interests in Cambodia, and which the United States had gone to great efforts to avoid in 1957. However, it was reported by US Ambassador Strom that although Sihanouk had been offered both military and economic aid by China, he had declined the offer of military aid stating that he was satisfied with the aid he received from the United States and France.[27]

This move was greatly welcomed by both countries, although they and Britain were painfully aware that Sihanouk had paved the way to call in Chinese support against Vietnam should he feel this necessary in the future. The most likely explanation for Sihanouk's rejection of military aid from China is found in his continuing policy of neutrality. Having significantly moved away from the West by recognising China, Sihanouk was anxious not to overstep the mark and this measure was in all likelihood an attempt to restore the balance of external forces in Cambodia. Such manoeuvres were typical of Sihanouk's policy, and a pattern emerges throughout his years of power, whereupon the Prince swings first to one side and then to the other in carefully orchestrated manoeuvres.

As the impact of recognition of Communist China began to settle, relations between Cambodia and Vietnam became increasingly crucial. Arguably, from this point on, US policy and interests in Cambodia were hostage to the tensions between Cambodia and Vietnam, and to a lesser extent, Thailand. Sihanouk, having established formal relations between Cambodia and China, began, in earnest, to play his game of threatening to call in Chinese help if the United States failed to keep Vietnam at bay, or if it reduced aid to levels that were unacceptable to Sihanouk. This delicate balance of power, which had, to date, proved Sihanouk's policy effective, characterised Cambodian foreign policy, much to the chagrin of the United States, until the overthrow of Sihanouk in a *coup d'état* in 1970.[28]

Sihanouk's neutrality had always been considered a thorn in the side of Vietnam. It is ironic, therefore, that the result of the Vietnamese incursion into Cambodia of 1958 should have had such drastic consequences for South Vietnam. Vietnam and China had a long history of traditional enmity. Saigon was livid that Cambodia had formally recognised China. Having always been suspicious of Sihanouk's neutrality, his recognition of China justified South Vietnamese fears that Sihanouk was in fact a 'Red' Prince.

Towards the end of 1958 and throughout 1959, the Viet Minh under the leadership of Ho Chi Minh began in earnest to support the insurgency in South Vietnam. South Vietnamese insurgents were taken to the North, trained and sent back South, along with supplies. The tracks that were used have become infamous as the Ho Chi Minh Trail, part of which crossed into Cambodian territory. Therefore, the increased influence of Communists in Cambodia seriously threatened South Vietnamese interests. Many of the border incursions and battles that were fought between Cambodia and Vietnam were motivated by the belief that Cambodia was a safe haven for North Vietnamese Communists.[29]

Sihanouk had always denied that Cambodian forces had allowed free passage to the North Vietnamese Communists. Whether Cambodia was aiding these forces officially is not clear. The border could not be controlled in its entirety. However, the economic benefits that these brigades could confer on the Cambodian peasants in the border regions, most certainly influenced some hamlets to aid the North Vietnamese and indeed the Viet Cong. Such admissions are now readily forthcoming. In a personal interview, a respected Cambodian politician and academic, Dr Lao Mong

Hay, said 'I have relatives who benefited from selling rice to the Viet Minh and the Viet Cong.'[30] Nonetheless, the Vietnamese government was convinced that Sihanouk was deliberately seeking to help the Communist movement against Vietnam. It is not surprising, therefore, that elements in the government in Saigon, particularly Diem's brother, Ngo Dinh Nhu, who directed the notorious secret police and security services, hoped to bring about Sihanouk's demise.

Intelligence reports explicitly warned both the White House and the State Department about these Vietnamese machinations in November 1958. The State Department was warned that the Saigon regime now aspired 'to engineer Sihanouk's abdication or otherwise arrange his removal from power ...'[31] This information caused mayhem at the US embassy in Phnom Penh. Strom emphatically discouraged such action, arguing that even if it was desirable there was 'no evidence that there is any cohesive group opposed to Sihanouk that would venture to plot his overthrow at present. On contrary his prestige very high as result his recent tours'.[32] Strom advised the State Department to take immediate action to disabuse Saigon of any such measures, and continued: 'I hope Department and Embassy Saigon will fully appreciate that if a serious report of Nhu's plotting should reach Sihanouk, he will assume US knowledge of it and will react violently to the gravest detriment of our position [in] Cambodia and with resultant bad effect in area.'[33] While some elements in the United States may have welcomed the idea of the overthrow of the Cambodian leader, the American embassy in Phnom Penh understood that Sihanouk's popularity, largely derived from his monarchical status, did not facilitate such manoeuvres in Cambodia.

In subsequent discussions with Nhu, Durbrow was briefed in detail on Nhu's complex plans to bring about Sihanouk's downfall.[34] Durbrow categorically told Nhu, under instruction from the State Department, that the United States had seriously considered Nhu's scheme and that it 'had no indication whatsoever that any such plan would succeed and made it clear that it would not have US backing'.[35] This may seem surprising considering the level of covert action undertaken by the United States in Southeast Asia, but it is likely that Washington was still smarting from the failed attempt to destabilise Sukarno in Indonesia.[36] Striving to avoid such an imbroglio, Strom urged the department that a stronger line had to be taken and further representations be made to the South Vietnamese government. Strom feared there would be continued attempts by Saigon to undermine Sihanouk's position and that such

> actions will probably be clumsy and thus dangerous. Even if not
> clumsy, such manoeuvres on part GVN, which closely identified in

RKG [Royal Khmer Goverment, Cambodia] mind with US, would not
be constant with friendly assurances which Sihanouk received in the
US. Nhu has made it clear that GVN would like to get Sihanouk out
of power and that only reason it is not at present considering forceful
coup is that it does not seem feasible.[37]

Although Durbrow seems to have acted in accordance with his direct
instructions from the State Department, he did not agree with the embassy
in Phnom Penh. Whilst the fight against Communism in Vietnam continued
to escalate, those involved closely in policy became increasingly frustrated
by the antics of neutralists. Durbrow was sympathetic to the government of
South Vietnam who were convinced that any efforts to resolve their
differences with Cambodia would be rejected by Sihanouk, indeed, they
were convinced that Sihanouk wished to destabilise the South Vietnamese
government. Saigon did not understand why the United States did not take
a firmer line with Sihanouk. The accommodation of Sihanouk's neutrality
was anathema to them, the question why the United States was supporting
policies that were detrimental to the containment policies of the West was
puzzling when set against more robust American policies elsewhere. This
was highlighted by Durbrow, who argued that while the US position on
Southeast Asia was clear to the Vietnamese it was:

> difficult to convince GVN maintain its moderation in face of RKG's
> provocative actions, chief of which was recognition of Communist
> China. GVN feels this move poses most dangerous threat to security
> and very existence of Free Vietnam and proves insincerity of RKG in
> its relations with its neighbours. GVN may talk about doing things,
> but it is Sihanouk/RKG who, by their actions, have caused
> deterioration of free world's position in Southeast Asia.[38]

Furthermore, Durbrow reminded the State Department that while Cambodia
was an important nation, the 'Embassy does not believe US relationships
with GVN and RKG can be equated. GVN is, generally speaking,
responsive to US suggestions while RKG, although appearing to be
responsive at times, pays lip service and then does as it pleases.'[39] Durbrow
was highly critical of Sihanouk's policy of neutrality, as far as he was
concerned, neutrality was simply a tool used by Sihanouk to further his own
interests and the United States should not be held hostage to such tactics.

Sihanouk considered his grievances against Vietnam legitimate, while
Saigon believed that Sihanouk was actively undermining the position of the
South Vietnamese government. It is particularly interesting that the two
American embassies seemed to support the governments of their respective
countries. The inability of both embassies to see the broader picture

objectively offers a variation of the theme of the 'diplomat's disease'. This did not bode well for the State Department, in its attempts to formulate a cohesive policy towards Cambodia.

As tensions between Cambodia and Vietnam continued to rise, the question of the equality of the relationships between the United States and Cambodia and Vietnam continued to be debated at the relative embassies. Sympathetic to Diem, Ambassador Durbrow had relayed to the State Department that in a conversation with him, Diem indicated that he was increasingly disillusioned with the United States stating 'it was unfortunate Vietnamese public opinion was becoming more apprehensive about US support of Sihanouk who obviously tended to favour ChiComs while Vietnam was true friend of United States.'[40] Angered by this attitude, Ambassador Strom argued 'this question of relative worthiness of Vietnam and Cambodia to receive US support had beclouded the real issue for months. On basis its record Vietnam is clearly the more worthy. However this is not question at issue nor has it been during last eight months.'[41] Strom continued to insist that the main US objective was to deny all of Southeast Asia to Communist control and that this would not be achieved without 'some *modus vivendi* among Thailand, Cambodia, Vietnam, but particularly between Vietnam and Cambodia'.[42] It is perhaps pertinent to suggest that the objective of the United States in denying Cambodia to Communist control, could not be achieved without some agreement between the embassies in Phnom Penh and Saigon.

## THE DAP CHHUON PLOT, FEBRUARY 1959

Vietnam now decided to act. While the Americans continued to debate how the problems between Vietnam and Cambodia should be resolved, tension between Cambodia and Vietnam reached new levels. The Vietnamese government ignored the representations made by Durbrow, and the ouster of Sihanouk became subsumed into mainstream Vietnamese policy towards Cambodia. Perhaps the best illustration of Vietnamese attempts to destabilise the regime in Cambodia can be found in the notorious episode known as the Dap Chhuon Plot. This debacle sheds important light on the impact of Vietnamese relations with Phnom Penh upon the interests of the Great Powers.

Furthermore, the question of US complicity in this affair, even if only by officials at a local level, begs serious consideration. It has been argued by Sihanouk that his recognition of China caused such alarm, that the United States decided to abandon its policy of trying to woo Cambodia away from a position of neutrality to a more concrete policy which entailed his ouster. In his autobiography, Sihanouk explains: 'As was to be expected, the

setting-up of diplomatic relations soon stirred the fires of CIA wrath.'⁴³
Chandler seems to agree with Sihanouk's analysis stating that 'the plot
would never have occurred had United States policy in 1958 not tilted
toward dissidents in Cambodia'.⁴⁴ However, this episode in Cambodian
history is perhaps most significant in showing how the United States was
unable to control its Vietnamese ally, and the frustration and difficulties that
this caused in formulating any policy towards Cambodia.

The Vietnamese government had made a shipment of mobile
broadcasting equipment to the Cambodian dissident, General Dap Chhuon.
Dap Chhuon, governor of Siem Reap, and military commander of the
northwest, ruled the town as a personal fiefdom. He had become
increasingly dissatisfied with Sihanouk's neutral politics, and saw
Sihanouk's recognition of China as the advent of a pro-Communist foreign
policy. David Chandler and R. B. Smith have both argued that Diem, Nhu,
and the Vietnamese Director of Political Intelligence, Tran Kim Tuyen, all
wanted to eliminate Sihanouk. It was agreed that Dap Chhuon would be the
instrument of destabilising the regime. Dap Chhuon had ambitions of
removing Siem Reap from Cambodia and establishing an independent state.

Both Chandler and Smith have implicated the United States in this plot,
indeed as has Sihanouk. Chandler contends that President Eisenhower was
informed of the plot, and both scholars argue that the CIA officer, Victor
Matsui, was the coordinating agent. It has also been purported that Vietnam,
Thailand and the United States had all supplied equipment and funds to Dap
Chhuon. It is argued that Sihanouk did not know about US complicity until
several months later, upon which, he protested to President Eisenhower in
writing.⁴⁵

It is beyond doubt that the United States had some knowledge of the
plot. However, the extent of involvement remains a point of contention.
Ambassador Strom had continued to counsel against such measures and was
worried about the effects such plans would have on the Cambodian
government, whom he believed would inevitably learn of such schemes,
owing to the laxity of Vietnamese security. Strom urged the State
Department to put pressure on the Vietnamese government to break contacts
with Dap Chhuon: 'I believe we must insist in a most categorical manner
that GVN break off all relations with Dap Chhuon conspiracy ... and that
GVN simultaneously take positive steps for settlement of its principal
differences with Cambodia.'⁴⁶

The State Department's response to Strom's warnings was rather
curious, considering the impact such a plot would have on US-Cambodian
relations. It is interesting that no further measures were deemed necessary
by the State Department, who argued that: 'another approach to GVN now
promises have little additional restraining effect, but might easily

antagonize Diem to detriment US interests'.[47] Furthermore, the State Department decided to refrain from trying to mediate between Cambodia, Vietnam and Thailand, expressing exasperation, and distancing themselves from Sihanouk: 'US arguments in favour dealing with Sihanouk frequently undermined by Sihanouk's erratic and emotional behaviour which particularly over past year has served merely confirm Vietnamese and Thai distrust.'[48]

It appears that the United States had decided to back away and allow the matter to run its course. Yet, as anticipated by Ambassador Strom, events in Cambodia took a sour turn. On 20 February 1959, Dap Chhuon sent a letter to Sihanouk's mother, the Queen, informing her of his decision to form a party in opposition to Sihanouk. The latter confirmed that he was informed of the plot by the Chinese and French representatives in Cambodia: 'We received warning from the Embassies of the People's Republic of China and France, that something nasty was afoot.'[49] Therefore, on 21 February, armed troops were dispatched to Siem Reap, although the town was taken over, Dap Chhuon escaped.

Two South Vietnamese agents had been arrested at Dap Chhuon's residence, and thus the South Vietnamese government became conclusively implicated. This resulted in Sihanouk calling a Heads of Mission meeting at Siem Reap where a tour of the house and evidence of the plot were presented to officials. The British Ambassador to Cambodia, Garner, reported: 'I have had some experience of this kind of exhibition in Communist China and I have no hesitation in saying that I think this one was quite genuine.'[50]

Although Sihanouk did not initially accuse Washington of complicity, he was outraged that the Americans had failed to inform him of the plot. He told Ambassador Strom that he had received information of the plot from other sources and questioned why the United States had not been forthcoming: 'our [US] intelligence must be just as good as those three Embassies. He asked if we had information on the plot and, if we did, why we did not also inform him.'[51]

Chandler argues that the United States were 'able to maintain a lofty tone with the Prince' but it is clear that the State Department felt it necessary to launch an aggressive line of defense. The Deputy Assistant Secretary of State for Far Eastern Affairs, Parsons, instructed Strom to express astonishment at the idea of US complicity in such a plot, and accused China of inspiring the whole affair: 'we can only assume they inspired by efforts our enemies to destroy mutual confidence between Cambodia and US. They evidently attempting attribute to US own motives and actions including subversion [of] Cambodian institutions.'[52]

However, this argument did not have any local credence and the British

Embassy refused to support this implausible line. Garner told the Foreign Office that this sort of argument was unlikely to succeed and confirmed 'I am afraid to say that evidence of South Vietnamese complicity seems to be incontrovertible ...'[53] At this point the United States decided it must distance itself from the plot and the State Department instructed Ambassador Durbrow to approach Diem and stress that Vietnamese involvement in such matters in Cambodia was to the detriment of Western interests:

> Mention to Diem we have no indication as yet Sihanouk has appealed or planning to appeal to ChiComs for assistance, and therefore all the more important at present crucial juncture GVN refrain from actions or statements which would tend to push Sihanouk further toward Communists and seriously prejudice salvaging free world position in Cambodia.[54]

These measures, by any standard, were too little, far too late. It is evident that the United States had decided not to interfere in the plot but neither did it choose to inform Sihanouk of the plot. It is unlikely that the plot was CIA inspired, although the Vietnamese secret services were receiving substantial material assistance and training from the United States and to a lesser degree from the British. On 3 March, Dap Chhuon was captured by Cambodian forces under the command of General Lon Nol, trying to cross the border into Thailand. The Cambodian government asserted that he later died in captivity from wounds inflicted during his capture.

The fact that France had informed Sihanouk of the plot was highly damaging to Great Power interests. To compound the difficulties faced by the United States, France expressed serious concern over the damaging effects the Dap Chhuon plot had on Western interests in Cambodia, and French officials – convinced of US complicity – decided to tell the British Ambassador that they thought American action had undermined the entire position of the West in Cambodia. The Foreign Office confirmed that 'the French have informed me that the Americans were most certainly involved in the Dap Chhuon affair although they may have only been maintaining links with Dap rather than plotting with him'.[55]

French representations were also expressed directly by the French Ambassador, Alphand, in Washington at a meeting with Christian Herter, the Acting Secretary of State. Ambassador Alphand was disenchanted with US methods and told Herter that the French government feared 'that if no quieting element is introduced Prince Sihanouk might request the protection of some neighbouring country – that is, Communist China, or the latter may of its own initiative exploit the situation to "protect" Cambodia and eventually control it'.[56] Having been effectively ousted by the United States in Indochina, a significant element of schadenfreude was apparent at what France saw as the Americans' inability to deal with Sihanouk. Nevertheless, France maintained that US 'influence was essential to calm the situation in this part of the world', otherwise, fearing the most disastrous results.[57]

The United States responded to French accusations bitterly. Herter told Alphand that he was not impressed with US-French cooperation in Cambodia. Herter accused France of deliberately seeking to embarrass Washington. Choosing to cite two examples, the French Ambassador to Cambodia, Gorce, was criticised because he had been at the scene of Dap Chhuon arrest, but had failed to inform the US Ambassador, until after the fact.

More seriously Herter accused Gorce of a breach of confidence, Gorce had given a copy of a letter from Sihanouk to President Eisenhower, in which Sihanouk had protested the complicity of America's allies in the plot, to his colleague in Vietnam who passed the letter on to President Diem and had thus placed the US in an ignominious position. Herter, in turn, accused France of working to the detriment of Western interests in Cambodia, he pointed out that 'these actions appear not to have been calculated to advance the cause of common Western interests in the area'.[58] Alphand assured Herter that this was not the intention of France and asserted that the United States and France should work more closely together and that he would 'report the lack of cooperation to Paris'.[59]

The lack of cooperation between France and the United States and the consequent tensions that arose cannot be considered in isolation. They were symptomatic of wider American-French relations throughout the world.[60] The return of de Gaulle to power in 1958 was not welcomed with enthusiasm by the United States. A resentful de Gaulle had blamed the US for prolonging France's agony in Vietnam, especially as the United States had accepted a compromise peace agreement in Korea. The return of de Gaulle to power gave new life to the French desire to lead an independent policy in Cambodia. France was more accepting of neutralist policy *per se*. Indeed, France was attempting to pursue a semi-neutralist policy in Europe. Therefore, France's marginalised position in Vietnam and French acceptance of Cambodian neutrality spurred the French in Cambodia to make up for the deficit in influence witnessed in Vietnam. French policy became progressively more radical and independent. By 1963 the French secret services had been explicitly ordered by de Gaulle to severe all relations with the CIA.[61]

British Ambassador Garner partly attributed the tensions in Cambodia to: 'the Americans' desire to increase their influence and push the French out'.[62] Historically France's colonial position facilitated huge influence and popularity with Sihanouk and therefore, French officials in Cambodia enjoyed privileges and access which were denied to the Americans, and which were strongly resented by them. A good example of this was the way in which French officials were allowed access into the Cambodian military in order to ensure that French equipment was being used properly, while their American counterparts were denied similar access.[63]

It is revealing that the French position was unscathed even enhanced by the Dap Chhuon plot. The fact that the French embassy had informed Sihanouk of the plot had earned it great favour. The Cambodian leader rewarded French cooperation by publicly praising France in a press release, notably failing to mention the United States. Sihanouk stated: 'The French government has adopted a realistic attitude and has understood that Cambodian neutrality is useful to the equilibrium and peace of Southeast Asia.'[64]

The United States cannot deny some involvement in the Dap Chhuon affair. However, it is most unlikely that the plot was inspired by the CIA or the State Department. The Vietnamese government had decided to act with, or without, US support to try and bring about the demise of Sihanouk's neutralist regime. It has already been argued that the United States was not able to control Vietnamese actions. Frustrated by its own inability to sway the Prince from pursuing a policy of neutrality that was increasingly less favourable to the West, the United States appeared to allow Vietnamese plans to go ahead. The failure of the plot, and French cooperation with Cambodia intelligence over this matter greatly damaged America's standing in Cambodia. Sihanouk remained in sole control of Cambodian affairs and his popularity was unquestionable.

After this plot, it became evident to the United States that some settlement of differences between Cambodia and her neighbours had to be achieved. America's interests in Cambodia had been seriously jeopardised by the actions of the Vietnamese and Thai governments. Other than leave Cambodia to Communist influence, the United States had no choice but to readjust its policy towards Cambodia, taking into account Sihanouk's grievances against his neighbours. This was by no means an easy task. Volatile events in Cambodia until the end of 1959, continued to develop in such a way as to undermine the United States.

## THE LACQUER BOMB, 31 AUGUST 1959

Relations between Cambodia and the United States had plummeted in the aftermath of the Dap Chhuon Plot. Indeed, Chandler has argued that the plot 'permanently damaged US-Cambodian relations'.[65] The US embassy had the unenviable task of trying to improve relations. Ambassador Strom, was disenchanted with Vietnamese actions and he insisted that it was in US interests to become 'more fully involved and more directly committed to the goal of better relations among the countries of Southeast Asia'.[66] However, taking into account Sihanouk's distrust of the United States, Strom argued that the best approach would have to be multilateral. Strom pressed that Washington needed the support of its Western allies, in particular France, who had remained in a high-standing position with the Prince.

Notwithstanding these advantages, Strom conceded that if a multilateral approach was not considered feasible by the State Department or indeed, by the other countries involved, the United States would have to press ahead with a unilateral policy, or risk losing Cambodia to Communist influence. Strom acknowledged that a unilateral policy which applied pressure to Thailand and Vietnam carried considerable risks for the United States *vis-à-vis* its relations with those allies, but he argued strongly that Cambodia should be maintained as a buffer state against Communist expansion: 'that the prospect of losing Cambodia to the Communists warrants bold action on the part of the United States'.[67]

The British embassy in Phnom Penh and the Foreign Office, agreed that the developments of the last year had led to a situation which warranted multilateral action. Hence, the Foreign Office had instructed the British embassy in Paris to work towards this end, using any means available to enlist French support. The Foreign Office, deemed this of such importance that the embassy in Paris was told to: 'consider that a major effort is required to align Western policies on Cambodia and to make sure that there is no further deterioration in Cambodia's relations with her neighbours or with the United States'.[68]

However, this consensus of opinion did not extend to the State Department. Although the Director of the Office of Southeast Asian Affairs, Eric Kocher agreed that the tensions between Cambodia and Vietnam were the 'most critical problem in our relations with Cambodia, namely disputes between that country and neighbouring Free World states', he could not agree with the recommended course of action put forward by the American embassy in Cambodia, nor by the Foreign Office.[69]

Unlike those on the ground in Cambodia, and those at the Foreign Office, Kocher, was adamant that Sihanouk's neutrality policy was not only an animus towards South Vietnam, but also actively undermined the position of the West in the whole of Southeast Asia. Kocher did not believe that Sihanouk should be rewarded for his neutralist 'antics'. Kocher highlighted the need to bring Sihanouk into line, and he reported to the Assistant Secretary of State for Far Eastern Affairs, Robertson, 'I believe that the Embassy places disproportionate emphasis on the need for a change in Free World policy toward Cambodia and does not fully take into account the other side of the coin, namely the need for a more rational attitude on the part of Sihanouk toward Cambodian relations with its neighbours.'[70]

In conjunction, Kocher argued that the United States should not seek to impose policy on Vietnam as this was against the primordial tenets of American foreign policy: 'it is not part of United States policy to impose our concepts on any sovereign government and I believe the substance of the embassy's recommendations is contrary to this principle'.[71] Such principles were admirable, but analysed against the background of American actions in neighbouring Laos, it seems unlikely that US policy would be governed by ethics, or even respect for international law. Moreover, during 1958 the United States had been intensively engaged in subversive policy in Indonesia, involved in an attempt to pressurise Sukharno.[72] It is much more likely that such arguments were presented as a guise to the actual problem of the limited pressure that the Americans could apply on President Diem.

Although sympathetic to the difficulties facing the State Department, the Foreign Office did not accept that the main problem rested with Sihanouk. It was clear to British policymakers that South Vietnam was responsible for attempts to destabilise the Sihanouk regime and therefore, it was no surprise, that the Prince had reacted vehemently. Indeed, the Foreign Office had become rather exasperated at the State Department's attitude, which did not accept that Vietnam had to be held accountable for its covert actions in Cambodia. Butler expressed this dissatisfaction clearly: 'One wonders whether it has sufficiently sunk into the State Department that Prince Sihanouk has a legitimate grievance against his neighbours and considers that he has one against the United States.'[73]

In addition, the Foreign Office, did not think that the United States had exerted enough pressure on the Vietnamese government: 'As regards the Vietnamese I am very doubtful whether the Americans have in fact done enough.'[74] There was considerable fear, that if Vietnamese meddling in Cambodian affairs was not halted, Cambodia would inevitably seek Chinese support.

The State Department continued to be intransigent about the proposed policy. Kocher cogently argued that the proposed policy had dangerous implications because it would 'carry the grave risk of confirming the opinion held by Cambodians (and other neutrals) that the acceptance of United States aid and the adoption of a strong, public anti-Communist policy by a nation automatically convert it into a pliant satellite of the United States'.[75] With specific reference to the proposed approach of the embassy, Kocher warned that such policy would involve the United States to act as mediator in disputes which could not necessarily be solved due to age-old animosities. While this was true, US mediation could have carried significant weight in reducing the tension between Cambodia and Vietnam and a promotion of a more conciliatory atmosphere would have served

Washington well. Ultimately, Sihanouk only sought security guarantees against perceived Vietnamese ambitions to encroach on Cambodia.

However, a secondary concern was highlighted by Kocher, he warned that 'United States readiness to become involved carries the risk of prompting Sihanouk to magnify minor incidents with the assurance of attracting attention and using them as leverage against Thailand and Vietnam'.[76] The Foreign Office, rather impotent in the face of State Department arguments conceded that: 'an opportunity of doing something to reconcile the Cambodians and the Vietnamese is now being missed'.[77]

Having rejected the recommendations of the US Embassy in Phnom Penh and the British Foreign Office, the State Department proposed a different approach to the problem of Cambodian and Vietnamese relations. The State Department decided that the first step would have to be a high level visit from the United States to the region in an informal attempt to encourage Cambodia, Vietnam and Thailand to adopt a more conciliatory stance towards each other. Consequently, the Deputy Assistant Secretary of State for Far Eastern Affairs, Parsons, was dispatched to the region. Advancing the merits of this visit, Kocher argued that 'these steps, while not constitution of United States involvement in Cambodian disputes, should demonstrate active United States interest in the problems of the area. Furthermore, they are intended to restrain the type of irresponsible and ill-advised action by the three countries concerned which constitute a major irritant to relations among them'.[78]

Several interesting themes are illuminated by the visit by Parsons to the region. The State Department had advocated this visit, not only to contribute to an easing of tensions between Cambodia and her neighbours, but also perhaps more importantly, Parsons was relegated to the task of trying to unify policy recommendations from the embassies in Saigon and Phnom Penh. The conflicting advice that the State Department had received from the embassies in Phnom Penh and Saigon had made it increasingly difficult to formulate policy on Cambodia, and had led to harm in the past. This division of US policy in Indochina had already been recognised by Britain as a problem in furthering the interests of the West in the region and in a telling remark, Butler stated: 'The trouble with the Americans is that, as so often, they speak with several voices in Indochina.'[79] This was not a problem unique to Indochina, it is testament to the general characteristics of US foreign policy throughout the world.

The visit by Parsons to the region was noteworthy for several reasons. Although Parsons was not able to identify any new problems, the State Department, for the first time, began to take seriously the effects of tensions between Cambodia and her neighbours, and the need for drastic action to halt Cambodia's drift eastwards. Furthermore, the difficulties that had faced the State Department in formulating policy and the extent of French obstructionism to furthering American interests in the region were clearly highlighted.

Addressing the issue of Cambodian-Vietnamese relations, Parsons concluded that the atmosphere was 'more thoroughly poisoned with emotion and suspicion than I had comprehended ...'[80] The former lack of appreciation of the importance of these regional conflicts by the United States had severely hindered the ability of the State Department to carry out its policy. This confirmed its tendency to ignore the dynamics of small-system conflicts within the broader picture of the conflict between East and West. In a fresh analysis of the problems between Cambodia and Vietnam, Parsons concluded that Cambodian hostility towards Vietnam, did not actually mean that Cambodia was embracing Communism, nor did it desire to. Parsons argued, that Cambodia 'is in my view anti-Communist and had a lively appreciation of Communist danger to Cambodia' but had threatened to call in Chinese support purely because it genuinely felt threatened by Vietnamese hostility.[81]

Nevertheless, Parsons explained Vietnamese hostility towards Cambodia in the context of the Vietnam War. Despite the historical tensions between Cambodia and Vietnam, Parsons argued that the South Vietnamese government was convinced that the Cambodian border area was a haven and breeding ground for their Communist enemies, and believed that Sihanouk was supporting their cause under the guise of his neutrality policy. He concluded that the Vietnamese government's:

> contempt for Sihanouk and Cambodians is undisguised and this obviously compounds difficulty. ... In fact I fear there persists a restless desire to get rid of Sihanouk, and Cambodians, fortified by ample evidence of maladroit GVN efforts to this end, are deeply suspicious of GVN and of us as friends of GVN. Atmosphere on both sides is thus thoroughly poisoned and no Vietnamese whom I saw showed any responsiveness to Durbrow's and my reiterated suggestions that they continued to seek basis for negotiation ...[82]

Added to these difficulties, Parsons also highlighted another serious factor that had undermined the US position in Cambodia. Parsons argued that the French in Cambodia, who enjoyed a privileged position with Sihanouk, had been actively undermining the standing of the United States in order to maintain their influence. He summarised:

> Apart from psychopathic attitude of each country toward the other, United States objectives are being frustrated, I believe by a second factor of some importance in Cambodia, namely attitude and

influence of French Ambassador Gorce and his number two. Neither of these officials are career diplomats but rather relics of colonial past and I heard no good of either as regards their narrow and self-serving attitude.[83]

In seeking to resolve these issues, Parsons had two immediate recommendations for the State Department. He stated that 'it is proven fact that Vietnam had sought to overthrow legitimate government of its neighbour and has thereby jeopardised free world position in Southeast Asia'.[84] Consequently he advised that the State Department should warn President Diem to forbid any Vietnamese involvement in plotting against Cambodia and ensure this by threatening to reduce aid to Vietnam if its involvement continued. Second, he believed the United States must put pressure on the Quai d'Orsay to 'cure French representation in Phnom Penh ... The French have considerable influence in Cambodia, notably with Sihanouk, and we must enlist support in counteracting what otherwise could be a disastrous turn of events for Cambodia, France and the United States.'[85]

In response to these fresh recommendations American policy shifted. Kocher agreed that the Vietnamese government had now to be warned against continued interference in the internal affairs of Cambodia and that a further US approach to President Diem was necessary; 'we believe that fundamental US as well as Vietnamese interests in the area require an acceptance of Sihanouk's continued possession of political authority in Cambodia, discontinuation of manoeuvres against him, and efforts by the GVN to work with him.'[86] However, Kocher continued to argue that any accusations or criticism of the Vietnamese government would have to be cautious and based on concrete proof of Vietnamese involvement in order not to damage US-Vietnamese relations.

Furthermore, Kocher was adamant that Washington could not threaten reduction of aid to Vietnam, 'cuts in aid would throw Vietnam further behind North Vietnam, not good for US interests'.[87] Kocher stressed again that South Vietnam was an ally of the United States whilst Cambodia refused to rally to the Free World cause. Furthermore, the cautious approach to Vietnam was indicative of the problems that the United States was encountering with the Diem regime, division of policy within Vietnam had reached such levels that meetings have been described as 'barely civil'.[88]

The added problem of French obstructionism did not surprise the State Department. Allegations of undermining the position of the United States were taken very seriously, and the State Department was determined that efforts would have to be made to bring French policy in line. The actions of the French Ambassador to Phnom Penh over the Dap Chhuon affair had been deplored by the United States and representations had been made at high levels in Washington by Herter, while Acting Secretary, as previously noted. Repeated representations had been made to France regarding Ambassador Gorce's behaviour, notably by Parsons and Robertson, to J. Dardian, the French Director General of Political and Economic Affairs at the Foreign Ministry, in February, on two occasions and also by the Under Secretary of State for Economic Affairs, C. Dillon, to the Secretary General of the French Foreign Office, L. Joxe, in April.[89]

Despite these numerous protests, French behaviour had not changed noticeably, the French government were not inclined to support the Americans in Cambodia, while US support for France in North Africa continued to lag.[90] Kocher agreed that a stronger line had to be taken with the French government, accusing France of deliberate malfeasance, notably through the actions of their Ambassador in Phnom Penh: 'Gorce on repeated occasions undertook unilaterally actions which had the effect of seriously undermining Cambodian confidence in the US and of further weakening Sihanouk's orientation toward the Free World.'[91] Kocher continued that the protest would have to 'emphasize that by reason of the favourable position enjoyed by France in Cambodia, French representatives there are in a particularly advantageous position to exert influence on Sihanouk' and therefore, the United States would 'urge the French Government to see that the extensive French influence in Cambodia is exercised so as to strengthen Sihanouk's orientation toward the Free World...Suggest that toward this end particular attention be given to selection and guidance of French representatives in Cambodia'.[92]

The importance of a coherent and cohesive strategy by the United States and France had long been advocated in vain by the British government. The British Ambassador in Phnom Penh, Garner, had acted as interlocutor on several occasions, but had been thwarted by the level of mistrust and rivalry between French and US officials. His frustration was clearly evident:

> The Americans should realise that it will pay them to work through the French ... and that the French should realise that it will be in their own interest to induce the Cambodians to allow the Americans a greater say in things; after all, if the Americans were ever ... to pack up and leave Cambodia, French interests here would inevitably go down the drain along with everything else.[93]

It is against this background that the State Department launched a new initiative to resolve the problems faced in keeping Cambodia in a position that was favourably inclined to the West. This initiative was marked by the change of the American Ambassador in Phnom Penh. Strom's replacement, William Trimble, was instructed to work more closely with his counterpart in Saigon, and to coordinate State Department policy towards Indochina.

Simultaneous to this initiative, the State Department sought to improve relations with France in pursuance of Free World interests in Cambodia.

The problems facing the United States in Cambodia, as identified by Parsons, were confirmed in a National Intelligence Estimate regarding Cambodia's international orientation which stated 'the counterbalancing of Communist influence in Cambodia has suffered because the French and the US have sometimes worked at cross purposes'.[94] Furthermore, the estimate concluded that the United States and Vietnam would have to accept that there was no alternative to Sihanouk in Cambodia because he remained 'the dominant figure in the Cambodian scene'.[95] The estimate warned that the tensions between Cambodia and Vietnam were unlikely to be resolved immediately but it was of paramount importance for the United States to become more involved in the disputes between the two neighbours, because 'a Thai or Vietnamese-sponsored move against the impulsive Sihanouk might drive him to some hasty action which could damage US interests in Southeast Asia'.[96]

In light of the above, and agreement by all parties concerned with American policymaking in Cambodia, the State Department sent an authoritative message to the embassies in Phnom Penh, Saigon, and Paris, which had been cleared at high levels, re-stating the Department's views on the problems facing the United States in Cambodia. It was agreed that the US would take further action to ensure that Vietnam did not interfere in Cambodia's internal affairs, and accepted that US involvement in specific issues would have to be considered although the 'Department as yet perceives no purpose to be served by formal direct US involvement this time and considers background role comprising primarily cautious exertion influence on both parties to take initiative (or desist from certain actions) most useful for present'.[97]

Furthermore, the Department stressed the need for France and the United States to cooperate in order to benefit the position of the West in the region, stating that it believed it was 'essential maintain close contact and coordinate major US actions with French in order to minimize French resentment and possibility further French unilateral actions harming US and Free World interests ...'.[98]

However, the Department warned that the likelihood of improved US-French cooperation was stymied by the 'probability French in Cambodia concerned primarily with maintenance French position including retention Sihanouk's favour and in view of past divergences US and French views on Southeast Asian problems ...'.[99] Notwithstanding this difficulty, the State Department instructed the various embassies to make the governments of Cambodia, Vietnam and France fully aware of 'US policy encourage improvement relations between GVN and RKG'.[100]

This new policy had direct results. One of the main developments after this decision to take a more direct role in Cambodian-Vietnamese relations, and to inform and work more closely with France towards this end, was a secret meeting of Sihanouk and Diem, in the first week of August 1959. This meeting was suggested by the American embassy in Saigon and agreed to by the American embassy in Phnom Penh, and was facilitated by the agreement of French officials 'who promised cooperation in attempting to improve relations between Cambodia and South Vietnam and Cambodia and the United States'.[101] Considerable mileage had been gained by this high-level meeting and all parties concerned had expressed positive views about *rapprochement*.[102]

However, the meeting was in vain. Despite the State Department's efforts to align South Vietnamese policy towards Cambodia, and the improvement of relations after the Diem-Sihanouk meeting, the South Vietnamese government did not change its policy towards Cambodia. This was highlighted by a further assassination attempt on Sihanouk which involved a bomb disguised as a gift to him. In common with previous Vietnamese efforts, this venture had also failed. The United States had not been informed of this latest venture and it was increasingly evident that US interests were being jeopardized by the scheming of Diem and Nhu. However, the reaction of the State Department to this disaster was notably different, and consequently, the bomb attack was not as damaging to American interests as would have been expected. It is highly probable that the State Department reacted with more vigour, because Diem and Nhu had failed to inform the United States of their plans, indeed, they had acted in direct opposition to what Washington had been trying to achieve.

On 31 August 1959, a bomb exploded in the Royal Palace killing the Cambodian Protocol Director and wounding several others. The bomb had been hidden in a lacquer box which was delivered as a gift to the Queen but the King and Queen had left the room shortly before the explosion. The Cambodian government was convinced that the Cambodian dissident Sam Sary was responsible for the attempted assassination attack with the backing of the Vietnamese government.[103] The American embassy in Phnom Penh reported that although they were by 'no means convinced GVN still backing Sam Sary, if it is, feel GVN is betting on man with no popular support and that it overlooks probability that in any revolutionary situation here most likely gainers would be Communists'.[104] The embassy therefore, strongly urged that the US intelligence services throughout Southeast Asia to 'redouble search for information who actually responsible for 31 August bomb attempt, since we need to know in order to formulate our own position'.[105] Furthermore, the embassy in Phnom Penh urged the State Department and Ambassador Durbrow in Saigon to 'discuss the matter candidly' with Diem.[106]

Durbrow was in full agreement with Trimble, and he stressed: 'if we are not to lose ground gained from Sihanouk-Diem meeting and if we want prevent possible serious deterioration relations and Cambodian swing to left I should see Diem soonest. Under instruction I should tell him how serious situation can become for whole Free World position Southeast Asia unless he as statesman joins us in overcoming Sihanouk's growing belief Sam Sary, with possible GVN connivance, carried out palace bombing.'[107]

Durbrow noted that although representations to Diem in the past had not been effective, the United States was now in a stronger position because it had obtained concrete evidence of Vietnamese involvement in the Dap Chhuon plot which the Vietnamese government had previously denied. Durbrow urged the State Department to allow him to take a strong line with Diem because he was of the 'firm belief "clever" Nhu has convinced Diem they can go ahead with their stupidities no matter what we say because we "need" Vietnam and would not dare take any drastic step to hurt them'.[108] The State Department responded rapidly to these requests and Durbrow met Diem on 25 September 1959.

Further to this meeting Durbrow saw Diem again on 7 October, and provided him with concrete information regarding Vietnamese plotting in Cambodia, Diem assured Durbrow that no such activities were authorised but that he would order an investigation. In a further *démarche* on 27 October, Durbrow under instruction questioned Diem about his investigations and although it was reported that the Vietnamese President did not admit the accuracy of US reports, he appeared to be 'very embarrassed' and Durbrow believed that there would be a reduction in Nhu's anti-Cambodian activities in the future.[109] Durbrow's reaction to this affair was vastly different to the Dap Chhuon Plot, his frustration with Diem and Nhu is underlined here. However, the envoy's faith that Vietnamese conspiracies would cease seems to be misplaced. Increasingly, in a variety of spheres, US representatives and envoys had difficulty to get Diem to listen to them for five minutes, let alone follow guidance.

Unlike previous occasions the US response was rapid, and indeed the State Department had not hesitated to confront Diem about the matter. Sihanouk was aware of this change in tactics by the United States and this boded well for relations with Cambodia. Both embassies in Phnom Penh and Saigon had acted cohesively and as a result the situation was dealt with far more effectively. This improved coordination between the embassies was highlighted by the meeting of Ambassadors Durbrow, Johnson (Laos) and Trimble in December 1959, in which they discussed the situation in Indochina and reported collectively to Parsons, on the interests and problems facing the United States in the region.[110] Parsons in a telegram to the ambassadors stressed his appreciation of their collective policy suggestions and made preliminary comments on proposed policy.[111] The new initiative by the United States to become more directly involved in Cambodian/Vietnamese relations and to work more closely with French officials in Phnom Penh, was rewarded by improved relations between Cambodia and the United States. The August bomb had not damaged relations further, but it must be stressed that as far as Sihanouk was concerned, the United States continued to be the recipient of genuine mistrust.

CONCLUSIONS

The years 1958 and 1959 are critical in providing an understanding of Sihanouk's neutrality policy. It is in this period that it became clear that the tensions between Cambodia and her neighbours would be the determining factor in how positive a position of neutrality Sihanouk took. Furthermore, the impact of this resulted in the United States having to reassess its policy towards Cambodia in order to take into account the regional disputes. This period also highlighted the fact that Sihanouk's neutrality policy could not be dispensed with but would have to be approached in a manner that would make him more favourable to the West, even if this was at the expense of weakening the relationship between the West and other nations in the region. This stands in contrast to US policy towards other leaders in Asia regarded as troublesome neutrals, including Sukarno and Nehru.

The problems that faced the United States in formulating policy towards Cambodia had important consequences. The inability to formulate a coherent and cohesive policy greatly affected US prestige in Cambodia. Divisions within the United States policy-making machine had to be addressed before it could hope to further its own interests in Cambodia. Furthermore, the division and differences between the United States and France also had a significant impact on Great Power interests. It became clear that successful implementation of containment policy largely depended on the ability of the United States and France to work together in pursuance of their collective objectives rather than seek their own self-serving interests.

Secret services exacerbated the problem of co-ordinating Western policy. Clearly American attempts to develop a substantial Thai and Vietnamese capability in this area had allowed both Bangkok and Saigon an enhanced sense of independence in terms of regional intervention. Even among the major powers there were doubts about the controllability of their own secret service activities. The American ambassador in Jakarta had recently endured the unpleasant experience of being perilously underinformed about the true nature of American policy towards Sukharno.

US diplomats had also been denying CIA activity in northern Burma for some years when this was transparently not the case. Ambassadors in the region could never be quite sure what sort of parallel policies were emanating from within their own embassies.

Yet by the end of 1959 American covert policies were not what Sihanouk believed them to be. The CIA seemed to be successfully applying the brakes in Bangkok. Here, the CIA Head of Station, Bob Jantzen was on particularly good relations with the premier, General Sarit. During their frequent late-night drinking sessions Jantzen worked hard to dissuade Sarit of his plans for a military incursion into areas of Cambodia claimed by Thailand.[112]

Finally, it is worthwhile to remember that the years 1958 and 1959 were important because they set a precedent which convinced Sihanouk that he could use neutrality successfully against the influence of Thailand and Vietnam in Cambodia. Sihanouk's conduct of foreign policy was therefore based on the assumption that he could score points against his neighbours by carefully balancing East against West. By 1960 he appeared to have proved the assumption to be correct.

## NOTES

1. Norodom Sihanouk and Wilfred Burchett, *My War with the CIA: Cambodia's Fight for Survival* (London: Penguin 1973); PRO FO 371 144344 1959, DU 1011/Cambodia Annual Review for 1958, from Garnet at British Embassy to Foreign Office, 27 Jan. 1959.
2. Sihanouk and Burchett (note 1) p.102
3. FRUS Vol.XVI 1958–1960, Telegram from Dept. of State to embassy in Cambodia, from Dulles, Washington, 1 July 1958, pp.232–3.
4. FRUS Vol.XVI 1958–1960, Telegram from embassy in Cambodia to Dept. of State, from Ambassador Strom, 7 July 1958, pp.233–5.
5. Ibid.
6. FRUS Vol.XVI 1958–1960, Telegram from embassy in Vietnam to Dept. of State, from Ambassador Durbrow, 9 July 1958, pp.235–6.
7. Ibid.
8. Michael Leifer, *Cambodia: The Search for Security* (London: Pall Mall 1967) p.105.
9. Kenneth Conboy, *Shadow War: The CIA's Secret War in Laos* (Boulder, CO: Paladin 1995) pp.28–36.
10. Leifer (note 8) pp.105–6.
11. Cambodian National Archives, *Cambodia Today*, May 1959, No.5, Ministry of Information Printing Press, Editorial by Norodom Sihanouk.
12. FRUS Vol. XVI 1958–1960, Telegram from Dept. of State to embassy in Cambodia, from Herter to Strom, Washington, 10 July 1958, pp.237–9.
13. David Haberstam, *The Making of a Quagmire* (NY: Random House 1965).
14. FRUS Vol.XVI 1958–1960, Telegram from embassy in Vietnam to Dept. of State, from Durbrow, Saigon, 9 July 1958, pp.235–6.
15. George Herring, *America's Longest War: The United States and Vietnam, 1950–1975* (Edgewood, NJ: John Wiley 1979).
16. FRUS Vol.XVI 1958–1960, Telegram from Dept. of State to embassy in Cambodia, from Herter to Strom quoting previous communication from Strom, Washington, 10 July 1958, pp.237–9.

17. FRUS Vol.XVI 1958–60, Telegram from embassy in Cambodia to Dept. of State, from Strom, Phnom Penh, 25 July 1958, pp.240–3.
18. Ibid.
19. Ibid.
20. FRUS Vol.XVI 1958–60, Memo of a conversation, Dept. of State, Washington, 5 Aug. 1958, pp.244–6.
21. Ibid.
22. Ibid.
23. Ibid.
24. Ibid.
25. FRUS Vol.XVI 1958–1960, Memo from Joint Chiefs of Staff to the Sec. of Defense, McElroy, Washington, 22 Aug.1958, pp.248–9.
26. Ibid.
27. FRUS Vol.XVI 1958–1960, Memo. from Director of the Office of Southeast Asian Affairs Kocher to the Asst. Sec. of State for Far Eastern Affairs Robertson, Washington, 3 Sept. 1958, pp.249–50.
28. Conboy (note 9) pp.281–3. Although Gen. Lon Nol was pro-American there seems little evidence that his coup was CIA-sponsored. Moreover Lon Nol proved to be an uncooperative ally.
29. For detailed analysis of the Vietnam conflict and the Ho Chi Minh Trail, see Herring (note 15) *passim*.
30. Interview with Lao Mong Hay, Executive Director of the Khmer Institute for Democracy, April 1998, Phnom Penh.
31. FRUS Vol.XVI 1958–1960, Paper prepared by Asst. White House Staff Sec., Eisenhower, Washington, 5 Nov. 1958, pp.256–7.
32. FRUS Vol.XVI 1958–1960, Telegram from embassy in Cambodia to Dept. of State, from Strom, Phnom Penh, 8 Nov. 1958, pp.257–8.
33. Ibid.
34. FRUS Vol.XVI 1958–1960, Letter from Ambassador in Vietnam, Durbrow, to Director of the Bureau of Intelligence and Research, Cumming, Saigon, 20 Nov. 1958, pp.260–64.
35. Ibid.
36. R. Audrey and George McT. Kahin, *Subversion as Foreign Policy: The Eisenhower and Dulles Debacle in Indonesia* (NY: New Press 1995); Matthew Jones, '"Maximum Disavowable Aid": Britain, the United States and the Indonesian Rebellion, 1957–8', *English Historical Review* 114/455 (1999).
37. FRUS Vol.XVI 1958–1960, Telegram from embassy in Cambodia to Dept. of State, from Strom, Washington, 21 Nov. 1958, pp.264–6.
38. FRUS Vol.XVI 1958–1960, Telegram from embassy in Vietnam to Dept. of State, from Elting, Saigon, 12 Dec. 1958, pp.269–70.
39. Ibid.
40. FRUS Vol.XVI 1958––1960, Telegram from embassy in Cambodia to Dept. of State, from Strom to Robertson, Phnom Penh, 16 Feb. 1959, pp.276–7.
41. Ibid.
42. Ibid.
43. Sihanouk and Burchett (note 1) p.103.
44. David Chandler, *The Tragedy of Cambodian History* (New Haven, CT: Yale UP 1991) p.99.
45. Ibid. p.100; R.B. Smith, *Cambodia's Foreign Policy* (Ithaca, NY: Cornell UP 1965) p.87; Sihanouk and Burchett (note 1) p.165.
46. FRUS Vol.XVI 1958–1960, Telegram from embassy in Cambodia to Dept. of State, from Strom to Robertson, Phnom Penh, 16 Feb. 1959, pp.276–7.
47. FRUS Vol.XVI 1958–1960, Telegram from Dept. of State to embassy in Cambodia, from Herter to Strom, Washington, 18 Feb. 1959, pp.278–9.
48. Ibid.
49. Sihanouk and Burchett (note 1) p.107.
50. PRO FO 371 144346 1959, DU 1015/37, Dap Chhuon report, telegram from Garner at

British embassy in Phnom Penh to Foreign Office, 3 March 1959.

51. FRUS Vol.XVI 1958–1960, Telegram from embassy in Cambodia to Dept. of State, from Strom to Robertson, Phnom Penh, 21 February 1959, p.280.

52. FRUS Vol.XVI 1958–1960, Telegram from Dept. of State to embassy in Cambodia, from Parsons to Strom, Washington, 21 Feb. 1959, pp.281–2.

53. PRO FO 371 144346 1959, DU 1015/37, Dap Chhuon Report, from Garner at British embassy in Phnom Penh to Foreign Office, 3 March 1959.

54. FRUS Vol.XVI 1958–1960, Telegram from Dept. of State to embassy in Vietnam, from Herter to Durbrow, Washington, 23 Feb. 1959, pp.285–8.

55. PRO FO 371 144346 1959, DU 1015/44, Minute by Butler at Foreign Office commenting on the Dap Chhuon Affair, 25 March 1960.

56. FRUS Vol.XVI 1958–1960, Memo of a conversation, Dept. of State, Washington, 3 March 1959, pp.293–5.

57. Ibid.

58. Ibid.

59. Ibid.

60. The relationship between France and the United States was not amicable in many parts of the world. Disagreement on the rearmament of Germany, the colonial wars in North Africa, are but two examples. France was convinced that the United States was likely to create a situation which would lead to a Third World War, while the United States accused France of a pusillanimous foreign policy. For an analysis of Franco-American relations see Frank Costigliola, *France and the United States* (NY: Twayne 1992).

61. Douglas Porch, *The French Secret Services: From the Dreyfus Affair to the Gulf War* (London: Macmillan 1995) p.409.

62. PRO FO 371 144345 1959, Internal Political Situation in Cambodia, DU 1015/25, French/American interests in Cambodia.

63. Ibid.

64. Cambodian National Archives, Ministry of Information Press, Cambodia Today, No.5, May 1959.

65. Chandler (note 44) p.99.

66. FRUS Vol.XVI 1958–1960, Memo from the Director of the Office of Southeast Asian Affairs (Kocher) to the Asst. Sec. of State for Far Eastern Affairs (Robertson), Washington, 12 March 1959, pp.297–300.

67. Ibid.

68. PRO FO 371 144346 1959, DU 1015/39, Telegram from Foreign Office to British embassy in Paris, 18 March 1959.

69. As note 66.

70. Ibid.

71. Ibid.

72. For a detailed account, see Kahin and Kahin (note 36) *passim.*

73. PRO FO 371 144346 1959, DU 1015/47, Telegram from Caccia at British embassy in Washington DC to Foreign Office, 27 March 1959, Minute by Butler.

74. Ibid.

75. As note 66.

76. As note 73.

77. Ibid.

78. As note 66.

79. PRO FO 371 144345 1959, Internal Political Situation in Cambodia, DU 1015/12, French and American roles. From British embassy in Saigon to Foreign Office, 30 Jan. 1959, Minute by Butler.

80. FRUS Vol.XVI 1958–1960, Telegram from embassy in Korea to Dept. of State, from Parsons reporting on his visit, Seoul, 5 May 1959, pp.310–13.

81. Ibid.

82. Ibid.

83. Ibid.

84. Ibid.

85. Ibid.
86. FRUS Vol.XVI 1958–1960, Memo from Director of the Office of Southeast Asian Affairs (Kocher) to Asst. Sec. of State for Far Eastern Affairs (Robertson), Washington, 9 May 1959, pp.315–20.
87. Ibid.
88. For a more detailed account of relations, see Herring (note 15) *passim.*
89. As note 86.
90. Frank Costigliola, *France and the United States* (NY: Twayne Publishers 1992).
91. As note 86.
92. Ibid.
93. PRO FO 371 144345 1959, Internal Political Situation in Cambodia, DU 1015/25. From Garner at British embassy in Phnom Penh to Foreign Office.
94. FRUS Vol.XVI 1958–1960, National Intelligence Estimate, NIE 67-59, Washington, 26 May 1959, pp.324–5.
95. Ibid.
96. Ibid.
97. FRUS Vol.XVI 1958–1960, Airgram from Dept. of State to embassy in Cambodia, from Dillon, repeated to Saigon and Paris, Washington, 5 June 1959, pp.325–9.
98. Ibid.
99. Ibid.
100. Ibid.
101. Ibid.
102. FRUS Vol.XVI 1958–1960, Editorial Note, p.329.
103. For a detailed description of the attack, and Cambodian allegations see Chandler (note 44) p.104 and Sihanouk and Burchett (note 1) pp.103–12.
104. FRUS Vol.XVI 1958–1960, Telegram from embassy in Cambodia to Dept. of State, from Trimble, Phnom Penh, 19 Sept. 1959, pp.330–32.
105. Ibid.
106. Ibid.
107. FRUS Vol.XVI 1958–1960, Telegram from embassy in Vietnam to Dept. of State, from Durbrow, Saigon, 22 Sept. 1959, pp.335–8.
108. Ibid.
109. Ibid.
110. FRUS Vol.XVI 1958–1960, Telegram from embassy in Vietnam to Dept. of State, from Durbrow, Johnson and Trimble to Parsons, Saigon, 13 Dec. 1959, pp.344–7.
111. FRUS Vol.XVI 1958–1960, Telegram from Dept. of State to embassy in Vietnam, from Parsons but signed by Dillon to Durbrow, Trimble and Johnson, Washington, 17 Dec. 1959, pp.348–9.
112. Thomas Powers, *The Man Who Kept the Secrets: Richard Helms and the CIA* (London: Weidenfeld 1977), pp.98–9; Joseph Buckholder Smith, *Portrait of a Cold Warrior* (NY: Putnam 1976) p.204.

# 8

# Late Imperial Romance:
# Magsaysay, Lansdale and the Philippine-
# American 'Special Relationship'

## EVA-LOTTA E. HEDMAN

Over four decades after his tragic death in a plane crash just outside Cebu
City in 1957, Ramon Magsaysay remains the single most mythologised
public figure in the history of the independent Philippine Republic. After
first rising to political prominence in his home province of Zambales as the
American-appointed military governor in the aftermath of the Japanese
Occupation, Magsaysay quickly captured a seat in the Philippine Congress
(1946) and, subsequent to chairing the National Defense Committee (1948)
and serving as National Defense Secretary (1950), won election to the
highest political office in the young republic (1953).

Meanwhile, Magsaysay also gained international repute alongside the
United States Armed Forces in the Far East (USAFFE) as a guerrilla turned
political and military reformer and, notably, as successful anti-Communist
crusader in the campaign against the Huk peasant rebellion in Central
Luzon.[1]

Widely hailed for his anti-Huk exploits and his pro-American outlook
alike, Magsaysay featured on the cover of *Time* magazine as the man with
an 'unchallenged reputation for honesty'[2] and received similar eulogies in
the editorial pages of *The New York Times* for his 'integrity, imagination,
courage and simplicity'.[3]

More than two decades later, a retired American intelligence operative
who had served 'in the covert side of the CIA' testified to Magsaysay's
lasting mystique:

> Magsaysay was a man of rigid honesty, sharp intelligence, and
> abundant energy. He was also a colorful, unpretentious, and earthy
> human being, and his few years of immersion in Manila politics had
> not dulled his instinctive understanding of the needs and problems of
> the people in the *barrios* and *sitios* – the villages and hamlets – of the
> rural hinterland. He not only sympathized with their difficulties, he

also understood the connections between popular grievances and the support gathered by the insurgency, while not forgetting that military effectiveness was also an essential ingredient of success. In addition to these and other qualities that he brought to the task, he was also a born leader, and instinctive democrat, and a firm anti-Communist. In short, he combined the essential qualities required to meet the crisis of the Philippine Republic.[4]

Interestingly, Magsaysay does not acquire such mythical proportions in the accounts by Magsaysay biographer Abueva and several (auto)biographies written by or about once-Magsaysay associates such as Eleuterio 'Terry Magtanggol' Adevoso, Manny Manahan, Francisco 'Soc' Rodrigo, and Jamie Ferrer.[5]

Instead, Magsaysay the legend receives his greatest eulogy from another figure of mythical proportions – Lt Colonel (ultimately Major General) Edward G. Lansdale, a former advertising man who first arrived in the Philippines towards the end of the Pacific War, stayed on with Army Intelligence and the Office of Strategic Services (OSS), and then returned to Manila in 1950, officially as Armed Forces of Philippines (AFP) advisor and Joint US Military Advisory Group (JUSMAG) liaison, only a week after Magsaysay had been made Secretary of National Defense.

In as much as these official postings provided a convenient 'cover' for Lansdale's actual assignments in the Philippines, they also, of course, contributed to the mystery that served to perpetuate his legendary status,[6] as did his larger-than-life appearances in two period novels, barely disguised as the folksy, harmonica-playing Colonel Edwin B. Hillandale in William J. Lederer and Eugene Burdrick's *The Ugly American* and, it is often surmised, as the young, idealistic American aid official Alden Pyle in Graham Greene's *The Quiet American*.[7]

In further testimony to Lansdale's enduring reputation as 'legendary North American avatar of counter-insurgency'[8] long after his activities in Vietnam (and Cuba and then Vietnam again) in the 1950s and 1960s, the Reagan administration sought him out in the 1980s for advice on how to counter the Sandinistas in Nicaragua and the New People's Army in the Philippines.

While Lansdale neither made US policy in the Philippines, nor 'created' Magsaysay the legend singlehandedly, he nevertheless enjoyed a great deal of discretion and influence – certainly more than his rank would suggest and probably more than any other single American at the time. This influence encompassed the direction and degree of US involvement in two (related) aspects of the young Republic's life – the counter-insurgency against the Huks and the promotion of Magsaysay as presidential material. On the one hand, Lansdale's appointment as AFP advisor and JUSMAG liaison allowed for close, direct and frequent meetings with Magsaysay. As a result, Lansdale also served as special adviser to the Civil Affairs Office (CAO) established by Magsaysay in March 1951 for purposes of expanding the counter-insurgency campaign. On the other hand, Lansdale's support for Magsaysay's presidential campaign was so widely recognised as to earn him the nickname 'General Landslide' on account of his activities in the Philippine elections in 1953. In years to come, Lansdale himself would have many occasions to espouse his own views on such joint politico-military adventures:

> We must not confuse our correct separation of the US military from partisan politics in our own country with our then remaining aloof from helping our allies fight the politico-military forces of the Communist enemy. These are entirely separate things. In our duty in the area, and on headquarters' staffs, we will often have the opportunity to give guidance to Southeast Asian military leaders. We should do so, as thoughtful and patriotic Americans desirous of building strong and free nations in the world.[9]

Beyond the (cold) world of covert action, the peculiar coupling of Magsaysay and Lansdale points to a familiar pattern in Philippine-American history. For example, the early years of American colonial rule from 1898 saw high-ranking colonial official W. Cameron Forbes (Director of Commerce and Police; Member of the Philippine Commision; Governor General), who developed one such 'special relationship' with young Cebuano politician Sergio Osmeña, 'defining the colonial channels of power in terms of his relationship with a 29-year-old Filipino provincial politico who was just emerging as a national leader'.[10] During the 1930s Commonwealth period, moreover, President Manuel Quezon appointed the US Army's retiring Chief of Staff, General Douglas MacArthur, as his 'military advisor,' thus writing another chapter in the contested history of Philippine-American relations.[11]

While historians have viewed these Filipino-American pairs in colonial relations as evidence of 'the cynically manipulative underside of the collaborative empire',[12] scholarship on the post-colonial period reveals, perhaps unsurprisingly, a relative lack of explicit analytical focus on the role and significance of such personalised aspects of 'international relations'. Yet such writings also span a wider spectrum of underlying theoretical assumptions as to the nature and direction of Washington-Manila relations. From the perspective of the most articulate formulation of the 'neo-colonial thesis' neither political maneuverings, nor personal relationships ultimately underpin the powerful structures of US 'strategic and economic domination' and its seemingly seamless success in 'further[ing] its own interests and those of its allies among the Filipino elite'.[13]

By contrast, the most recent published study to revisit such relations in the early post-colonial period claims that they demonstrate but 'illusions of influence' – despite all the good intentions of 'US officials' and 'policies' – in the Philippines.[14] Dressed up in terms of 'political economy' and 'political culture,' this argument appears upon closer scrutiny to rest upon the rather disingenuous treatment of the very politics ('US policies' vs. 'Philippine corruption') and personae ('US officials' vs. 'Filipinos') rescued from other, more structuralist accounts of Philippine-American relations.

The most persuasive and meticuluously documented account of Philippine-American relations in the post-World War II period avoids these pitfalls. This short essay highlights both how, within the context of the Cold War, successive Filipino presidents (and Ferdinand E. Marcos in particular) worked US government officials to political advantage, and how short-term interests such as 'protecting American bases and businessmen's profits' prevailed at the expense of long-term ones of political stability and development in the Philippines.[15]

Rather than piecing together yet another account of how Magsaysay benefitted from Lansdale/American support/intervention while trying to separate truth from fiction, this essay will instead concentrate on the mythologisation of Magsaysay. Interestingly, this legend does not seem to enjoy much in the way of popular elaboration or circulation in the Philippines today. For example, the 'Spirit of Magsaysay Movement' that proclaimed continued commitment to civic and social reforms upon his death, and the Progressive Party that fielded former 'Magsaysay Boys' for the presidency as well as several senatorial slates, faded quickly from the public eye in the late 1950s. Instead, the annual Ramon Magsaysay Awards, typically celebrated as Asia's own Nobel Prize, hosted by the Manila-based Foundation bearing his name serve as the most tangible reminders of this reformist legacy. Otherwise, only during Corazon C. Aquino's bid for the presidency in 1986 did his name gain wider popular circulation again with the revival of his old election-campaign jingle 'Mambo Magsaysay'.[16]

By contrast to these relatively faint traces of Magsaysay the reformist-cum-politician in the Philippines, his role in the history of the early Republic has entered the annals of counter-insurgency campaigns studied at military academies and, largely due to Lansdale, have become the stuff of legend elsewhere.[17] Instead of claiming that Lansdale somehow captured Magsaysay once and for all, this essay explores his mythologisation of the Filipino within the context of US covert action and American liberal imperialism writ large. Beyond merely observing that 'Magsaysay became the central character in one of Washington's most durable legends',[18] we here examine Lansdale's autobiography *In the Midst of Wars* for clues as to this imperial enchantment with – as opposed to mere political propaganda use of – 'the Guy'.

## COVERT ACTION

With the 'loss' of China and the outbreak of the Korean War bringing the Cold War to Asia in the early 1950s, the United States increasingly turned to *militarised* covert action in the region.[19] Against the inroads made by Communist organisation and national mobilisation – or what one author once referred to 'as the now obscure little wars in Malaya, the Philippines, [and] Burma'[20] – in the region, American foreign policy thus first began developing the counter-insurgency doctrines and experiences that have since played such a major – and controversial – role in shaping post-World War II world politics. With Eisenhower relying more heavily on the CIA than his predecessor and becoming 'especially attracted to its capacity for covert actions,' moreover, US covert action also involved more frequent and widespread violence during this early period than perhaps at any other time since 1945.[21]

> In no part of the Third World were the Eisenhower administration's *militarised* interventions – whether direct or by proxy – so extensive (or have they been so little chronicled) as in the newly emerged ex-colonial states of Southeast Asia.[22]

In this context, fighting the Huks in the Philippines held particular significance 'as the beginning of active counterinsurgency by the US'.[23] Despite the large presence of conventional military forces as signalled by the JUSMAG and its close relations with the newly-established Philippine Army, 'unconventionality was the keynote of that part of the US mission which had the greatest share of influence upon the Philippine approach.'[24] Against this backdrop, then, Magsaysay gained a reputation not simply as an effective Secretary of National Defense but as the famed 'Huk-fighter' who first and, as it turned out, perhaps more successfully than anywhere else since, adopted a deliberate counter-insurgency strategy against a Communist-led and peasant-supported guerrilla war.

According to two of Lansdale's closest men, Filipino Colonel Napoleon D. Valeriano (AFP) and American Lt Colonel Charles T. T. Bohannan, for example, Magsaysay, during his stint with National Defense (September 1950 to February 1953) was '[p]robably the first to use twentieth-century knowledge and technique in a deliberate, rigorous exploitation of this approach to counterguerrilla warfare...'[25] As for the significance of the Philippine case from this very early stage of American counter-insurgency doctrine and practice to its fuller development under Kennedy and, more recently, Reagan, one recent study argues that:

The Huks' defeat is still regarded as a success for United States 'psywar' and antiguerrilla tactics. Strategists applied Philippine 'lessons' in Vietnam, and continued to construe parallels to brushfire wars in the 1980s. Counting only works available to the public, the military and its support organizations have produced almost two dozen studies of the winning tactics employed by the anti-Huk campaign.[26]

In the preface to Lansdale's autobiography (re-published in 1991), moreover, former CIA director William E. Colby argued that '[h]is thoughtful recounting of events shows us appropriate forms for American activity to take in Third World countries, lessons that were learned the hard way in the Philippines.'[27]

Such tactics ranged from the Nenita death squads to so-called civic action projects and thus aimed both at fighting the enemy and undermining his social support base through a strategy of counterinsurgency. In the Ranger/Commando tradition of the Indian Wars and the Civil War that served as inspiration for their American advisors, the 'counter-guerrilla' – or 'Cold Warrior' – 'was to be a professional soldier, trained in techniques of raiding, scouting, and harassment....'[28] In order to pursue such techniques in insulation from the conventional military's chain-of-command, Magsaysay thus established the Civil Affairs Office (CAO) as a psychological warfare division under his own staff rather than under the General Staff where some officers remained resistant to such innovations. Significantly, Lansdale notes, the CAO 'wasn't too unlike the enemy's organization, where political officers in Huk squadrons were in touch with the Politburo'.[29]

In as much as the CAO paralleled the enemy's organizational structure, 'counter-insurgency' on the whole evolved very much as 'the mirror-image of guerrilla war.'[30] If the 'myth of savage warfare' called for the kind of fighting that 'combines the amoral pragmatism and technical expertise of the gunfighter with the skill in handling natives that belongs to the "man who knows Indians"', then, it has been suggested, American military planners and practitioners in search of a strategic doctrine for fighting post-colonial insurgencies in the Cold War found a 'perfect *counterpart*' in Mao's little red book on guerrilla warfare. Akin to 'the doctrine of Indian fighting – you need "White savages" to combat "Red"',[31] counter-guerrilla warfare thus demanded so-called unconventional methods against a new form of (Communist) Red savagery. Viewed in this light, the references to advances in military tactics and to remnants of local 'superstitions' in the infamous *asuang* (ghost) story retold below assume particular significance for purposes of fighting an effectively dehumanized enemy:

> A combat psywar squad was brought in. It planted stories among town residents of an *asuang* living on the hill where the Huks were based. Two nights later, after giving the stories time to circulate among Huk sympathizers in the town and make their way up to the hill camp, the psywar squad set up an ambush along a trail used by the Huks. When a Huk patrol came along the trail, the ambushers silently snatched the last man of the patrol, their move unseen in the dark night. They punctured his neck with two holes, vampire-fashion, held the body up by the heels, drained it of blood, and put the corpse back on the trail. When the Huks returned to look for the missing man and found their bloodless comrade, every member of the patrol believed that the *asuang* had got him and that one of them would be next if they remained on that hill. When daylight came, the whole Huk squadron moved out of the vicinity. Another day passed before the local people were convinced that they were really gone.[32]

Whether or not this peculiar encounter actually convinced anybody of either the arrival or departure of an *asuang* in this locality is perhaps beside the point. However, this carefully reconstructed event underscores the extent to which the anti-Huk campaign – and, by defition, the famed Huk-fighter Magsaysay – have been identified with notions of progress familiar and often palatable to 'Cold Warriors' and nation-builders alike. On the one hand, the mention of 'a combat psywar squad' anchors the violence described above to 'specialist' technology and 'tactical' innovation associated with the modernization of coercive state apparatuses. Beyond the obvious objection that no such highly institutionalized military/intelligence bureaucracy existed in either Washington DC or Manila at the time, the more interesting observation here concerns the assumed role and significance of these very squads and their exploits within the broader framework of legal-rational state- and nation-building. In this regard, the maverick activities of Lansdale and Magsaysay are often counterposed against the JUSMAG/AFP chain of command in such ways as to reify the distinctions drawn between 'conventional' and 'unconventional' warfare and thus to maximize the individual prowess of our two heroes.

On the other hand, the references to 'planted stories ... of an *asuang* living in the hills where the Huks were based' and the subsequent killing and blood-letting of a Huk guerrilla cannot but conjure up images of a 'backward' Filipino peasantry susceptible to 'superstition' and ideological mystification alike. Although anthropologists no doubt would be quick to point out the inconsistencies between local beliefs about *mga asuang* and the above psywar vampire-like projections, in Lansdale's account the psywar experts appear, once again, 'as men who know Indians' (better than themselves)', and yet at the same time the bearers of rational enlightenment and a civilizing mission.

'THE FRONTIER'

If counterinsurgency provided the action for the Magsaysay legend, then the epic battlefield itself was to be found somewhere 'on the "ideal boundary" between two cultures, one "civilized and cultivated", the other one "wild and lawless".' In the American imagination, 'that "ideal boundary" is, of course, the "frontier"....'[33] In fact, Lansdale had quite literally left behind his wife and two little boys in an aborted renovation project of a house where he had torn down walls but left the remodeling and 'interior decoration' unfinished. In departing for his new assignment in the Philippines, he also abandoned a comfortable teaching position at a war academy with its orderly classroom routine.[34] Lansdale's first wistful glimpse of the Philippines upon his return in September 1950 captures this sense of escape from the domestication and routine of life in America to a place not yet entirely gridded by modern development: 'Lordy... they haven't yet finished paving highway 54.'[35]

Once installed in his quarters in the JUSMAG compounds with all its trappings of American suburbia, Lansdale vividly recalls the many and frequent 'sudden departures for unknown destinations'[36] in the provincial Philippines. On an inspection trip accompanying Magsaysay to the AFP's Economic Development Corps (EDCOR) site in Kapatagan, Lanao, for example, Lansdale revelled in the following 'touching scene':

> Amidst the clamor of music, shouts, and barking dogs, the faces of the welcomers were alight with pleasure at seeing the newcomers. It struck me suddenly that they must have felt lonely in what they believed to be a spot at the end of the world. The scene was touching.[37]

Whereas the EDCOR project signalled efforts to promote progress and rationalization associated with both Manila and Washington DC, the charming disorder of this 'spot at the end of the world' nevertheless seems to assure that such modernist expansion remained sufficiently incomplete so as to retain a certain heroic romanticism. A brief 'R&R' trip to Panay seemed to have offered a similarly enchanted moment with Lansdale happily 'lounging about on a tropical island' and, in yet another instance of bucolic bliss, exchanging 'some of the songs currently popular in Manila' for 'some of the local folk songs':

> I had spent a brief holiday on the island of Panay at a friend's farm, sleeping in the grass under the trees and swimming at the nearby beach. Fishermen and schoolchildren visited the farm, finally winding up their visit by singing some of the local folk songs. I had taken out

> a harmonica and accompanied them, then played some of the songs
> currently popular in Manila. It was a happy, relaxing interlude in the
> war for me, lounging about on a tropical island, barefoot, dressed only
> in a pair of shorts.[38]

Yet neither guerrilla resettlement visits, nor 'R&R' interludes provided the
ultimate escape. Instead, war did. As suggested by Lansdale himself: 'It was
close to playing hooky, to go to war.'[39] Similarly, in what appears as a
rejuvenating birthday celebration in Lansdale's ruminations, war itself
offered what have been referred to as the perfectly 'unordered spaces'
against which 'to stage the wanderings and disorientations, the quests and
conquests and conversions, the ordeals and sacrifices and triumphs that are
the stuff of romance'.[40]

> We drove to this fight through a provincial morning heavy with the
> sweetness of mango blossoms, past high school youngsters playing
> softball in a clearing, onto a dirt trail where I hit a ford across a deep
> stream driving too fast, slapping up a great cascade of water which
> conked out the engine. From the dense and tall greenery of the
> sugarcane surrounding us came the close-by din of rifles and
> automatic weapons. Magsaysay popped under the hood and wiped dry
> the carburetor and spark plugs, while I stood guard, wondering if the
> closest firing was friend or foe.... The sounds of combat died away as
> Huk guerrillas wandered out of the cane, hands up in surrender. It was
> over. We returned to Manila and the work awaiting us there. What a
> way to spend a birthday![41]

Although Magsaysay appears as Lansdale's 'native counterpart' here and
thus arguably still remain 'representative of racial character' within this
'Asian' context, his evident skill at automobile repairs serves as a reminder
of an exceptional 'latent gift for American-style progress'.[42] Recalling a
familiar theme in American literature, this account also celebrates male
companionship in the midst of dangerous terrain and violence thus hinting
at a 'love passing the love of women, which binds together in the New
World wilderness a pair of males, one white, one nonwhite'.[43]

Similarly, in as much as the consummation of such relationships must
remain, at least in the grand narrative, perpetually deferred, the story retold
above also echoes another recurring trope in American literature, that of
'regeneration through violence'.[44] As an imperial continuation of dominant
colonial fantasies 'making death rather than love the central theme' in
American fiction,[45] the Philippines as imperfectly mapped frontier became
similarly invested with morbid longings. Unsurprisingly, the Philippines
thus also emerged as a site of the phantasmagoric in Lansdale's colourful
recollections:

> To the superstitious, the Huk battleground was a haunted place filled
> with ghosts and eerie creatures. Some of its aura of mystery was
> imparted to me on my own visits there. Goose bumps rose on my arms
> on moonless nights in Huk territory as I listened to the haunting minor
> notes of trumpets playing Pampanguena dirges in the barrios or to the
> mournful singing of men and women known as *nangangaluluwa* as
> they walked from house to house on All Saints' night telling of lost
> and hungry souls. Even Magsaysay believed in the apparition called
> *kapre*, a huge black man said to walk through tall grass at dusk to
> make it stir or to sit in a tree or astride a roof smoking a large cigar.[46]

It was thus within this context of 'a world at war – starkly divided, partially
wild and mysterious, dramatically dangerous',[47] that Magsaysay, both
trusted 'native' companion and yet also, unmistakably, spiritually at home
on the late imperial frontier, gained his larger-than-life reputation.

'THE GUY'

Much has been written on Magsaysay's role in the Philippine anti-Huk
campaigns and on their significance for the subsequent development of
counter-insurgency doctrine and practice alike. Beyond such *realpolitik*
considerations, however, the above discussion underscores the extent to
which Magsaysay, or 'The Guy' as he became known at the time, emerged
as a legendary figure of mythical proportions. In as much as the stuff of this
legend centered on the late imperial frontier, it provided an alternative
mythical foundation for Magsaysay beyond 'the all-encompassing narrative
of the Free World and the American Century', which, it has been argued,
'quickly became very boring'.[48]

Instead, it served to identify Magsaysay with 'a swashbuckling politics
and a world in which neither epic heroism nor chivalry is dead'.[49]
Unsurprisingly, Magsaysay the legend thus appears not unlike his most
enthusiastic American chronicler and *alter ego*, Lansdale, himself once
described as 'a folk hero, a military miracle man and a wrecker of United
States policy'.[50]

In addition to the many testimonies from contemporary observers as to
'the warm and intimate friendship' between the two men,[51] Lansdale's own
recollections are also replete with references to his strong personal
identification with Magsaysay:

> At the time, Magsaysay had just turned forty-three. He was about my
> height, a bit huskier than I, and six months older. I already knew that
> we shared things in common; each of us was the second son in
> families of four boys, although he had sisters and I didn't, and we each

had worked for a living while going to college in the lean years of the depression.[52]

While noting that they were both 'the second son in families of four boys' and that they had both 'worked for a living while going to college...,' this listing of 'things in common' omits any mention of the very ties that might have threatened to undermine the close identification between two men destined for the late imperial frontier – that is, to their own wives and kids. Beyond such recognition of the familiar, enchantment thus beckoned on this very frontier. As Lansdale remarked with reference to Magsaysay: 'He opened a new dimension in my life....'[53] And what a life it was:

> With the election over, I accepted Magsaysay's invitation to join him for a rest at this father's farm in Zambales province, where we both unwound from the tensions of the recent past. Laziness, sleep, skinny-dipping in a nearby river, fish-fries and corn-roasts on its bank, and nightly serenades by neighbors with their guitars and *bandurrias* (the 15-string musical instrument of the old Philippines) soon worked their restorative magic.[54]

As noted above, the Magsaysay legend recalls familiar themes from the 'Frontier Myth' – 'with a metaphoric extension of the Frontier categories to a new situation in which Asians become figurative Apaches and the Philippines become a symbolic equivalent of Boone's Kentucky or Houston's Texas'.[55] In this vein, the legend also echoes recurring tropes of an enduring literary tradition that harks back to American colonial society with its racial conflicts and violence and, it has been argued, displays a commensurate fascination with death rather than 'the great passions portrayed in classic European fiction'.[56]

Indeed, this tradition tends to pair off male companions on the frontier of civilisation in apparent opposition 'to the "stickier" and more sentimental kinds of relationships involving women, whether that of mother and child, husband and wife, or passionate wooer and mistress'.[57] Although introducing the possibility that such male couples might bridge endemic racism and violence with their 'austere, almost inarticulate, but unquestioned love',[58] this outcome remains forever deferred. Of course, such white/non-white male pairings abound in American literature and popular culture from the classic novels of James Fenimore Cooper and Mark Twain to *The Lone Ranger* (and Tonto) comic strip and television series, to more recent cult movies such as Quentin Tarantino's *Pulp Fiction*.

Studies of Philippine-US relations have tended to focus almost exclusive attention on the nature and direction of military, economic and political domination, the brief discussion above has explored a different approach to perhaps the most infamous 'special relationship' forged between represntatives of the governments in Manila and Washington DC in the post-colonial period. In this regard, Magsaysay and Lansdale appear as yet another variation on a theme familiar since American colonial fiction and still discernible in contemporary popular culture: 'an archetypal relationship which... haunts the American psyche: two lonely men, one dark-skinned, one white....'[59] Within the context of the Cold War, Landale noted more than once, 'counterinsurgency is [only] another word for brotherly love'.[60]

> There were Americans who believed in these dedicated Filipinos and acted upon that belief. As they did, such Americans were accepted as brothers, not outsiders.[61]

If such notions of brotherhood recall the words of William Howard Taft, first US Civil Governor General of the Philippine Islands, as he referred to his colonial subjects as 'little brown brothers' a half-century earlier, it is the stuff of late imperial romance that binds Lansdale to Magsaysay on this closing frontier:

> He and I walked over to the empty highway. The town was out of sight down the road. We started toward it, a Filipino in a vividly colored sport shirt and farmer's straw hat, an American in khaki uniform and air force blue cap.[62]

## NOTES

I wish to thank Professor George McT. Kahin for the generosity with which he shared research material and good stories on Lansdale. While this essay shows little evidence of Professor Kahin's careful research and vast knowledge of South East Asia and American foreign policy, it nonetheless owes much to his legendary intelligence and humanity.

1. See, for example, Robert Shaplen, 'Huks, Foe in the Philippines', *Colliers*, 7 April 1951, and 'Letter from Manila', *New Yorker,* 7 April 1951; and T. Durdin, 'Filipino Emerges as a New Asian Leader', *New York Times Magazine*, 22 Nov. 1953. During his 1951 visit to the US, Magsaysay reportedly met with publishers and editors of the *New York Times, New York Herald Tribune, Life, Time* and *Look.* See Jose V. Abueva, *Ramon Magsaysay: A Political Biography* (Manila: Solidaridad 1971) p.213, fn.20.
2. 'Cleanup Man', *Time*, 26 Nov. 1951, pp.33–4.
3. Editorial, *New York Times*, 19 June 1952.
4. Douglas S. Blaufarb, *The Counterinsurgency Era: US Doctrine and Performance* (NY: MacMillan 1977) p.29.
5. See, for example, Abueva (note 1); Eleuterio 'Terry Magtanggol' L. Adevoso, *A Personal Story - 50 Years* (Metro Manila: Guaranty Press 1989); Nick Joaquin, *Mr. Rural Reform: The Times & Tidings of Manny Manahan* (Manila: College Assurance Plan 1990); Fransisco Soc Rodrigo, *Mga Bakas ng Kahapon (Memoir)* (Quezon City,1991); Isagani R. Cruz, *Jaime N. Ferrer: Once a Hunter, Always a Hunter* (Metro Manila: Jaime N. Ferrer Fdn 1994).
6. In Lansdale's own words: 'I didn't admit that I was a chief CIA agent out in the Far East... the hell with what I really was. It didn't matter too much about my position, in a way.' Edward Geary Lansdale, *In the Midst of Wars: An American Mission to Southeast Asia* (NY: Harper & Row 1972) pp.xxii.

7. William J. Lederer, *The Ugly American* (NY: Fawcett Crest 1958) and Graham Greene, *The Quiet American* (London: Heinemann 1955). Years later, Lansdale wrote: 'I am never about to write the truth of some past events – the way they turned out made nice history for the nations involved and I am happy to keep history in the fiction class.' *In the Midst of Wars* (note 6) p.xxiv.
8. Van Gosse, *Where the Boys Are: Cuba, Cold War America and the Making of a New Left* (London: Verso 1993) p.39.
9. Lansdale lecture at the US Army War College, cited in Abueva, *Ramon Magsaysay* (note 1) p.191, fn.21.
10. Michael Cullinane, 'Playing the Game: The Rise of Sergio Osmeña, 1898–1907', Ruby R. Paredes (ed.) *Philippine Colonial Democracy* (Quezon City: Ateneo de Manila UP) p.70.
11. Alfred W. McCoy, 'Quezon's Commonwealth: The Emergence of Philippine Authoritarianism', in Paredes, *Philippine Colonial Democracy* (note 10) p.141. For a discussion of Quezon in the first years of American colonial rule, see Michael Cullinane, 'The Politics of Collaboration in Tayabas Province: The Early Political Career of Manuel Luis Quezon, 1903–1906, in Peter Stanley (ed.) *Reappraising an Empire: New Perspectives on Philippine-American History* (Cambridge, MA: Harvard UP 1984) pp.58–84.
12. Stanley, in his edited volume *Reappraising an Empire* (note 11) p.5.
13. Stephen Rosskamm Shalom, *The United States and the Philippines* (Quezon City: New Day 1986) pp.xiii and xvi.
14. Nick Cullather, *Illusions of Influence: The Political Economy of United States-Philippines Relations, 1942–1960* (Stanford UP 1994).
15. Raymond Bonner, *Waltzing with a Dictator: The Marcoses and the Making of American Policy* (NY: Times Books 1987) p.441.
16. Mark Richard Thompson, 'Cory and "the Guy": Reformist Politics in the Philippines,' *USFI Field Staff Report 16* (Indianapolis: Universities Field Staff Int. 1988–89).
17. Once again, Lansdale's commentary is revealing: 'I decided that Asia needed its own heroes – so I've given them a whole bookful of them, with us/uns merely being companionable friends to some great guys.' Lansdale (note 6) p.xxiv.
18. Cullather (note 14) p.98.
19. See Audrey R. and George McT. Kahin, *Subversion as Foreign Policy: The Secret Eisenhower and Dulles Debacle in Indonesia* (NY: The New Press 1995).
20. Blaufarb (note 4) p.21.
21. See Kahin and Kahin (note 19) p.7.
22. Ibid. p.9.
23. Blaufarb (note 4) p.23. Blaufarb continues thus: '[B]ecause the experience was clearly different from conventional combat and because the program was undertaken by the Philippine government encompassed, at least embryonically, the wide gamut of activity which became characteristic of American counterinsurgency thinking.' Ibid. p.23.
24. Ibid. p.38.
25. Col. Napoleon D. Valeriano and Lt. Col. Charles T.R. Bohannan, *Counter-Guerrilla Operations: The Philippine Experience* (NY: Praeger 1962) p.29. Both Valeriano, former Philippine Constabulary turned Huk hunter in command of the infamous Nenita Unit, and Bohannan, First Lieutenant in the G-2 intelligence section of the US armed forces in the Philippines when Lansdale returned in Sept. 1950, worked very closely with Lansdale first in the Philippines and later in Vietnam.
26. Cullather (note 14) p.91.
27. William Colby, 'Preface' in Lansdale (note 1) p.xix.
28. Richard Slotkin, *Gunfighter Nation: The Myth of the Frontier in Twentieth-Century America* (NY: Harper Perennial 1993 ed.) (first pub. by Atheneum 1992) p.458. Another revealing autobiography by retired CIA agent Joseph B. Smith, who also served in the Philippines, is titled *Portrait of a Cold Warrior* (Quezon City: Plaridel Books 1976). Smith's volume was one of the few CIA autobiographies not submitted for clearance by the CIA.
29. Lansdale (note 6) p.70.
30. Van Gosse (note 8) p.37.
31. Slotkin (note 28) pp.446–7, 453. In his memoir, Lansdale repeatedly refer to 'savage Huk attacks'.

32. Lansdale (note 6) pp.72–3.
33. Leslie Feidler, *Love and Death in the American Novel* (NY: Anchor Books 1960) p.179.
34. Supposedly one of Lansdale's favorites, the following Thomas Paine epitath is perhaps worthy of note in this context: 'Where liberty is not, there is my country.'
35. Lansdale (note 6) p.4.
36. Ibid. p.41.
37. Ibid. p.55.
38. Ibid. p.83.
39. Ibid. p.15.
40. John McClure, *Late Imperial Romance* (London: Verso 1994) p.3.
41. Lansdale's account of a visit to a Pampanga sugar plantation in early 1951 (note 6) pp.86–7.
42. Citations from Slotkin (note 28) p.449.
43. Feidler (note 33) p.509.
44. Ibid. This is also the suggestive title and central thesis of Richard Slotkin's book, *Regeneration through Violence: The Mythology of the American Frontier, 1600–1860* (Ohio: Wesleyan UP 1973).
45. Leslie Feidler, *Love and Death in the American Novel* (NY: Anchor Books 1960), (1992 ed.) p.509.
46. Lansdale (note 6) p.72.
47. Citation from McClure, *Late Imperial Romance* (note 40) p.3.
48. Van Gosse (note 8) p.52.
49. McClure, *Late Imperial Romance* (note 40) p.41.
50. *Christian Science Monitor* review of Lansdale, cited in Cecil B. Currey's Introduction to *In the Midst of Wars* (note 6) p.xxi.
51. Citation from Abueva (note 1) p.172, fn.31.
52. Lansdale(note 6) p.33.
53. Ibid. p.37.
54. Ibid. p.122.
55. Slotkin (note 28) p.54. Although this particular comment is in reference to the early American colonial expansion into the Philippines at the turn of the century, it remains relevant to the late imperial period discussed here.
56. See Feidler (note 33) p.509.
57. Ibid.
58. Feidler (note 33) p.192.
59. Ibid.
60. *Washington Star* reporter Mary McGrory repeating Lansdale's words back to him in 1965, cited in Currey's Introduction to Lansdale's *In the Midst of Wars* (note 6) p.xvii.
61. Brig. Gen. Edward G. Lansdale, 'Lessons Learned: The Philippines, 1946–1953 (ALERT No. 6A)', reprint of a lecture at the Foreign Service Institute, Washington DC, 26 Sept. 1962 (Armed Forces Information and Education, Dept. of Defense 1962) p.2.
62. Lansdale (note 6) p.39.

# 9

# British and Malaysian Covert Support for Rebel Movements in Indonesia during the 'Confrontation', 1963–66

## DAVID EASTER

For many years it was widely assumed that British and Malaysian strategy during the 1963–66 Confrontation or undeclared war with Indonesia was entirely defensive. While Jakarta tried to break up Malaysia by supporting insurgents in Borneo, London and Kuala Lumpur refrained from taking offensive counter action. Recent works have modified this picture by showing that during the conflict British troops secretly carried out 'Claret' cross-border patrols up to a depth of 10,000 yards into Indonesian Kalimantan (Jakarta's part of Borneo).[1] However, there was another, even more aggressive side to Britain's and Malaysia's strategy: from 1964 the two countries covertly aided rebel movements in Indonesia in an attempt to weaken and undermine the Confrontation campaign. Using the fragmentary sources of evidence that are available this essay traces the development of this policy.[2]

The Confrontation had its origins in the process of British decolonisation in South East Asia. In November 1961 Prime Minister Harold Macmillan and his Malayan counterpart, Tunku Abdul Rahman, reached an agreement that the British colonies of Sarawak, North Borneo and Singapore should achieve independence by merging with Malaya and the British-protected Sultanate of Brunei to create a Federation of Malaysia. Neighbouring Indonesia strongly opposed this project and worked to prevent Malaysia's formation, at first covertly by supporting and encouraging an abortive revolt in Brunei in December 1962, and then overtly by announcing in January 1963 a policy of 'Confrontation' against Malaya.[3] Confrontation involved using diplomatic pressure and propaganda to try to dissuade Britain and Malaya from setting up Malaysia. There was also a military component to the campaign; from April 1963 onwards small-scale guerrilla raids were carried out into Sarawak and North Borneo from Kalimantan.

Confrontation posed a serious challenge to the formation of Malaysia and it raised questions in London and Kuala Lumpur of how best to respond. One tempting option was to retaliate by striking back at Indonesia's weak points. Economic stagnation and resentment at Javanese domination had created fertile grounds for subversion in the other Indonesian islands. Already in 1958 the United States had tried to exploit this discontent by using the CIA to support revolts against the Indonesian President, Achmed Sukarno, centred on Sumatra and the Celebes.[4] Britain and Malaya had assisted the CIA's operations: American transport planes refuelled at Changi RAF base in Singapore before air-dropping weapons to the rebels in Sumatra.[5] The revolts had in the end failed to topple Sukarno but they suggested a strategy that Britain and Malaya could use to blunt the effectiveness of Confrontation.

Even before Indonesia formally declared its policy of Confrontation this idea was being put forward in London. On 27 December 1962, in the aftermath of the Brunei revolt, Philip de Zulueta, Macmillan's Private Secretary, advised the Prime Minister that 'maybe the best solution from the purely military point of view would be to encourage a subversive movement inside Indonesia-Borneo'.[6] In Kuala Lumpur the Tunku was thinking along similar lines. A telegram to London on 24 January 1963 reported that the Malayan Premier was confident that if he really tried he could make trouble for Sukarno at home.[7] The Tunku was described as being 'clearly tempted' to act in Sumatra. Later in May, he informed a British official that rebels in the Celebes were attacking Indonesian government forces everywhere.[8] The Tunku gave no indication that he was giving support to the rebels, but he made it obvious that he felt the only solution for Indonesia and future security for Malaysia lay in the overthrow of Sukarno.

These various expressions of interest appear to have led to an examination of the possibilities of aiding rebel movements in the outer Indonesian islands. A British Ministry of Defence (MOD) briefing paper later recalled that 'Since the beginning of Confrontation we have made a particular study of dissident elements in Kalimantan itself and other Indonesian islands, especially the Celebes.'[9] However, despite this study little concrete action seems to have been taken at this point, possibly because in June–July 1963 the Malayans became heavily involved in diplomatic efforts to remove Indonesian hostility to Malaysia. It briefly appeared that a negotiated solution to Confrontation might be possible.

In the event hopes of reconciling Sukarno to Malaysia proved illusory and when the new federation was formally established on 16 September 1963, Indonesia responded by intensifying Confrontation.[10] Diplomatic relations between Jakarta and Kuala Lumpur were severed and Sukarno announced the cutting of all trade relations between the two states. On 25

September he declared that Indonesia would 'crush Malaysia'.[11] The Indonesian guerrilla raids into Borneo looked set to continue or even increase.

It was concern over the possible military effects of these raids that caused a renewal of British interest in giving support to rebel groups in Indonesia. As Borneo and Kalimantan shared a 970-mile long jungle frontier it was relatively easy for Indonesia to infiltrate guerrillas and large numbers of British and Malaysian troops would be needed to patrol the border. The Chiefs of Staff (COS) feared that if they were limited to a defensive strategy, more and more forces would have to be deployed in Borneo at the expense of Britain's other global commitments.[12] On the other hand if Britain took overt military action, such as bombing Indonesian targets, it might provoke international condemnation.

In these circumstances giving covert support to rebel groups appeared an attractive alternative. On 19 September 1963 the COS approved a Planning Staff report which concluded that if Indonesian aggression remained covert, and British military action was accordingly restricted, the only effective counter, apart from defensive operations in Borneo, was for Britain to carry out covert subversive operations against Indonesia.[13] The report suggested that such operations could be used 'to stimulate disaffection wherever possible and so to divert and dissipate Indonesian resources'. On 24 September the COS discussed possible covert operations against Indonesia.[14] Lord Mountbatten, the Chief of the Defence Staff, had in mind subversion to pin down the maximum number of Indonesian soldiers, *coup de main* raids and propaganda. Admiral Sir Varyl Begg, the British Commander-in-Chief in the Far East, was asked to examine the potential of covert action.

In Kuala Lumpur there was also renewed interest in supporting Indonesian rebel groups. On 9 October the Tunku told Begg and Lord Carrington, the visiting British Minister without Portfolio, that he was in touch with Indonesian dissidents and that he felt they should be given money and assistance.[15] Nevertheless, there was a significant difference between British and Malaysian aims in any possible covert action. The Tunku openly said to Admiral Begg and Carrington that he wanted to encourage and help the dissidents to break up Indonesia. Sumatra could then join Malaysia and the other islands in the Indonesian archipelago become independent states. Later there could be a federation of all 'Malaysian' countries. These expansionist geopolitical ambitions went far beyond the limited British goal of trying to weaken the Confrontation campaign and they were regarded with dismay in London.

Another complication was the ambivalent attitude of the United States. Although the Americans deplored Confrontation they had publicly reversed their previous opposition to Sukarno and were trying to find some way of establishing a *modus vivendi* with him. Hence the State Department refused British requests to cut off all economic aid to Indonesia and it pressed for further Indonesian-Malaysian negotiations. At the same time however, Dean Rusk, the American Secretary of State, was privately urging Britain to consider taking covert retaliatory action against Indonesia.[16]

The seemingly schizophrenic nature of American policy was confusing to British ministers but they eagerly responded to Rusk's suggestions of covert retaliation. During talks at President Kennedy's funeral on 26 November Rusk asked the new Prime Minister, Sir Alec Douglas-Home, 'Why could not something be done in Sumatra?'[17] Douglas-Home revealingly replied that 'this had been an idea of his for two years but he had not been able to persuade others that it was a good one'. Similarly, on 19 December Rusk asked Duncan Sandys, the Commonwealth Relations Secretary, if Britain had considered retaliation against Indonesia.[18] Sandys explained that for the moment Britain would concentrate on Malaysia but 'he would like to consider some counter-subversion in Sumatra'.

The issue of covert action was also being raised more and more within the British government, at both ministerial and official level. At the end of November Mountbatten seems to have submitted to Defence Secretary Peter Thorneycroft a memorandum on covert action, which incorporated the views of Begg.[19] In response Thorneycroft asked Mountbatten to mention the subject at a meeting of the Cabinet Defence and Overseas Policy Committee (DOPC) on 4 December. The actual minutes of the meeting contain no reference to covert action but they do show that ministers were worried that Britain's strategy allowed a few guerrillas to tie down a large number of British troops.[20] There were calls for the strategy to be re-examined and the committee asked the Foreign Office, the MOD and the Commonwealth Relations Office (CRO) to provide guidance for policy in case of open conflict with Indonesia.

The first draft of this paper was produced by James Cable, Head of the Foreign Office's South East Asia Department.[21] Cable emphasised that if Britain overtly attacked Indonesia without sufficient *casus belli* she would be exposed to international censure and the threat of retaliation by the Communist powers. The United States might not support her and 'the outcome could scarcely differ from that of Suez'.

Furthermore, although a conventional attack could destroy the Indonesian regular forces, Cable did not believe it would defeat the guerrillas. He suspected that even the complete occupation of Kalimantan would not achieve this. As an alternative Cable suggested offensive operations against Indonesia by Asian irregular forces claiming to be part of an Indonesian resistance movement. This would excite less international disapproval than the bombing of Indonesian targets and would divide rather than unite the Indonesians. Cable did not think that it would be possible to overthrow the Indonesian government by these means but he argued that it would intensify existing political and economic strains within the country.

Cable's draft paper was discussed by Foreign Office officials on 13 December and there are references to a contemporaneous but separate consideration of covert action by Sir Bernard Burrows, Head of the Joint Intelligence Committee (JIC).[22] The conclusions of these official discussions are not known, but at a DOPC meeting on 19 December ministers did talk about covert action.[23] They were told that at an earlier NATO Council meeting, Robert McNamara, the American Defense Secretary, had privately expressed concern that the Indonesians were likely to gradually increase their covert pressure in Borneo. McNamara had warned that Britain would find it increasingly difficult to deal with this unless she was prepared to adopt a retaliatory policy of the same kind. Alarmed by these comments the DOPC asked Rab Butler, the Foreign Secretary, to consider means of 'countering more positively' Indonesian pressure in Borneo.

Accordingly on 14 January 1964 Butler presented a memorandum to the DOPC, which looked at the possibilities of taking either offensive military action or promoting negotiations between Malaysia and Indonesia.[24] Like Cable before him, Butler feared that overt military action would not stop the guerrilla raids and would lead to international criticism. Nor did he believe that negotiations offered a way out of the conflict as he thought Jakarta was likely to insist on unacceptable terms. Butler therefore concluded that Britain should follow a 'strategy of attrition'; defending Borneo against Indonesian incursions and hoping that internal stresses would eventually cause Indonesia to weary of Confrontation. Giving covert support to rebel groups in Indonesia would obviously be a way in which London could aggravate internal stresses in that country and Butler intended to cover this point at a DOPC meeting.[25] In order to preserve secrecy he would only raise orally the 'question of retaliating in kind to Indonesian campaign of subversion and guerrilla raids'.[26]

Aside from Butler's submission the DOPC had also been given on 13 January 1964 a report by Thorneycroft, who had just returned from talks in Kuala Lumpur.[27] Thorneycroft had slightly different views on policy towards Confrontation to those of Butler. The visit to Malaysia had convinced him that if Britain relied on a drawn out defensive strategy in Borneo it would cause increasing military difficulties. Instead Thorneycroft wanted to make a forceful approach to the Americans to put maximum pressure on Sukarno to desist from Confrontation. In case this failed he also wanted plans to be drawn up for offensive military operations and for covert action. Under the latter rubric Thorneycroft seemed to include subversion and support for dissident groups in Indonesia; in a conversation with the Tunku on 6 January the Defence Secretary had suggested that 'fomenting difficulties within Indonesia' might be a possible option.[28]

So despite their differences both Thorneycroft and Butler were raising the possibility of taking covert action as an integral part of Britain's strategy in Confrontation, and as we have seen other senior ministers, such as Sandys and Douglas-Home, were in favour of this approach. Further impetus for covert action was provided by the news on 14 January that, without consulting the British, the United States was sending Attorney General Robert Kennedy to meet Sukarno in Tokyo for talks.[29] At a DOPC meeting later that same day ministers were worried that Washington might try to push forward a compromise solution to Confrontation that would damage Britain's interests.[30]

At the very least the Kennedy mission seemed to show that Britain could not rely on using Washington to strong arm Sukarno into ending Confrontation as Thorneycroft had hoped. The second part of Thorneycroft's proposals, preparing for offensive action against Indonesia, therefore took on a new importance. On the Defence Secretary's instructions Begg had drawn up a list of possible overt military measures that Britain could take.[31] On 21 January 1964 Begg also discussed covert operations with the COS and Sir Dick White, Chief of the Secret Intelligence Service.[32] The next day White and Begg attended a meeting of the DOPC.[33] The committee decided that White should start contingency planning for covert operations against Indonesia.[34] Prior political approval would be necessary before any particular covert operation was launched.

At some point between January and July 1964 this prior political approval was given. Possibly the decision to go ahead was taken in March – certainly at that time Britain was coming under pressure from the Tunku to start covert action. On 25 March White gave the DOPC a progress report on British plans for covert operations.[35] Whatever the order of events a MOD paper on 6 July recorded that

> … we have joined with the Malaysian Government in giving some encouragement to the dissident elements involved [in Celebes and other Indonesian islands]. Tactical operations across the border in Kalimantan are designed to make similar use of any opposition to the Central Government.[36]

A few days later, on 14 July 1964, Douglas-Home, the Tunku and the Australian and New Zealand Prime Ministers, Sir Robert Menzies and Keith Holyoake, were briefed on covert action at a meeting in London.[37] Tan Sri Ghazali Shafie, the Permanent Secretary at the Malaysian Ministry of

External Affairs, told them that his government 'had received very valuable assistance in drawing up plans for subversive operations against Indonesia'. He went on to say that

> So far as current operations were concerned, these were proving more difficult in Sumatra, which was under strict police control, than in Celebes, where a strong independence movement had developed

Indeed, Ghazali suggested that

> ...we might soon have to consider when it would be opportune for the Celebes to declare their independence, together with such questions as the military assistance which we should be prepared to offer them at that time, the support which we could give them by political warfare operations and the extent which we should be prepared to accord political recognition to their independence.

Ghazali's latter comments suggest that, unlike the British, the Malaysians still hoped to use covert action as a way of breaking up Indonesia.[38] There was other evidence for this. When Carrington had visited the Tunku in Kuala Lumpur in mid-April he had found that the Malaysian leader '... seemed obsessed with the belief that Indonesia was wide open to subversion and would soon disintegrate; he was convinced that Sumatra would fall into his lap like a ripe plum'.[39]

If the Malaysians had more ambitious and aggressive goals for covert action than the British this did not stop the two countries from co-operating in giving assistance to rebel groups in the outer Indonesian islands. But what form did this assistance take? Available British documents give no information on this but some clues are perhaps provided by Indonesian public statements. During United Nations Security Council debates on the Confrontation in September 1964 the Indonesian representative, Sudjarwo Tjiondronegoro, cited several instances of alleged British subversion against Indonesia.[40] He claimed that in the town of Tawau, in North Borneo, Britain had set up an organisation to promote smuggling and to provide rebel groups in Kalimantan with arms and money. Fifty Indonesians from eastern Kalimantan had been trained in Tawau in handling weapons, psychological warfare and in inciting people to revolt. In central Celebes the Indonesians had discovered in August a haul of 573 Lee-Enfield rifles, 6 Bren guns, 6 mortars and 30 tons of ammunition dropped in shallow waters. These weapons were supposedly intended for a dissident group led by Andi Selle, an Indonesian army officer who had rebelled against the central government. Another batch of British arms had been uncovered in eastern Sumatra in July.

Of course Tjiondronegoro's allegations could have simply been Indonesian propaganda and certainly the British government tried to dismiss them as such. On 14 September Sir Patrick Dean, the British Permanent Representative to the United Nations, told the Security Council that he was authorised by his government 'categorically to deny the charge that we have attempted to subvert the Indonesian Government'.[41] But Dean's denial was clearly untrue – Britain was attempting to subvert Indonesia and the location and timing of the alleged incidents does fit with what we know of British and Malaysian covert action.

Covert action remained an important if limited element of British strategy in the Confrontation even after Douglas-Home's government was replaced by a Labour administration in October 1964. This point is made evident by a memorandum, JA(65)9 (Final), drawn up in February 1965 by the Joint Action Committee, an official body with the same composition as the JIC which co-ordinated covert action.[42] Approved by senior Labour ministers in February and March, JA(65)9 (Final) was intended to be a general statement of Britain's aims in the conflict that could provide guidelines for more detailed tactical planning, especially for psychological warfare and propaganda from Singapore.[43] The paper defined Britain's short-term aim as getting Indonesia to call off Confrontation.[44] In the long term Britain would want to see a non-Communist and non-aligned Indonesia living in good relations with Malaysia.

To successfully achieve these goals British policy-makers would have to maintain a precarious balance; being neither too soft nor too harsh on the Indonesians. So although JA(65)9 (Final) stated that British armed forces would have to repulse and deter Indonesian attacks, it also warned that overt military retaliation would stoke up Indonesian resentment against Britain and Malaysia and reduce the chances of a peaceful settlement. The paper also recommended that Britain should favour the Indonesian Army, as much as this was consistent with the defence of Malaysia, as the Army was the one force in Indonesia capable of resisting the growing strength of the Indonesian Communist Party, the PKI.

These considerations placed restrictions on covert support for rebel groups in Indonesia. JA(65)9 (Final) directed that 'covert propaganda and clandestine operations' should aim to

> Aid and encourage dissident movements or tendencies inside Indonesia (in Atjeh, Sulawesi [Celebes], Kalimantan etc) with the short term objective of dissipating Indonesia's military effort against Malaysia.

At the same time the paper advised that London must recognise the possibility that

> ... in the long term effective support for dissident movements in Indonesia may be counter-productive in that it might impair the

capacity of the Army to resist the PKI and it may encourage secessionism; therefore [Britain should] attempt, by covert means, to make it clear to the Indonesian Army that any support for dissidents is no more than a tactical response to 'confrontation'.

JA(65)9 (Final) shows clearly the limited nature of British aims in covert action. Yet within a few months the MOD began to challenge these limitations, partly because of the military situation in Confrontation. Although Britain had given covert support to dissident groups in Indonesia and had initiated from April 1964 short-range cross-border patrols by British troops into Kalimantan, its strategy had mainly been defensive.[45] British forces had concentrated on repelling Indonesian raids into Borneo and had not taken overt military counter action against Indonesia. Consequently, just as the COS had feared in September 1963, Britain had been compelled to commit large numbers of units to the defence of Malaysia and this commitment was placing increasing strain on Britain's military resources.

On 6 July 1964 the COS discussed the problem with Defence Secretary Denis Healey.[46] Admiral Sir David Luce, the Chief of the Naval Staff, told Healey that increasing Indonesian pressure on Borneo and Malaya meant that 'our forces were now stretched to the limit'. Luce and the other COS wanted to take more offensive military action to wrest the initiative from Sukarno and Healey sympathised with their position.[47] He said that Britain was reacting in a most expensive way to Confrontation and he asked for a study of ways of doing it more economically. However, the Defence Secretary did not just want to look at overt military measures; he suggested to the Chiefs that one possible alternative was 'subversive action on a large scale to disintegrate Indonesia'.

The MOD was also putting forward a political case for intensifying covert action. In a memorandum for Healey on 12 July Mountbatten claimed that even if Sukarno died (the Indonesian leader was known to be suffering from ill-health), a unitary Indonesia under PKI or perhaps even army leadership was likely to carry on Confrontation.[48] So

> ...one turns to the possibilities of disintegration of Indonesia. Native opposition forces are unlikely to be able to secede in any of the islands without extensive military help from outside. However, there may be some limited benefit from an all out psychological warfare campaign, backed up perhaps by limited military assistance to dissidents

Healey's reply to Mountbatten's memorandum, on 19 July, indicated that a study of more aggressive forms of covert action was under way. The idea of using dissident groups to break up Indonesia was item C in Mountbatten's paper and Healey noted that 'action is being taken to probe the possible action in your C'.[49]

If such a study was being done it was very probably blown off course by events in August 1965. On 9 August the Tunku effectively expelled Singapore from the Malaysian Federation. London was aghast at this move, which left the vital British military base in Singapore adrift in a mainly Chinese island state and cast serious doubts on the stability and unity of the rest of Malaysia. Indeed Singapore's separation caused ministers in London to radically reappraise British policy towards Confrontation. Notably Healey performed a complete U-turn. In a letter to Prime Minister Harold Wilson on 13 August he advised that the government should adopt a policy aimed at negotiating an end to Confrontation and the withdrawal of British forces from Borneo 'even at the expense of serious strain on our relations with Malaysia.[50] Other ministers seemed to agree. On 31 August the Cabinet Overseas Policy and Defence Committee (OPDC) decided that in forthcoming Quadripartite talks with the United States, Australia and New Zealand, Britain should try to persuade the allies that it had to seek an early end to Confrontation and, in time, abandon the Singapore base.[51]

Against this background it is likely that any study of more aggressive forms of covert action would have been placed in abeyance. The topic was soon revived though, for the tentative new British policy of trying to negotiate an exit from Confrontation fell at the first fence. The Americans had abandoned their efforts to work with Sukarno and at the Quadripartite talks on 3 and 7 September, they and the Australians vehemently opposed any suggestion of Britain withdrawing from Singapore or making early moves to negotiate an end to Confrontation.[52] Under pressure from the allies Wilson's government had to promise not to launch a diplomatic initiative in the dispute.[53]

Thwarted in their plans for appeasement, British policy-makers switched back to considering taking a tougher line against Indonesia. A report on the Quadripartite talks produced by officials in the Foreign Office, CRO and MOD on 20 September 1965, observed that there were now arguments for 'sharpening our reaction to Indonesian confrontation'.[54] This would prove to the allies and Indonesia that Britain was not cooling in the defence of Malaysia and show that Singapore's separation had not weakened British resolve. Studies of a possible sharper reaction were in fact already in hand, and on 23 September ministers in the OPDC gave their approval to this planning.[55]

A Foreign Office briefing paper given to Foreign Secretary Michael Stewart ahead of the OPDC gave some idea of the form a sharper reaction could take.[56] It suggested that as part of a sharper reaction Britain could keep up vigorous patrolling on and over the border in Borneo, use propaganda and deception to create a sense of unease in Indonesia and exploit by political warfare the internal political divisions in the country. In addition there was 'Covert support for dissident movements in Indonesia, which helps in a small way to distract the Indonesian Government from confrontation.'

The Foreign Office and the CRO were not confident that these types of measures would make Sukarno change his mind about Confrontation, and they feared that the longer he remained in power, the greater the danger there was of him being succeeded by an effective and implacably hostile PKI government.[57] So even if the situation in Malaysia and Singapore did not deteriorate Britain would still need to review its policies in the future. It would have to consider options ranging from seeking talks before the position became even worse to '... making a determined effort to break up Indonesia because, however chaotic and unstable the consequences, this would be preferable to a strong and menacing communist state of 100 million people.'

Once again though events in South East Asia seem to have disrupted British planning for intensified covert action against Indonesia. On 30 September 1965 an Indonesian air force lieutenant general attempted a *coup d'état* in Jakarta. The coup was swiftly put down by the Indonesian Army but there were signs that Sukarno and the PKI had been implicated in it. In retaliation the Army savagely turned on the PKI, massacring thousands of its cadres, and began to challenge Sukarno for power.

The tumult in Indonesia raised hopes in London that Sukarno might be replaced by a more amenable government which would call off Confrontation. As a result the Foreign Office and the CRO lost interest in a sharper reaction and they began to explore ways of improving relations with Indonesia.[58] Healey and the MOD still attempted to win support for a sharper reaction at an OPDC meeting on 22 December but this was blocked by the two overseas ministries.[59] In any case the MOD now tended to conceive a sharper reaction in terms of a proportionate overt military response to Indonesian aggression rather than increased support for Indonesian dissident groups.

By the spring of 1966 the hopes of the Foreign Office and the CRO seemed to have been borne out as the Indonesian Army began to take effective control of the country. In March Sukarno's powers were greatly reduced and there was a corresponding decrease in Indonesian activity in Borneo. Encouraged by these developments on 4 April Stewart submitted a paper to the OPDC, which attempted to redefine British policy and tactics.[60] Stewart proposed that while Britain should make it clear that it would continue to defend Malaysia and Singapore against Indonesian attack, it should also demonstrate that it was ready to respond to any sincere Indonesian initiative to end Confrontation.

To this end Stewart wanted to offer Jakarta £1 million in emergency economic aid and lift an export embargo on Rolls-Royce engines for Fokker aircraft ordered by Indonesia. He also asked that while Britain's relations with the new regime were 'in the present delicate and potentially hopeful stage', military and political warfare measures to counter Confrontation should be reduced to the minimum level consistent with the safety of British forces and the security of Malaysia and Singapore. Any contact with dissident movements '... for tactical reasons or as an option in case of future implacable hostility on the part of more securely established Indonesian Government, should be discreet, limited, and non-commital; it is not our policy to seek to dismember Indonesia.'

On 6 April 1966 the OPDC gave general consent to Stewart's new policy line.[61] In doing so it abandoned any ideas of increasing support for rebel groups as part of a more aggressive campaign of covert action against Indonesia. It is highly probable that within the next few months London and Kuala Lumpur suspended all aid to the rebels as the military government in Jakarta demonstrated that it did wish to improve relations. There was a rapid détente between Indonesia and Malaysia and on 11 August the two countries signed an agreement to establish normal diplomatic relations and end Confrontation.

British support for Indonesian rebel groups during Confrontation was a natural consequence of the strategy that London followed in the conflict. In essence this was the strategy of attrition that Butler had put forward in January 1964; Britain repelled Indonesian raids into Borneo and hoped that eventually Jakarta would tire of Confrontation. Nonetheless this strategy, and the self-restraints it imposed, created serious problems for Britain. The Indonesians were able to steadily increase their covert pressure on Borneo and Malaya, forcing Britain to commit more resources to Malaysia's defence.

The only way in which London could counter this pressure was to clandestinely strike back at Indonesia and this was done via the 'Claret' operations and the secret support for rebel groups in the outer islands. The aid to the dissidents was thus one of the very few tools that Britain could use against the Confrontation campaign and therein lay its importance in overall British strategy.

Britain's aims in supporting the rebels were cautious and limited. The Foreign Office hoped to use them to weaken Confrontation – it did not wish to dismember Indonesia. Yet as the Indonesian pressure increased and as the PKI became more powerful the MOD and the Foreign Office did consider whether Britain should help the rebels to disintegrate the sprawling Indonesian state. However external events prevented these ideas from being taken any further. In this the British attitude seems to have been different to that of the Tunku who appeared ready to break up Indonesia and frequently cast covetous eyes on Sumatra.

## NOTES

1. P. Dennis and J. Grey, *Emergency and Confrontation* (Sydney: Allen and Unwin 1996); E. Smith, *Counter-Insurgency Operations: 1, Malaya and Borneo* (London: Ian Allan 1985); R. Gregorian, 'CLARET Operations and Confrontation, 1964-66', *Conflict Quarterly* 11/1 (1991).
2. Many British government documents relating to these issues are still retained. Furthermore minutes of relevant meetings of the Cabinet Defence and Overseas Policy Committee do not give a full account of what was discussed.
3. For Indonesian complicity in the revolt see Public Record Office (PRO) PREM 11/3869 Tel 256 Selkirk to FO, 8 Dec. 1962 PRO DEFE 11/391 Tel 375 Selkirk to FO, 20 Dec. 1962.
4. *Foreign Relations of the United States Vol.XVII Indonesia* (Washington DC: US GPO 1994); A. Kahin and G. Kahin, *Subversion as Foreign Policy* (NY: New Press 1995).
5. PRO FO 371/187583 Minute by Longmire, 25 Feb. 1966. T. Bower, *The Perfect English Spy* (London: Heinemann 1995) pp.228–9.
6. PRO PREM 11/4346, Minute de Zulueta to Macmillan, 27 Dec. 1962.
7. PRO DO 169/237, Tel. 103 Kuala Lumpur to CRO, 24 Jan. 1963.
8. PRO DO 169/240, Tel. 764 Kuala Lumpur to CRO, 2 May 1963.
9. PRO DEFE 13/632, 'Brief for discussion with Sir Robert Menzies' by MOD, 6 July 1964.
10. Brunei did not join Malaysia.
11. PRO FO 371/169719, Tel 3871 FO to New York, 27 Sept. 1963.
12. PRO CAB 148/16 DOP(O)(63) 3: Annex COS 329/63, 27 Sept. 1963.
13. PRO DEFE 5/143 COS 313/63, 18 Sept. 1963.
14. PRO DEFE 11/484, Minute Mountbatten to Thorneycroft, 30 Sept. 1963.
15. PRO DO 169/242, Bottomley to Pritchard, 11 Oct. 1963.
16. PRO PREM 11/4350, Tel. 1553 Home to FO, 26 Sept. 1963.
17. PRO PREM 11/4905, 'Extract from Record of a Conversation at HM Embassy Washington…on November 26 1963', 26 Nov. 1963.
18. Ibid. 'Record of Conversation between the Foreign Secretary and the United States' Secretary of State…on December 19, 1963', 19 Dec. 1963.
19. The actual submission from Mountbatten to Thorneycroft on 29 Nov. is retained but Thorneycroft's reply is in PRO DEFE 13/387, Minute Hockaday to Mountbatten, 4 Dec. 1963.
20. PRO CAB 148/15 DO(63), 3rd Meeting (2), 4.12.63.
21. PRO FO 371/173503, Cable to Golds, 10 Dec. 1963.
22. Ibid. Minute Waterfield to Arthur, 12 Dec. 1963.
23. PRO CAB 148/15 DO(63), 5th Meeting (2), 19 Dec. 1963. PRO FO 371/175263, Bottomley to Golds, 19 Feb. 1964.
24. PRO CAB 129/116 CP(64) 5, 6 Jan. 1964.
25. PRO FO 371/179118, Memo by Cable, 4 Jan. 1964. PRO CAB 148/1 DO(64) 1, 7 Jan. 1964.
26. PRO FO 371/175266, Memo by Cable, 7 Jan. 1964.
27. PRO CAB 148/1 DO(64) 5, 13 Jan. 1964.
28. PRO DEFE 13/631, 'Note of Meeting with Tunku Abdul Rahman, Prime Minister of Malaysia, on 6 January 1964', 8 Jan. 1964.
29. PRO FO 371/175261, Tel. 584 FO to Washington, 14 Jan. 1964; Tel. 613 FO to Washington, 14 Jan. 1964.
30. PRO CAB 148/1 DO(64), 1st Meeting (1), 14 Jan. 1964.
31. PRO DEFE 11/485, Minute by Sec. COS COS 19/64, 16 Jan. 1964.
32. Ibid.; Mountbatten to Thorneycroft, 21 Jan. 1964. PRO DEFE 11/488, Minute Watkins to COS, 2 March 1964.

33. PRO CAB 148/1 DO(64), 2nd Meeting (3), 22 Jan. 1964.
34. PRO DEFE 13/631 'Copy of Minute from SEC/CABINET to 'C', dated 24 Jan.1964', not dated.
35. PRO FO 371/175084, Tel. 526 Head to CRO, 16 March 1964. PRO FO 371/175085, Pritchard to Head, 20 March 1964. PRO DEFE 11/488, Note Watkins to COS, 20 March 1964. The actual minutes of the DOPC meeting make no reference to covert operations; see PRO CAB 148/1 DO(64), 16th Meeting (2), 25 March 1964.
36. PRO DEFE 13/632, 'Brief for discussions with Sir Robert Menzies' by MOD, 6 July 1964.
37. PRO DEFE 25/158, 'Extract of Note of a Meeting held on 14th July at 9am.', 22 July 1964.
38. The Australians and New Zealanders shared the British point of view on this. Mountbatten, who attended the meeting, told the COS that 'The Tunku... outlined the various political activities which were being taken to aid Sumatra and Celebes to break away from Java. This had alarmed the Australian and New Zealand Prime Ministers considerably.' DEFE 32/9, 'Confidential Annex to COS 47th Meeting/64, Held on 14th July', 22 July 1964.
39. PRO FO 371/175066, 'Report by Lord Carrington on his visit to South East Asia, April 7–18 1964', 24 April 1964.
40. PRO FO 371/175087, Tel. 1824 Dean to FO, 9 Sept. 1964. United Nations Security Council Official Records 19, Aug.–Dec. 1964, 1149th Meeting, 14 Sept. 1964.
41. FO 371/175088 Tel 1875 Dean to FO, 14 Sept. 1964.
42. PRO PREM 13/430, Minute Trend to Wilson on 'Malaysia', not dated.
43. Ibid Minute PM/65/32, Stewart to Wilson, 26 Feb. 1965. Minute Healey to Wilson, 1 March 1965. Minute Moon to Wright, 5 March 1965. PRO FO 371/181503, Golds to King, 1 April 1965.
44. PRO DEFE 5/162 COS 162/65, Appendix 1, 20 Sept. 1965.
45. PRO DEFE 4/169 COS(64), 33rd Meeting (7), 5 May 1964. PRO CAB 148/2 DO (64) 34, 28 April 1964.
46. PRO DEFE 25/212 MM/COS 5/65, 'Minutes of a Meeting...between the Secretary of State for Defence and the Chiefs of Staff on Tuesday, 6th July 1965 at 2 pm.', 6 July 1965.
47. Ibid. PRO DEFE 11/593, Minute Vice Chief of Defence Staff to Mounbatten, 2 July 1965.
48. PRO DEFE 13/475, Minute Mountbatten to Healey, 12 July 1965.
49. Ibid.; Minute Healey to Mountbatten, 19 July 1965.
50. PRO PREM 13/431, Healey to Wilson, 13 Aug. 1965.
51. PRO CAB 148/18 OPD(65), 37th Meeting (1), 31 Aug. 1965.
52. PRO FO 371/181529, 'Record of a Meeting held in the India Office...on...3 September 1965', 10 Sept. 1965; 'Record of a Meeting held in the India Office...on...7 September 1965', not dated.
53. PRO PREM 13/431, 'Discussions with Mr Ball', 8 Sept. 1965. PRO PREM 13/589, 'Record of a Conversation between the Prime Minister and the United States' Under Secretary of State, Mr George Ball...on...September 8, 1965.' Not dated.
54. PRO CAB 148/22 OPD(65) 131, 20 Sept. 1965.
55. PRO CAB 148/18 OPD(65), 41st Meeting (3), 23 Sept. 1965.
56. PRO FO 371/181529 'Brief for Secretary of State for the OPD Meeting at 10 am on 22 September' by Peck, 21 Sept. 1965.
57. PRO FO 371/181530, Memo by Joint-Malaysia Indonesia Department on 'Action against Indonesian Confrontation', 1 Oct. 1965.
58. Ibid.; Pritchard to Head, 27 Oct. 1965. PRO FO 371/181457, Brief by Peck for Burrows, 29 Nov. 1965.
59. PRO CAB 148/24 OPD(65) 191, 14 Dec. 1965; OPD(65) 192, 20.12.65. PRO CAB 148/18 OPD(65), 55th Meeting (3), 22 Dec. 1965.
60. PRO CAB 148/54 OPD(O)(DR)(WP)(66) 6, 4 April 1965.
61. PRO CAB 148/25 OPD(66) 19th Meeting, 6 April 1966.

# PART III

# THE MALAYAN EMERGENCY

# 10

# Corpses, Prisoners of War and Captured Documents: British and Communist Narratives[1] of the Malayan Emergency, and the Dynamics of Intelligence Transformation[2]

## KARL HACK

*I hadn't the slightest idea how to penetrate the MCP, nor had he the director, nor the handful of British officers who were serving under me, I don't think that we got any penetration achieved at that time, not until the intentions of the Communist Party became a little bit more obvious, and then it became a little bit late.*
From Guy Madoc, Deputy Director MSS in 1947, speaking in 1980s.[3]

*The importance of intelligence in the Malayan Emergency campaign cannot be exaggerated ... In a country covered with dense jungle, where evasion is easy and contact with the enemy cannot be made without secret information, it is essential that intelligence should be gained from the Communist forces without their knowing. Intelligence, therefore, to use semi-technical language, must be 'alive' as well as 'blown' or 'dead' .... At present the opposite occurs. The bulk of our reliable information is obtained not from agents or police friends or contacts but instead from corpses, prisoners of war and captured documents.*
From 'Intelligence Services and Related Counter-Measures' in Malaya, Appendix IX of a Cabinet Paper C(51)59, of 21 Dec. 1951.

*The small number of CTs [Communist Terrorists] in the vast area of dense jungle in Malaya can seldom be found without intelligence information*[4]
From Director of Operations Report, Sept. 1957.

These three quotations raise an important question about the Malayan Emergency: how was intelligence transformed? Counter-insurgency intelligence in Malaya was ineffective in 1948. In 1952 it had large numbers of officers handling documents and surrendered enemy personnel (SEP), but not enough agents able to give information on which operations could be planned. By 1957 Police Special Branch had become central to the defeat of a now-ailing Communist insurgency, running hundreds of SEP and agents, and had catalogued most insurgent names and locations.

The question of how this transformation was achieved is approached in three ways. First, by contrasting intelligence at its worst (1948–49) and best (post-1954). This contrast highlights those developments which were key to intelligence transformation.

Second, it will be argued that, in explaining these key changes, there should be increased emphasis on an incremental, rather than a 'Big Bang', model of change. The foundations for intelligence transformation, for achieving the contrast between these periods, should be located in the objective ethnic and social terrain of Malaya, and the gradual refinement of 'population control'. 'Population control' seen not as mere repression, but as the disciplined application of coercive and persuasive power, including breaking up larger enemy formations by relentless military activity, resettlement, detention without trial and food control. In Malaya, such coercive measures lay at the heart of the campaign, with 'hearts and minds' tactics – aimed at ameliorating discontent and inducing insurgents to surrender and co-operate – serving an important auxiliary function.

This contribution's emphasis on objective conditions, and gradual change, contrasts with the existing 'British' (or more properly 'Anglo-Saxon', as it includes Australian and Canadian) historiography. This predominant 'British' school stresses sudden changes in leadership in 1952, when General Sir Gerald Templer was appointed as the first and only joint Director of Operations and High Commissioner. His new team is seen as transforming intelligence and a previously stalemated campaign.[5] Yet it will be argued that this British 'story' in effect rests on oral history and the shaping power of memory as much as it relies on historical analysis. There are other, competing stories, not least the Communist one, which need to be reconciled in our final account.

The third approach is thus to try and integrate the dominant and divergent British and Communist stories about 1949–54 into one internally coherent analysis. In so doing, it will be argued that Templer did have an important impact – but not necessarily the one claimed for him by British memory. That his era (1952–54) did see British intelligence increase in efficiency, but only after the Malayan Communist Party's (MCP) insurgency had entered a decline. A decline reflected in their very different telling of the story.

The conclusion will be that the insurgency was successfully undermined by a British campaign and intelligence apparatus working well below peak efficiency, and still suffering serious leadership problems. In a refinement of my previous considerations of the Malayan Emergency, I therefore argue intelligence transformation involved strong elements both of incrementalism and of the 'great leap' forward which came with successive leadership changes.

## THE GOOD AND THE BAD – INTELLIGENCE IN 1948–49 AND POST-1954

The Malayan Emergency was declared by the British authorities in Malaya on 16–18 June 1948. It was not declared because of intelligence *per se*, but because five murders on plantations on 16 June confirmed a pattern of spiralling violence.[6] The Malayan Security Service (MSS) was responsible for intelligence in Malaya. It suffered from divided focus, Indonesia's war of independence making Britain nervous of Malay 'extremism', from small numbers, from its separation from the police and so from ordinary police information, and from the legacy of World War II.

The war of 1941–45 had ruptured British intelligence structures. The torture and brutality of the Japanese *kempeitai* (military police) tainted the very idea of agents and intelligence. Even worse, some Asian Special Branch officers passed from British to Japanese control, and then back again.[7] Other local officers failed to get rid of habits developed to limit the material given to the Japanese, such as feeding translated Chinese newspaper reports as if they were from agents.[8] The war, in sum, left a legacy of poverty, black marketeering and crime, and raised the MCP and its anti-Japanese guerrillas to the status of heroes.[9] In the early Emergency, guerrillas quite explicitly compared British tactics to Japanese behaviour.[10]

There were relatively few gains for British intelligence from World War II, but three need noting. First, wartime inflation and postwar shortages made the black market a pervasive evil, so that 'everything' up to the highest level, could be bought.[11] Second, a small but important group of men from Force 136 (Britain's wartime clandestine organisation for Asia) had served as liaison officers with the Malayan National Liberation Army's (MNLA) wartime precursor. That is, the Malayan People's Anti-Japanese Army (MPAJA).[12] These men could be expected to have an understanding of guerrilla mentalité, if not their own contacts. Some ex-Force 136 went on to reach high positions, such as Claude Fenner and Ian Wylie, who both spent time in Special Branch headquarters.

Finally, the wartime Malayan People's Anti-Japanese Army killed many 'running dogs', whose families then had no reason to love the MPASA. Since most police and officials were Malay, most MPAJA Chinese, this reinforced ethnic divisions, but it also made the Communists enemies among the Chinese. In one case, a beautiful Chinese seamstress whose father had been executed became an excellent government informer. People who had worked for the Japanese – voluntarily or not – also had good reason to serve with the security forces against their erstwhile enemies.[13] The seamstress, who the Communists were also extorting money from, risked going out hooded with Special Branch officers in order to identify suspects. In another such operation, two *orang asli*[14] informers stood in a jeep, its glaring headlights hiding their identity from villagers. They identified more than 60 suspects who had been seen in insurgent jungle camps, who were then bound and trucked off, and their houses fired.

Not atypical of the British 'counter-terror' of the early Emergency, this sort of operation and information helped to sort 'the goats from the sheep', pushing the guerrillas into the jungle. Thus early antics, with MNLA visiting *kampongs* (villages) for celebrations and food, had to be replaced by a sophisticated and vulnerable supply system between jungle and village, a system kept going by dedicated members of the *Min Yuen* (mass or people's organisation). This process of separating out insurgents from the villages was itself crucial. Once it had happened, however, the sort of information required to locate and ambush insurgents in the jungle was less likely to come from informers outside of the *Min Yuen* and MNLA. Informers could still indicate that the MNLA visited particular routes, premises and individuals, perhaps to order food or collect subscriptions, but privileged and specific information on MNLA plans, camps or movements had to come mainly from the *Min Yuen*.[15]

The 1941–45 war also boosted a tendency for poor Chinese to flee state pressure, cyclical unemployment and low wages by flight to Malaya's jungle frontier. Now also fleeing Japanese oppression and food scarcity, the numbers of jungle fringe 'squatters' – growing vegetables and food – spiralled to over 500,000. Here was a group outside normal administration, speaking a different language from the majority of administrators, who mostly learned Malay. A group, in short, outside the reach of intelligence, whether of the administrative or police sort.

Thus burdened, and lacking adequate training, the small Malayan Security Service failed to recognise the full extent and importance of the MCP decisions of March to May 1948. These were to change from a 'united front' approach of labour organisation and penetrating political parties to one of preparing for revolutionary war. They programmed spiralling violence into the pre-existing pattern of MCP pressure, matched by British counter-pressure, arrests and labour control. The MCP had anticipated a full British response to these new tactics would come only after September.[16] In June they were thus caught off-guard themselves, being forced to hastily reassemble wartime anti-Japanese guerrillas and new recruits into an army. Ultimately called the Malayan National Liberation Army (MNLA) and organised into regiments and independent platoons, this peaked at around 7,000 in 1950–51.[17]

Intelligence continued to be Britain's 'Achilles heel' in 1948–49, despite an August 1948 reorganisation. The Malayan Security Service – a small, non-executive, urban-based[18] intelligence bureau[19] – was dissolved. Intelligence was transferred to the Singapore and Federation of Malaya's separate police forces. It became the responsibility of their 'Special Branches', set up under each force's Criminal Investigation Department (CID).[20] Thus intelligence could now more easily be checked against information from ordinary policing. Yet Special Branch was still under-manned. In 1948 Malayan Special Branch had 12 officers and 44 inspectors – most of them expatriate or Malay – to face several thousand mainly Chinese insurgents and several hundred thousand MNLA sympathisers and organisers. The expansion of the overall police force from under 10,000 to 70,000 simultaneously placed strains on the whole structure.[21] A position made worse by tensions within the police between new British recruits with Palestinian experience, those who had been 'in the bag' (prisoners) in the 1939–45 war, and those 'not in the bag'.[22]

Forced to compete for personnel, and finding recruitment of Chinese-speakers difficult, Special Branch continued to perform poorly. It also failed to establish a dedicated intelligence training institute, instead sharing general Criminal Investigation Department training.[23] In 1948–49, Special Branch thus failed to generate intelligence which was of operational use to the army in any quantity. What it did achieve was mainly background intelligence on Communist personnel, formations and aims. Battalion intelligence officers and patrol leaders complained they were starved of information. Preparing a single patrol might mean visits to the Labour and Chinese departments and multiple other sources, and snooping round a plantation on the pretence of being a purchaser of rubber latex, in order to assemble information on Communist haunts and routes. Even worse, Far East Land Forces intelligence often talked vaguely of bandit groups rather than specific units and locales, so some battalions simply rode 'to the sound of guns'. A large proportion of troops were committed to sweeps of areas – sometimes including plantation and jungle – with inadequate direction.[24]

In summary, by early 1950 intelligence was still wracked by the lack of sufficient personnel (especially Chinese-speaking), and by the absence of strategy and tactics which could produce adequate operational intelligence. Chinese of all classes still had good reason to withhold information: relatives in the jungle; lingering admiration for the MCP's wartime anti-Japanese activities; fear; and distrust of a police force raised from Malaya's largest grouping, the Malays. Policing was considered 'a low class and distasteful profession'.[25]

Yet by 1957 Special Branch had drawn up an order of battle of insurgent numbers, names, locations, organisation, and plans.[26] In 1952–54 a pattern had emerged in which combined Special Branch-military-police operations targeted individual camps of resettled villagers, or small areas. Since the MCP had opted for a rural-based guerrilla strategy – despite most Chinese living in towns, where they earned Malay animosity by controlling much of

Malaya's economy – the squatters were the MNLA's blood supply. A single guerrilla required five pounds of rice a week to survive, which increasingly had to be smuggled through checkpoints in bicycle rims or under garments.[27] The jungle was no substitute. One British report on wartime conditions gave a bleak picture of the hardships jungle life could impose, with anaemia, running and persistent ulcers, and malaria all rampant. For large groups, 'it was quite impossible to live off the jungle'. Access to *orang asli*-grown tapioca, and food grown on the jungle edge, was essential.[28]

The *Min Yuen* thus acted as the umbilical cord between the squatters, the MNLA's sustaining force, and the jungle. From 1950–52 most squatters – over 330,000 out of half a million by September 1951 – were resettled in camps.[29] No fewer than 600,000 workers were regrouped (concentrated together on an existing site). The resettlements were later more optimistically re-labelled 'New Villages', with land titles available after December 1951. The main intelligence problem thus became to create information which would enable guerrillas to be ambushed as they came into the space between jungle and camp.

Surrendered or captured enemy personnel (SEP and CEP) were still needed, to provide the initial information, namely a picture of local MCP and MNLA organisation.[30] Indeed, until 1952, SEP, CEP and captured documents ('corpses', as one document put it) – were the most plentiful sources of information, and they continued to be important thereafter.[31]

These sources enabled security force operations to be matched to MNLA areas of operation. Then additional agents had to be secured, people in current contact with the MNLA, who could give 'live' information on future plans. From 1952–56 techniques for securing such agents were refined. Food operations and prior resettlement were the crucial pre-requisite to this learning process. Increasingly, operations featured intensified arrests, policing and food denial: cans were punctured, rice pre-cooked or served communally, food movements controlled. It could take up to three months before insurgents used up local stockpiles, but ultimately they would be compelled to replenish supplies.[32]

As food operations intensified, these not only blocked MNLA supplies, but gave New Villagers an 'excuse' to deny foodstuffs by saying it was impossible to buy them, or to get them past checkpoints.[33] With controls beginning to bite, some suppliers could be spotted, given enough rope to hang themselves with, and then confronted. Sometimes mass arrests would remove the most reliable *Min Yuen* first, forcing the guerrillas to rely on less committed, more vulnerable supporters.

Finally, resettlement might weaken Communist counter-intelligence. Not only by arrests, but because the creation of a security force and Home Guard-saturated zone reduced the opportunity for killer squads to eliminate traitors.

Increasing government control provided everyday opportunities for Chinese to contact administrators without arousing suspicion, for instance during duties as Home Guards. Brian Stewart notes how Operation 'Letter Box', which involved interviewing villagers individually, could sow doubts among Communist supporters.[34] Communist counter-intelligence was thus being undermined. Yet as far back as 1945 a Force 136 report (written by British officers who had spent time with the guerrillas), noted that: 'Some of our men, armed with pistols, would frequently patrol or be stationed in the *kampong* [village, here a village used for supplies] to eliminate informers. The *kampong* people, *to protect themselves, insisted that this should be done* [my emphasis].'[35] In this way, up to 100 Chinese a month were being murdered by early 1950, before resettlement took off.[36] As it did so, Communist killer squads and supporters were likely to be decreasingly effective at taking out 'running dogs'. This inability was likely to breed increased vulnerability, fear of exposure, and even self-serving betrayal, among supporters.[37]

Once compromised, meanwhile, the MNLA's suppliers could be turned. Used as agents, they could provide information from the men they supplied, information used to ambush these same fighters.[38] In addition, SEP could be attached to patrols, to help identify Communist tracks and haunts in the area between resettlement camps and jungle.

Intelligence, in the form of securing large numbers of additional informers, and agents with operationally-useful information, in this way centred on resettlement and a 'population control' approach. An approach which included measures such as issuing identity cards, powers to detain without trial and the death penalty for carrying weapons. It could only became effective, however, after the advent of the 'Briggs Plan', put into place by the first Director of Operations (April 1950 to December 1951), Lt-General Sir Harold Briggs. This made squatter resettlement systematic rather than sporadic, insisting resettlements should receive full government administration. Furthermore, the refining of these techniques took place, and could only take place, from 1952 onwards. At this stage quantitative resettlement had reached a point (over 70 per cent of resettlement complete) where energies could be released for qualitative improvement. Special Branch's 1949–51 expansion under the guidance of the first Director of Intelligence (William Jenkins) was also bringing it to a size more capable of exploiting the new situation, and a further and rapid expansion took place in 1952–53.[39]

The Briggs Plan also set up 'War Executive' committees at District, State and Federal levels. The latter combined civil and military leaders, such as the local District Officer and battalion commander, and a Special Branch officer. As Brian Stewart argues, these had the benefit of being able to order and co-ordinate concrete action. They might not have been possible at all in many non-colonial settings, since the colonial 'District Officer', a civil servant knowledgeable and authoritative in a defined locality, provided the essential link downwards.

The Briggs Plan took effect gradually and not without setbacks: by late 1951 most squatters had been moved, but often to camps inadequately sited and protected; in 1952–54 extra barbed wire, lighting and amenities were provided; and by the late 1950s some were thriving settlements.

This ongoing refinement of resettlement areas and food control was destined to create a pattern of improvement to which the MCP had no effective response, even before the refinement of British techniques.[40] In its 'October 1951 Resolutions' the MCP Central Committee reversed the previous year's decision to fight resettlement to the end, choosing instead to reduce attacks on civilian-related targets, and increase political subversion and supply and planting work.[41]

The Secretary-General of the Communist Party, Chin Peng, re-emphasised this dilemma as recently as February 1999. At a workshop with historians in Canberra, he recalled that even Chin Peng was 'forced by circumstances' to retreat 'one step after another', from Pahang in the south, through Perak, to the Thai border in the north (1952–54). Not by plan, but because of security force pressure, and because his headquarters group could neither find nor buy enough food to sustain itself.[42] Thus, though population control was imperfect – New Villagers spent much of the day working outside the fence, and many villages lacked perimeter lighting even in late 1951 – it was a crucial if incipient improvement by late 1951. Already, in 1951 to 1952, it was forcing the MNLA to reduce average unit size, and persuading them to change tactics.[43]

By 1954 aspects of intelligence other than resettlement, food control and jungle fringe patrols were also gaining prominence. These included setting up jungle forts, because since 1952 the remaining guerrillas were retreating into deep jungle. A combination of SAS, helicopter and aircraft-supported deep jungle patrols, and jungle 'forts' (often a few rough huts arranged in a triangle or other close formation, with surrounding growth cleared) was used from 1953.[44] These acted as trading posts, and allowed the *orang asli* to be courted with medical aid, rewards for information, and protection. This could break *orang asli*-Chinese guerrilla bonds, which in some cases went back to an exchange of essentials such as salt for tapoica during the Japanese occupation.[45] Border operations also increased in importance with the 1952–54 'Little Long March' of the Communist Politburo and some regiments to the north. There the main Communist forces were to remain, only finally reaching a peace agreement in 1989.

Finally, as the 'Little Long March' stranded increasingly small MNLA units to the rear, and government operations bled these left-behind groups of men and sustenance, increasingly high-level SEP came out in the late 1950s. These gave additional material for propaganda and air-dropped leaflets targeted at particular groups.[46] A few re-entered the jungle to coax out colleagues. Others were recruited to the 'Special Operations Volunteer Forces', units of SEP led by European officers, which were found to be useful mainly in areas they were personally familiar with.[47] Even at this late stage, however, the tightening noose of patrols and controls – as government security forces could be concentrated against fewer targets and areas – was vital. This was especially important for Special Branch, which had to optimise use of its most scarce resources, high-quality Chinese and Chinese-speaking officers.

In summary, intelligence up to 1952, by when the Communist campaign was already in serious trouble, relied mainly on recruitment of more intelligence personnel, and on SEP, CEP, and 'corpses'. Early informers also played an important role, especially in helping to separate the 'goat from the sheep'. As the MNLA retreated into the jungle and reorganised, however, larger numbers of agents, in direct contact with the MNLA or *Min Yuen*, were needed. The pre-conditions for securing these were in place by 1952. Resettlement was now moving from a quantitative to a qualitative phase. With the uniformed police expansion coming to an end as well, priority could go to expanding Special Branch. In 1952 alone Special Branch inspectors and police lieutenants rose from 114 to 195, rising again to 297 the following year.[48]

Techniques for intelligence operations were then refined. Combined Special Branch-police-army operations, with resettlement as a prerequisite, food control at their core, and securing agents taking priority over military operations, remained the most effective route to operationally-useful intelligence after 1951–52.[49] As the Director of Operations' Report of 1957 put it in emphasising the crucial importance of ambushes: 'Such ambushes are only likely to be possible if the CTs ['Communist Terrorists'] are forced to contact their suppliers in or near villages or their places of work in order to obtain food or other supplies.'[50]

Thus most of the contrast between early and late intelligence performance was achieved in a space of a few years (1950–54). If we can confirm how this was achieved, we will be able to offer a more analytical conclusion on the factors facilitating and frustrating intelligence transformation.

THE CONTINUITY OR INCREMENTAL THESIS VERSUS THE 'BIG
BANG' MODEL OF CHANGE

*Malaya could still be lost if a new and wholehearted effort is not made. The
chain of direct and indirect consequences flowing from such an event would
be far graver for Britain, for the standard of living of its people, and for the
whole western position in Asia than is generally realised.* From *The
Economist*, 24 Nov. 1951.

*the communist hold on Malaya is as strong, if not stronger, today as it has ever
been. This fact must be faced.* From DEFE11/46 (1471) British Defence Co-
ordinating Committee (Far East) to Chiefs of Staff, 15 Nov. 1951.

*owing to the enemies concentration of and rigid control over the masses the
party is confronted with numerous difficulties ...[with mass organisations]
...At present, certain difficulties in our procurement of supplies are closely
connected with these weaknesses.* From the MCP's Oct. 1951 Resolutions.[51]

The predominant, British explanation and experience of the Emergency is
that in late 1951 there was stalemate. A plan for effective 'population
control' had been devised, but its implementation was ineffective.
Emergency incidents and security force casualties peaked in 1951, High
Commissioner Sir Henry Gurney was ambushed and killed on 6 October,
resettlements were often on poor land with inadequate perimeter defences.
British leadership was hit by the successive death of Gurney, the retirement
of Briggs and departure of the Director of Intelligence, all between late
1951 and early 1952. This is matched by a majority – though not unanimous
– British tradition that Templer's arrival in February 1952 'energised' the
campaign.[52]

Templer arrived in late February 1952, as both High Commissioner and
Director of Operations. Combining these roles enabled him to eliminate
disputes. He made a whirlwind country-wide tour round New Villages and
security force posts. A new Director of Intelligence[53] (DOI) – Jack Morton
– was appointed. For the first time the DOI was now authorised to
coordinate military as well as police intelligence, and Templer emphasised
absolute control of all intelligence by Special Branch. Their needs were to
have priority should army operations threaten to expose their agents.[54] Guy
Madoc, who had received full intelligence training and experience in
London and Thailand (1947–50) was promoted to head Special Branch as
'Senior Assistant Commissioner', Police Department E. This was itself a
new department, as Special Branch was taken away from CID control.
Madoc managed to get a dedicated intelligence training school running
efficiently within a few months.

The British version thus argues Templer's leadership – by example, by administrative action, by personnel selection and management – 'energised' the floundering Briggs Plan's 'population control'. It made a plan which was right in theory work in practice. The crucial changes thus came in a 'Big Bang' – a 'Great Leap forward' – catalysed by Templer. Had Gurney continued the British version suggests the campaign would have stalemated or worsened.[55] By extension, intelligence changes might have been delayed or remained unthought of: Special Branch might have remained under CID control.

Templer's era is also supposed to have seen dramatic improvements in 'hearts and minds' policies. These measures, especially the extension of elections from town and village level (1951–52) through to all-Malayan elections (1955) were accompanied by new amenities for New Villages. Schools, medical posts, government-sponsored strains of pig, piped water, all these and more started appearing.

According to the most sophisticated variant of this story, the MCP's 'October 1951 Resolutions' had provided a 'window of opportunity'. That is, by ordering a switch in 'Number One Urgent Task' – from military to 'mass organisation' and subversion – it temporarily reduced pressure on the security forces. This window was to close quickly, as at the end of 1952 the MCP called for military action to be given a greater priority again. Fortunately, Britain had meanwhile taken the opportunity to add measures which would minimise discontent amongst squatters and Chinese. The radical discontinuity was thus Templer's achievement of a combined model of population control with new 'hearts and minds' measures. Measures covering both political and civil fields, both votes and the village pump. The addition of the carrot to the stick, of 'hearts and minds' policies to a coercion approach, was in this way crucial.

By contrast, I have argued elsewhere that the Emergency was not headed for protracted stalemate in 1951–52, and that the British version's apparently radical discontinuities did not have the precise effects claimed. Instead, the mature 'population control' approach of Briggs was gradually starting to work by late 1951, and could only become more effective as resettlement consolidated. Readers should refer to my previous articles in *Intelligence and National Security* and in the *Journal of Southeast Asian Studies* for details.[56]

These articles question the British story of stalemate in late 1951. They argue there was policy continuity, and that 1951–52 proved a watershed. By early 1952 the physical act of resettlement, and the process of raising an extra 60,000 police and up to 250,000 Home Guard, were mostly over.[57] Energy could now begin to be transferred from quantitative to qualitative tasks: from raising police to training; from trucking people to new resettlements to turning these into well-protected areas with desirable amenities.[58]

This is how Gurney saw things on 3 October 1951, immediately before his death on the 6th.[59] Just a few days later Director of Operations Directive Number 17 focused on tightening food control and security around resettlements. By November at the latest the government was looking to increase the role of Chinese Village Home Guards.[60] Such incremental improvements in the policing and protection of resettlement areas – continuing even in the period October 1951 to February 1952 – were to underpin later Special Branch operations on which increased 'live' intelligence depended.

More importantly, there is an alternative to the predominant (but not monopoly)[61] British story: a Communist interpretation.[62] At least in so far as this is represented by Chin Peng, the Secretary-General of the MCP from 1947.

Chin Peng was born in 1922 in Sitiawan, a small town situated next to a major tin-mining area in the Malayan state of Perak. His parents were middle class, in that they ran a bicycle and vehicle sales and spare parts business. As a prewar student, he gravitated to Communism as the best way of combating the Japanese. Rising in the Perak wartime guerrillas, he became Perak State Secretary (1943), and liaison officer with Britain's Force 136. Following the war, he replaced Secretary-General Lai Tek, who fled in 1947 when his exposure as a traitor (a French, British and Japanese agent) seemed imminent. Chin Peng thus played a major role in the decisions which led to full-scale insurgency in 1948, while still in his early twenties.

Chin Peng has a 'little smile always on his face', startling frankness, and the ability to charm people with his intelligence and understanding of their needs. Gerald de Cruz, who worked with Chin Peng in postwar Communist propaganda, has described him as 'the perfect gentleman', with 'a core of steel', a warm and lovable devotee of Communism.[63] He speaks good English, in addition to Chinese and Malay. Since 1989, when the Communist remnants (by then split into several factions) agreed to cease hostilities, he has been hoping to stake his forces' claim to history – that they accelerated Malayan independence by at least 10 to 25 years – by giving interviews and writing his biography.[64]

Chin Peng's understanding of the conflict seems to be that the Briggs Plan was causing considerable problems by 1951. This existence of two opposed memories or stories was demonstrated in an encounter at Canberra in February 1991, where Chin Peng was holding a workshop with historians. Some of these sought to extract from Chin Peng an account which could be squared with the 'British' version – which in turn owes

FIGURE 6

Chin Peng (Secretary-General of the Malayan Communist Party, 1947–) and Leon Comber (ex-Malayan Special Branch Officer) at Canberra – February 1999.
*Source*: Author.

much to the memory of participants such as Guy Madoc.[65] Australian Lt-General John Coates began the relevant session by asking Chin Peng what he considered the Communist high-point.[66] Other participants asked whether he did not think the MCP achieved a high point later than 1950, or whether he viewed Gurney's assassination as particularly significant.

This was because Chin Peng's suggested high-point was around 1949–50, before Briggs' arrival. At this point the MNLA still hoped it might liberate small towns, perhaps even a large area of rural South Kelantan. Even before resettlement, however, food shortages prevented large formations being maintained for more than short periods. The largest forces were broken up. They were 'forced' to disperse, and the emphasis changed to small-scale attacks. Chin Peng stressed mounting food problems, combined with Malaya's unfavourable geography: there being no areas distant from authority and yet populous, as in China. Pressed on Gurney's 6 October 1951 assassination he said it made them 'happy … [but] … we don't take this as a turning point'.[67] No one or two individuals could decide the fate of a campaign, 'even myself'.[68] Where the British story makes Gurney's death a necessary evil, the removal of a man who obstructed change, or who might have turned Chinese policy damagingly harsh, Chin

Peng saw it as just one engagement, albeit a spectacularly successful one.[69]

What seems to have happened is that the Communists' numbers increased from 1949 to mid-1951, as population control drove out those fearful of arrest or angered by resettlement. As one 'subscription-collector put it, 'great changes in far-off places [China and Indo-China] had heightened the morale in Malaya' by early 1950.[70] Yet the food supply problem was not resolved. The Briggs Plan and the Communists' August 1950 instructions to resist resettlement thus brought the number of incidents to a 1951 peak. However, in October 1951 the Communists concluded their sabotage and anti-resettlement policies were alienating support. The resolutions of that month changed the emphasis in their plans, but this failed to prevent, and may even have accelerated, their decline as improving resettlement further garrotted supplies in 1951–54.

FIGURE 2
EMERGENCY INCIDENTS BY YEAR

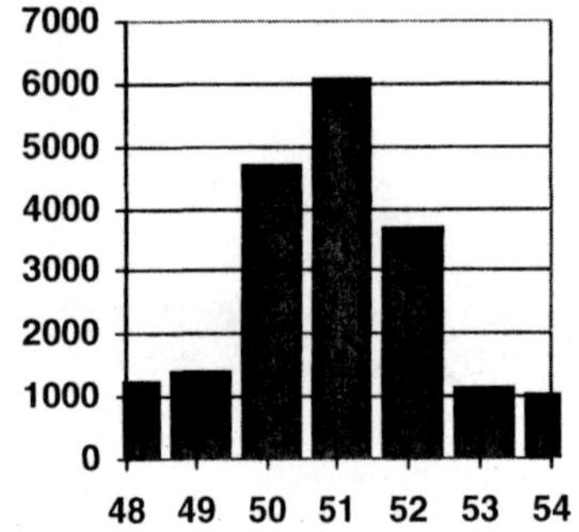

FIGURE 3
SECURITY CASUALTIES BY YEAR

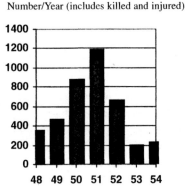

Number/Year

Number/Year (includes killed and injured)

*Source*: Adapted from Director of Operations Report dated Sept. 1957[71]

The British story thus does not fit with the Communist account, especially in its emphasis on dramatic change around 1952. This is part of a general trend for Chinese versions to differ from the British, especially over the emphasis the British story puts on 'winning hearts and minds'.[72] A classic example of the entirely different perspectives taken is the case of the town of Tanjong Malim. Brian Stewart's account in this volume confirms the British version that, following a 'brutal massacre' of a government repair party on 24 March 1952, Templer showed the Chinese British determination. The victims included a British World War II hero – Michael Codner.[73] Tanjong Malim's inhabitants, however, yielded no information, A 22 hour curfew and draconian cuts in rations were imposed, followed by

FIGURE 4
EMERGENCY INCIDENTS
MONTHLY FIGURES FOR 1952

FIGURE 5
TOTAL 'COMMUNIST TERRORIST' LOSSES
MONTHLY FIGURES FOR 1952

Number/Month

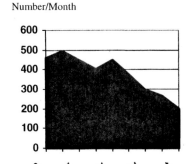

Number/Month

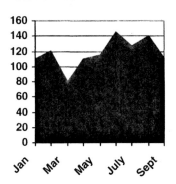

*Source*: Adapted from Rhodes House, Oxford: Young Papers, Mss Brit Empire s486/2/3,
'Combined Intelligence Staff' (52) (7) (Final), 30 Sept. 1952, Appendices A and G.

questionnaires. Templer promised to open these himself, and to lift the
curfew if information was forthcoming. Thus Templer demonstrated his
energising quality, his attention to intelligence, and applied pressure in a
way calculated to persuade, if not exactly woo, Chinese hearts and minds.

Tanjong Malim is indeed a good, if extreme, example of how Templer
tightened existing population control. Nevertheless, the significance
attributed to Tanjong Malim by the Communists, and many Chinese in
general, is likely to be different. Chin Peng has recalled how he first cycled
with 30 men to Tanjong Malim on 15 February 1942. Discovering none of
the Communists sent to the British for training had returned, and learning of
the British surrender at Singapore that same day 'we set up our forces'. Like
many other Emergency hotspots, Tanjong Malim thus lay at the centre of
wartime anti-Japanese resistance.[74] So from the Communist perspective a
village of war heroes and their helpers was subjected by Templer to an
example of population control of the most rigid kind: To what Loh Kok Wah
has termed a 'Foucaltian nightmare' of control and alienation, and Cheah
Boon Kheng has described as Templer's reign of fear and resentment.[75] Just
how much information such exercises produced has, furthermore, been
questioned.[76]

Thus the British story – at least in its 'hearts and minds' mode – cannot
be fully reconciled with the Communist account of why insurgency was
defeated. Chin Peng has in addition stressed that objective conditions in
Malaya defeated the MNLA, especially ethnicity, geography (the
combination of good communications in populated areas and lack of

sustenance in the jungle), and the lack of outside help. As Chin Peng put it, 'we didn't receive any outside aid ... not even a bullet'. A rebellion launched when it seemed history was moving their way, with Communism sweeping China and the Soviet Union emerging as an outside superpower, remained physically isolated from that tide.[77]

This stress on objective constraints also emerges from 1998 interviews with Chin Peng carried out by Qiu Qi Deng, from the Chinese-language journal *Yazhou Zhoukan*. Qiu described Chin Peng's historical role thus: 'The History of the MCP is part of the flowing river of history ... Chin Peng's movement in history's rivers forms a part of his role in history. In the rushing current, he might have been unable to reach for his ideals and dreams.'[78]

The phrase 'flowing river of history' is used by Qiu Qi Deng to evoke Chin Peng's memories, a supposed 'host of feelings of love and hate' flooding back.[79] Yet the metaphor accurately reflects the *Yazhou Zhoukan's* interviews with Chin Peng in a second sense. For Chin Peng clearly felt he was part of the anti-colonial flow of history, accelerating independence, and the Communist flow, preventing Britain from sending more forces to Korea. Yet he also believed Malaya's direction at that time, its racial and geographic constraints, prevented his movement from bringing it fully into the wider flow of events.[80] When commenting on Communist failure, he tends to relate it to objective conditions more than subjective British or Communist leadership. Other Communists and ex-Communists, such as Guo Ren Hui (a member of the MCP's Singapore Town Committee), have echoed this view of Communism being frustrated by objective circumstances, or being ahead of its time for ethnically-riven Malaya.[81]

The picture Chin Peng has portrayed, consistently since the 1989 peace agreement,[82] is thus of an MCP constrained by a lack of Malay support. A picture of a guerrilla army increasingly pushed from pillar to post by population control, increasingly unable to buy food even when the money was available, and again and again disrupted by security force offensives.

Chin Peng's memory matches the evidence of contemporary Communist documents. The October 1951 Resolutions' only answer to resettlement was to circumvent it – rather than defeat it as ordered a year earlier in August 1950 – by increasing 'mass' work (supplies), political work and planting.[83] In Canberra he described earlier orders to contest resettlement to the end as 'impossible' and 'too optimistic'.[84]

The MCP thus decided, probably in early 1952, to move its headquarters to Perak, Chin Peng's home state. On arrival, however, it was told that the local organisation could not provide sufficient food or protection for the headquarters. 'Step by step' it then made the move north, to the Thai border.[85]

Even before this retreat, the October Resolutions' defensive emphasis on mass organisation and political work implied (according to one British intelligence estimate) a transfer of over 1,500 MNLA fighters to other, less frontline activities. This represented about 25 per cent of the MNLA's estimated average 1952 strength of under 6,000.[86] Emergency incidents and indicators remained near peak levels in late 1951, but as the October Resolutions filtered through in the period up to mid-1952, incidents started to fall. By mid-1952, just three or four months after Templer's arrival and before intelligence or police re-training had advanced far, the improvements in statistics for incidents, security force casualties and other indicators were becoming dramatic.[87] By the end of 1952, monthly incidents were running at a quarter of their peak figures.

Adding together the statistics, the documents on the October Resolutions, and Chin Peng's testimony, it seems a combination of the maturing Briggs Plan and a lack of any effective Communist counter-strategy was already proving fatal. At the very least, the Communists miscalculated in 1951 that their economic sabotage and anti-resettlement policy was unsustainable in its current form, at the most, they were right and it was unsustainable. Either way their decisions – not to contest resettlement but only to subvert it, to move northwards, and to shift emphasis slightly towards supply and political work – together represented a watershed.

Thus both the British and Communist sides have stories of stagnation and trials for late 1950 to early 1952. But only on the Communist side was this associated with a defensive drift in policy (downgrading military action relative to mass organisation, a retreat northwards) and increasing difficulty securing public support.

It seems plausible that the Communist memory might be a better guide than British memory, not in general, but for the specific issue of why *they* took critical decisions in this period.

If this picture is accurate, it calls for a careful reassessment of the role Templer played in increasing intelligence efficiency. There is no doubt that his 1952–54 tenure was an important period in this process. For instance, Special Branch training school was set up in 1952, running over 4,000 courses by late 1954.[88] Co-ordination was improved, and it is in this period that techniques for securing agents on the 'Outer Ring' of the MNLA forces (around New Villages) were refined. It is simply that what might be called the 'Big Bang' theory of intelligence change – emphasising Templer and his team – may overstate the relative importance of British leadership in winning the campaign. It may also over-emphasise the importance to intelligence transformation of changes in organisational structure. By contrast, it underestimates the role of campaign strategy, and 'objective' conditions such as ethnic and social terrain, if not 'subjective' factors such as flaws in Communist strategy and tactics.

A case can thus be made for a high level of continuity in intelligence development. Intelligence had already shown signs of improvement by early 1952, and – and more importantly – 'New Village' development was just starting to open up fresh possibilities.

Malaya's Cabinet had been told as early as December 1951 that a CID investigation against the *Min Yuen* was underway, that early signs of improvement were there, and that the priority was to gain agents capable of 'pumping' for 'live' information, rather than 'dead' or blown' information from SEP, CEP and documents.[89] Furthermore, Templer and his new Director of Intelligence's first actions were of mixed wisdom. Increasing the number of Military Intelligence Officers (MIO), separating Special Branch totally from CID,[90] and establishing a training school seem to have been important. The MIOs were soldiers placed with and under Special Branch. These were translaters of intelligence as well as producers in their own right. They ensured police intelligence was converted into a form useable for military operations. The extension of the Director of Intelligence's powers to include co-ordination of military as well as police intelligence, and to chair a combined civil-military Federation Intelligence Committee, also helped to optimise the use of resources.

Yet in April 1952 DOO Directive number 21 ('S.B Intelligence Targets') downplayed the targets which were to prove most profitable for agents – the 'outer ring' of *Min Yuen* and sympathisers. Instead it directed Special Branch to prioritise the MNLA and Party 'inner ring' of political and propaganda leaders. People who were always to prove among the hardest targets to crack. By contrast, Clutterbuck has described how the slow perfection of combined Special Branch-food operations received a boost in August 1952, not as a result of instructions from a new higher leadership, but as a result of experimentation by local commanders and committees.

In August 1952 the local Gurkha commander (Brigadier Mark Henniker, 63 Gurkha Infantry Brigade) and the District War Executive Committee in Seremban District, Negri Sembilan (about 25 miles square), began Operation 'Hive'. Planned as far back as June, this involved using intense intelligence preparation, followed by arresting suppliers, and only then planning ambushes as Communist supplies ran low and agents provided leads. Military units placed around the area prevented the local MNLA from simply fleeing. According to Clutterbuck, this early example was then gradually refined, with improvements in food searches, central cooking, longer durations, and the eventual realisation that entire Communist districts had to be targeted. Otherwise district or branch committees could rebuild their organisation again when pressure was released. Although the

precise importance of Clutterbuck's chosen examples might be questioned
– similar innovations may have been going on in different areas – his
general picture seems clear. In June 1954 a standard policy was laid down
for such 'federal priority' operations, and by 1956 Clutterbuck argues these
reached peak efficiency.[91]

In short, the development of Special Branch-food-military operations
around New Villages into a, if not the, main source of procuring agents
emerged organically from 1952, from the opportunities provided by
resettlement's gradual improvement, and from refinements in techniques
suggested by intelligence and military officers at all levels. It certainly
happened mainly under and after Templer, but also after the Communist
campaign had gone into decline, and not obviously as a result of one or two
key organisational changes or initiatives from the very top.

Before concluding, we need to note that our two main stories –
Communist and British – do not necessarily provide all the answers. In
particular, it is possible to question whether both under-emphasise the role
of Communist leadership, and the damage wreaked on it by successive
waves of treachery, and of Japanese and British action.

Chin Peng seems to trace Communist frustrations not mainly to
shortcomings in leadership cadres, or strategy, but to 'objective conditions':
ethnic cleavages; a geography that was unsuitable to insurgency; and
Marxism being before its time in Malaya. Marxist notions of historical
determinism and objective conditions combine to imply that it was not so
much that the MCP leadership failed to win, as that they could not win. Yet
in one case at least, an intelligence coup had had a devastating effect on the
MCP's leadership ranks. This was the British, and then Japanese,
recruitment of the triple agent Lai Teck (Secretary-General, 1939–47).[92]

Secretary-General from before World War II to March 1947, Lai Tek,
betrayed his comrades to the Japanese and British alike. Originating from
Indochina, he had been handed to the British by French intelligence, and
then planted in the MCP by Special Branch.[93] Yoji Akashi estimates the
minimum number of comrades personally betrayed by Lai Teck at 105.
How much damage this treachery did, when combined with large-scale
British arrests and deportations, cannot be easily be calculated.[94] What can
be stated is that successive betrayals of cadres and members of the Central
Committee and Singapore Town Committee left a relatively young and
inexperienced leadership.

In 1948 these new leaders failed to anticipate the quick British response
to their strategy of increased violence, especially in managing labour
relations. Hence they were caught unprepared in June. When questioned,
Chin Peng himself explained this miscalculation as due to inexperience and
youth.[95] The MCP then focused on guerrilla warfare when Malays

dominated the countryside, and reduced mass support by an economic sabotage campaign which nevertheless failed to stop Malaya becoming Britain's most important source of dollar earnings. Malaya's jungles, furthermore, could never sustain large numbers unless the squatter areas were held, so that Coe has harshly concluded that the leadership 'led the faithful into the wilderness'.[96]

FIGURE 7
THE THREE-FACED SPY[97] – LAI TEK

*Source*: Imperial War Museum, London, Harry Miller Papers.

CONCLUSION

The model of intelligence transformation offered here is necessarily complex. First, one can suggest there are two predominant stories about the Malayan Emergency, Communist and majority British. Just as Marc Ferro recognised the Russian Revolution had different chronologies in the cities, forests and clearings, and steppes, so too the Malayan Emergency had different narrative threads.[98] Indeed, Chin Peng and Templer's stories are separate in a literal way. With jungle communications sometimes taking months, Templer's impact could only seep through to Chin Peng in 1952–53. Yet from October 1951 Chin Peng already seems to have been moving towards the trajectory which would ultimately take him to the Thai border.

The following conclusions must also be somewhat tentative, since this study's focus on two narratives is in part a heuristic device. As more sub-plots (Malaysian Chinese, Indian, Malay) are interwoven, the result will be a more fractured picture. Chin Peng, for instance, cannot stand alone as a 'type' and representative of Communism, not least because from 1953 the MNLA remaining in Malaya, and Communists in Singapore, were increasingly left to their own devices. With these caveats in mind, we can summarise the results of the exercise so far.[99]

The Communist story, backed up by contemporary Communist documents and some British intelligence analyses, seems to show their campaign reaching a turning point in 1951–52. By 1952 the Communist leadership had accepted it could not destroy resettlement, and despite increasing attempts at subversion, was set on a path leading it to withdraw its headquarters north, and its remaining units into deeper jungle. At this stage the critical forces were the objective geographic, social and ethnic terrain (a Communist Chinese-led insurgency facing a mainly hostile Malay population), and strategy, in the shape of the Briggs Plan's population control. That is, an approach centred on resettlement, measured coercion and good civil-military coordination, but ameliorated by political, civil and military 'hearts and minds' measures.[100]

This account has attempted to integrate parts of both the British and the Communist interpretations. The British story, with its emphasis on Templer's energising impact and 'hearts and minds' approach, reflects a real sense of frustration in late 1951: at the lack of more tangible success; that a High Commissioner could be assassinated; and at inefficiencies and disputes at leadership level. It confirms that British efficiency peaked *after* the campaign had passed its high-water mark in 1951–52, if not because a previous slackening of pace facilitated retraining and other improvements.

It also reflects the fact that leadership changes – specifically the arrival of Briggs, the appointment of Jenkins as Director of Intelligence (1950), and most famously Templer's era, did see leaps forward in organisation. Briggs turned sporadic relocation into a campaign-winning and systematic resettlement, backed by joint war executive committees and a framework of locally-based battalions. Jenkins, as the first Director of Information in 1950–51, then oversaw early Special Branch expansion, and understood the vulnerability of the *Min Yuen*. As Cabinet was told in December 1951, Jenkins had 'established a firmer framework and already military commanders report an increased flow of information'.[101] He was obstructed, however, by disputes with Gray as Commissioner of Police, who was ultimately backed by Briggs and Gurney, and still insufficient numbers of Chinese recruits.

Templer thus inherited a Special Branch of increased size and improved technique, and a winning strategy. He improved the efficiency of this winning formula, giving his new Director of Intelligence wider powers and chairmanship of the coordinating Federation Intelligence Committee, and allowing the creation of Special Branch training school. The systematisation of military intelligence officers, now attached under Special Branch at most localities, also improved the translation of intelligence into military action. Special Branch growth, meanwhile, was further accelerated.[102]

The British story thus shows how the sense of crisis and fluidity surrounding leadership changes helped new leaders to overcome forces favouring *stasis*. Thus, even if the campaign was changing in nature in 1951–52, without Gray's removal as Commissioner of Police, it might have been difficult to achieve police and Special Branch change as rapidly. Gray had opposed Special Branch's separation from CID, and viewed Jenkin's ideas on prioritising the *Min Yuen* with suspicion.[103] In addition, propaganda still needed overhauling in 1952.[104] Again, in this sense Templer, as an ex-Director of Military Intelligence, was an excellent choice.[105]

By contrast, the Communist interpretation, with its stress on the pre-Templer period and the effects of the Briggs Plan and geography, reminds us not to underestimate the importance of ethnic and geographic factors, and population control. For intelligence in the crucial period, before the MCP's October 1951 Resolutions, relied principally on corpses, CEP and SEP. The willingness of the SEP to help the security forces was to be vital, and was noted incredulously by British forces. This must in turn be related to the position of the insurgents.

These were mainly Chinese rural guerrillas, surrounded by Malay *kampongs*. They drew inspiration from Chinese traditions of anti-Japanese resistance. Yet as the war became more distant and the British offered at least some compromises to nationalism, the relevance of this tradition must have begun to fade. They were also separated in sympathies from many of traditionally or commercially orientated Chinese in the towns, whose aspirations focused on profit and community, and who organised themselves in clan associations and chambers of commerce.

British policy fed on this favourable ethnic terrain with military 'hearts and minds' tactics. It offered captured or noncooperating Communists the threat of judicial execution, but promised those who helped potentially enormous rewards. SEP were used for lecture tours, to help turn other captured Communists, to penetrate the MCP mindset, and even to write a 'new management' version of the Communists' *Freedom News* (after its 1951 capture).[106] Once in British hands good – or at least loyal – Communists were soon likely to become dead Communists, traitors could thrive. The rewards supplemented another useful side-effect of betrayal: the removal of colleagues who would otherwise seek the death of a new 'running dog'.

Finally, time may have been critical in allowing the percentage of Chinese in the police to rise from minimal in 1948 to nearly ten per cent in 1952. Time reduced the effects of the war, which had rendered guerrillas anti-Japanese heroes – not so much Communists as 'the people who resisted the Japanese' – and their betrayers and government agents as 'running dogs'. Put another way, the attraction of Communism, for some at least, may have been the way it located them in narratives of anti-Japanese struggle, and of Chinese history, and as time went on these narratives became less compelling.[107]

In addition, the lack of special attention to Templer in the Communist story may reflect the fact that the main post-1952 boost to agent recruitment came from elsewhere: not so much from Templer's 1952 changes, as from a gradual maturation of tactics for exploiting New Villages. A process Templer's Special Branch Directive of 1952 did not to pick up on, and which was an organic development from the Briggs Plan.[108] It was Resettlement which allowed the security forces, by rigorous population control measures, to create a field of information around a set of New Villages, turning Communist suppliers into agents, and undermining the ability of MNLA counter-intelligence. Many of the improvements attributed to Templer – arming more Home Guards, elected Village Committees, improving New Village security and amenities, even selected collective punishments – were in place or planned before his arrival.[109] The improvement in intelligence from 1952 was real, but at a fundamental level it grew naturally from past policy and present experimentation.

Combining 'British' and Communist narratives has thus helped to produce a nuanced understanding of intelligence transformation. One which sees intelligence success as having been made possible by a mix of objective ethnic and social conditions, strategy in the shape of the Briggs Plan's 'population control', the occasional and efficiency-boosting leaps forward which accompanied leadership changes, and incremental learning and development.

## NOTES

Acknowledgements: This study would have been impossible without the help of Chin Peng, who generously allowed historians to 'interrogate' him for two days, and Leon Comber (a former Malayan Special Branch officer, now at Monash Asia Institute, Monash University). The Canberra Workshop with Chin Peng was organised by Professor Anthony Reid, with C.C. Chin assisting. The Nanyang Technological University generously funded my attendance in mid-semester. Edmund Lim Wee Kiat translated the *Yazhou Zhoukan* (15–21 June 1998), and Wang Zhenping helped with nuances in the same. Finally, I need to thank all those people who have generously discussed their experiences of the period with me.

Where not otherwise indicated, sources are from the Public Records Office, Kew Gardens, London.

1. Narratives, stories or even myths in the sense that accounts attempt not only to impose order on facts – a central narrative – but also meaning. The dominant British 'myth' makes participants characters in a story of Phoenix-like resurrection from 1951's despair, victors in one scene in a wider Cold War drama, and actors in a morality play that has, as its moral, the need for unified, vigorous leadership (preferably under one supremo) or 'hearts and minds' tactics. This sort of story can fit into a Whig interpretation of Empire: the British won their counter-insurgencies because of superior foresight (the French and Americans not so). Or (as with Richard Stubbs), it can provide a didactic tale about counter-insurgency, stressing the need to combine stick and carrot, bullet and bridge-building. The story-telling (there is no reason why stories cannot be true) thus has many functions at the levels of individual, military and state history.

2. For more detail, see my 'Intelligence and Counter-Insurgency in the Era of Decolonisation: The Example of Malaya', in *Intelligence and National Security* 14/2 (Summer 1999) pp.24–55, and 'Iron Claws on Malaya': The Historiography of the Malayan Emergency', *Journal of Southeast Asian Studies* 30/1 (March 1999) pp.99–125. This piece provides a shorter summary, new material from the Public Record Office in London and a Canberra Workshop with Chin Peng; and a greater recognition of the late (late 1952–55) perfection of agent-recruiting procedures.

3. Rhodes House, Oxford, Granada End of Empire series, Malaya Vol. 2, p.95ff.

4. See AIR20/10377: Director of Operations Report, Sept. 1957, p.55 for quotation. Henceforth this is called DOO Report, 1957.

5. For a fuller analysis of British historiography, see my 'Iron Claws on Malaya' (note 2). Examples which include the idea of a late 1951 stalemate include: Anthony Short, *The Communist Insurrection in Malaya 1948–1960* (London: Frederick Muller 1975), who stresses Templer later 'energising' the campaign; the Australian Lt.-Gen. John Coates, *Suppressing Insurgency: An Analysis of the Malayan Emergency* (Boulder, CO: Westview 1993); and the Canadian Richard Stubbs, *Hearts and Minds in Guerrilla Warfare: The Malayan Emergency 1948–1960* (Singapore: OUP 1989). The latter emphasises the addition of 'hearts and minds' tactics after 1952 as the winning addition. See also John Cloake, *Templer: Tiger of Malaya* (London: Harrap 1985); and Noel Barber, *War of the Running Dogs* (London: Arrow 1989). Malaysian works sometimes share these interpretations, e.g. Dato' J.J Raj, *The War Years and After* (Petaling Jaya: Pelanduk 1995).

   However, two types of British works are slightly different. Those which sell British counter-insurgency as an effective paradigm emphasize 'population control' as central to an overall 'British' model, highlighting Templer's personality less. See Sir Robert Thompson (also a British adviser in Vietnam), *Defeating Communist Insurgency: Experiences from Malaya and Vietnam* (London: Chatto 1972); and Richard Clutterbuck, *Conflict and Violence in Singapore and Malaysia: 1945–1983* (Singapore: Graham Brash 1984).

   Neither is the majority British view the only one. Some more junior figures in the British 'Establishment', especially those with service in Malaya mainly before Templer, see him in a more equivocal way. See, for example, Victor Purcell, *Malaya: Communist or Free?* (London: Gollancz 1954), and Leonard Rayner, *Emergency Years: (Malaya 1951–1954)* (Singapore: Heinemann Asia 1991). Leon Comber, who formerly served as a Special Branch officer in Johore, made this point about the 'minority' [my term] British memory, shared by some more junior government officers, in e-mails to the author. In a more unusual 'Anglo-Saxon' approach, the American sociologist Lucien Pye stressed the social and personal motivations of insurgents (as opposed to being primarily nationalistic or ideological), in his *Guerrilla Communism in Malaya: Its Social and Political Meaning* (Princeton UP 1956).

6. Three British planters and two Chinese assistants were killed on 16 June in Perak, catapulting government into declaring a nation-wide Emergency by the 18th. The issue of how well intelligence performed in the Emergency outbreak is highly controversial. Some idea of the issues can be found in A.J. Stockwell, 'A widespread and long-concocted plot to overthrow government in Malaya', *Journal of Commonwealth and Imperial History* 21/3 (Sept. 1993)

pp.66–89; Coates (note 5) p.7, 25–6; Cloake (note 5) p.197; D. Mackay, *The Domino That Stood: The Malayan Emergency: 1948–60* (London: Brassey's 1997), p.31, 159, fn10; Stubbs (note 5) pp. 66–9; and Short (note 5) pp.39–61, 79–90. The MSS *did* warn in 1947–48 that squatters should be moved, and that the MCP might turn violent. The FO warned in early 1948 that international communist policy seemed to be shifting. But there was no hard evidence of plans, and MSS warnings were overshadowed by equal concentration on militant Malay nationalists

 7. Singapore National Archives: Oral History Department, A. Khan transcript A000150/13. Ahmad Khan records being given the choice between joining Japanese Special Branch or death.

 8. Singapore National Archives: Oral History Department, R.Corridon, transcript A00044/15, pp.27–30.

 9. Even moderate, English-educated Chinese such as Chin Kee Onn (who later became a novelist and a government information officer) initially regarded the guerrillas (sometimes known as 'jungle people') as 'unseen heroes'. See Chin Keen Onn, *Malaya Upside Down* (Kuala Lumpur 1946: repr. KL Federal Publishers, 1976). It would be interesting to know if the British copied Japanese methods (excepting torture). The less obvious included: infiltrating disguised Japanese or apparently harmless Malays, Indians and Chinese onto outer jungle paths; setting up a bogus Communist organisation; and using around 10 prostitutes at Ampang near Ipoh to extract information. One hopes the MCP were correct about the latter, as following the discovery that one girl returned 'home' to 'parents' in a police station, they were killed by *changkol* (a sort of hoe). Imperial War Museum, London: Capt. G.A. Garnoss-Williams Papers, Vol. II, pp. 63–4.

10. Rhodes House, Oxford, Brewer Papers, Box 1, File 4, diary of an insurgent, entry for 6 Nov. 1948: 'The British are operating in the same way as the Japanese – torturing the people'. Other accounts suggested the British were worse, as they burned houses as well as detaining people, e.g. 'A', diary of Lam Meng, 6 Nov. 1948, 'their tactics were worse than the Japanese'.

11. E-mail from Leon Comber to author, 12 July 1999.

12. The title MNLA ('Malayan *National (Min-tsu)* Liberation Army') was adopted in early 1949, when 'Malayan People's Anti-British Army' was dropped. The term *min-tsu* was translated as 'Races' by Special Branch. Thus most works (including some earlier articles by this author) use 'MRLA', though in Canberra in Feb. 1999 Chin Peng confirmed preference for 'National'. It is also preferred by C.C. Too, *New Straits Times*, 3 Dec. 1989; and Lee Ting Hui, *The Open United Front: The Communist Struggle in Singapore, 1954–1966* (Singapore: South Seas Society 1996), pp.38–9, endnotes 100–101, both authors with specialist knowledge of the MCP.

13. E-mail from Leon Comber to author, 12 July 1999. Wylie became Deputy Commissioner of Police. Fenner joined Security Intelligence Far East, being seconded to open SB Training School in 1952.

14. *Orang asli* are the forest-dwellers of the interior. These two were specifically identified as *Jakun* (or *Orang Melayu Asli* or proto-Malay), who may have formed about 33 per cent of a total then variously estimated as 38,000–100,000. AIR20/10377, Director of Operations Report, Sept. 1957, p.18 estimated 50,000–60,000. A few *orang asli* were resettled, some collaborators in the jungle given shotguns, but a distinct *orang asli* security force organisation had not been formed by independence. See John Leary, *The Dream People: The Orang Asli in the Malayan Emergency, 1948–1960* (Ohio U. 1985) esp. pp.2, 61, 63, 142–3.

15. Rhodes House, Oxford: MSS Litton, Indian Ocean s113, letter of 8 March 1949. In this latter case, the informers were *orang asli*.

16. At the ANU Workshop, Canberra, 22–23 Feb.1999, Chin Peng confirmed this, stressing the March–May policy was to gradually step up violence to maintain strikes against 'scabs' and disruption, and to begin assembling the core for a future army. He added the MCP Central Committee only expected to meet again around August, and that there was therefore no concrete plan for guerrilla warfare.

17. Short (note 5) pp.65–94; CO 1030/16; Rho: MSS Indian Ocean s251, Dalley Papers. Short (note 5) pp.139–40. Coates (note 5) p. 45, note 49.

18. Coates(note 5) p.41, note 8. The MSS had bases in Singapore, Kuala Lumpur (Selangor, national capital), Penang, Ipoh (Perak) and Seremban (Negri Sembilan).
19. Coates (note 5) p.24, suggests MSS's separate status and lack of rural presence prevented it drawing conclusions from rural police detection of rising violence, but post-war Malaya's record of crime, gangsterism, KMT and secret societies, made attributing rising crime to Communism problematical. Stockwell 'A long-concoted plot' (note 6); Susan L. Carruthers, *Winning Hearts and Minds: British Governments, the Media, and Colonial Counter-Insurgency, 1944–1960* (London: Leicester UP 1995) Ch.2.
20. See *The Federation of Malaya Annual Report: 1947* (Kuala Lumpur: Government Printer 1948) p.97, and *1948*, p.124. The MSS and then SB were parts of a range of intelligence agencies, including that of the Army's Headquarters Malaya Command, which issued weekly intelligence appreciations.
21. The larger figure included part-time police, for details on numbers see my, 'Intelligence and Counter-Insurgency' (note 2), pp.149–50, notes 42–3.
22. The particular phrasing used I have taken from Leon Comber.
23. See Guy Madoc interviews in Rhodes House, Granada End of Empire, Malaya Vols. 2 and 4.
24. For a good guide to early problems, see Riley Sunderland, *Antiguerilla Intelligence in Malaya, 1948–1960* (Santa Monica, CA: RAND Corp. 1964).
25. Rhodes House, Oxford, Granada Papers, Madoc Interviews, pp.12–13, where Madoc (who was a general officer who rose to Officer Superintending Police Circle prewar) commented that often 'a Chinese detective was a pretty low member of society', though things improved a little postwar. Presumably he meant post-1948.
26. See for instance, AIR20/10377, Director of Operations Report, Sept. 1957 [henceforth DOO Report, 1957], p. 27, para. 96, and map (App. D) of insurgent locations.
27. Richard Clutterbuck, 'Communist Defeat in Malaya', in *Counterinsurgency Case History: Malaya 1948–60* (Ft Leavenworth, KS: US Army Command and General Staff College 1965) pp.27–8. For pictures of 'two female Chinese' concealing rice, see: http://arkib.gov.my/gif/daura02.gif.
28. Imperial War Museum: Capt. G. A. Garnons-Williams Papers, Vol. II, pp.30–1. This contains Lt. Col. F. Spencer Chapman and Major Broome's report on the guerrillas up to May 1945.
29. ISEAS: Tan Cheng Lok papers folio 24, 'Appendix "C"' to the Agenda [probably for the Federal War Committee], 10 Nov. 1951, 'Resettlement'.
30. Food control measures included reducing rations, licensing food movements, reducing stocks in shops and puncturing tins. Also communal cooking of rice (dry rice lasted a long time), searches for MNLA food dumps, spraying jungle crops, and patrols to increase insurgent movement.
31. See CO1020/51, DOO Directive No. 21, 'SB Intelligence Targets', para. 1, April 1952; and C(51)59, 21 Dec. 1951, secret appendix IX to Cabinet paper for the quotation.
32. The *Annual Report on the Federation of Malaya: 1954* (Kuala Lumpur: Government Printer 1955) p.4, stated that, 'Food supplies remained the greatest problem facing the terrorists.'
33. Rhodes House, Young Papers, 'Progress of the Emergency', c1953, Operations Info. Branch, Police.
34. Templer originally used questionnaires against Tanjong Malim in early 1952, but Chinese members of the MCA Representatives Committee also suggested house-to-house visits, so as not to exclude the illiterate, see Singapore, Institute of Southeast Asian Studies, Tan Cheng Lock Papers, 3.274, minutes of a meeting of MCA representatives with Templer, 21 April 1952.
35. Imperial War Museum: Garnons-Williams (note 28).
36. Coates (note 5) p.40.
37. See Richard Clutterbuck, *The Long, Long War* (London: Cassell 1966) pp.93–4. See also Yoji Akashi, 'Lai Teck, Secretary General of the Communist Party of Malaya, 1939–1947', *Journal of the South Seas Society* 49 (1994) pp.87–95 esp. p.77, for MCP willingness to kill members feared tainted after arrest in 1943–44. British propaganda made use of the fear of elimination, see King's College London Archives, Stockwell Papers 7/1-7, eg., Leaflet 1534 (22 Jan. 1953).
38. Clutterbuck (note 5) chs 11–12 (pp.195–219). See also DOO Report 1957, p.15, para. 55 (a). on 'Agents', defined as 'Communist supporters who remain in touch with the CTs'.

39. By 1952 there were just under 100 officers. Inspectors and police lieutenants rose during the year from 114 to 195, rising again to 297 the following year. The latter figures suggest dramatic improvements in Chinese recruitment to Special Branch in 1951–53. See Hack, 'Intelligence and Counter-Insurgency' (note 2) pp.150, endnotes 42–3 for more on numbers and Chinese issues.

40. For the Briggs Plan increasing information and facilitating food control, PREM8/1406, 4 June 1951, MAL C(51) 1, 'Combined Appreciation of the Emergency Situation' by High Commissioner and DOO.

41. For a full analysis of the Oct. Resolutions, see Hack, 'Intelligence and Counter-Insurgency' (note 2) pp.133ff.

42. Workshop with Chin Peng, Canberra, 23 Feb. 1999.

43. See Hack, 'Intelligence and Counter-Insurgency' (note 2) p.138 for MNLA unit size, and *passim* for changing plans in Oct. 1951.

44. See AIR20/10377, Director of Operations Report, Sept. 1957, p. 18. By 1957 there were 11 forts (for an estimated 50,000–60,000 *orang asli*, with medical and trading centres, and an intelligence network was established using *orang asli* enrolled as auxiliary police. By 1956 only 300–400 *orang asli* were estimated as under MNLA influence.

45. Imperial War Museum: Garnons-Williams (note 28).

46. See for instance Cloake (note 5) p.239. Templer recorded a message in Jan. 1954.

47. DOO Report 1957, p.21. Formed 1953, by 1957 there were 10 platoons each of around 23 men, usually used versus selected targets under SB control.

48. Hack, 'Intelligence and Counter-Insurgency' (note 2), pp.150, endnotes 42–3. A police constable in 1951 earned $104 a month (Slightly more in SB), a rubber tapper might earn up to $7 a day. See Defe 11/46 (1471). It would be interesting to know if the MCA bounties Stewart's Ch.12 mentions were important in the better post-1952 recruitment figures.

49. By 1954, most insurgent eliminations were based on SB information. See Coates, *Suppressing Insurgency* (note 5), p.125. In 1957 the DOO still saw food operations as central to combating the few remaining 'hostile' MNLA area by 'screwing down the people in the strongest and sternest manner', see WO216/901, DOO to Templer, 15 March 1956; and DOO Report 1957, p.15, para.55 (c). Until late in the Emergency, penetration was only significantly achieved for this outer ring of MNLA sympathisers.

50. DOO Report 1957, p.15, para.55 (a). Later on, weak-spots might be left in food operations, as 'honey-pots' into which MNLA would re-emerge to be ambushed. Madoc was a pre-war Malayan policeman (1930ff), Deputy Dir. MSS, trained in Bangkok and London c.1947–50, Assistant Superintendent SB 1950, Dir. SB 1952, DOI 1954–58.

51. Oct. Resolutions, p.72, introducing the 'Urgent Tasks of the Party' and explaining the interconnection between the government's 'starvation policy' (also p.143ff) and masses organisation.

52. See note 2 above for more comment on the historiography.

53. Templer's initial idea was for one man to have executive responsibility for all intelligence, but after talking to Sir Percy Sillitoe and the JIC (London) he agreed a single coordinator, with a committee, was better. Executive responsibility might have bogged down an individual, or imposed pressures to act for each department. See CO1022/51, S.E.V. Luke to D. Reilly, 29 Jan. 1952.

54. Morton, a former head of Security Intelligence Far East (the regional MI5 branch in Singapore) was made non-executive DOI in 1952, but had Templer's support and chaired the Federation Intelligence Committee (FIC). This included the SAC, SB, Head of Communist Section SB, and representatives of the Commissioner of Police, military intelligence and civil departments including Labour and Chinese Affairs. It reported to the DOO and Deputy DOO Committee, advised by a Combined Intelligence Staff with a core of three military intelligence representatives and one SB. In effect the FIC coordinated intelligence under Morton and with Templer's backing (the two dined together frequently), and was paralleled by Intelligence Committees at lower levels. See CO1022/51, Charter for the Federation Intelligence Committee and Combined Intelligence Committee, 1952, various drafts.

55. Hack, '"Iron Claws on Malaya"' (note 2), *passim*.

56. See Richard Stubbs (note 5) *passim*; for articles by Hack see note 2.

57. Coates (note 5) pp.88–91, of around 500 resettlement areas only 6 were ever abandoned. ISEAS: Tan Cheng Lock papers folio 24, 'Appendix 'C' to the Agenda [probably for the Federal War Committee], 10 Nov. 1951, 'Resettlement', states that by 30 Sept 1951 (about 15 months after the Brigg's Plan's launch) 333,712 people were resettled in 315 villages, leaving an estimated 110,965 and 116 villages to go.

58. Cabinet was told that police retraining was now essential, see C(51)59, 21 Dec. 1951, secret Appendix IX to Cabinet paper for the quotation, found in CO1022/51. Earlier Gray had not prioritised this, but with nearly a million people to regroup or resettle, most in 18 months, as well as the peak of MNLA sabotage, there were practical constraints.

59. See Hack, '"Iron Claws on Malaya"' (note 2) pp.110–11, which draws on a long Gurney letter to the Colonial Office, written on 3 Oct. 1951.

60. ISEAS: Tan Cheng Lock Papers 24, 'Appendix 'A' to the Agenda [for Federal War Council planned for 15 Nov. 1951], dated 10 Nov. 1951, 'The Co-operation of the Peoples of Malaya Against Communism: Federation Policy'; and 'Appendix 'B': DOO Directive No. 17, Protection of Concentrated Villages and Resettlement Areas', 12 Oct. 1951. The latter included measures for police wives and volunteers to search all women leaving camps. The British story often seems to make Templer overwhelmingly responsible for things such as accelerated arming of Home Guards. In fact, DOO Directive no. 17 laid down a progression from unarmed status, through weapon issue from police stations, to weapon retention in houses. Appendix "D" of 12 Nov. 1951 also reported Home Guard strength 'growing daily' and 'growing responsibility' expected for food control and security.

61. See note 5 for British historiography in its majority and minority forms, and Hack, '"Iron Claws on Malaya"' (note 2), for more details.

62. This case for a Communist story is necessarily tentative, pending the results of Chin Peng's biography, and more work by Chinese-speaking scholars. For similar Communist views see: Mr Guo Ren Hui (Singapore National Archives: Oral History Records, 1980 interview, transcript, pp. 104-111). Guo Ren Hui was a former Singapore Town Committee member. Communist and left-wing versions seem to use Marxist notions of historical determinism to excuse their failure: the ethnic and class basis in Singapore; geography being unsuitable to insurgency; or Marxism having been premature or before its time in these countries.

63. The quotations are from Rhodes House, Oxford: Granada End of Empire volumes, Malaya, Gerald de Cruz. Gerald de Cruz perceived Chin Peng, with whom he played ping pong and slept in the same room, in much the same way as he appeared to the author in 1999.

64. For Chin Peng's details I have used C. C. Chin's 'Brief Biography', which was provided at the Canberra Workshop and discussed with the Secretary-General. See also John Coe, 'The *Rusa Merah*: Reflections on a Revolutionary', in *The Beagle, Records of the Northern Territory Museum of Arts and Sciences* (1988) 5/1, pp.163–73. For Chin Peng's (reported) views on independence, see *Yazhou Zhoukan*, 15–21 June 1998, though he has made similar claims, including at the Dec. 1989 talks which arranged an end to hostilities. Chin Peng's memoirs have been underway for several years. Chin Peng's penchant for citing Spencer Chapman, however, highlights the need to distinguish what is his testimony from that picked up from mainly British books.

65. The questioners were in fact Anthony Short (for instance on the impact of Gurney's death) and Richard Stubbs. Guy Madoc was a highly successful Head of SB from 1952–54. He has helped many historians – including this one as well as Short – and endorses the idea of SB transformation under Templer and himself, with MIOs, separation from CID control, and SB training school all stressed. He also supported the idea Gurney death was fortuitous, indeed necessary, for things to be turned around. Most of these opinions are common (see Brian Stewart in this volume) but not unchallenged. A minority British memory, shared by Leonard Rayner and Leon Comber among other participants, seems to place more stress on continuity.

66. Lt.-Gen. John Coates (retired), a former Chief of the General Staff of the Australian Army, and author of *Suppressing Insurgency*.

67. Workshop with Chin Peng, Canberra, 23 Feb. 1999.

68. Ibid.

69. For a full discussion of the British memory, and how it is not fully supported even by British intelligence analysis of late 1952, see Hack, '"Iron Claws on Malaya"' (note 2), pp.137–40.

70. Institute of Southeast Asian Studies, Tan Cheng Lock Papers XI, Tan Chin Siong to Tan, 18 June 1950, from purporting to be from 'a subscription collector who has taken refuge'. He argued insurgent fighting technique also improved in 1949, and the way resettlement initially increased Communist numbers.

71. AIR20/10377, 'Review of the Emergency', DOO, 12 Sept. 1957.

72. For instance: Stubbs emphasises Britain winning 'hearts and minds' in 1952–54, Chin Kee Onn, Cheah Boon Kheng, Loh Kok Wah and others see repression and control as overwhelmingly dominant. For further comments on this, see my '"Iron Claws on Malaya"' (note 2) pp.115–23.

73. Actually 12 people died, but arguably Codner was the critical one, in that he assured media attention. See Stubbs (note 5) p.165; and D.Mackay (note 6) pp.125–27. Codner was one of the men involved in the famous 'wooden horse' escape from the German POW camp 'Stalag III' in WW2. Now an Assistant District Officer, he was ambushed while trying to get a sabotaged water pipe restored on 24 March 1952. The case received wide publicity. Other villages received draconian punishments before and after (though not in large numbers), but Templer had the edge in publicity management if not harshness.

74. For Chin Peng and Tanjong Malim, see *Yazhou Zhoukan*, 15–21 June 1998. Note the elements of Chin Peng's recall: the Communists had supplied men for training, but these were lost in the British defeat of Singapore; the Communists had to set up their own units with weapons taken from the battlefield; and the recall of the road to Tanjong Malim, Perak (his home state) as a starting-point in his war story.

75. For Cheah, Loh and other examples of a Malaysian Chinese version, see my '"Iron Claws on Malaya"' (note 2), pp.115–23 and p.101, footnote 7 Even Chin Kee On, an English-educated teacher who later became a government information officer, has Kung Li, hero of his novel *The Grand Illusion* say the government had far to go to win Chinese hearts and minds in 1952.

76. Short (note 5) p.341, suggests the ambush may have been carried out independently of the villagers anyway, by a mobile Communist unit. See also Clutterbuck (note 5) p.179.

77. Workshop with Chin Peng, Canberra, 23 Feb. 1999.

78. *Yazhou Zhoukan*, 15–21 June 1998.

79. The metaphor may also draw on the poetic image of trying to cut the river with a sword, which will only lead to more sorrow. Chin Peng, however, usually appears jovial, in absolute control, constantly aware of others' meaning and views, and considered in his replies. On the other hand, his desire to write his memiors, and willingness since 1989 to give occasional but generous interviews and attend in Canberra, indicate an acute concern with his, and the movement's, place in history.

80. Workshop with Chin Peng, Canberra, 23 Feb. 1999. See also the interviews with Chin Peng in *Yazhou Zhoukan* (15–21 June 1998), kindly translated by Edmund Lim, with further help from Wang Zhenping); and Richard Collin, paper on interviews with Chin Peng given at the School of Oriental and African Studies, London, 16 June 1992.

81. Ibid.

82. For this article I have drawn mainly on the Canberra Workshop, but Richard Collin – who interviewed Chin Peng in 1991/92 – reported in the same vein. Particularly on Chin Peng's emphasis on the Brigg's Plan, versus his dismissiveness of most other actors. He told Collin Templer's attitude may even have helped the MCP. Collin (note 80).

83. For Aug. 1950, see John Coe, 'Beautiful Flowers and Poisonous Weeds: Problems of Historicism, Ethics and Internal Antagonisms: The Case of the Malayan Communist Party' (U. of Queensland, Unpub. DPhil, 1993), pp.166–7.

84. Workshop with Chin Peng, Canberra, 23 Feb. 1999.

85. Ibid.

86. See Hack, 'Intelligence and Counter-Insurgency' (note 2), pp.137–40.

87. See Hack, '"Iron Claws on Malaya"' (note 2), pp.112–15.

88. See Hack, 'Intelligence and Counter-Insurgency' (note 2) p.151, notes 56–7.

89. C(51)59, 21 Dec. 1951, secret appendix IX to Cabinet paper for the quotation, found in CO1022/51.

90. Madoc emphasises the separation of SB from CID, but Leon Comber has argued the

connection did not overly hinder SB before. Clutterbuck, *Conflict and Violence* (note 5), p.178, states a separate SB was created in Aug. 1950. Presumably he means SB was more clearly separated from CID at that time, the latter concentrating on crime. Organisationally they were part of the same department until 1952.

91.  Clutterbuck (note 5) Ch.11, esp. pp.212ff, *passim*. Clutterbuck also highlights an MIO's debriefing report on Hive (by Capt. H. S. Latimer) which he says proposed a pattern of operations, 'which proved … with only minor improvements, to be the battle-winning pattern for the remaining seven years of the Emergency', see p.217.

92.  Yoji Akashi, 'Lai Teck' (note 93), pp.87–95.

93.  Most of the following on Lai Teck is taken from Yoji Akashi, 'Lai Teck, Secretary General of the Communist Party of Malaya, 1939-1947', *Journal of the South Seas Society* 49 (1994) pp.87–95. See also Cambridge University Archives: British Association of Malaya Collection V, Crime, No. 5, Onraet, for a translation of, 'A Written statement on Lye Teck's case, issued on 28 July 1948 by MCP Central Committee. Margin (possibly written by Onraet, a prewar head of SB) reads: 'Lye Teck brought over by SB from Indo-China with concurrence and advice of the French after a visit of AHD Dickinson … [in] 1932'. The MCP has him arriving in 1934 or 1935.

94.  Even in WW2, when SOE had admired the guerrillas' organisation, morale, discipline and courage, it had noted they were 'indifferent shots' with poor 'intelligence work, planning, leadership and tactical grasp', 'surprisingly incompetent' at getting a job done. Messages taking months to travel from camp to camp. 'It took them half a year to porter a W/T set from the coast to the mountains and another three months to collect batteries.' This was the assessment of a sympathetic SOE officer assessing the potential of the guerrillas to help an Allied invasion. Quotations and information from: Imperial War Museum (note 28).

95.  Workshop with Chin Peng, Canberra, 23 Feb. 1999. Chin Peng said the leadership was 'inexperienced' and 'very young' when asked why the Party thought Britain would not launch a full scale attack until Sept. 1948, despite the Communists increasing their labour violence from March–May. The Central Committee had intended to plan strategy later in the year, and had no plan ready in June.

96.  Coe, 'Beautiful Flowers and Poisonous Weeds' (note 83), p.399.

97.  In *Yazhou Zhoukan*, 15–21 June 1998 Chin Peng's interviewer puts this phrase in quotations, but it is not absolutely clear if this means he is quoting Chin Peng or not.

98.  Marc Ferro, *The Russian Revolution of February 1917* (London: RKP 1972, translation from the French) p.xv.

99.  For an example of individuals sown skilfully into an overall narrative, and to some extent representing wider classes of person and experience, see Orlando Figes, *The People's Tragedy: The Russian Revolution of 1891–1927* (London: Jonathan Cape 1996), where Prince Lvov, General Brusilov, the writer Maxim Gorky and others are interweaved. By comparison, Emergency history often concentrates on a single 'British', 'Communist', 'radical' or 'Chinese' version.

100. Political meaning Britain's clear commitment to independence for Malaya, starting with making local politicians 'Members' (quasi-ministers) in 1950, and elections from town level up starting in Dec. 1951. Civil meaning amenities. Military meaning rewards for information (payable even to SEP), rehabilitation programmes and surrender terms. The latter included dropping 'safe-conduct' leaflets and, in effect, not prosecuting co-operators for crimes, while nonco-operators could face death.

101. C(51)59, 21 Dec. 1951, secret appendix IX to Cabinet paper for the quotation, found in CO1022/51.

102. This is the normal stress on MIOs, though of course some aimed to produce and process as well as merely 'translate' intelligence, and the best came with Chinese-language skills. E-mail from Leon Comber to author, 13 July 1999.

103. CO1022/51, J.D. Higham for Mr Paskin (both CO), 21 June 1952, 'The Special Branch of the Police is … now being remodelled on the lines that Sir William Jenkin advocated and Sir Henry Gurney opposed'.

104. C(51)59, 21 Dec. 1951, secret appendix IX to Cabinet paper for the quotation, found in CO1022/51. In Dec. 1951 the Film Unit had 63 mobile vans but had 'failed to produce any

propaganda of importance', the 'Special Emergency Information Department's (SEID) press information and pyschological warfare was criticised, and the Black Propaganda department boasted 'occasional hours' by the head of the SEID, one full-time Chinese cyclostyler and 'the part-time co-operation of one Chinese literary expert'.

105. ISEAS: Tan Cheng Lock Papers 5.261, Tan to Maxwell, 11 March 1952. As early as 1 March Templer had made the Chief Secretary (already chairman of the Resettlement Committee) responsible for resettlement 'aftercare'.

106. First appearing on 15 Aug. 1951 under 'new management', it featured high-level defector and ex-union leader Lam Swee, writing about the 'Imperialistic Feudalistic MCP'. There is a copy in Cambridge University Archives, British Association of Malaya Collection V, Crime, Onraet.

107. This theme of MPAJA/MNLA roots being Chinese and anti-Japanese in focus goes to the heart of its weakness as a Malayan national movement. Its repeated attempts to court Malays were vitiated by this Chinese core to its origin and ethos. See for instance Singapore National Archives: Oral History Department, transcript of Mr Guo Ren Hui, pp.1–4; and Workshop with Chin Peng, Canberra, 22 Feb. 1999 (session led by C.C. Chin), for Chin Peng coming to Communism after deciding the Kuomintang were ineffective as anti-Japanese forces. He joked he could have ended up an officer in the KMT.

108 CO1022/51, J.D. Higham for Mr Paskin (both CO), 21 June 1952. The minute asked if Templer's Directive on SB targets indicated a major change from *Min Yuen* to 'inner ring' targets.

109. ISEAS: Tan Cheng Lock papers 24, 'Appendix 'A' to the Agenda [for Federal War Council planned for 15 Nov. 1951], dated 10 Nov. 1951, 'The Co-operation of the Peoples of Malaya Against Communism: Federation Policy'; 'Appendix 'B': DOO Directive No. 17, 'Protection of Concentrated Villages', 12 Oct. 1951; Appendix ''D', 12 Nov. 1951; and Appendix E Chinese and the need for village elections. See also folio 24, 'Extract from a letter by Col. H.S. Lee', 26 Nov. 1951, for a high MCA official emphasising quality not quantity, and increasing Home Guard roles.

# 11

# Content, Credibility and Context: Propaganda Government Surrender Policy and the Malayan Communist Terrorist Mass Surrenders of 1958

## KUMAR RAMAKRISHNA

It is said that the threat represented by the Malayan Communist Party (MCP) to the security of the Federation of Malaya was effectively neutralised by 1954, and subsequent years up until the official end of the Malayan Emergency in July 1960 represented nothing more than a mere 'consolidation' or mopping up process.[1] This perception is flawed, however. While it is true to assert that by 1954 the physical capacity of the MCP to capture power by military means was virtually nil, that did not mean that it was no longer a threat. While the less committed terrorists had been eliminated or had left the jungle, remaining at large were the smaller number of highly indoctrinated 'hardcore' terrorists.[2] The latter (about 2,100 by April 1957) were not merely engaged in subversion of 'political organisations, youth and labour', they were capable of spearheading a re-intensification of the armed struggle should external and domestic factors have permitted.[3]

In particular, it was reckoned that only 170 ranking terrorists (district and state committee members and secretaries, and the Central Committee) were keeping 'the Emergency alive'.[4] Hence it was extremely vital that these hardcore terrorists and their leaders, who posed a 'residual threat' to the security of Malaya, were eliminated.[5] Intriguingly, this occurred in 1958: the MCP was rent asunder by mass surrenders which so depleted its ranks that Secretary-General Chin Peng demobilised the party at the end of that year. Thus 1958 marked the virtual end of the shooting war.[6]

The search for explanations for the 1958 surrenders immediately runs into problems. Stock analyses as to why the federal government eventually prevailed against the MCP usually highlight *inter alia*, the intelligence provided by police Special Branch;[7] resettlement of the rural population into compact and defended New Villages, which not merely secured the 'hearts and minds' of the public, but also cut the MCP off from its supply lifeline;[8]

the MCP's own strategic weaknesses and tactical errors;[9] and British counter-insurgency style emphasising minimum force.[10] While these perspectives certainly shed important light on why the tide of the military campaign shifted decisively in the government's favour by 1954, they do not elucidate why it was in 1958 of all years that terrorist morale cracked. This article suggests that an examination of the role of government propaganda, in particular psychological warfare to the terrorists, can offer a precise explanation as to why the 1958 collapse occurred.

It is a curious fact that although it has been accepted that the government's psychological warfare in the Emergency was effective,[11] the subject, while certainly covered in the literature, has yet to receive thorough, systematic study. Moreover, its contribution to the course and outcome of the Emergency is regarded as ancillary to the factors mentioned in the preceding paragraph.[12]

This study argues instead that rather than being a peripheral factor, the government surrender policy – which as the late Sir Robert Thompson noted, was the 'main base' of psychological warfare[13] – played a critical role in precipitating the 1958 surrenders. We shall see that there were in fact five distinct phases in the evolution of surrender policy in this period: September 1949 to August 1950; September 1950 to August 1955; September 1955 to February 1956; March 1956 to August 1957; and September 1957 to July 1958.

In tracing the evolution of official surrender policy throughout these phases, this analysis will argue that the effectiveness of the policy in precipitating terrorist defections to the government's fold, was contingent on three factors: the content of policy, the credibility of the government in the eyes of the terrorists, and the strategic and political context.

## CONTENT, CREDIBILITY AND CONTEXT OF THE GOVERNMENT SURRENDER POLICY

Propaganda to the terrorists in the Emergency assumed several forms: leaflets and voice aircraft broadcasts were the more direct ways for the government to communicate with the terrorists, while lecture tours by Surrendered Enemy Personnel (SEPs) to rural villagers, especially Chinese, were a more indirect yet equally important means of communication with the 'People Inside'.[14]

In assessing the effectiveness of surrender policy, it is suggested that three factors were important: content, credibility, and context. Content refers to the substance of the policy, and three aspects were important. The first was *scope*: whether the offer of pardon was made to all terrorists, or only those not guilty of involvement in capital crimes, for instance. Also crucial was *promised treatment*: exactly what SEPs could expect if they gave up, such as detention, repatriation or rehabilitation. Last but by no means least was *phrasing*. Hence drafters had to decide whether to use or omit potentially loaded words such as 'surrender', 'detention' and 'investigation'.

Credibility was the second factor determining the appeal of the surrender terms. British propagandists always held that credibility was the *sine qua non* of effective propaganda. Thus the job of the propagandist was not to dissemble, but to present the audience with verifiable facts so that they would gradually trust him. Once the propagandist enjoyed this trust and was by implication credible, the audience would willingly listen to what he had to say.[15]

As regards the government surrender policy in the Emergency, it could be said that its effectiveness was in part a function of the degree to which terrorists actually *believed* government assurances in its leaflets about the treatment they could expect on surrender. As we shall see, to build credibility, the government's task was not merely to make guarantees through its propaganda media about the treatment potential SEPs could expect if they gave up, it had to painstakingly ensure that it indeed provided the treatment it promised. The consequences of a lack of credibility were serious: although a surrender leaflet offered generous terms to the terrorists, it would still fail to elicit the desired response if the terrorists utterly lacked confidence in the government's good faith.

The third factor determining the effectiveness of surrender policy was context. It was a cardinal rule among British wartime propagandists that propaganda was only an auxiliary weapon, the handmaid of official policy and strategy. In other words, propaganda could not function in a vacuum. If policy and strategy were effective, propaganda working in tandem with them could produce results. On the other hand, if policy and strategy were defective, propaganda asserting that all was well would be dismissed.[16] We shall note in this regard that in the early years of the Emergency, the ineffectiveness of the strategy of large-scale military operations mortally prejudiced the 1949 amnesty.

A corollary of the idea of propaganda needing to be co-ordinated with policy and strategy was the so-called 'psychological moment'. This referred to the optimal timing for the release of propaganda to the audience.[17] Hence, we shall see that the 1957 *Merdeka* amnesty was effective partly because it was in operation when the psychological moment, the recognition by the remaining terrorists that further struggle was futile, arrived. Having elaborated on the troika of content, credibility and context, it behoves us now to examine how these factors affected the potency of the government surrender policy between September 1949 and July 1958.

## PHASE 1: SEPTEMBER 1949 TO AUGUST 1950

The Japanese occupation of Malaya between February 1942 and September 1945 seriously damaged British imperial prestige in Malaya. This resulted in the ejection of the sanguine pre-war view that Malaya, whose rubber and tin were crucial to imperial prosperity, would remain in the British orbit 'for the indefinite future'. Consequently, in April 1946 a unitary Malayan Union was inaugurated, which in superseding the separate pre-war political structures, was meant to prepare the country for eventual self-government. Most significantly, the Union obliterated the sacrosanct principles of Malay state sovereignty and conferred common citizenship not only on the indigenous Malays but also the immigrant and increasingly settled Indians and Chinese.

The Union was vociferously opposed by the Malay elites who formed the United Malays National Organisation (UMNO), and it was eventually replaced in February 1948 by a federation which preserved state sovereignty and made it more difficult for non-Malays to become citizens.[18] While the occupation had marked the nadir of British fortunes in Malaya, it had positively enhanced the MCP's prestige, as the Communists (in their incarnation as the Malayan People's Anti-Japanese Army) had assiduously cultivated the image of champion of the oppressed Malayan Chinese.

Capitalising on this clout, the Communists infiltrated Malayan social, labour and political bodies in a bid to capture power immediately after the Japanese surrender, a strategy greatly aided by the social and economic dislocation of post-war Malaya. By March 1948, however, the economy was recovering and social discontent was gradually alleviated, factors which among others contributed to the assessment by the Central Committee of the Party that the strategy of 'open and legal struggle' was not likely to succeed. Arrangements were thus made to adopt a more militant approach, and disturbances on estates and mines escalated.[19]

In this charged context, the federal government, increasingly alarmed by the growing lawlessness in Malaya, declared a state of Emergency on 18 June 1948, proscribing the MCP on 23 July.[20] Among the considerable Emergency powers that the government arrogated to itself was the right to impose the death penalty on anyone bearing arms illegally.[21]

The MCP subsequently launched a terror campaign (closely backed up by propaganda) aimed at dislocating the economy, capturing arms and sparking a popular revolt against the government as a prelude to the eventual annihilation of British imperialism in the peninsula. Pointedly re-naming their forces the Malayan Races Liberation Army (MRLA) from February 1949, the Communists caused much mayhem.[22] Between 16 June and 31 December 1948, for instance, they killed 482 security forces and ordinary civilians, and wounded 404 others.[23] By April 1949, however, the Central Committee realised that this strategy was unsuccessful: the government had not collapsed, the European planters in particular had not abandoned their estates and fled, and most damagingly, the expected popular uprising against British imperialism in Malaya had not materialised. The MCP subsequently withdrew into the deep jungle to re-organise, re-emerging with a renewed offensive in October.[24] It was during the MCP's tactical pause between April and October 1949 that the government sought to seize the initiative, at least in the propaganda arena. Following preparations in August, therefore, High Commissioner Sir Henry Gurney[25] inaugurated the first formal surrender terms: an amnesty on 6 September 1949.

Intended to attract the 'lukewarm adherents' who had decamped into the jungle, corrode the trust between the terrorist rank and file and its leadership, and enable the security forces to build up an intelligence picture of the MCP organisation,[26] the amnesty declared that the government recognised that some terrorists had been forced to join the Communists. Thus: 'The law has been altered to enable such persons to surrender without being executed for carrying arms...[and] have still managed to avoid becoming assassins or committing the other more dastardly crimes against defenceless persons planned by the Communist leaders.' The leaflet then exhorted terrorists to 'come in to surrender as quickly as you can', because 'this offer will not be open indefinitely'. The leaflet finally declared: 'Do not be afraid of harsh treatment when you come in. Your circumstances will be fully understood by the Government.'[27]

As far as content was concerned, the scope and promised treatment parameters prejudiced the effectiveness of the amnesty. With regards to scope, the 1949 surrender terms were not an unqualified guarantee of clemency: it promised non-prosecution only to SEPs who had not been involved in capital crimes, or who did not have 'blood on their hands'. However in the 15 months since the start of the Emergency, most terrorists, including the so-called 'lukewarm adherents' to whom this amnesty had been directed, had had more than enough time to get their hands 'bloody' to some extent. Wavering terrorists were thus unsure as to what degree of participation in capital crimes would be perceived by the government as warranting prosecution. This uncertainty thus deterred them from coming out.[28]

As to promised treatment, the amnesty leaflet, apart from urging terrorists not to fear 'harsh treatment', did not provide clear enough details on what exactly would happen even to SEPs who were perceived by the government to qualify for clemency.

It might be asked why Gurney did not authorise a more explicit leaflet which spelt out what SEPs could expect on surrender. Gurney had a problem. By December 1949, it became clear to the police that some SEPs who had emerged were actually guilty of having 'blood on their hands', and were thus liable for prosecution. However, Gurney recognised that prosecuting these SEPs would dry up the flow of surrenders. At the same time, he felt that he could not be seen to be letting them off without punishment for their crimes, as this would anger public, especially European planter opinion. The planters had suffered many casualties at the hands of the terrorists and were insistent that the government arrest and prosecute them all. In such a climate, therefore, explicitly assuring terrorists that they would not be prosecuted if they surrendered was politically impossible.[29]

In fact, six months later the Joint Information and Propaganda Committee attempted to revise the 1949 amnesty so as to state explicitly that SEPs who voluntarily surrendered and were found not to have 'blood on their hands' would 'after examination, either be repatriated, or sent to a Rehabilitation and Training Centre with a view to his returning as a respectable and useful member of society'. However, in July 1950 it was decided not to put out the revised terms for fear of antagonising the planters. Instead it was agreed to simply publicise the treatment given to SEPs in the government's Taiping Rehabilitation Centre, which had been opened in 1949.[30]

The reason why the content of the amnesty was problematic was because of the government's low stock with the terrorists. Up to 1951, the dearth of adequate intelligence on the identities of terrorists, the circumstantial reality that most MCP terrorists appeared to be Chinese, and the notion that a firm hand was needed to deal with the Chinese villagers, compelled the harassed police and army to regard all Chinese as potential terrorists and subject them to rough treatment.[31] Moreover, the brunt of the emergency regulations, especially those authorising individual and collective detention and deportation, fell most heavily on the rural Chinese:[32] as late as December 1951, of the 25,641 detained under emergency regulations, a massive 22,667 were Chinese.[33] Hence one estimate suggested that as many as 70 per cent of the MCP recruits comprised rural Chinese anxious to escape from police repression.[34]

Because the sum total of government deeds communicated not concern but rather indifference bordering on callousness, the bulk of the terrorists, who were rural Chinese, simply did not trust the government at this point, and widely believed Communist propaganda that they would be executed once the government no longer had use for them.[35] Hence until they were told exactly what they could expect if they gave up, and were given reason to believe that they would indeed receive such treatment, they were not willing to cross over.

There was a final reason why the 1949 amnesty flopped: the strategic context. While there were a good proportion of terrorists who were in reality waverers who had been press-ganged into the jungle or had wanted to elude the Police, many other terrorists had willingly joined the MCP because they were convinced that the Party could deliver on its promises of material benefits and social status.[36] To such convinced terrorists, it was demonstrably clear in the first three years that the security forces, which were hampered by poor intelligence and the ill-judged tactics of large-scale sweeps and bombing, were not winning the war. Hence there was little incentive to even consider whether they qualified for amnesty when in their eyes they appeared to be backing the winning horse.

The 'psychological moment' for an amnesty, the moment when the physical circumstances of the terrorists compelled them to be most receptive to government surrender propaganda, was clearly not at hand. In sum, the deficiencies of content, credibility and context all militated against the effectiveness of the 1949 surrender terms. This was borne out by the poor returns: while 155 terrorists surrendered in the last three months of 1949, the surrender rate in 1950 was very disappointing, and in the last six months of the year the monthly surrender rate fell below 10.[37]

## PHASE 2: SEPTEMBER 1950 TO AUGUST 1955

The government's surrender policy thus limped along from September 1949 to September 1950, when Hugh Carleton Greene arrived from the British Broadcasting Corporation (BBC) to re-organise government propaganda in Malaya. In doing this Greene drew upon his considerable wartime propaganda experience.[38] Following a careful analysis of the state of the shooting war he set up the Emergency Information Services, one aim of which was to attack the morale of the *Min Yuen* (the Communist logistics organisation) and the MRLA. To this end, Greene fully appreciated the significance of a momentous decision taken by Gurney a month before his arrival. In August, Gurney had finally decided that SEPs with blood on their hands would not be prosecuted *immediately*. Gurney was not saying that culpable SEPs would escape punishment; they just would not be punished at the moment, and he deliberately omitted specifying exactly when they would be prosecuted.

This decision afforded the Emergency Information Services a great deal of flexibility which Greene took full advantage of. He thus articulated the policy of 'fair treatment'. In terms of scope, 'fair treatment' assured all terrorists – with blood on their hands or not – that they would not be ill-treated if they came out. The emphasis was on getting SEPs to 'explain what *has* happened to them in Government hands and what their comrades can therefore *expect* to happen to them if they surrender'. At the same time, however, because the fair treatment policy did not constitute a new amnesty, Greene ensured that no promises of non-prosecution were ever made to the terrorists.

To publicise this policy, Greene sent out teams of SEPs on lecture tours to the rural areas where terrorist informants were able to see that SEPs appeared to be well treated in government hands. In addition, Greene put out leaflets with photographs of groups of SEPs apparently none the worse for wear. The idea was to inform terrorists via spoken and written propaganda that SEPs were well treated, and by actually parading SEPs in the rural areas, *confirming* that what the government said in its propaganda was true.[39] Greene was thus trying to build up the government's credibility in the eyes of the terrorists, so as to secure their confidence in the government's benevolent intentions toward them.

As Greene was revamping surrender policy in 1950 and 1951, the strategic context was also improving. The arrival of Lt-General Sir Harold Briggs[40] in April 1950 as the first Director of Operations, heralded the intensification of the resettlement of exposed rural Chinese into compact and defended Resettlement Areas; the adoption of more effective small-scale security force patrolling on the jungle fringes; and the inauguration of food control measures in mid-1951 to curtail the supply line to the terrorists. Briggs also oversaw the improvement in intelligence gathering and processing which greatly aided security force operations.[41] In sum, a carefully-conceived content promising nothing more than 'fair treatment', and the steadily improving strategic context by 1951 combined to improve slightly the surrender rate: while only 74 terrorists surrendered in the last eight months of 1950, 136 gave up in the first eight months of 1951.[42]

Greene's policy of assuring terrorists of only fair treatment on surrender was carried on by Gurney's successor General Sir Gerald Templer, who became High Commissioner and Director of Operations in February 1952.[43] In May, Templer illustrated to the Conservative Secretary of State for the Colonies, Oliver Lyttelton, how the content of surrender policy was operationalised in propaganda. SEPs in leaflets or lecture tours were not allowed to say: 'It is the generous policy of the government to free men like me.' They were only authorised to state: 'I am now a free man.' In other words, the aim was to create only an 'impression of policy' for terrorist consumption. Templer reiterated that no promises of non-prosecution were ever made in government leaflets.[44]

In fact, in 1952 and 1953 Templer was under some pressure to modify the content of surrender policy to include an unequivocal promise that all SEPs who came out of the jungle would not be 'hanged or imprisoned' for past crimes – in short, an amnesty. Some police and administration officials argued that such a clear and explicit declaration on the fate of SEPs would generate mass surrenders. On the other hand, others countered that an 'easy surrender' policy was utterly immoral: it would enable a man 'with several brutal murders to his discredit' to 'walk out of the jungle and get a job as a washer-up in a police mess'. For his part, Templer refused to alter the content of existing policy. He argued that it was unwise for the government to promise all SEPs non-prosecution, thereby committing itself to releasing even SEPs guilty of 'particularly dastardly and notorious crimes', and provoking public opprobrium. Besides, Templer, clearly influenced by Greene's report, opined that the 'psychological moment' for an amnesty capable of generating mass surrenders was not yet at hand. The government thus persisted with the 'fair treatment' policy.[45]

Templer also had to work on improving the government's credibility, which had been seriously damaged in January 1952 over the Goh Ah Khoon affair. Goh, a mere rank and file terrorist, had been arrested in May 1951 and initially classified as an SEP, a fact which had been publicised. Following subsequent investigation, however, he was reclassified as a captured enemy person (CEP) and prosecuted, but the fact of his reclassification was not publicised. Thus the public and hence the terrorists were still under the impression that Goh was an SEP. The government thus inadvertently projected the message that it prosecuted SEPs. The effects were serious: one SEP immediately committed suicide in his cell, while the MCP gleefully propagated the line that the government milked SEPs and then executed them. It was admitted that the government's credibility with the wavering terrorists would need 'many months' to recover.[46]

Templer moved to tighten control of SEPs to prevent a repeat of the Goh imbroglio. SEPs were made the responsibility of Special Branch and in August 1952 Templer quietly reiterated to the police that no SEP should be prosecuted 'save in exceptional circumstances'. Instead, all SEPs were put to work for the government for three months, and then they were kept on, released or sent to Taiping Rehabilitation Centre. The latter details were still not publicised to terrorists, however, who were only told that they could expect fair treatment if they gave up. Nevertheless, apparently well-treated SEPs continued to be paraded in public, enabling terrorists to *infer* that the possibility of their not being prosecuted if they gave up was very real indeed.[47]

Furthermore, Templer's memorable personality and personal integrity, deliberately projected via a highly visible public profile, proved to be a key factor in repairing government credibility not merely with the public but even the terrorists.[48] Thus in March 1954, one SEP, who came out after hearing a voice aircraft broadcast in Mandarin by Templer that 'it was safe to surrender', opined that 'all jungle men knew they could trust General Sir Gerald Templer'.[49]

Finally, as far as the context was concerned, the steady progress begun under Briggs greatly intensified under Templer: detention and deportation figures began a long and steep decline; the bulk of the Resettlement Areas became New Villages with better security and amenities; the security forces were steadily becoming highly proficient in jungle fighting; while food denial schemes aimed at destroying precise MCP district organisations were elaborated and were having telling effects. Meanwhile, the MCP itself found by 1953 that its indiscriminate terror campaign of June 1948 to October 1951 had practically destroyed its chances of building a base among its natural constituency, the rural Chinese. Hence, instead of mass support, the MCP only elicited mass aversion, which its official cessation of indiscriminate terror in October 1951 did nothing to dispel.[50]

By the time Templer left at the end of May 1954, therefore, the tide of the military campaign had turned decisively in the government's favour, a fact reflected in the improving terrorist surrender rate. While between 1949 and 1951 the surrender rate had been a paltry average of 15.5 per month, this jumped to 21.3 in 1952, Templer's first year as High Commissioner. Between January and June 1953, moreover, the average rose to 29.4 and peaked at 32.5 in the last six months of the year.

However, the rate dropped first to 25.3 between January to March 1954, and then to 13 in the period April to June.[51] The fall in the surrender rate was attributable to two reasons: by 1954, the uncommitted in the MCP rank and file had been excised, leaving behind a harder core of 'tougher' hardcore terrorists. Second, events in Indochina, especially the Viet Minh victory over the French at Dien Bien Phu in May 1954, allowed MCP propagandists to propagate the idea that if the Viet Minh could succeed, the MCP could as well, and that 'when a certain time came', aid would reach the MCP from the Viet Minh.[52]

PHASE 3: SEPTEMBER 1955 TO FEBRUARY 1956

In January 1955, with Donald MacGillivray[53] as the new High Commissioner and Lt-General Sir Geoffrey Bourne[54] the new Director of Operations, the leader of the powerful United Malays National Organisation-Malayan Chinese Association (UMNO-MCA) Alliance political party, Tunku Abdul Rahman,[55] promised that should the Alliance win the federal elections scheduled for July, it would declare an amnesty for all terrorists. Tunku made the promise on the assumption that an amnesty would hasten the end of the Emergency, and in so doing persuade the British to grant self-government to Malaya sooner than later.[56]

Tunku's announcement greatly disquieted MacGillivray and Bourne, who felt that there was no evidence to support the view that declaring an amnesty would precipitate the collapse of the MCP. They thus prevailed upon Tunku to desist from public discussions of an amnesty on the premise that the current surrender policy already embodied 'a very considerable degree of amnesty'.[57]

Furthermore, in order to forestall further pressure from the Alliance for an amnesty, the government decided in early March to flesh out its policy of fair treatment. It was announced publicly for the first time that all SEPs were held for three months in order to assist government operations and after that they either joined the security forces voluntarily or were rehabilitated.[58] It has to be emphasised that this was a most significant announcement for the terrorists in the jungle: the government all but admitted that although it never explicitly said so in its propaganda to the terrorists, in practice it never prosecuted SEPs, even if they had blood on their hands.

Moreover, Chin Peng was from the start of 1955, a very worried man. He knew full well that the strategic initiative in the shooting war had long passed from the MCP, and huge cracks were appearing. Under heavy pressure from the security forces, together with improved food denial schemes, the Pahang terrorist organisation had collapsed by the end of 1954, and by early 1955 high-ranking terrorists, even state committee members, were coming out.[59] Moreover some SEPs revealed that the Indochina ceasefire of July 1954 had compelled them to lose hope that at some point external forces would arrive to help the MCP.[60] In view of this general recognition of military defeat, the January discussions of an amnesty had greatly rattled the Central Committee, compelling it to decry such a 'plot' designed to 'sway' terrorist 'minds from long-term warfare'.[61]

Chin Peng would also have worried about the government's tacit admission in March 1955 that in practice no SEP had ever been prosecuted, as this might persuade some terrorists to give up the struggle. Finally, Chin was aware that a conference of Commonwealth Communist Parties in Britain in 1954 had directed that the Emergency in Malaya be resolved by the 'method of peace'.[62] It was in these circumstances that the MCP launched its 'political offensive', sending out the so-called Ng Heng letter dated 1 May 1955 asking for peace negotiations.

The Ng Heng letter was received by certain interests including the government in Malaya in late June. The government immediately rejected the peace offer on the grounds that the MCP knew that it was losing as the surrender rate was back up to almost one a day; that it was under pressure to modify its tactics in line with international Communist policy; and most importantly, given the federal elections the following month, it was obvious that the Communists were trying to prevent other Malayan political parties from positioning themselves as the people's champions. If that were to happen, the 'wind will be taken right out of the Communists' sails'.[63]

Nevertheless, even as the government was rejecting Ng Heng it was fully conscious that the strategic and political context necessitated a modification of its surrender policy. Hence in late June and into July 1955 the Government considered a fresh amnesty, as it was felt that it would represent a timely counter-move to 'offset the propaganda value of the Communists' negotiation proposals' as well as 'convince neutral opinion that the government were not seeking to prolong the shooting war but were prepared to make a positive proposal to end it'.[64]

There was another consideration: MacGillivray argued that with respect to the terrorist rank and file, 'it would seem that this might be the psychological moment to make a fresh offer', in order to 'drive a wedge between them and their leaders'. Certainly, immediately after receipt of the Ng Heng letter, government propaganda informed the terrorists that their leaders were proposing to give up the struggle.[65] This effort prompted 'repeated discussions and uncertainty and even controversy among units in the jungle'. In response local Communist leaders exhorted the rank and file to 'be more resolute and definite' in trusting the Central Committee and to 'definitely not waver'.[66]

MacGillivray calculated that it would take several weeks for news of Ng Heng to thoroughly seep through to the terrorist rank and file in the jungle. Once this time had passed, however (perhaps by August 1955) an amnesty could be declared. In addition, he admitted that there was considerable merit in the Alliance view that any fresh amnesty offer should not be made before the July federal elections, but rather afterwards by an elected Malayan government.[67] There was a final crucial factor. The British were extremely keen to ensure that Chin Peng did not succeed in winning over the Emergency-weary public with his definition of an MCP peace: the emergence from the jungle of the Communists with their rights intact and enjoying the fullest liberty to take part in the Malayan political process. The government thus had to define an alternative version of peace and secure the public's acceptance of it, meaning the emergence from the jungle of a defeated enemy with its rights sharply curtailed.[68] It was in this respect that the terms of the 1955 amnesty were crucially important.

In fact, given the tense strategic situation in Southeast Asia at the time, the content of the 1955 amnesty leaflet was not easily arrived at. MacGillivray disagreed with the opinion of the Chiefs of Staff Committee that the leaflet announce how SEPs would be 'held in detention' once they came out. Warning that the term 'detention' might have a deterrent effect on the terrorists, he suggested that the word 'investigation' be used instead. He insisted that this approach represented the 'best possible compromise between the aim of making the amnesty successful and the need to leave the Federal Government with a free hand in dealing with hard core Communist terrorists'.[69]

Furthermore, the phrase 'if any of them wish to go to China, their request will be given due consideration', apparently 'suffered many birth pangs before it was born'. It was eventually decided against expanding the sentence to include other countries in Southeast Asia like Thailand and Indonesia so as not to alarm them.[70]

In the event, after 'much discussion' between Kuala Lumpur and London, the text of the amnesty was finally agreed upon by late August,[71] and it was thereby declared on 9 September 1955. Addressed to 'all who have taken up arms against the Government of the Federation of Malaya and those who have consorted with them', the leaflet declared: 'Those of you who come in and surrender will not be prosecuted for any offence, connected with the Emergency, which you have committed under communist direction, either before this date or in ignorance of this declaration.' The heart of the leaflet was as follows:

> The Government will conduct investigations on those who surrender. Those who show that they genuinely intend to be loyal to the Government of Malaya and to give up their communist activities, will be helped to regain their normal position in society and be reunited with their families. As regards the remainder, restrictions will have to be placed on their liberty but if any of them wish to go to China their request will be given due consideration.

The leaflet also stipulated that while there would be no general ceasefire, local ones would be arranged by the security forces who would also be on the alert to assist terrorists who wanted to accept the offer.[72] It was also decided not to have a time limit for the amnesty, though this was not mentioned in the leaflet.[73]

Because by 1955 the terrorist rank and file comprised harder core Communists who were more suspicious of government motives, establishing credibility was more difficult than in previous phases. A 1956 study showed that many of these harder core SEPs had feared that if they gave up they would be beaten up, poisoned, tortured or simply disappear. They asserted that there should be more government propaganda promising good treatment of SEPs.[74] Nevertheless, even among this harder core, there were gradually increasing signs of confidence that the government kept its promises.[75]

In terms of context, moreover, this phase of the government surrender policy was dominated by Chin Peng's shrewd political machinations. Three days after the declaration of the amnesty, he sent out letters to prominent Malayans proposing that he and Chief Minister Tunku Abdul Rahman meet for talks. Tunku received notice of this in late September, and following consultations with MacGillivray and Bourne, agreed to meet Chin Peng to clarify the terms of the amnesty, not negotiate new peace terms.[76] Following preliminary protocol meetings in Klian Intan, Perak, between MCP propaganda head Chen Tien and government representatives, the date and place of the talks were fixed: Baling, Kedah on 28 and 29 December 1955.[77]

In fact, once Tunku had agreed to meet him at Baling, Chin Peng immediately let it be known among the rank and file that it was no point accepting the amnesty terms when in a few months at Baling he would be able to secure even better exit terms for them. This had the effect of utterly nullifying the appeal of the Alliance amnesty.[78]

The content of the Alliance amnesty also posed problems. At Baling, Chin Peng, balking at the amnesty stipulations that SEPs would have restrictions placed on their liberty, rejected it outright. He counter-offered that the MCP would be willing to cease hostilities in return for 'recognition of the M.C.P., no detention, no investigation and no restriction of movement' of terrorists who came out of the jungle. While Tunku clarified that SEPs who wished to be repatriated would not be investigated, he insisted that those who did not want to recant Communism and wished to remain in Malaya would have to be. The fundamental difficulty between Tunku and Chin Peng, however, was over the 'primary question' of recognition of the MCP. Tunku insisted that he would never recognise the MCP and indeed wanted it dissolved. Chin Peng refused, and the talks broke down.

However, Tunku did extract from Chin Peng the significant concession that should the Chief Minister secure control of internal defence and security from the British, the MCP would cease hostilities.[79] Tunku subsequently announced on 30 December that the amnesty and all other surrender terms in force prior to the amnesty would be withdrawn on 8 February 1956.[80] The cumulative result of Chin Peng's machinations and the Baling outcome was that the 1955 Alliance amnesty proved a disappointment: by the time it was withdrawn on 8 February 1956, only 74 SEPs had been generated.[81]

## PHASE 4: MARCH 1956 TO AUGUST 1957

In early 1956, captured documents showed that the morale of the terrorists had been 'severely shaken' by the failure of the Baling talks and the end of the 1955 amnesty, but there were no large-scale surrenders as the rank and file were trying to absorb the implications of these events. At the same time, to avoid 'uncontrollable disappointment' among the terrorists, the Central Committee launched an intensive internal propaganda campaign, suggesting that the MCP had scored a moral victory at Baling. The propaganda also described how, as time passed, the will of the government and the public to continue the struggle would weaken, compelling them eventually to seek an accommodation on the MCP's terms. The rallying cry to the comrades was thus to 'hold on' for that inevitable day. This became the MCP's so-called wait-and-see policy which was clearly discernible by mid-1956.[82]

The rapidly-developing political context aside, there were further changes in the content of surrender policy. When the 1955 amnesty and indeed all previous surrender terms were withdrawn on 8 February 1956, the government recognised that it had to replace them with something new. This was not easy. After the Baling stalemate, the government did not want to return to the pre-amnesty surrender terms of guaranteeing fair treatment of all SEPs and appear weak. Yet neither could the government afford to offer a 'very mild inducement to surrender' if it wanted to get its hands on SEPs and secure operational intelligence.[83] Eventually, in mid-March 1956, a new surrender policy was formulated. Leaflets dropped on the jungle emphasised that this new offer was not a continuation of the 1955 amnesty. Rather: 'These terms are only for those of you who have genuinely foresworn Communist terrorism and have not been guilty of acts of atrocity or murder.' The leaflet added: 'When you come out, the Government will treat you fairly. Those of you who have genuinely given up the struggle against the lawfully established Government of the people will be helped to regain your freedom and be reunited with your families or if your prefer, repatriated to China.'[84]

There was no time limit placed on this new offer. The content of the new terms was immediately problematic. While the government, by stipulating that the offer was open only to those who had not been guilty of capital crimes, succeeded in communicating its resolve to get tough with the MCP following its rejection of the 1955 amnesty, it unwittingly narrowed the scope of the offer so drastically as to render it ineffectual. This was because the remaining terrorists, being the harder core, had virtually to a man been guilty to varying degrees of involvement in some form of atrocities. In other words, practically no remaining terrorist qualified for pardon under the March 1956 surrender terms.

Subsequently, in July 1956 it was decided to adopt a 'less stringent interpretation of the exclusion clause', meaning that apart from 'no more than a score' of brutal terrorists who had been guilty of 'notorious crimes', everyone else could be offered the pre-1955 amnesty terms of fair treatment on surrender.[85] Unfortunately, the problems with the content of the March 1956 surrender policy, when coupled specifically with the MCP rank and file's 'wait-and-see' attitude, meant that the average monthly surrender rate in 1956 dropped below that for 1955, from an average of 20.66 to 11.25.[86] Nevertheless, the government persisted with the March 1956 terms into 1957.

PHASE 5: SEPTEMBER 1957 TO JULY 1958

To appreciate the impact of the final significant change in the government's surrender policy in September 1957, it is necessary to examine the strategic and political context, beginning in late March 1956, about three months after the Baling Talks. The head of MCP propaganda, Chen Tien, sent a letter to several prominent Malayans and organisations offering to re-open negotiations with the government on terms which would enable the terrorists not to 'suffer political indignity or personal retaliation'. The MCP, aware that since Baling several public organisations had urged the government to make peace with the Communists, hoped to put pressure on Tunku to re-consider his tough stand at Baling.

However, Tunku rejected this new offer, accusing the Communists of attempting to renege on their promise at Baling to lay down arms once he had secured control of internal defence and security (which he had done on 1 March 1956 when the Emergency Operations Council was formed).[87] Lambasting the MCP for its bad faith, he declared that he would only meet the MCP to 'make arrangements for their unconditional surrender'.[88]

Then in September 1956, Chin Peng wrote to the 8th Chinese Communist Party Congress in Peking, welcoming international mediation to resolve the Emergency. However, when Tunku got wind of this later that month, he flatly rejected any notion of 'international mediation' in the Emergency, reiterating that he wanted nothing less than the MCP's unconditional surrender.[89] Tunku then went on the offensive himself two months later, via Operation 'Iceland', the biggest mass leaflet drop since the 1955 amnesty. Directly addressing the rank and file, Tunku urged them not to be 'duped' by their leaders that there was 'still some hope', and specifically rebutted four of Chin Peng's 'lies'.

First, he countered that it was pure fiction that Chin Peng had almost succeeded at Baling and would do so the next time, and informed them that their Deputy Secretary-General, Yeong Kwo, who had planned the so-called 'political offensive', had been killed by the security forces.

Second, apart from emphasising the inexorable decline in the MCP's military fortunes, Tunku also pointed out that Chinese Premier Chou Enlai himself had told all overseas Chinese to be loyal to the governments of their respective domiciles, which really meant that China was not going to intervene in Malaya.

Third, Tunku debunked the Central Committee's myth that independence was not coming in 1957. Assuring them that no one outside the jungle believed this, he pointedly declared: 'You say that you are fighting for independence. My Party and I have achieved it.' He emphasised that he was in possession of all 'the facts of the situation, including your leaders' secret views of the situation, which they never let you know'. Finally, Tunku promised that instead of weakening in resolve as the Central Committee was claiming, the government and the people of Malaya were determined to fight the MCP 'until it is destroyed and terrorism is utterly stamped out', and that independence or *Merdeka* would not change this determination.[90]

'Iceland' must have had some effect because only four months later, in March 1957, the MCP again called for peace negotiations. This time, the Central Committee sent out a cyclostyled letter to several Chinese guilds. In content it was 'absolutely identical' to Chen Tien's offer of March 1956, exactly a year earlier. Essentially it called for all terrorists to be given the same privileges as other citizens; that they should be allowed to stand for elections; and that they should not be punished. Tunku's response was that the MCP statement was 'an old piece of propaganda'.[91]

Nevertheless, despite Tunku's apparently blasé dismissal of the MCP offer to negotiate, public pressure to end the Emergency was mounting. At the end of June 1957, the Malayan Trade Union Congress (MTUC) urged the government to open fresh talks with the MCP so as to end the 'colossal drain' on the country's finances. The MTUC argued that it was important to have a 'give and take' attitude, and warned that perhaps the British were using the prolongation of the Emergency to keep its forces in Malaya. If that was the case, Malaya's independence would be nothing but a sham.[92]

Tunku countered in mid-July 1957 that as long as 'Government sticks to its guns' the MCP would capitulate. Later in the month he announced, for the first time since the start of the Emergency, that the war would be over by the end of 1958. He even predicted that he expected to receive a letter from Chin Peng offering the complete surrender of the MCP.[93] Then in late July he announced a 'secret plan' to defeat the 'Reds' by end-1958. This involved an 'intensified psychological warfare campaign' involving all cabinet ministers and Alliance federal, state, town and village councillors fanning out throughout the country to enlist the support of the public in eliminating the remaining terrorists.[94] Significantly, by this time, the public (even those in districts that had traditionally been pro-Communist) were deserting the MCP in droves, sensing that the end was truly in sight. Hence in Tanjong Malim 2,000 people, escorted by security forces, plunged five miles into the jungle and for four hours, called out for five remaining terrorists to surrender. The Chinese chairman of Tanjong Malim's pro-government Good Citizen's Committee, declared that it was 'stupid' of the terrorists not to give up.[95] Then on 28 August 1957, Tunku announced at his last press conference before *Merdeka*, that the government would be giving the terrorists one final chance to give up after Malaya became independent on 31 August.[96]

Against this context of an intense political battle between Tunku and Chin Peng, the content of the government surrender policy received fresh refinement. The *Merdeka* amnesty was subsequently announced on 3 September. Its key terms were: 'Those of you who genuinely desire to give up the armed struggle may come out of the jungle and may ask any individual to help you to do this...You will NOT be prosecuted for any offence connected with the Emergency which you have committed under communist direction before this date.' What treatment could SEPs expect?

> Those who show that they genuinely intend to be loyal to the elected Government of Malaya and to give up their communist activities will be helped to regain their normal life and to be reunited with their families, if they so wish. As regards the remainder, they will be repatriated to China (with their families if they so wish) and will not be made the subject of any investigation or interrogation but will be given fair treatment while waiting for repatriation.

The leaflet also warned that there 'would be no relaxation of Security Forces operations, so accept this offer before it is too late'.[97] In contrast to the 'Iceland' drop of November 1956, it was decided that the *Merdeka* amnesty offer would be codenamed 'Greenland'. It was publicly announced that there was a time limit: the offer would be open only until 31 December 1957.[98]

The *Merdeka* amnesty seemed to produce results. On 16 December, Tunku announced that 122 terrorists had given up since 3 September. Moreover, while the surrender rate in the first eight months of 1957 had been eight a month, dropping to seven in September as terrorists were coming to grips with the new surrender terms, in October and November the rate had skyrocketed to 40 a month. Moreover, for the first time in the Emergency, the number of SEPs considerably exceeded the total number of terrorists killed or captured. More ominously for the MCP, 36 of the 122 SEPs who had come out were at least branch committee members or above.

Tunku thus decided to extend the amnesty for another four months.[99] Subsequently, on 27 March 1958, he announced at a press conference that 215 terrorists had given up since the inauguration of the *Merdeka* amnesty, the largest number for any similar period since the Emergency began. Again, included in this number were very senior Communists. It was thus decided to extend the *Merdeka* amnesty a final time, to 31 July. After this date, the government would revert to the old policy of guaranteeing merely 'fair treatment'.[100]

Then on 9 July it was announced that 118 terrorists, including 25 ranking Communists, had given up in Perak alone since October 1957. The surrender snowball had started in October when five terrorists surrendered and agreed to covertly help Special Branch by bringing out the rest of their comrades. The operation had taken seven months, and utterly smashed the south Perak Communist organisation.[101] Tunku then announced that from January to August, 160 terrorists, including 33 ranking Communists, had surrendered in Johore. In particular, for the first time in the Emergency, a Central Committee member, Hor Lung, had surrendered, and greatly assisted Special Branch in encouraging the large scale surrenders in Johore. By the end of 1958, the MCP South Malaya Bureau had ceased to exist. In sum, by the end of 1958, there were only 868 terrorists left in the whole of Malaya and 485 of these were on the Thai side of the border.[102] To all intents and purposes, therefore, the shooting war was over by 31 December 1958.

The Perak State government held that the *Merdeka* amnesty had been a key factor in the 'final destruction of militant Communism as a potential threat to the security of the country'.[103] To be sure, the success of the amnesty lay in intrinsic and extrinsic factors. Intrinsically, the content of the amnesty text had been formulated only after the Baling script had been studied afresh by government experts for several months. Thus the scope of the surrender terms was wide: unconditional pardon was offered to *all* terrorists regardless of what they had done before the date of the amnesty.

Moreover, the phrasing of, and promised treatment contained in, the amnesty text reflected a sensitivity to Chin Peng's opposition at Baling to any mention of 'prosecution', 'interrogation' and 'investigation'. In fact, the text emphasised that SEPs who refused to recant Communism would simply receive fair treatment while awaiting repatriation to China, and would not be subject to 'investigation' or 'interrogation'. In addition, the Chinese word for 'repatriation to China' was specially chosen to avoid the negative connotation usually associated with the process. Furthermore, unlike previous surrender terms, the word 'surrender' was replaced by the phrase 'come out of the jungle', while the leaflet was addressed to the rather dignified-sounding 'M.C.P. personnel'. The whole idea had been to frame the text and terms in 'a most palatable language' to the hardcore terrorists and their leaders.[104]

By the time of the *Merdeka* amnesty, the government had painstakingly managed to establish some credibility with the hardcore terrorists through its careful public treatment of SEPs. It was thus very significant that when some of these hardened Chinese SEPs were interviewed in 1958 they acknowledged that a major factor why they had come out was that they trusted Tunku to keep his word with respect to the extremely, almost unbelievably liberal amnesty terms.[105]

Moreover, as Hugh Greene had suggested seven years before, the success of the *Merdeka* amnesty in effecting mass surrenders was in no small way due to the strategic context. The security forces were completely on top by 1957, while the introduction from mid-1956 of central cooking drastically worsened the food supply situation for the terrorists. While small amounts of food, especially uncooked rice, had still managed to trickle out to the terrorists despite food denial, central cooking meant that all rice in New Villages and estates was centrally stored and cooked. Consequently there was no longer even any uncooked rice for villagers to surrender to the terrorists later. The effect on terrorist morale was profound.[106]

In sum, by September 1957, the terrorists and even some leaders were essentially waiting to see if the Central Committee could secure better exit terms than what the government could offer. Chin Peng's ability to secure better exit terms than the *Merdeka* amnesty hence represented the most crucial feature of the political context in 1957.

The Tunku-Chin Peng political endgame began on 1 September 1957, when the MCP posted a manifesto in Thailand, which was received by Malayan newspapers in early October. In the document, Chin Peng once more reiterated that the MCP would lay down arms in return for participation in the democratic process within constitutional limits. Again Tunku replied publicly on 5 October that the only thing he would accept was the complete surrender of the Communists, and if Chin Peng wanted to discuss this, he could write to him directly.[107] Chin Peng did so on 12 October, suggesting that a further meeting could result in a 'just and fair agreement' to end the Emergency.[108] Tunku received this on 8 November and reiterated that if Chin Peng genuinely wanted to surrender he would make arrangements for talks under the *Merdeka* terms. It was forecast in late November that any further talks with Chin Peng would be held in December 1957.[109]

However, it shortly became obvious that just as he had done two years earlier in 1955, Chin Peng had thrown up the hope of peace talks to nullify the effect of the *Merdeka* amnesty on the terrorists. In other words, Chin Peng was calculating that the terrorists would ignore the *Merdeka* offer in the expectation that he would be able to secure even more generous exit terms at the forthcoming peace talks.[110]

Subsequently, on 6 December 1957, Tunku issued an ultimatum to Chin Peng. Declaring that he was fed up of waiting, the Prime Minister announced that Chin Peng had until 31 December to send an emissary to discuss protocol for the talks, or else the whole thing would be off.[111] Chin Peng replied to Tunku on 9 December, informing him that he would be sending two lieutenants for preliminary discussions, but insisted that the question of surrender did not arise. On 21 December, the very day Tunku received this reply, he immediately announced that he could not 'see any possibility of coming to terms until Chin Peng is prepared to surrender'.[112] Tunku therefore dismissed any possibility of meeting Chin Peng for further talks.[113]

It is suggested when Tunku declared that there would no longer be further talks with Chin Peng, the psychological moment for the optimal functioning of the *Merdeka* amnesty was reached. This was because from that date onward, the remaining terrorists recognised that the only terms they could come out under were the *Merdeka* terms. Chin Peng would not be able to secure better terms because the government was not going to give him a forum to demand better terms. Tunku had thus trumped Chin Peng, and terrorist morale collapsed, precipitating the mass surrenders of 1958.

In sum, far from representing the mopping up phase of the Emergency, the years after 1954 were crucial in that the government still had to eliminate the residual threat posed by the smaller group of hardcore terrorists left in the jungle. In this connection, an examination of the role of government propaganda in the specific form of surrender policy, in contrast to other perspectives, provides an explanation as to how and why the climactic mass surrenders of 1958 occurred. While the surrender policy passed through several stages, the potency of government surrender policy in the form of the *Merdeka* amnesty was explicable because after 21 December 1957, the three crucial factors of government credibility, the attractive content, and the favourable political and strategic contexts, finally intersected.

## NOTES

1. Charles Townshend, *Britain's Civil Wars: Counterinsurgency in the Twentieth Century* (London /Boston: Faber 1986) p.164; Donald Mackay, *The Malayan Emergency 1948–60: The Domino that Stood* (London/Washington: Brassey's 1997) p.140; Robert Asprey, *War in the Shadows*, 2nd ed. (London: Little, Brown 1994) p.573.
2. Public Record Office (PRO) WO 291/1783, F.H. Lakin and Mrs G.J. Humphrey, 'A Study of Surrenders in Malaya during Jan 1949 to June 1954', ORS (PW) 11/54 , July 1954; *The Communist Threat to the Federation of Malaya* (Kuala Lumpur: Government Printer 1959) p.19.
3. *Straits Budget (SB)*, 25 April 1957.
4. Ibid.
5. PRO CO 1030/10, 'Review of the Emergency Situation in Malaya at the end of 1956', 12 Feb. 1957. Hereafter DOR 1956.
6. Anthony Short, *The Communist Insurrection in Malaya, 1948–60* (London: Frederick Mueller 1975) pp.490–92; Aloysius Chin, *The Communist Party of Malaya: The Inside Story* (Kuala Lumpur: Vinpress 1995) pp.50–51.
7. Richard Clutterbuck, *Conflict and Violence in Singapore and Malaysia 1945–1983*, rev. ed. (Singapore: Graham Brash 1984); Mackay, *Malayan Emergency* (note 1) pp.128–9.
8. Richard Stubbs, *Hearts and Minds in Guerrilla Warfare: The Malayan Emergency 1948-1960* (Singapore: OUP 1993); Karl Hack, 'Screwing Down the People: The Malayan Emergency, Decolonisation and Ethnicity' in H. Antlov and S. Tonnesson (eds.) *Imperial Policy and Southeast Asian Nationalism* (Surrey: Curzon Press 1995) pp.83–98.
9. Anthony Short, 'The Malayan Emergency' in R. Haycock (ed.) *Regular Armies and Insurgency* (London: Croom Helm 1979) pp.65–6; Brian Crozier, *The Rebels: A Study of Post-War Insurrections* (Boston: Beacon Press 1964) pp.166–8.

10. Thomas R. Mockaitis, *British Counterinsurgency, 1919–1960* (London: Macmillan 1990).
11. Crozier (note 9) p.214; J.B. Perry Robinson *Transformation in Malaya* (London: Secker 1956) pp.153–5.
12. The most comprehensive if rather general survey of government Emergency propaganda is provided by Thompson. Robert Thompson, *Defeating Communist Insurgency: Experiences from Malaya and Vietnam* (London: Chatto 1966) Ch.8. See also Susan Carruthers, *Winning Hearts and Minds: British Governments, the Media and Colonial Counterinsurgency 1944-1960* (London/NY: Leicester UP 1995) pp.90–95; Stubbs (note 8) pp.120–21, 180–84; Short (note 6) pp.419–23.
13. Thompson, ibid. p.90.
14. Stubbs (note 8) pp.120–21, 183–4; Malcolm Postgate, *Operation Firedog: Air Support in the Malayan Emergency, 1948–1960* (London: HMSO 1992) pp.117–21.
15. R.H.S. Crossman 'Psychological Warfare', *RUSI Journal* 97/587 (1952) p.324. Crossman was the leading Allied propagandist in World War II, and between 1940 and 1943, as Head of the Political Warfare Executive German Section, worked closely with Hugh Carleton Greene of the BBC German Service. Greene later re-organised Malayan Emergency propaganda. Michael Tracey, *A Variety of Lives: A Biography of Sir Hugh Greene* (London: Bodley Head 1983) pp.73–9, 127–32.
16. Sir Robert Bruce Lockhart, 'Political Warfare', *RUSI Journal* 95/577 (1950) p.195; Crossman, ibid. p.320.
17. R.H.S. Crossman, 'Supplementary Essay' to D. Lerner, *Psychological Warfare against Nazi Germany: The Sykewar Campaign, D-Day to VE-Day* (Cambridge: MIT Press 1971) pp.338–40.
18. A.J. Stockwell 'British Imperial Policy and Decolonization in Malaya, 1942–52', *Journal of Imperial and Commonwealth History* [hereafter *JICH*] 13/1 (1984) pp.68–9.
19. For the origins of the MCP, see Cheah Boon Kheng (ed.), *From PKI to the Comintern: The Apprenticeship of the Malayan Communist Party* (Ithaca, NY: Cornell UP 1992). On the MCP during the Occupation, see F. Spencer Chapman, *The Jungle is Neutral* [1949] (Singapore/Kuala Lumpur: Times Books Int. 1997) and Paul H. Kratoska, *The Japanese Occupation of Malaya 1941–1945* (St Leonards, NSW: Allen and Unwin 1998) pp.95–103. On the MCP's united front activities in 1946–48, see Cheah Boon Kheng, *The Masked Comrades: A Study of the Communist United Front in Malaya, 1945–48* (Singapore: Times Books Int. 1979). On the controversial origins of the Emergency, see M.R. Stenson, *Industrial Conflict in Malaya: Prelude to the Communist Revolt of 1948* (London: OUP 1970), and A.J. Stockwell '"A Widespread and Long-Concocted Plot to Overthrow the Government in Malaya?" The Origins of the Malayan Emergency', *JICH* 21/3 (1993) pp.66–88.
20. Stubbs (note 8) p.61; Stockwell, ibid. p.77.
21. *Communist Banditry in Malaya: The Emergency June 1948–December 1949* (Kuala Lumpur: Dept. of Public Relations 1950) p.2.
22. Anthony Short, 'Communism and the Emergency' in Wang Gung Wu (ed.) *Malaysia: A Survey* (London/Dunmow: Pall Mall Press 1964) p.153; Edgar O'Ballance, *Malaya: The Communist Insurgent War, 1948-60* (Hamden, CT: Archon 1966) p.89; J.N. McHugh, *Anatomy of Communist Propaganda* (Kuala Lumpur: Dept. of Public Relations 1949) p.41.
23. *Communist Banditry* (note 21) pp.19–20.
24. PRO WO 106/5990, 'Review of Emergency in Malaya June 1948–Aug 1957', 12 Sept. 1957.
25. Gurney had served in Kenya, Jamaica, East Africa and the Gold Coast between 1921 and 1946, before becoming Chief Secretary in Palestine between 1946 and 1948. He was assassinated by the MCP in Oct. 1951.
26. Rhodes House Library, Oxford (RHO) MSS.Brit.Emp.s.486, 'Surrender Policy', March 1953; PRO CO 537/4868, 'Political Intelligence Report from Commissioner-General's Office', 16 Sept. 1949.
27. See the September Amnesty leaflet, found in RHO MSS.Ind.Ocn.s.276.
28. RHO MSS.Brit.Emp.s.486, 'Surrender Policy'; PRO WO 291/1509, F.H. Lakin, 'Psychological Warfare Research: its Role in Cold War', AORG 5/56, 1956.

29. A.J. Stockwell (ed.) *British Documents on the End of Empire (BDEEP), Series B, Vol. 3, Part II, Malaya: The Communist Insurrection, 1948–1953* (London: HMSO 1995) doc. 203.

30. The Joint Information and Propaganda Committee (JIPC) had been set up in February 1950 in order to ensure that all Government propaganda assets were co-ordinated and that Communist propaganda, particularly from China, was countered. PRO CO 537/6579, minutes of the 1st JIPC meeting, 10 Feb. 1950; 9th meeting, 23 June 1950; and 10th meeting, 7 July 1950.

31. RHO MSS.Ind.Ocn.s.320, D. Gray to W.J. Watts, 17 Dec. 1951.

32. R.D. Renick Jr, 'The Emergency Regulations of Malaya: Causes and Effect', *Journal of Southeast Asian History* 6/2 (1965) pp.17–23.

33. *BDEEP Malaya Part II* doc. 257.

34. Institute of Southeast Asian Studies (Singapore) TCL.11.5, Tan Chin Siong to Tan Cheng Lock, 18 May 1950.

35. PRO CO 537/6015, Tom Driberg interview with SEP Lam Swee, 1 Nov. 1950. Lam had been a high ranking Communist in Johore who defected to government in June 1950. He was later recruited into Emergency Information Services.

36. PRO WO 291/1781, F.H. Lakin and G.J. Humphrey, 'A Study of the Reasons for Entering the Jungle within a Group of Surrendered Chinese Communist Terrorists in Malaya', ORS (PW) 8/54, 17 June 1954.

37. Short (note 6) p. 221; PRO CO 537/7255, Hugh Carleton Greene, 'Report on Emergency Information Services', 14 Sept. 1951. Hereafter Greene Report.

38. Greene had been BBC German editor from 1940–46. Prior to that he had been the chief correspondent of the *Daily Telegraph* in Berlin, and had worked in RAF Intelligence for a few months in 1940. After the war he had been Controller of Broadcasting in the British zone of Occupied Germany, and had then been Head BBC East European Service in 1949. He returned from Malaya in late 1951, and in 1960 became BBC Director-General.

39. PRO CO 537/7255, Greene Report.

40. Briggs, an Indian Army officer, had served with distinction in Eritrea, the Western Desert, Iraq and Burma (1940–44), before becoming GOC-in-Chief, Burma Command (1946–48) where he also dealt with insurgency.

41. *BDEEP Malaya Part II* doc. 216; Stubbs, *Hearts and Minds* (note 8) pp.105, 124.

42. PRO CO 537/7255, Greene Report.

43. Templer had been Director, Military Government 21 Army Group (Germany) in 1945–46; Director, Military Intelligence, War Office 1946–48, Vice-Chief Imperial General Staff (1948–51); GOC Eastern Command (1950–52). After Malaya he was CIGS (1955–58).

44. PRO CO 1022/49, inward tel. 593 from Templer to Lyttelton, 12 May 1952.

45. Ibid.; *Daily Telegraph*, 23 June 1952 and 30 Jan. 1953; *Scotsman*, 7 Jan. 1953; PRO CO 537/7255, note dated 24 Jan. 1952 on Information Services meeting scheduled for 28 Jan. 1952.

46. PRO CO 1022/14, *The Security Forces' Weekly Intelligence Summary* w.e. 7 Feb. 1952. SEPs were defined as 'enemy personnel who willingly surrender to the forces of law and order at a time when they could otherwise willingly have made good their escape'. CEPs were defined as 'enemy personnel who come into our hands otherwise than an SEP'. PRO CO 1022/49, 'Commissioner's Instruction No. 3: the Treatment of Surrendered Enemy Personnel (SEP) and Captured Enemy Personnel (CEP)'.

47. PRO CO 1030/22, 'Surrender Policy', 12 Aug. 1954, and 'Surrender Offer to Communist Terrorists', 13 March 1956; CO 1022/49, A. Gann to J. Higham, 1 Sept. 1952, and 'Commissioner's Instruction No. 3'; RHO MSS.Brit.Emp.s.486, 'Surrender Policy'.

48. A.D.C. Peterson to the *Listener*, 14 Aug. 1969. Peterson was Director-General Information Services, Malaya (1952–54); *SB*, 11 Sept. 1952.

49. *Daily Telegraph*, 27 March 1954.

50. Liddell Hart Centre for Military Archives (LHCMA) Maj.-Gen.Dennis Edmund Talbot Papers, Lt.-Gen. Sir H. Stockwell, 'Appreciation of the Situation in Malaya', 15 Oct. 1953. For a fuller discussion of the significance of the Oct. 1951 MCP Directives, see Stubbs (note 8) pp.148–50.

51. PRO WO 291/ 1783, 'A Study of Surrenders in Malaya'.
52. Ibid.; PRO WO 291/1788, F.H. Lakin, 'Some Effects of International Affairs on Communist Terrorists in Malaya', ORS (PW) 17/54, 7 Dec. 1954.
53. MacGillivray had been in the Colonial Service since 1928, serving in Tanganyika (1929–38), Palestine (1938–47), and Jamaica as Colonial Secretary (1947–52). He was Deputy High Commissioner in Malaya (1952–54).
54. Lt.-Gen. Geoffrey Bourne had been GOC British Troops Berlin (1949–51) and then CO 16th Airborne Division (Territorial Army), before coming out to Malaya.
55. Tunku Abdul Rahman was a member of the Kedah royal family, and was Director of Education (Kedah) and Director of Passive Defence during the Occupation. After the war he resumed his law studies at the Inner Temple, and was called to the Bar. He became President of UMNO in Aug. 1951. The Malayan Chinese Association (MCA) had been formed in Feb. 1949 by Dato Tan Cheng Lock. UMNO and the MCA had decided to form the Alliance Party to contest the federal elections, after an *ad hoc* experiment at electoral co-operation during the 1952 municipal elections in Kuala Lumpur proved successful.
56. PRO CO 1030/22, inward tel. 17 from MacGillivray to Lennox-Boyd, 7 Jan. 1955. Alan Lennox-Boyd was Secretary of State for the Colonies (1954–59).
57. *Weekly News Summary* [hereafter *WNS*], week ending 22 Jan. 1955.
58. *Scotsman*, 7 March 1955.
59. PRO WO 291/1786, F.H. Lakin and G.J. Humphrey, 'A Study of Surrenders amongst Communist Terrorists in Malaya, June–Nov 1954', ORS (PW) 15/54, 18 Nov. 1954; WO 291/1699, D.F. Bayly Pike, 'Interrogation of 112 Surrendered Communist Terrorists in 1955', ORUFE 4/56, May 1956.
60. PRO WO 291/ 1788, 'Some Effects of International Affairs'.
61. *WNS*, w.e. 4 Feb. 1956.
62. RHO MSS. Brit.Emp.s.527, Granada interview with C.C. Too, Aug. 1981. Too was Head of Government Psychological Warfare from 1956 to 1983.
63. *WNS*, w.e. 25 June 1955.
64. PRO FO 371/116940, 'The Question of Offering an Amnesty to the Communist Terrorists in Malaya', 30 July 1955.
65. PRO FO 371/116939, inward tel. 378 from MacGillivray to Lennox-Boyd, 30 June 1955.
66. *WNS*, w.e. 4 Feb. 1956.
67. PRO FO 371/116939, inward tel. 378 .
68. LHCMA Talbot Papers, 'Considerations concerning a Declaration of Amnesty', 25 Aug. 1955.
69. PRO FO 371/116940, inward tel. 497 from MacGillivray to Lennox-Boyd, 24 Aug. 1955; H. Macmillan to Prime Minister, 23 Aug. 1955.
70. PRO FO 371/116940, inward tel. 539 from MacGillivray to Lennox-Boyd, 6 Sept. 1955.
71. PRO FO 371/116940, inward tel. 497 from MacGillivray to Lennox-Boyd, 24 Aug. 1955.
72. LHCMA Talbot Papers, 'Declaration of Amnesty', 9 Sept. 1955.
73. PRO FO 371/116940, inward tel. 539.
74. PRO WO 291/1699, 'Interrogation'.
75. PRO WO 291/1786, 'A Study of Surrenders' (note 59).
76. *WNS*, w.e. 1 Oct. 1955; *Federation of Malaya Annual Report 1955* (Kuala Lumpur: Government Press 1956) p.5.
77. PRO CO 1030/27, Secret 'Note', n.d.; inward savings 1545 from MacGillivray to Lennox-Boyd, 20 Dec. 1955; CO 1030/30, 'Report by Chief Minister of the Federation of Malaya on the Baling Talks', 1956.
78. PRO CO 1030/10, 'Review of the Emergency Situation in Malaya at the end of 1955', Jan. 1956.
79. A.J. Stockwell (ed.) *BDEEP Malaya, Series B, Vol. 3, Part III: The Alliance Route to Independence, 1953–1957* (London: HMSO 1995) doc. 391.
80. *WNS*, w.e. 31 Dec. 1955.
81. *WNS*, w.e. 11 Feb. 1956.
82. PRO CO 1030/10, DOR 1956.
83. Ibid.

84. PRO CO 1030/22, inward tel. 190 from MacGillivray to Lennox-Boyd, 15 March 1956.
85. PRO CO 1030/10, DOR 1956.
86. *Federation of Malaya Annual Report 1956* (Kuala Lumpur: Government Press 1957) pp.439–40.
87. In Jan./Feb. 1956 Tunku had gone to Britain and secured full control of internal defence and security, as well as a promise that Malayan independence would come by the end of Aug. 1957. Subsequently Tunku as Chief Minister became the Chairman of the Emergency Operations Council, which among others included the director of operations.
88. *WNS*, w.e. 7 April 1956.
89. *WNS*, w.e. 29 Sept. 1956; PRO CO 1030/412, inward tel. 161 from MacGillivray to Lennox-Boyd, 18 March 1957, CO 1030/412.
90. *WNS*, w.e. 17 Nov. 1956.
91. PRO CO 1030/412, inward tel. 177 from MacGIllivray to Lennox-Boyd, 23 March 1957; Federal Government Press Statement, 23 March 1957.
92. *SB*, 4 July 1957.
93. *SB*, 18 July 1957.
94. *SB*, 1 Aug. 1957.
95. *SB*, 29 Aug. 1957.
96. *SB*, 4 Sept. 1957.
97. National Archives of Singapore (NAS) Department of Information Services (DIS) 176/58, *Merdeka* Amnesty leaflet.
98. *SB*, 11 Sept. 1957.
99. *SB*, 25 Dec. 1957.
100. NAS DIS 176/58, Amnesty leaflet; *Straits Times* [hereafter *ST*], 10 July 1958.
101. *Malaya: Journal of the British Association of Malaya* (Aug. 1958) pp.16–18.
102. *Malaya* (Oct. 1958) p. 20; PRO AIR 23/8698, AVM V.E. Hancock, 'Tenth Report on the RAF Operations in Malaya, 1 Jan.–31 Dec. 1958'.
103. *ST*, 30 Dec. 1958.
104. *SB*, 18 Sept. 1957.
105. NAS DIS 176/58, 'Psychological Warfare Section Monthly Report', March 1958.
106. Tan Sri Dato Mubin Sheppard, *Taman Budiman: Memoirs of an Unorthodox Civil Servant* (Kuala Lumpur: Heinemann Asia 1979) pp. 202-22.
107. PRO CO 1030/412, inward tels. 268 and 271 from MacGillivray to Lennox-Boyd, 5 Oct. 1957.
108. PRO AIR 23/8697, AVM V.E. Hancock, 'Ninth Report of the RAF Operations in Malaya, 1 Jan. 1957–31 Dec. 1957'; *SB*, 13 Nov 1957.
109. Hancock Report 1957 (ibid.); PRO CO 1030/412, inward tel. 445 from MacGillivray to Commonwealth Relations Office, 6 Dec. 1957; *SB*, 4 Dec. 1957.
110. PRO AIR 23/8697, Hancock Report 1957.
111. *SB*, 18 Dec. 1957.
112. *SB*, 25 Dec. 1957.
113. PRO AIR 23/8697, Hancock Report 1957; *Federation of Malaya Annual Report 1957* (Kuala Lumpur: Government Press 1958) pp.470–71.

# 12

# Winning in Malaya:
# An Intelligence Success Story

## BRIAN STEWART

It was an honour to participate in the conference on the Clandestine Cold War in Asia and I was particularly delighted to have this opportunity to join in a discussion on the intelligence aspects of the Malayan Emergency, since the operational successes of the security forces and the bravery and effectiveness of the civilians, officials and others have been widely recognised but the contribution made by those involved in intelligence work has tended for the usual reasons to be less well known. Anthony Short has suggested: 'other things being equal the key to counter insurgency in Malaya was Intelligence' but this point is seldom acknowledged publicly.

Perhaps some lack of emphasis on intelligence was inevitable. It has been well said that 'success has many parents but failure is an orphan'. Intelligence seldom gets mentioned when all goes well while headlines blazoning 'failure of intelligence' appear frequently when things go wrong. I have also noticed serious historical studies that do not even have the word *intelligence* in their indices!

There are undoubtedly cogent reasons why the role of intelligence is often overlooked in accounts of operations which include the complexity of the business itself; the difficulties of tracing its impact and, above all perhaps, the problems of gaining access to authoritative sources on the subject. When I recently visited the Public Records Office I could find no files on the Joint Intelligence Committee's discussions about the Emergency and this contribution lacks as a result, therefore, the normal buttressing of footnotes that you are entitled to expect in an academic paper. These notes are based on my own personal experience as a participant in the successful battle against dedicated Communist guerrillas not on the official records, nor indeed on any other books except Anthony Short's magisterial work which provided me with a framework.[1]

I do not wish to argue that intelligence was the main ingredient responsible for the successful ending of the Malayan Emergency, still less that the intelligence community was always right. Indeed records show that at the beginning of the Emergency neither the Malayan Security Service (MSS) nor the Criminal Investigation Department (CID) predicted the armed insurrection. The machinery had been set up to fight a different battle and even two days before the insurrection began the MSS was suggesting that military aid would not be needed to assist the police, even though Anthony Short has stated that it acknowledged that 'the danger today increases as long as the power of the communists increases'. This was a balanced but unhelpful assessment of little use to decision makers.

An assessment immediately after the conflict started was extraordinarily optimistic, though critics might say complacent; both about the weaknesses of the Malayan Communist Party (MCP) and about the ease with which it could be cut off from its support bases and defeated. Malcolm MacDonald, the Governor-General, and others were uncomfortably aware that the MSS seemed incapable of providing either good factual intelligence or realistic assessments. Yet, although the weaknesses of the intelligence machinery were recognised, the only immediate action taken was to set up a co-ordinating staff. MacDonald was still highlighting the need for more and better intelligence in April 1949 although surprisingly sanguine about the operational situation.

There were many reasons for the manifest failures of the intelligence machine, including the facts that the MSS was too small and that the background of the Director, Colonel John Dalley, led him to concentrate on Malay nationalist activities and downgrade Communism as a threat. More importantly, perhaps, the MSS had a source at the highest level in the MCP and therefore assumed that it would know if the MCP planned an insurrection. It was unfortunately wrong.

This is not the place for a detailed discussion on the problems of intelligence assessment and prediction. However, it is worth remarking that intelligence officers are no better equipped with a magic crystal ball by which to predict future events than diplomats, economists, journalists or politicians. While they can be expected to discover the facts and any plans that exist, they are no less subject to the uncertainties of future events and the vagaries of human nature than anyone else. My thesis is simply that the eventual victory over the Malayan Communists owed much to intelligence. In spite of the bad start mentioned above, the development and improvement of the intelligence machine, exploiting the conditions imposed by the Malayan government under the Emergency Regulations, enabled the intelligence community to interact with maximum effect with the officers of the administration and the security forces at every level: federal, state and district.

The Malayan Communist Party (MCP) had an overwhelming intelligence advantage in 1948 in that they could easily find agents from among the disaffected elements within the Chinese community, with Chinese nationalism as a common bond against the other races. The government had to work much harder to recruit reliable and effective agents. Lt-General Sir Harold Briggs who was appointed as Director of Operations in April 1950 described the existing state of intelligence as 'our Achilles heel'. The intelligence picture had been transformed by 1952, by which time a Special Branch training school had been brought into operation; military intelligence officers had been seconded to Special Branch; the Chinese Affairs Department had been reconstituted and operational intelligence was increasingly effective leading to kills; ambushes; defections and successful *psywar* operations against the Communist Terrorists (CTs).

The MCP's original advantages, of operating among a rural Chinese population, who were at best, from the government's view point, neutral at worst disaffected and active helpers of the MCP and its military arm, the CTs, were progressively reduced as resettlement, food controls and curfews cut them off from their support bases, while potential Chinese agents outside the jungle became more confident that they could trust government officers to be discreet and professional. As a result of 'crash' language training courses, which were among the responsibilities of the Chinese Affairs Department and highly successful, potential agents were able to communicate directly with European officers and, as the Emergency continued, the Special Branch's penetration of the MCP's organisation reached impressive levels and assessments became useful and reliable. Intelligence was no longer the Achilles heel.

I realise that I am stating what should be a blindingly obvious truth when I stress the importance of close co-ordination of operations and intelligence in Malaya, but anyone who has been involved in efforts to bring together the activities of different governmental departments and agencies will recognise that effective co-operation is not easily achieved. It is particularly difficult in the situation we are considering when the civilian administration; the security forces and the intelligence community are all involved, since each component has its own priorities and its own way of doing things or, to use the jargon of the business school, its own *corporate culture*. In Malaya, however, the three sectors were brought together in what was probably a uniquely effective way and I was tempted to give this contribution the title of 'The Three-legged Stool' to emphasise this. Whatever other factors contributed to victory, it seems clear that success was built on the solid foundation provided by the three groups acting in consort and in support of each other, thus ensuring the best and most timely use of intelligence for operational purposes, as well as effective assessments.

My opportunities to observe this co-operation at first-hand arose from the fact that I was serving throughout the Emergency in the reborn Chinese Affairs Department, where I was employed not on normal administrative duties but, as one of the tiny minority of Malayan Civil Service (MCS) officers who had been taught Chinese, in a liaison role bridging the gap between the government and the Chinese community. The job was rather like that carried out by those Indian Civil Service officers who a generation before had been seconded to the Indian Political Service. We were advisers rather than administrators and whatever influence we achieved was derived not from legal powers but through the personal relationships we were able to build within the Chinese community and with colleagues in the government.

The small cadre of Chinese speakers in the MCS in the years before the war had been mainly employed in what was called the Chinese Protectorate dealing with specialist fields such as Chinese education and immigration, social welfare, secret societies and labour issues. London's wartime plans for post-war Malaya included the abolition of the Chinese Protectorate, which was seen in London as a divisive anachronism. A small rump of the Chinese Protectorate was established in Singapore and Kuala Lumpur but the two Secretaries for Chinese Affairs had minimal authority, and little responsibility except for advice on secret societies; banishment enquiries and control of publications with the aim of keeping subversive literature out of the territory.

When the Emergency started there was not only a serious shortage of Chinese-speaking MCS officers, who could communicate effectively with the mass of the Chinese population whose command of English and Malay was often rudimentary, but in addition the abolition of the Protectorate had led to the unhappy consequence that the bridges between the government and the Chinese community had withered away, leaving the government badly out of touch. This was a critical shortcoming when the vast majority of those fighting, or supporting the fight to turn Malaya into a Communist state were ethnic Chinese whatever the motive, inspired by the triumph of the Communist Party of China. Whether impelled by a racial pride in China's new place in the world, proud of Chinese language and culture, frightened, or apathetic, the problem was a Chinese one.

The Malayan government soon woke up to the fact that there was a need to revive a serious Chinese Affairs Department but Malcolm MacDonald ruled that it should not be given back its pre-war paternalistic powers. He thus begged the question as to how, without any clearly defined role or legal powers, its officers could operate effectively in a government dedicated to preserving Malay privilege and in an atmosphere where the Malays were deeply suspicious of the Chinese and envious of their wealth. The account given by Anthony Short of the plenary meeting of government and community leaders on 17 October 1951 illustrates the point. The Malay Chief Ministers refused to attend, since they considered that with Chinese leaders present they could not speak freely on the subject of the Chinese community and its failure to play a proper part in the fight against the CTs. The Malays had a point since, if they had spoken their minds, they would have caused great embarrassment, and seriously reduced the chances of collaboration between the Chinese and Malays.

The embryonic Chinese Affairs Department was well aware of the security risks posed by the Chinese rural dwellers who were in most cases squatters without land rights, but whose desire for tenure could not be granted without infuriating the Malays, who were determined to evict the squatters. This situation was, of course, a gift for MCP agitators. There were other issues for the Communists to play up including the usually very low standard of the rural Chinese schools, which enjoyed little help from the government, and the obstructions placed by the Malays in the way of granting citizenship rights to Chinese. These were all subjects in which I became closely involved as a Secretary for Chinese Affairs engaged in the campaign to win the 'hearts and minds' of the Chinese.

The Chinese Affairs officers for the most part succeeded, despite their lack of legal powers and in the face of the prevailing pro-Malay policies, in re-establishing effective links to the Chinese community from peasants to millionaires. The Chinese on the whole seemed to welcome the return of the *Dai Jin* (great men) or *Foo Mo Goon* (mother and father officials) as the old Chinese Protectorate Officers had been known.

It was more difficult to ensure the confidence of the Europeans in the MCS and police, or of Malay officials. The task of balancing on the tightrope between a Malay-biased government and a largely alienated Chinese community was not made easier by the polemics of Victor Purcell, a senior pre-war Chinese Protectorate officer turned academic who portrayed the Templer regime in highly critical terms, or of Han Suyin, who took a very jaundiced view of the fight against Communism in her popular novels. Purcell, it may be worth noting in view of our current discussion, remarked in his book *Malaya: Communist or Free?* (1954) that the real rulers of Malaya were the Special Branch. Thus we have Short and Purcell agreeing at least on the important role of the intelligence community: one with approval and the other with disapproval.

I had just passed my language exams when the Emergency broke out and was involved at once on my return from China in the development of the now toothless Chinese Affairs Department. I was posted to Malacca in 1952 and managed to persuade the Resident Commissioner that the title of Secretary for Chinese Affairs Malacca was more likely to gain me access at the age of 27 to the elderly Chinese leaders in the area than the title of 2nd Secretary [C] in the Settlement Secretariat. I was fortunate in having a Resident Commissioner who understood the importance of face! My colleagues in the Malay States were not so lucky: some never advanced beyond 'Resettlement Officer'.

The only statutory titles which I managed to claw back for the sake of a *poo bah* style board outside my office were Registrar of Marriages and Protector of Chinese, which at this stage meant no more than Director of the *Po Leung Kuk* or Institute for the Preservation of Virtue, which housed young ladies and trained them to keep them out of prostitution, and Superintendent of Chinese Schools. The educational one was the most relevant of these titles. This list of titles hardly suggested the sort of power wielded by a District Officer, with numerous legal duties, such as Collector of Land Revenue and Licensing Officer in many spheres.

I took as my first task the building of intimate and confidential relations with the newly formed Malayan Chinese Association (MCA), which was then headed by Tan Cheng Lock (who was later knighted) the father of the first Finance Minister of Malaysia, Tun Tan Siew Sin. Yet I had also to ensure that my information and advice to the government, as represented by the Resident, was seen as unbiased and untainted by my close friendship with the leaders of the Chinese community. The job of Secretary of Chinese Affairs (SCA) Malacca gave me a good vantage point from which to observe the workings of the machinery set up to fight the Emergency on the ground, and what I observed then is the basis for my remarks on the parts played by intelligence and psychological warfare that follow. It was, however, a worm's eye view since I was operating at settlement and district level and my federal contacts were personal rather than official.

The position of the MCA in the 1950s was crucial to the developing scene. As SCA Malacca I dealt with the MCA not only at district and settlement level but also at national level in the sense that Tan Cheng Lock, who was a resident of Malacca, was happy to turn to the SCA Malacca for advice and second opinions, and indeed for drafting duties when there were speeches to be made. The leadership of the Chinese community at these three levels included some very different types. There were the rough and ready leaders of villages and of particular Chinese linguistic groups, Cantonese, Hakka, Hokkien, possibly barely educated and speaking only rudimentary Malay in addition to their mother tongue. The subtleties of government policy were not for them. They expected the SCA, whom they still knew in colloquial Chinese as their 'father and mother official', to temper the wind to the shorn lamb and defend the Chinese right or wrong.

Their loyalties were not by even the greatest stretch of the imagination to the Federation of Malaya or the Queen, but to their own community and family against a background of some ill-defined concept of the defence of Chinese culture. Our job was to make them understand at least that the British colonial government was attempting to see fair play and that resettlement was not a punishment but a necessary defence. These were people, however, with whom one could deal on practical matters, such as finding land and money for improving Chinese schools or encouraging Chinese recruits into uniform to join the fight against Communism. They were also people one had to handle delicately when refusing to accept any sort of present, since a strict adherence to the rule book would have led to criminal prosecution for the offender, while a mere refusal to take the gift left the SCA without hard evidence to refute any calumny that a bribe had been received.

The leaders at settlement level were usually better educated business-men, commodity dealers or wealthy gold merchants. However, it was still never very easy to move the conversation from the particular to the general. The SCA was expected to see justice done to the Chinese when curfews and other security restrictions caused hardship, but there was little disposition to join in debates about constitutional matters; only plentiful complaints in private that Britain was abandoning them to the mercies of the Malay majority.

The problem at federal level for Cheng Lock and his like was that they were wealthy *baba* Chinese whose ancestors had left China centuries before and whose knowledge of the Chinese language was derived from home rather than from school. The *babas* knew English and Malay but the Chinese classics and the Chinese written language had formed no part of their education. Tan Cheng Lock was a useful leader of the MCA, courageous enough to speak up against Communism, able to carry on a dialogue with his opposite numbers in the Malay and Indian political parties in the Alliance and the British officials. Yet his *baba* background gave him little leverage with the majority of the Chinese whose first and often only language was Chinese and whose links to China were close and recent. He was thus weakened in his ability to relate to the Chinese as a whole in contrast to Tunku Abdul Rahman, the UMNO leader, whose feudal aristocratic background did not prevent his communicating easily with his fellow Malays at all levels.

Cheng Lock provided a useful bridge between the Chinese and the government, which was not seriously challenged during the run up to *Merdeka*, but he was not able to offer charismatic leadership to the Chinese most of whom came from very different backgrounds. His influence was limited by his lack of knowledge of things Chinese in general and in effect he was a non-executive chairman, representing the Chinese in talks with the Malays and British but unable to deliver much positive grassroots support to the government. He was at sea in Chinese politics and many of the Chinese policies in which he acquiesced were undone in Malaysia and Singapore by Lee Kuan Yew, who knew full well the dangers which unrestricted Chinese nationalism in schools and universities posed in a plural society.

History may be kind to Cheng Lock on the grounds that for all his shortcomings he had the courage to speak against Communism and presided over the creation of the MCA thus enabling the Alliance, combining racial parties based on the Malay, Chinese and Indian communities, to be established as a multi-racial political group which would take over from the colonial power on independence day and rule for at least the next 40 years. The conclusion may well be, however, that Cheng Lock was little more than a figure-head, convenient for the government but hardly an 'alternative Malayan Chinese leader'. Nevertheless he helped the colonial government to work out a compromise between the Malays and the Chinese and that has endured.

A Lee Kuan Yew figure with more political subtlety, imagination and drive would have proved too strong meat for the Malays as the expulsion of Singapore from Malaysia in 1965 showed. Cheng Lock, by contrast, elderly, courteous and barely political, provided a non-threatening figurehead – a King Log rather than a King Stork – at a time when Malayan politics were in their infancy. The main objectives were to prepare for a democratically-elected independent government, to beat the Communists, as well as finding a reasonable balance between the various communities in a plural society where the Malays were the original rulers but others needed to have their rights assured.

It is important first of all, however, to accept that there were specific factors that made acquiring and using intelligence during the Malayan Emergency easier than it was, for instance, for the Americans in Vietnam. The British were the colonial power and had been in the country since the founding of Penang at the end of the eighteenth century so they had an intimate knowledge of the territory. A formula for independence had been agreed by the leaders of all sectors of the population. There was little mileage to be had from attempts to stir up emotion against the 'colonial oppressors' when they had already made clear their intention to relinquish their authority.

Another Malayan advantage was that the majority of the population were Malay Muslims, who were opposed to Communism both on account of its atheism and of the fact that its chief advocates in Malaya were ethnic Chinese, who were widely resented as a community for their economic success. A high proportion of the Chinese in Malaya, although proud of the new international respect earned by the People's Republic of China, were also opposed to Communism both because they knew from relatives in China the suffering it had inflicted on so many there and because they valued the opportunities offered by private business, activities which were anathema to Communist teaching.

Few, however, came off the fence to give active support to the government and the most important task for all those in the Chinese Affairs Department was to persuade more of the ethnic Chinese in Malaya to help actively in the battle against the communists. The bulk of our efforts went into the *hearts and minds* campaign. The department was strongly supported in this work by General Sir Gerald Templer, a former Director of Military Intelligence (DMI), who had the greatest respect for the profession and like the Duke of Wellington before was aware of the importance of good intelligence. Templer also insisted that every effort should be made to involve the public in the collection of intelligence and encouraged the SCAs to get actively involved in all aspects of intelligence work.

General Templer gave his personal attention, for example, to the planning of a scheme called Operation 'Letter Box', which was intended to have a psychological impact on the Communist Terrorists (CTs) and make them uncertain as to whether they had been betrayed, as well as to provide new intelligence about local supporters and the planned operations; whereabouts and tactics of the CTs.

The basis of the scheme was that a New Village would be visited by a government team of Chinese speakers from a variety of departments. The visit would take place in the morning, just before the lifting of the night curfew, and the village gates would remain closed while the team, drawn mostly from outside the police, interviewed every adult in the village. The formula was a refinement of Templer's action in Tanjong Malim after a brutal CT massacre when the village had its curfew lifted only after the residents responded constructively to an intelligence questionnaire. I, as SCA, was the co-ordinator of Operation 'Letter Box' in the villages chosen for these experiments.

I participated personally in the dawn operations, explaining to the villagers that we had come to give them the chance to help themselves by giving us information about the local CT activities; that they would not be identified as informants, but all the written information would be collected at headquarters and used to mount operations against the CTs, whose activities had led to all the miserable restrictions of curfews and food controls which had been imposed. The intelligence questionnaires ran to two A4 pages in the Chinese language and invited the villagers to describe any suspicions they had about terrorist activity in the vicinity and what they had heard of CTs and their supporters and methods in and around the village.

The interviews took place in private on a one to one anonymous basis and at the end the villager was asked to complete a written questionnaire (to which they were not required to put their name). The villagers were assured by their interrogators that the Communists would have no means of discovering the identity of those who gave information.

Although little hard intelligence was received as a result of these operations, the CTs did not know that and local sympathisers and supporters slept uneasy in case they had been identified. The operations took up relatively little resources, since we borrowed Chinese staff from all departments for the dawn sweeps and those involved were back on duty by midday. Operation 'Letter Box' was more of a *psywar* than an intelligence gathering operation. Intelligence was a bonus, the main objectives were to encourage the waverers; to sow fear and doubt in the minds of the CT sympathisers and to shake the confidence of the CTs themselves in the benevolence of the environment in which they operated. The operations certainly kept the Communists and their supporters off balance, since they could never be certain what intelligence had been revealed by the hundreds of villagers interviewed.

It has often been emphasised by people with less admiration for General Templer's performance than I have, that much of the success achieved in his time was due to plans, such as those for resettlement and food denial, which had been worked out before he arrived. This is, of course, broadly true but without 'the Tiger's' energy, infectious enthusiasm and drive the plans might not have been carried out so effectively. He also brought with him from his experience as a former DMI a full appreciation of the importance of intelligence work and of the necessity of co-ordinating it with the rest of the government machinery. The business of intelligence, from collection through analysis and assessment, was of considerable interest to him and he ensured that the voices of Special Branch and the Chinese Affairs Department were given far more weight in the War Executive Committees than might otherwise have been the case.

The details of the structure of these War Executive Committees are fully described by Short. Templer's arrival and his interest in co-ordination and his experience put life into them and made a great contribution to their success. The permanent members of the committees at the district level were the local MCS officer who took the chair; the senior policeman and senior military commander; the head of the local Special Branch and the Secretary for Chinese Affairs. The three legs of the stool were thus assembled in a strong combination: the administrative head of the area, the local operational commanders and the Special Branch and Chinese Affairs officers who presented both political and operational intelligence. This permitted opportunities for rapid assessment and discussion of information from all available sources and decision-taking in the light of the fullest possible knowledge of the intelligence of the day.

The intelligence community was linked much more clearly to all branches of the government than is normally the case and I became directly involved in the collection of secret intelligence because of my knowledge of Cantonese. Those Chinese who were prepared to risk their lives by helping the police wanted, not surprisingly, to increase their chances of survival by dealing directly with an expatriate officer rather than with a local Chinese who might betray them. I found myself, therefore, interpreting for my police colleagues in some of their most sensitive conversations with Chinese agents. One case I remember well was of a highly productive agent who insisted, against all advice, on taking a large cash advance against the credit which was building up in his secret account. The agent was murdered very shortly thereafter by the Communist terrorists, who rightly assumed that the man's sudden wealth was in some way connected with a series of successful ambushes which had been mounted against them along their lines of communication and supply in the jungle.

The most satisfying outcome of my participation in the collegiate interdepartmental committee work was that it enabled me to develop the idea for a project, later designated the 'White Area Scheme', whereby we proclaimed that it had been decided not to impose on the central district of Malacca the curfews, food controls, resettlement measures and other miseries which restricted districts throughout Malaya because the people had been so co-operative and provided so much useful information on the communists. The objective, as with Operation 'Letter Box', was partly psychological, since it was far from true that everyone was co-operating.

This was an experiment which came to fruition with some difficulty against considerable opposition from the representatives of the security forces. They took the entirely understandable view that the central district of Malacca and its rural Chinese should be subjected to the same restrictions as the other two Malacca districts, since the CTs were receiving support from the rural population in the central district. The SCA argued in the Settlement War Executive Committee and District War Executive Committee that there was no danger in continuing to allow the central district to enjoy its freedom, but that there might be significant dividends to be gained from pretending that the area's freedom had been earned by co-operation with the government thus encouraging other districts to show more positive co-operation. The SCA's suggestion was, of course, unwelcome from the narrow security view point but Sir Gerald Templer, who was a supporter of the 'ideas' men in Chinese Affairs, ruled that the experiment should take place. Maximum publicity was given to the rewards of loyal co-operation to encourage others to seek ways of ingratiating themselves with the government in order to break free from the Emergency restrictions.

The experiment was by any definition a success. It did no identifiable damage to local security operations; it encouraged the local headmen to work more closely with the SCA and other elements in government to ensure that their 'white' status was preserved and provided an opportunity to start reducing Emergency restrictions in other districts where the security situation was favourable. In effect we declared a victory in central Malacca. The CTs did not challenge our declaration. The population were flattered, if perhaps surprised, by their new found reputation as loyal anti-Communists and the MCP was left uncertain as to just how much of our publicity was true and how much was bluff. The same uncertainty helped to bring some of the population off the fence.

The operation also gave the local MCA an opportunity to claim that the great fortune enjoyed by central Malacca was due to the lobbying of the MCA on behalf of the rural Chinese. In short, there was no downside to the operation and in the intelligence context it provided new incentives for co-operation with the government. It is, of course, impossible to quantify the results but it certainly provided hope to the MCA and their rural constituents that the tide had turned and provided a precedent for lifting restrictions in other districts where, for whatever reason, the security situation had improved.

In Malacca terms, the SCA saw the experiment as beneficial above all in helping the local MCA to improve its image with the rural population. There was no specific intelligence objective. The objective was 'hearts and minds' and that it certainly achieved. I cannot speak authoritatively for the rest of the Federation, since my responsibilities and knowledge were limited to Malacca, but the experiment seemed to provide a helpful precedent for all. The 'White Area' policy was in effect a way of declaring a victory in the hope that the rewards earned by the rural Chinese for their supposed loyalty would prove sufficiently attractive to encourage the public to collaborate more readily with the government in order to maintain their privileged position, curfew and food control free, and to persuade neighbouring districts of the benefits of collaboration by giving the impression that the fortunes of war had changed dramatically in favour of the government, demoralising the CTs and heartening the population.

There had been no resounding security victory in central Malacca and it was mere chance that, as the area nearest the port city, it had been the last to be considered for the full rigours of resettlement and other Emergency regulations. Whatever else it achieved, Operation 'White Area' provided a precedent for declaring victories elsewhere in Malaya and thus adding to the discomfiture of the CTs.

I want to turn now to the subject of the use of psychological warfare in the Emergency since General Templer reinforced the intelligence effort by introducing Emergency Information Officers, who worked with officers from the police, the army and the Chinese Affairs Department to exploit any propaganda opportunities. Immediately a CT surrendered or was captured, for example, material was prepared describing the happy family reunion of the ex-CT. Voice aircraft, newspapers and pamphlets were all brought into play to persuade the CTs in the jungle to surrender and see their families again. In Malacca we actually established a Chinese newspaper, *The Fortress*, to put across every form of government message. General Templer stamped his mark on this aspect of operations too and imported a future chief of the BBC, Hugh Carleton Greene, to conduct the *psywar orchestra*.

The 'surrendered enemy person' (SEP), or defector in normal intelligence parlance, was a major source of intelligence as well as a psychological weapon. Each SEP whether of high or low rank raised the spectre of treachery, and lowered morale and operational efficiency in the jungle. The combined forces of intelligence and psychological warriors concentrated considerable resources on publicising pictures of the SEP in the bosom of his or her family to encourage further defections and to give the lie to MCP propaganda that no mercy would be shown to CTs who fell into the hands of the security forces. Other ploys included safe conduct passes and searchlights to help potential defectors to navigate out of the jungle. Most Chinese Affairs officers were closely engaged in this type of activity helping the Emergency Information Officers and Special Branch to exploit every surrender arranging, for example, tours by SEPs to talk to the villagers about their experiences.

It is certainly true that the Intelligence Branch, initially the CID but later on separated into CID and Special Branch, relied heavily on the opportunities offered by the imposition of food control and curfew and the creation of the New Villages to talent spot potential agents. The CTs were camped in the jungle and dependent on support from those, above all Chinese, with legitimate reasons to operate in the jungle. The Chinese working in the logging industry provided therefore a prime target for the CTs seeking medicine, food and other supplies from the towns and conversely were an attractive target for intelligence officers seeking to talent spot, cultivate and recruit agents. The motivation of those recruited for intelligence work was more likely to be financial than ideological and, although there might be times when both motives were present, the main inducement was usually financial. This was both a strength and a weakness. A strength in that no suspicion of anti-Communist sympathy was attached to the candidate. A weakness in that greed could lead to an insistence on payment in cash which on occasion could lead to the agent drawing fatal attention to himself by free spending.

By focusing on those working in the forest fringes, the security forces were able to identify the routes between the CT camp and the area where the logger arranged to cache supplies, or to receive instructions from his CT contacts. With the knowledge of the place and the time of the next CT supply operation, it was often possible to mount a successful ambush operation. The method had one obvious drawback. The CTs were as aware as the British intelligence officers that their jungle movements were only known to a few people outside their camp and the loggers, as prime targets for recruitment by the Intelligence Branch, were prime suspects for the role of informer.

The method worked, however, and the combination of food restrictions, resettlement and curfew gave the security forces opportunities for successful ambushes, which would not have been possible had the jungle fringes been alive with Chinese farmers who, reluctantly or willingly, could be forced to act as an intelligence screen and a supply force for the CTs. The arrival of Chinese-speaking British military intelligence officers provided a further resource for dealing with the rural Chinese in their own language. Some of them had been known to me in Macao as fellow language students but I had no personal experience of their work in Malaya.

I was not directly involved in penetration operations. There were clearly successes in this area but the main ones in which I took part were in persuading CT leaders to surrender and turn their coats. Much effort went into the psywar campaign to disturb the leaders and the rank and file by claiming that they were being betrayed by informers and defectors who were now living comfortable lives and able to see their families. Immediate and rapid exploitation of any surrender was an important priority. Voice aircraft would drop pamphlets bearing pictures of the happy SEP reunited with his family and promising the same treatment to anyone who gave himself up. The psywar campaign caused dissension and mutual suspicion in the CT camps and, even if fear prevented any mass defection, the seeds of doubt were sown. The thought of defection became a strong element in the mind of CTs discouraged by poor conditions, insufficient food, ill-health and little evidence that they were winning the battle.

Much has been made of the general 'hearts and minds campaign' to persuade the general population of the benevolence of the government; but the locally focused campaigns for the hearts and minds of individual CTs conducted by the security forces and their colleagues in the Information Department (like C. C. Too) and the Chinese Affairs were probably as important, if not more so, than the general campaign. We dealt with local affairs, local personalities, and by every channel possible preached the gospel that a defector would be guaranteed fair treatment. We were not, of course, allowed to offer amnesty: the final verdict on the individual Surrendered Enemy Personnel was made by judicial review in the light of all the circumstances.

It is probably impossible to make any meaningful judgement about which part of the intelligence machine was the most effective. My own experience was of state and district level operations which certainly had considerable success in the production of operational intelligence, which led to successful ambushes and attacks on CT camps. An important aspect of intelligence gathering was the rapid local debriefing of the SEP and speedy tactical exploitation of their information about camps, supply routes, methods and CT supporters, in order to launch immediate operations which might catch the local CTs off their guard before they became aware of the defection.

Simultaneously the psywar operators were making parallel plans to exploit the intelligence of the defection once the military response had been given adequate time. It is unfortunate from the research point of view that it is so difficult to get access to the records of the huge and successful psywar and deception operations that were the fruits of the co-ordinated work in the War Committees and their supporting agencies.

One of my principal contributions to the 'hearts and minds campaign' centred on the fact that almost all the uniformed local forces, both police and army, were manned by Malays and when, as was inevitable, there was friction between the police and the local population it was easy for Chinese troublemakers to claim that the problem was due to deliberate anti-Chinese attitudes. As Secretary for Chinese Affairs, I was perpetually involved in the war of words between the government officials, usually British or Malay, presenting the allegations of the Malay side and MCA representatives putting forward the complaints of the Chinese population. These cantankerous exchanges gave the Communists and their foreign supporters plenty of opportunity for anti-government propaganda suggesting that the police and army were anti-Chinese. In the heat and fog of operations there were plenty of unfortunate incidents when troops exceeded their powers and houses were burnt down and so on.

The mass of the local Chinese population remained on the touch-line and continual appeals to the Chinese to join the uniformed forces were ignored so that as a result it was calculated that out of a total of 70,000 in the police force, only 800 were Chinese, with all the rest Malay, Indian or other racial minorities. The leaders of the Chinese community, when exhorted to do more to help the government, tended to quote the old Chinese proverb: 'You do not use good steel to make nails and you do not use good sons to become soldiers.' There was in addition to this classical Chinese philosophical attitude to involvement in military affairs, a more practical objection – the pay was too low! I eventually managed to persuade the leaders of the MCA in Malacca that something had to be done. It was not only helping the Communists but also making the Malays extremely resentful because their sons were having to risk their lives to protect the Chinese whose own children refused to join the security forces.

The MCA eventually agreed to put their hands in their pockets and to give a monthly allowance to the families of every Chinese who joined up. The results of this arrangement were highly satisfactory and the recruiting teams who came to Malacca were astonished at the queues of young Chinese hoping to enrol. Their puzzlement continued, since I had thought it wiser not to draw the attention of the authorities to this unofficial bounty for those Chinese prepared to overcome their traditional objection to uniformed service! In another rather similar initiative I managed to persuade the MCA that we should raise the money to build decent Chinese schools throughout the settlement whether in the New Villages or the old ones.

This scheme to establish a Chinese Education Fund was easy to sell to the Chinese business people, who were possibly feeling a twinge of guilt about the lack of tangible support being given by the Chinese community to the war effort, but it was less easy to persuade the few non-Chinese organisations and one western Agency House complained, with some justification, that the Education Fund constituted a sort of tax which was being levied illegally. Ultimately, however, all agreed and we were able to build 13 basic but effective, rural schools to replace the squalor of the country schools which preceded them.

On this occasion too, I thought it sensible not to bother other government departments with boring details about the mechanics of the fund-raising! The scheme had, in addition to its specific objective of providing decent schools for which government funds were not available, the merit of demonstrating to the Chinese community that contrary to communist propaganda the government was not opposed to the promotion of Chinese education and culture.

Other hearts and minds initiatives which originated from the SCA's office in Malacca and Penang included building cheap houses, providing playing fields, and rallying the Chinese community to participate fully in such affairs as the celebration of Queen Elizabeth's Coronation and the re-invention of the Chinese Dragon Boat Festival, which is now described in Penang's tourist literature as the 'traditional' Water Festival.

Perhaps the most exotic was the creation of civics courses in Malacca, whereby every month 50 or 60 rural Chinese leaders were brought up to Malacca, housed and fed by the MCA in Chinese temples, and lectured by government officials on government policies and democracy. The highlight of the course was a bus ride to Kuala Lumpur where the students were entertained to tea by Lady Templer at King's House. Whatever else the civics courses achieved, they countered the MCP propaganda about the high-handed, indifferent, brutal, colonial oppressors. The students may not have understood all that they were taught, but they could hardly fail to recognise that government was interested in them and their problems, while the visit to King's House was of course an amazing experience for them to describe to their relatives and friends. It was, of course, also an outstanding example of Templer's sympathetic support for all imaginative attempts to win hearts and minds.

I apologise for what may seem to be an unwarranted emphasis on the contribution of the Chinese Affairs officers to the 'hearts and minds' and intelligence initiatives. Since, however, the Department and its work were little known and still less understood even at the time, I trust that this attempt to put the spotlight on it may be felt to be justified. This brief note touches on and I hope gives some flavour of the aspects of intelligence and *psywar* activity during the Malayan Emergency about which I have personal knowledge. Some accounts of the Malayan campaign record little about the intelligence activities that contributed so much to the ultimate victory and I am delighted that an effort is now being made to draw attention to the work that was done by the intelligence community.

## ACKNOWLEDGEMENT

Anyone who writes on the Malayan Emergency must, as I happily do, acknowledge their great debt to Anthony Short whose authoritative work, *The Communist Insurrection in Malaya 1948–1960* (London: Frederick Muller 1975) was beside me as I composed this preliminary outline on one small aspect of the period which he covers so magisterially.

# Abstracts

## US Humint and Comint in the Korean War: From the Approach of War to the Chinese Intervention
### MATTHEW M. AID

Little has been written about the intelligence aspects of the Korean War, 1950–53, least of all about the role of American Humint and Comint during the conflict. Newly declassified documents show that the American Humint and Comint organizations performed poorly during the early stages of the Korean War, in part because US intelligence organizations in the Far East had been allowed to atrophy in the years after the end of World War II. The documents reveal that the American intelligence infrastructure in the Far East was fragmented and poorly managed, and required more than a year to revitalize following the North Korean invasion in June 1950.

## A Mission of Espionage, Intelligence and Psychological Operations: The American Consulate in Hong Kong, 1949–64
### JOHANNES R. LOMBARDO

After the Communist victory in China in late 1949, the Cold War manifested in Asia as a reoccurring confrontation between the United States and the People's Republic of China (PRC). For the British colony of Hong Kong, its location on the southern coast, its relative degree of openness and the intensity of the Cold War in Asia, turned the colony into a miniature battleground of ideological conflict. This openness facilitated the operations of foreign agents in Hong Kong, particularly agents run by Nationalist Chinese, the United States and the Communist Chinese. The British government had a more accommodating policy towards Beijing, and authorities in Hong Kong were often at odds with American activities there. Nevertheless the British discreetly facilitated American intelligence gathering and propaganda operations. The activities of the American Consulate in Hong Kong – the largest consulate anywhere in the world – during the 1950s and early 1960s are examined, together with their impact on the divergent policies of the US, UK and also to some degree, Taiwan, towards Communist China.

## Taiwan's Propaganda Cold War:
## The Offshore Islands Crises of 1954 and 1958
### GARY D. RAWNSLEY

This study examines the propaganda and psychological warfare that originated – often with CIA assistance – in the Republic of China on Taiwan during the 1954 and 1958 offshore islands crises. It suggests that while Taiwan enjoyed several advantages over its propaganda rivals, it failed to take advantage of them. For example, the government decided to ignore completely American advice, especially about the limitations of propaganda. The analysis concludes that propaganda from Taiwan was designed more to service Taiwan's interests in the United States than to intimidate the Communist regime in Beijing. The American intelligence community knew that Chiang Kai-shek's optimism in a military recovery of the Chinese mainland, with American support, was misplaced.

## The SIS Singapore Station and the SIS Far Eastern Controller
### PHILIP H.J. DAVIES

This contribution examines the development of the British Secret Intelligence Service (SIS) regional headquarters, or 'controlling station' in Singapore between 1945 and 1965, and the status of regional 'controlling stations' within Britain's regional administrations on one hand, and her central intelligence machinery on the other. It is argued that the development of the SIS in Singapore brings into sharp relief the basic relationship between that agency and the overt workings of British government. That relationship constitutes what in American intelligence literature is called a 'pull architecture' in which operational goals and priorities are laid upon operational agencies rather than set by those agencies themselves. This is examined both in terms of the intelligence machinery in Singapore under the Commissioner-General for the UK in Southeast Asia, and in terms of the central intelligence tasking and dissemination mechanisms in London.

## Legacies of Secret Service:
## Renegade SOE and the Karen Struggle in Burma, 1948–50
### RICHARD J. ALDRICH

This essay examines the issue of the long-term legacies of the encouragement of local resistance activity against occupying forces. While such strategies can prove effective in the short-term, they can also bequeath a legacy of uncontrollable, heavily armed populations with a taste for disobedience. Moreover, the special organisations set up to support such activity can also prove difficult to control. These issues were explicitly debated in Asia during 1945 by elements of Mountbatten's SEAC HQ. This essay examines the case of Burma in 1948, when ex-SOE officers returned to Burma to assist their wartime allies, the Karens, in their fight against the central government. The latter were supported by a British Military Mission. This also represents an example of 'privateer' secret service activity, which remains a somewhat neglected field.

## Bombs, Plots and Allies:
## Cambodia and the Western Powers, 1958–59
### MONA BITAR

During 1958 and 1959, Prince Sihanouk enhanced his policy of neutrality in order to counter the threat which he perceived from his neighbours, Thailand and especially South Vietnam. Crucially, Sihanouk held the United States and other Western allies accountable for actions undertaken by both Thailand and Vietnam. It is asserted that the relationship between Cambodia and the United States was terminally linked to Cambodia's difficult relationships with her neighbours. A key question is why Sihanouk held the United States, and more specifically the CIA, responsible for Vietnamese aggression. Ultimately, Sihanouk's irritation led to his decision to recognise Communist China. Ironically, the CIA stations in both Bangkok and Saigon were exerting themselves to secure restraint on the part of their local allies, though not always with success. The importance that these regional issues exerted upon all those involved in United States policymaking has not hitherto been fully appreciated, and many have tended to see the conflicts of this region in an exclusively Cold War framework.

## Late Imperial Romance: Magsaysay, Lansdale and the Philippine-American 'Special Relationship'
### EVA-LOTTA E. HEDMAN

More than four decades after his death in a plane crash outside Cebu City in 1957, Ramon Magsaysay remains the most mythologised public figure in the history of the independent Republic. While Magsaysay the reformist-cum-politician left but faint traces in the Philippines, Magsaysay the anti-Huk fighter has entered the annals of counter-insurgency campaigns studied at military academies and has become the stuff of legend elsewhere. This brief essay explores the mythologisation of Magsaysay within the context of US covert action and American liberal imperalism writ large. To that end, the essay returns to already published material on Lansdale, including his autobiography, *In the Midst of Wars*, for clues to this imperial enchantment with 'The Guy'.

## British and Malaysian Covert Support for Rebel Movements in Indonesia during the 'Confrontation', 1963–66
### DAVID EASTER

This essay examines the British and Malaysian response to Indonesia's guerrilla campaign of 'Confrontation' in Borneo. In particular it shows that from 1964 Britain and Malaysia covertly aided rebel groups in the outer Indonesian islands in an attempt to weaken the Confrontation campaign. The essay also reveals differences beween London and Kuala Lumpur over the political aims of covert action, with the Malays seeking to break up the Indonesian state.

## Corpses, Prisoners of War and Captured Documents: British and Communist Narratives of the Malayan Emergency, and the Dynamics of Intelligence Transformation
### KARL HACK

British accounts of the Malayan Emergency argue intelligence underwent a major transformation in 1952–54, as part of a campaign-winning infusion of new leadership. This article uses the recent statements of Chin Peng, Secretary-General of the Malayan Communist Party from 1947, to construct a contrasting Communist analysis. One which sees the insurgent campaign as flagging by 1951, before intelligence reached its peak. It then tries to reconcile these contradictory British and Communist narratives. In so doing, it suggests a more incremental pattern of intelligence development. A pattern which was punctured by occasional efficiency boosting leaps forward, following key events such as the systemization of 'population control', and various leadership changes.

## Content, Credibility and Context:
## Propaganda, Government Surrender Policy and the Malayan Communist Terrorist Mass Surrenders of 1958
### KUMAR RAMAKRISHNA

This essay argues that while previous analyses of the Malayan Emergency are able to shed light on why the tide of the military campaign had swung in the government's favour by 1954, they cannot precisely explain why the disastrous mass Communist surrenders of 1958 – which all but ended the Emergency – occurred. The essay suggests rather that an examination of the content, credibility and context of the government surrender policy between 1949 and 1958 helps illuminate this issue. In particular it argues that by 1958, the extremely liberal *Merdeka* amnesty terms, together with increasing government credibility with the terrorists and a favourable strategic and political context, precipitated the MCP collapse.

## Winning in Malaya:
## An Intelligence Success Story
### BRIAN STEWART

This study discusses the key role played by the Malayan government's intelligence community in the victory over the Malayan Communist Party. It argues that the successful development of the community's skills owed much to Templer and, in particular, to his insistence that intelligence was given due weight in the War Executive Committees and to the encouragement he gave to the work of the Chinese Affairs officers. The personal experience of the author as Secretary for Chinese Affairs Malacca is described and examples given of concrete steps taken during the 'hearts and minds' campaign and other successful psychological warfare activities.

# About the Contributors

**Matthew M. Aid** is a senior manager of a Washington DC financial research and investigative firm. He is the author of 'Not So Anonymous: Parting the Veil of Secrecy About the National Security Agency', in Athan G. Theoharis (ed.), *A Culture of Secrecy* (Lawrence: UP of Kansas 1998). He is currently writing a history of the National Security Agency (and its predecessor agencies) covering the period 1917 to the present.

**Richard J. Aldrich** is a Professor in the School of Politics and Director of the Institute of Asia-Pacific Studies at the University of Nottingham. He was a Fulbright Fellow at Georgetown University in 1992 and is co-editor of the journal *Intelligence and National Security*. His publications include *The Key to the South: Britain, the United States and Thailand During the Approach of the Pacific War, 1929–1942* (Singapore: OUP 1993) and *Intelligence and the War Against Japan: Britain, America and the Politics of Secret Service* (Cambridge: CUP 2000). He is completing a study of relations between intelligence services during the Cold War.

**Mona Bitar** is a doctoral student at the University of Nottingham researching British and American policy towards Cambodia 1954–65. She is currently employed by Cambridge Management Consulting in London.

**Philip H.J. Davies** is the author of *The British Secret Services* (Oxford: ABC-Clio, Rutgers: Transaction 1996), and has a detailed analysis of the relationship between MI6 and the machinery of British central government forthcoming in the journal *Public Administration*. He is currently Lecturer in Sociology at the University of Reading.

**David Easter** is an Occasional Teacher in the Department of International History at the London School of Economics where he has recently completed a doctorate on British Policy during the Confrontation with Indonesia. His research interests are in twentieth century British and South East Asian history and the Cold War.

**Karl Hack** is a Lecturer at the Nanyang Technological University, Singapore. His *Defence and Decolonisation: Britain, Malaya and Singapore, 1941–1968* is forthcoming with Curzon Press. He is also writing a book on the role of intelligence in the creation of modern Malaysia and Singapore. His research interests include low-intensity conflict, general decolonization in the Southeast Asia, and fiction pertaining to the latter.

**Eva-Lotta E. Hedman** is a Lecturer in Comparative Politics and South East Asia Studies in the School of Politics at the University of Nottingham, where she also serves as a Deputy Director of the Institute for Asia-Pacific Studies. Having published several articles on the politics of civil society and social movements in South East Asia, she has recently completed work on civil-military relations and paramilitary mobilization in the Philippines.

**Johannes R. Lombardo** received his PhD from the University of Hong Kong in 1997 and held a Sir Edward Youde Memorial Fellowship. His research subject as 'United States Foreign Policy towards the British Crown Colony of Hong Kong during the early Cold War period, 1945–64'. His research was supported by grants from the Harry S. Truman Library and the Hong Kong America Research Centre.

**Kumar Ramakrishna** has recently completed a doctorate on propaganda during the Malayan Emergency at the Department of History, Royal Holloway College, University of London.

**Gary D. Rawnsley** is a Lecturer in Politics and Deputy Director (China) of the Institute of Asia-Pacific Studies at the University of Nottingham. He is the author of *Radio Diplomacy and Propaganda* (Macmillan 1996), *Taiwan's Informal Diplomacy and Propaganda* (Macmillan 1999), and is the editor of *Cold War Propaganda in the 1950s* (Macmillan 1999). He is currently completing a study of critical security and the media in Taiwan with Ming-Yeh T. Rawnsley, to be published in 2000 by Ashgate Press.

**Ming-Yeh T. Rawnsley** is an Associate Research Fellow in the Institute of Asia-Pacific Studies, University of Nottingham, and an experienced print and television journalist. She has published extensively on the media in both English and Chinese, and is the author of *Viewing the Media* and *A Study Room in England* (Chinese 1999). She is currently completing a study of critical security and the media in Taiwan with Gary Rawnsley.

**Brian Stewart** CMG joined the Black Watch in 1941 straight from Oxford. He landed in Penang in September 1945 and served in the Malayan Civil Service until 1956. He returned to Malaysia as Director of the Rubber Growers Association and then became an Honorary Lecturer in the University of Hong Kong.

# Index